D1060403

Contents

Introduction

The history of knives goes all the way back to the beginning of the human race. The first simple tool, made more than two million years ago, was a sharp edge on the side of a piece of flint. Clearly recognizable stone knives date from the Paleolithic period from 500,000 to 10,000 BC. This period is referred to as the Stone Age: *paleo* is Greek for 'old' and *lithos* means 'stone.' Stones with very sharp

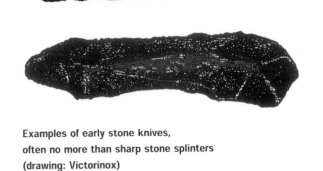

Examples of early stone knives, often no more than sharp stone splinters (drawing: Victorinox)

edges were used for hacking, cutting and scraping animal hides. Some excavated stone tools still have clear traces of chipped-off stone splinters. In the late Paleolithic (about 40,000 to 10,000 BC) the shaping of tools became more sophisticated. Stone and bone needles stem from this period, as well as specially shaped stone spear points and spears.

In order to cut as thinly as possible, stone blades were shaped on both sides. In the late Stone Age, fire was used to heat the pieces of flint to make them easier to work. People were still nomadic at this stage, living from the animals they hunted, the fish they caught and grass seeds, fruits, plants and roots they collected.

In the Mesolithic, or the middle period of the Stone Age, from 10,000 to 4,000 BC, the Great Ice Age came to an end. Excavations show that, during

Stone knives from the middle period of the Stone Age (drawing: Victorinox)

this era, hunters and their tools became more specialized: harpoon tips for fishing and flint axes started appearing.

In the Neolithic, from 4,000 to 2,000 BC, the climate grew milder. People did not need to follow herds of wild animals anymore and, as the need for a nomadic existence faded, they started establishing groups. Hunting and fishing still provided important sources of protein, but the focus slowly shifted towards agriculture and stockbreeding. Working tools became more sophisticated. Stone knives were sanded smooth and handles were made of wood or animal hide to protect the fingers. The first utility articles made of clay date from this period.

During the Bronze Age, from 2,000 to 700 BC, people in what is today Europe started making knives from brass and bronze. (In the Middle East, bronze had been used since 5,000 BC.) Iron was known, but rare and the technique for extracting iron from the ore and hardening it was still unknown. A bronze knife consisting of ninety percent copper and ten percent tin was worth much more at this time. Most copper came from

Stone axes and a knife from a later period of the Stone Age (drawing: Victorinox)

mines in the Balkans. Despite the primitive trade flow, bronze reached regions as distant as Denmark. Tin for the alloy came mostly from Anatolia in Turkey.

During the Bronze Age, people lived mostly from agriculture and stockbreeding. They built stronger settlements to protect themselves against enemies.

Many bronze knives have been found on excavations of sites from this era. Blades were made with an extension or "thorn," to which a handle could easily be attached, and the shape of the knives in general was beginning to look a lot like the ones used today.

In the Iron Age, from around 1,000 BC, people started to make knives and hunting gear from iron.

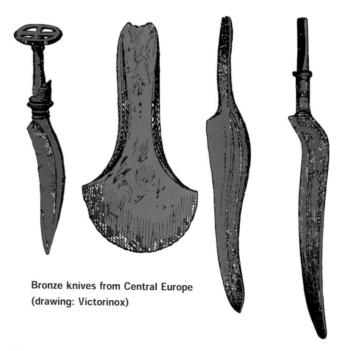

Bronze knives from Central Europe (drawing: Victorinox)

The Greek and Roman armies had iron swords and knives. Knives became a part of everyday life among common citizens as well. A good knife was a valuable possession.

Iron objects from this era were not of very high quality, however, as the technique for smelting (melting) iron was still unknown. Instead, the ore was heated until it was glowing hot and pulverized. The small bits of iron were then reheated and forged together. Bellows were not invented until later. Air currents, quickly forced out over a fire from animal hides, made the fire burn much hotter and iron could be smelted.

The first known iron casts date from this period. "Damascus," a technique that originated in India and spread to the Middle East, dates from the Iron Age. The word came from the Syrian city of Damascus. It is the process of smelting various types of iron together. By folding the "package" of steel in a specific way before smelting it, smiths were able to achieve patterns. Over the centuries, this technique was refined.

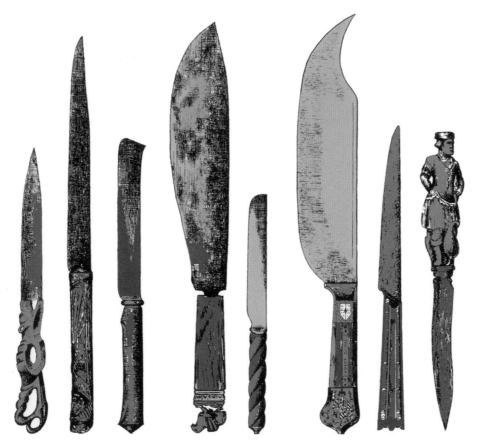

Examples of iron knives from the eleventh to the sixteenth centuries (from left to right) (drawing: Victorinox)

There were many ironworking centers in Europe during the Middle Ages, such as Toledo in Spain and Sheffield in England. But by the end of the nineteenth and the beginning of the twentieth century, the Damascus technique had been nearly forgotten in Europe. This is largely due to the developments of firearms. Around the turn of the century, people started using nitroglycerine instead of black gunpowder. This produced a far greater gas pressure, against which the Damasteel from this time was not resistant.

But nowadays, with special techniques and steel types, Damasteel is freely used again. Modern Damasteel looks better and is harder and more varied than any our forefathers could have dreamt of.

This hand-drawn image was taken from the 1984 publication *The Knife and its History*, released at the centenary anniversary of the industry, with kind permission from the Swiss company Victorinox.

Ultramodern folding knife from mosaic Damascus by Fogarizzu

A

AKSYONOV

www.rusartknife.urbannet.ru/gallery.html

Portrait of Andrey Vasil'evich Aksyonov with his master sign on the right and the logo of the Russian Knifemakers' Guild below.

Andrey Vasil'evich Aksyonov was born on 9 November 1954 in Moscow. He had been interested in Russian history since his early youth. In school, he studied art and practiced woodcarving, sculpture and graphic arts and made some very beautiful wooden swords for himself and his friends.

Later, he became fascinated by iron and steel. At sixteen he started working as an apprentice machine fitter in the 'Calibre' tool factory. There he started studying engraving techniques and learned to make tools to work with wood and metal.

His interest in weapons forging started when he was asked to make sabers for a film. As there was hardly any modern information available on the subject, he frequented the Museum of History, the Kremlin Weapons Museum and the Soviet Military Museum, and started collecting cards and books about weapons. Based on these, he made aluminum blades for sabers, swords and daggers, and wooden handles. For decoration, he studied the jewelry trade and learned to work with leather and engrave special materials such as mammoth ivory.

In 1987 Aksyonov met the famous Russian weapons forger Borisovich who introduced him to the world of knife makers and he went to work professionally. He got involved with a group of Russian knife makers who were trying to rediscover the nearly forgotten technique of of Damascus and his insight into weapons as a part of the Russian culture grew.

Today, there are plans to reopen the 16th century weapons manufacturing school in Moscow as a subdivision of the Kremlin's Weapons Museum.

The sheath of the Rimskiy dagger in detail

The Majestic sabre
by Aksyonov

The forging masters of the Weapons Museum made many items that still inspire local and international knife makers today. The 'Russian Chambers' gallery was built in 1994 and Aksyonov has been working there ever since as a master knife maker. He is a member of the Russian Knifemakers' Guild and of the Society for Weapons History. He has received many awards for his work and takes part in many national and international knife exhibitions. Aksyonov is a master in creating sabers and swords of a quality comparable to the old Russian treasures. These knives were photographed by the 'Russian Palace' gallery in Moscow.

MAJESTIC

This majestic saber is shaped like a Russian battle saber of the sixteenth and seventeenth centuries and is decorated in accordance with the traditions of the Moscow Weapons School from this period. The top ring is decorated with the Russian orthodox icon of the archangel Michael. The lower rings contain depictions of great Russians: the first prince, Ryurik, the first emperor, John III, and Tsar Peter the Great. The symbol of the Russi-

an Empire and the family emblem of the Russian Tsar, Alexey Mihaylovich, are on the shutter of the sheath.

This Damascus blade was forged by Damascus smith Bichkov, from Susdal. It is made of ancient 'Demidov' iron and some modern steel types. The gold-coated motif on the 29.9 inch blade was done by Aksyonov's friend Golovin from Tula, also a member of the Russian Knife Manufacturer's Guild. Aksyonov carved the handle from a walrus tusk that his son had brought back from an archeological expedition to the Kamchatka peninsula. Aksyonov and his friend and fellow knife maker Timofeev collected the fresh water pearls while on summer holiday in Karelia. The turquoise and garnets, collected during archeological expeditions, came from Karelia as well. The total length of the saber is 36.2 inches. Aksyonov spent fourteen months working on this saber, first put on display in April 2004 at the Belford Festival of the Kremlin.

Detail of the sabre

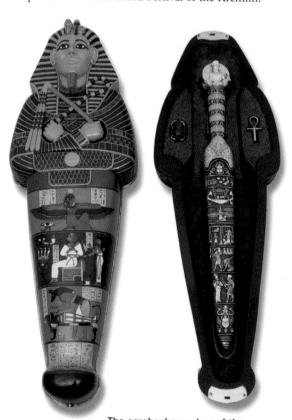

The sarchophagus box of the
Pharaoh dagger

**The Rock Lobster
by Jens Anso**

REVOLUTION

The Revolution has a 3-inch, claw-shaped blade. The total length of the fully opened knife is 6.7 inches and the length of the handle is 4 inches. The knife has a linerlock latch with hand-polished double bolt rods or liners made of stainless steel 6AL4V, guilloched on the outside. Flame hardening gave them a bronze color. The blade is made of polished stainless RWL-34 steel, tempered by a special freezing technique to 60 HRC. Anso chose mammoth ivory with a dark patina for the handle. The chic handle plates are somewhat smaller than the casing and were cut away to protect the ivory against dents and chips. The screws used to attach the handle plates were filed down to look decorative and then tempered by flame. The back spacer is also made of RWL-34 steel.

ROCK LOBSTER

This folding knife is intended for fishing. Its total length is 9.4 inches when opened and it has a 4-inch long RWL-

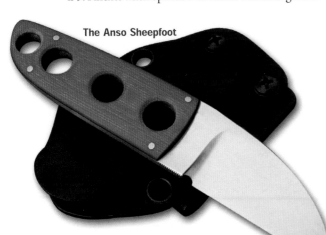

The Anso Sheepfoot

34 steel blade, with a round Spyderco hole instead of a thumb stud. Anso holds a license from Spyderco to use this patent. This knife has a framelock with titanium casing plates 0.122 inches thick. The handle plates are made of Fibermascus and attached with Torx screws. A carry clip is attached to the right handle plate.

The Tukan knife

SHEEPFOOT

The name of the Sheep-foot Model comes from the typical shape of the blade: the back runs in an arch to the tip and the cutting side is completely smooth and horizontal. It is an integral knife, which means that the blade and the core of the handle are made of one sheet of steel, in this case of stainless RWL-34. The total length of the knife is 5.3 inches, with a 2.0-inch long blade. Holes drilled in the handle ensure a stable grip and make the knife lighter. The handle plates are made of red G10 synthetic material.

TUKAN

The Tukan is mostly an integral knife with a typical claw-shaped blade 4 inches long. The total length is 10 inches. As additional support for the delicate work, a finger slot was used, rather than a bolster. This part of the handle is not part of the blade. The knife was made of a single piece of RWL-34 steel, with a Fibermascus, a type of laminated fiberglass.

The emblem of AvR Knives

AVR/AAD VAN RIJSWIJK
www.avrknives.com

Aad van Rijswijk was born in 1949 and grew up in Schiedam. After finishing school he worked as a weapons technician with Arthur Dorst in The Hague. His work and his hobby as a sharpshooter regularly took him to weapons fairs, where he saw a great variety of handmade knives and got hooked. He has been making exceptionally high quality private collector's knives full time since 1991. After a learning and orientation period at, among others, the well-known firm Hill Knives in Rotterdam, his perseverance started to pay off.
AVR folding knives have integral casings, called Interframes, which are manufactured from one piece of steel. AVR has four basic models that can be altered to suit the needs of the client. One lovely quality, the spring tension of these knives, can be adjusted with a small Allen screw. Solid kni-

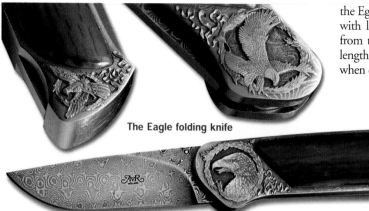

The Eagle folding knife

the Egyptian style because the Egyptians of old worked with lapis lazuli. The case is engraved with symbols from this period in white and yellow gold. The total length of the knife is 6.5 inches and it is 3.9 inches long when closed.

FORK & KNIFE

This knife and fork are made of stainless Damasteel and done in Art Nouveau style. The engraving on the pommel of the handle was inspired by a female figure by the artist Alfons Mucha. The handle is made of walrus ivory. This knife and fork are currently on display in Via Montenapoleone, the busiest shopping street in Milan.

ves can be custom made. AVR works with two Belgian engravers: Dany Hermine and Eduard Vos. For the handles, Aad van Rijswijk uses mainly prehistoric ivory, mother-of-pearl and semi-precious stones that he personally selects in Oberstein.

Aad uses ATS-34 stainless Damasteel, 250-layer Damascus with a ladder structure, and Wild Rose Damasteel, bought in Germany. Both steel types were tempered to 59 HRC. This full-time knife smith, who is currently living in Vlaardingen in the Netherlands, is a member of the German, Italian and American Knifemakers' Guilds.

INTEGRAL

This semi-integral knife is made of stainless Damasteel. The blade is double

The Damascus cutlery

EAGLE

This knife was for an American client who wanted a folding knife with the history of his Italian-American origins on it. The knife is made of stainless Damasteel and the handle plates are made of mammoth ivory. The engravings were done three-dimensionally from yellow, white and pink gold. The front was engraved with an American eagle as well as a Roman helmet with crossed swords. The other side symbolizes freedom, with a flying eagle and a dove of peace. The total length of the knife is 6.5 inches and the casing is 3.9 inches long.

EGYPTIAN

This interframe folding knife is made of stainless Damasteel. The inlay plates of the handle are made of lapis lazuli from Afghanistan. It is very difficult to find good quality lapis lazuli, which is currently mined in the mountains of Afghanistan using explosives, which create a countless number of hairline cracks in the material, rendering it unusable. The knife was made in

ground. The engraving on the bolster and on the back of the bolster is Simera, a symbol of Satan used in religious art. The handle is made of mammoth

The Egyptian

ivory. This material is more than 15,000 years old and comes from Siberia. The total length of the knife is 10.2 inches.

The Integral hunting knife

The Mother of Pearl knife

JAPANESE WARRIOR

This folding knife is an interframe as well and the blade is made of ATS-34 steel. The plate inlays in the casing are made of mother-of-pearl. The very fine engravings on the bolsters were done in Japanese style. The total length of the knife is 6.5 inches and the handle length is 3.9 inches.

MOTHER-OF-PEARL

This is an integral knife made of one plate of ATS-34 steel. The blade was ground on both sides. The handle plates were made of mother-of-pearl and attached with mosaic pins. The bolsters were engraved with golden Simeras. The total length is 9.8 inches.

SHAVING SET

Now and then, Aad van Rijswijk gets some special requests, such as this razor. This gave him the idea to make an exclusive set, consisting of a razor with a blade made of stainless Damasteel, a stand and a shaving brush. The handles of the knife, the brush and the stand itself are all made of mammoth ivory. The brush is made of rock rabbit hair. This set is on display in Milan, like the Knife & Fork set.

The shaving set

The Japanese
Warrior folding knife

B

The ivory was carved by Galina Pozdeeva. A walnut case with hand-carved hunting scenes and a miniature portrait of a wild boar come with the knife. The guard, pommel and finishing work were done by Pavel Shribokov.

FANG

The Fang hunting knife has a lovely arched shape. This integral knife has a wide bolster with a deep contour that serves as a finger slot and integrated guard. It was designed and made by Albert Kalegin. Alexey Zadvornov did the engraving work. Alexey Krasnoperov assembled the knife and applied the finishing touches. The total length of the knife is 7.1 inches. The stainless steel blade is 3.15 inches long. The handle is made of birch burl wood with a particularly beautiful vein structure.

HAPPINESS OF A MOTHER

This knife was beautifully engraved by Gennady Makarov, with a depiction of a lynx with a youngster in a forest, surrounded by exotic flowers. Trees were engraved in the guard and pom-

BASKO

www.basko.guns.ru

The emblem of Basko

Basko from Izhevsk is a cooperative institution that exports the work of several Russian custom knife makers. It has been in existence for only ten years and it represents its members at a great number of European and American knife exhibitions. The knives are exclusively handmade and only one version of each knife is made. The engraving is done by specially trained engravers. The material used is of the highest quality stainless steel, Damasteel, and mammoth ivory. Usually, two or three Russian knife makers work together, each contributing a major part of the project as is common among knife makers of the Russian Guild.

BOAR

This big, handmade hunting knife is 8.8 inches long. The blade, the guard and the pommel are made of stainless steel. One part of the blade is ground hollow and the other part depicts the head of a wild boar. The steel engravings were made by Sergey Krupin. The blade is 4.4 inches long and the handle is made of mammoth ivory. A complete hunting scene of a piglet and sow is depicted in the middle.

The Fang

Happiness of a Mother with an engraving of a lynx wits its young

mel. The knife is 8.8 inches long and the blade is 4.4 inches in length. The handle is made of mammoth ivory. Andrey Nikiforov designed and finished the knife. A case made of painted and engraved walnut wood comes with it.

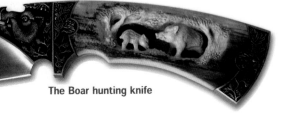

The Boar hunting knife

MAMMOTH HUNTER

The Otter as an art object

The Mammoth Hunter is a collector's item with a design from the Stone Age. The 5.4 inch blade is made of Damasteel with the structure of a chipped stone knife. The entire knife is 9.25 inches long. The handle is made of mammoth ivory. The knife

The Mammoth Hunter

beautifully decorated three-dimensionally with an otter hunting fish in a combination of engraving and etching by Anatoly Tolmachev. The open-work handle is made of mammoth ivory and depicts another otter swimming between water plants, chasing a big fish. This engraving was done by Alexander Vakhrushev. The total length of the knife is 8.8 inches.

ROSE

This hunting knife, designed by Andrey Nalyubin, won an award in the custom knives category at the International Weapon Exhibition (IWA) in Nuremberg, Germany. The total length is 9.25 inches. The blade was made of stainless Damasteel and is 5.35 inches long. The engraving of a three dimensional polarbear was done by Boris Stepanov. Alexander Vakhrushev made and engraved the handle of mammoth ivory. The knife was finished by Konstantin Telegin.

The Mammoths

stands on a rough piece of mammoth ivory attached to a block of walnut wood. A miniature mammoth made of white mammoth ivory stands in the front. It was designed by Vitaly Tolochenko. The metalwork was done by Alexey Kopanev and engraver-sculptor Irina Ivanova did the carving. The knife was finished by Alexey Krasnoperov and Andrey Mayev.

MAMMOTHS

This knife was designed by Oleg Baranov. The total length is 8.8 inches. The length of the stainless Damasteel blade is 4.4 inches. The steel was made and engraved by Rustam Farrakhov. The sculptor Galina Pozdeeva carved the mammoth in the handle. The knife leans against a rough piece of mammoth tusk. It stands in its entirety on a block of walnut wood. All of the finishing touches were done by Andrey Nikiforov and Andrey Mayev.

OTTER

This beautiful knife was designed by Dmitry Gordenko. The stainless steel blade is 4.4 inches long. It was

The Rose, an award winner at the IWA 2003

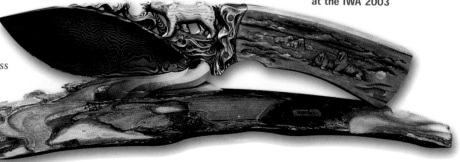

A depiction of the Stone Age

SPIDER

Vitaly Matyushin designed this beautiful knife. The longer you look at it, the more details you see. The blade is 4.4 inches long. The open-work steel bolster depicts a spider on tree leaves, creeping up on a fly. On the blade is an etching of a fly that had already been caught. The engraving was done by Vitaly Matyushin. The total length of the knife is 8.8 inches. The handle is made of a polished piece of walnut branch. Pieces of metal that serve as pins were placed in the handle. The knife was finished by Dmitry Gordenko.

STONE AGE

This depiction of a knife that looks like a Mammoth Hunter and a primitive axe, designed by Vitaly Tolochenko and Oleg Baranov, is called 'Stone Age.' The axe head as well as the knife blade were made of Damasteel by Alexey Kopanev. The total length of the knife is 9.25 inches and the blade is 5.4 inches long. The handle of the axe is made of walnut wood and is 23.8 inches in length.

The small mammoth, made of mammoth ivory, was done by Irina Ivanova. It was assembled and finished in its entirety by Pavel Shirobokov and Andrey Mayev.

The Spider

The Wolf Knife

WOLF

The Wolf is a design by Konstantin Telegin, which he made with Alexander Zverev and Alexander Vakhrushev. The 4.4 inch long, stainless steel blade was engraved by Alexander Zverev. The guard and pommel were made and engraved by Konstantin Telegin. Alexander Vakhrushev made the handle from

The Wood-grouse

mammoth ivory. The total length of the knife is 8.8 inches and it comes in an engraved walnut case with a painted cover.

WOOD-GROUSE

There are many different depictions of the grouse on this knife, beautifully engraved and etched into the stainless steel of the blade and into the handle of mammoth ivory by Vitaly Matyushin. The total length is 8.8 inches and the blade is 4.4 inches long. It comes in an engraved walnut case, adorned with a miniature oil painting of a wild grouse. The handle was engraved and cut by Alexander Vakhrushev and Alexander Fionin did the finishing touches.

BEAUCHAMP

www.beauchamp.cjb.net

Gaetan Beauchamp is from Stoneham in the Canadian province of Quebec. He lives in a picturesque valley on the river Huron, which runs through his

Emblem of Gaétan Beauchamp

back yard. His career as a knife maker had an unusual start. In 1990 he saw his friend scratching away on a piece of ivory using the scrimshaw technique. Beauchamp tried it and did so well that he got hooked. As the quality of his work improved, it became difficult to find a good knife maker who could mount his scrimshaw handles onto beautiful knives. So Beauchamp learned to make knives himself. Today he is better known for his knives than for his scrimshaw designs. His most popular creations are uniquely shaped fighting knives.

Beauchamp prefers a dark background, such as water buffalo horn, for his scrimshaw. Most scrimshaw pieces are done on a light background of ivory or bone. The artists use small tools such as a jeweler's needles because the work consists of scratching and picking out the surface of the material. The cuttings and pickings are then filled in with ink. Work done on a dark surface is called reverse scrimshaw. In order to do this the artist must think in negative, cutting into the dark surface, making the lighter lines stand out. Beauchamp uses oil paint to color the lines. With this difficult and time-consuming method, it can easily take him up to two hundred hours to create a piece of art. Beauchamp's talents are not limited to scrimshaw. His fantastic knives are made of ATS-34, 440C steel and Damasteel. He mostly uses stainless 416 steel for the bolsters. Most knives come in a beautifully crafted leather sheath, made by his wife, Denise Bryar from unique leathers such as elk, emu,

Portrait of a lion pair in reverse scrimshaw

hough it is recommended to ask a supplier for an official certificate in order to prevent potential problems at customs. Once in a while ivory comes from India and Sri Lanka, where elephants are used in forestry. This ivory can be imported with a so-called CITES (customs) declaration and is referred to as legal ivory.

SMALL AMBER HUNTER

This semi-integral hunting knife of ATS-34 steel is similar to the Small Hunter. The handle parts are of amber, a yellow-brown and transparent (fossil) resin from pine trees, mainly found off the Baltic coast and in Columbia. This knife is 7 inches long with a 3-inch blade.

The Bali-Song emblem of Benchmade

BENCHMADE
www.benchmade.com

The Benchmade Knife Company of Clackamas, Oregon was founded in 1988. The company uses

Small Amber Hunter

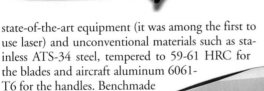

state-of-the-art equipment (it was among the first to use laser) and unconventional materials such as stainless ATS-34 steel, tempered to 59-61 HRC for the blades and aircraft aluminum 6061-T6 for the handles. Benchmade introduced the Designer series in 1991, combining designs from top custom knife makers with modern production methods to produce designer knives at affordable prices. Benchmade produces two

types of edges: a plain edge that can be re-sharpened and a partially serrated, or Combo Edge, for cutting through fibrous material such as ropes, nets or webbing.

The AFO stiletto

Benchmade blades come with a satin smooth finish, giving the surface a slightly matte appearance. There are further variations such as: stonewash, in which the blade is placed in a tumble apparatus with steel balls; scotchbrite, where the steel is roughened in miniscule grinding cases; or bead blasting, which dulls the surface so that it does not reflect any light – very important with tactical knives. A highly polished finish gives the steel a mirror-like shine and protects it against corrosion. A special protective polymer coating, applied at high temperature and burned in, also prevents glare or corrosion. The company slogan is: "Make it cool, make it solid, make it happen and definitely make it Benchmade."

AFO (ARMED FORCES ONLY)

The AFO (Armed Forces Only), is made for the military, police and emergency services. It is a stiletto, whose blade jumps out of the side of the handle under spring pressure, controlled by a colored metal button on top of the blade pivot. The 4.71 inch handle is milled from solid 6061, T-6 aluminum. The 3.75 inch, Teflon-coated, ATS-34 steel blade is 0.125 inches thick, and comes with either a smooth or a serrated edge.

The Benchmade Ambush and Mini-Ambush

Later models are of stainless 154-CM steel, tempered to 58-60 HRC. The opened knife is 8.46 inches long and it weighs 4.85 ounces. The latter models are standard equipment for the American Navy and part of the survival kits of the American Air Force.

AMBUSH

The Benchmade Ares

Benchmark co-owner Mel Pardue from Repton, Alabama, designed this folding knife. The Ambush and the smaller Mini-Ambush have stainless AUS-8 steel blades that can be flicked out of the handle with one hand with a thumb stud and fixed in position with a sliding stud under the blade pivot. This system is called the Rolling Lock, actually the foregoer of the Axis locking system. The handles of both knives are made of anodized airplane aluminum 6061-T6. The total length of the 6-ounceAmbush is 9.25 inches with a blade length of

3.95 inches. The 2.7 ounce Mini-Ambush is 6.95 inches long, with a 2.95 inch long blade and a 4-inch handle.

ARES

The Ares is a folding knife with the new Axis Lock system, designed by the custom knife makers Bill McHenry and Jason Williams. The bar runs abeam through the inner stainless 410-steel casing and can be used on both sides. As soon as the knife is opened, the steel bar moves under spring pressure in line

The Benchmade Axis-720

behind the toe of the blade. To fold the blade back, push the bar to the back to release the lock. The spearpoint blade of the Ares is made of stainless ATS-34 steel, tempered to 59-61 HRC. The length is 3.6 inches and it is 0.114 inches thick. The 4.7 inch long handle is made of twin colored synthetic G-10 material. The folded knife is 8.2 inches long, and weighs 4.4 ounces. It comes with a smooth or a partially serrated edge and a detachable carry clip that can be placed on either side of the handle.

AXIS-720

Mel Pardue designed this tactical folding knife with a non-reflective, synthetic protective layer on the stainless ATS-34 steel blade with an Axis locking system. The inner casing is of stainless 410-steel. The handle plates are of

The Benchmade Bali-Song butterfly knife

the light 6061-T6 aluminum, anodized black. The total length is 7.62 inches. The handle is 4.37 inches long and the knife weighs 4.3 ounces. The Bowie-shaped blade is 3.25 inches long and 0.115 inches thick with a thumb stud on both sides for easy opening. The knife has a detachable carry clip

BALI-SONG

The Benchmade Bali-Song was one of the first butterfly knives to appear on the market. The 4.3 inch long, 0.125 inch thick blade is made of stainless 440C steel, tempered to 58-60 HRC. The total length of the opened knife is 9.4 inches and it weighs 4.1 ounces. The handle, of 6AL-4V titanium, is 0.51 inches thick. This knife is forbidden in some countries.

CBK (Concealed Backup Knife)

The CBK (Concealed Backup Knife) push dagger

CBK stands for 'Concealed Backup Knife.' This is actually a push dagger, made upon request of various law enforcement agencies. The 2.5 inch long, 0.125 inch thick blade, made of stainless 440C steel features a chisel-shaped cut. The dagger is 5.47 inches in total length and weighs 2.32 ounces. It comes with a tactical sheath which can be carried in many different ways. This push dagger is banned in some countries.

Griptilian

The Benchmade Leopard folder, designed by Pat Crawford

The Griptilian series was designed by Mel Pardue, Bill McHenry and Jason Williams. The stainless 440C steel blade has a droppoint shape with an overall oval contour and a thumbhole for opening the knife and the Axis locking system. The total length of the knife is 8.07 inches. The blade is 3.45 inches long and 0.115 inches thick. The 4.62 inch handle is made of black Noryl GTX, a modern shock resistant synthetic material that is not very flexible and lightweight, or from colored Valox – fiberglass strengthened synthetic resin with excellent hardness and strength. It can be pressed into any shape and is available in any color imaginable. The weight of the Griptilian is 3.25 ounces. The Mini-Griptilian is actually not so small, as the handle length is 3.94 inches and the blade is 2.8 inches long.

Model 813 Mini-Tsek

Leopard

Pat Crawford designed the Leopard. The blade is made of ATS-34 steel and the inner casing is of 420 steel and has a classic linerlock system. Holes drilled into the handle make the knife a little lighter. The handle plates are made of 6061-T6 aluminum. The knife's total length is 8.35 inches, with a 4.75 inch handle and a 3.6 inch blade.

Mini-Tsek

The Model 813 Mini Tsek has an adjustable clippoint blade made of 440C steel and is

The Griptilian by Benchmade

0.097 inches thick. Thumb studs are fitted on both sides of the blade so that the knife can be opened with the left or the right hand. The 3.1 ounce knife is 7.62 inches long when opened and has a 3.16 inch blade. The left side of the 4.46 inch handle, made of stainless 410-steel plates, serves as a linerlock as well. There is a detachable steel carry clip on the handle on the right-hand side.

The Benchmade Monochrome

Monochrome

This knife, with a Monolock locking system, was designed by Steirer Eisen, the new Austrian knife designer at Benchmade. It was actually based on the linerlock, but it is a little bit heavier, with the heavy liner forming a part of the inner casing. The 3.04 inch long,

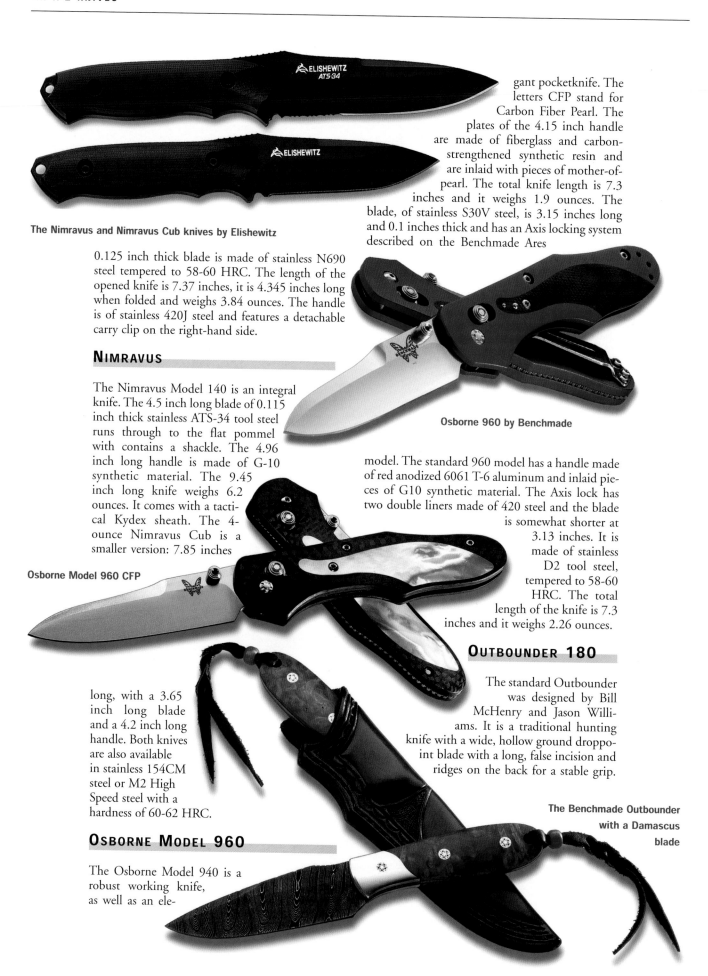

The Nimravus and Nimravus Cub knives by Elishewitz

gant pocketknife. The letters CFP stand for Carbon Fiber Pearl. The plates of the 4.15 inch handle are made of fiberglass and carbon-strengthened synthetic resin and are inlaid with pieces of mother-of-pearl. The total knife length is 7.3 inches and it weighs 1.9 ounces. The blade, of stainless S30V steel, is 3.15 inches long and 0.1 inches thick and has an Axis locking system described on the Benchmade Ares

0.125 inch thick blade is made of stainless N690 steel tempered to 58-60 HRC. The length of the opened knife is 7.37 inches, it is 4.345 inches long when folded and weighs 3.84 ounces. The handle is of stainless 420J steel and features a detachable carry clip on the right-hand side.

NIMRAVUS

The Nimravus Model 140 is an integral knife. The 4.5 inch long blade of 0.115 inch thick stainless ATS-34 tool steel runs through to the flat pommel with contains a shackle. The 4.96 inch long handle is made of G-10 synthetic material. The 9.45 inch long knife weighs 6.2 ounces. It comes with a tactical Kydex sheath. The 4-ounce Nimravus Cub is a smaller version: 7.85 inches

Osborne 960 by Benchmade

model. The standard 960 model has a handle made of red anodized 6061 T-6 aluminum and inlaid pieces of G10 synthetic material. The Axis lock has two double liners made of 420 steel and the blade is somewhat shorter at 3.13 inches. It is made of stainless D2 tool steel, tempered to 58-60 HRC. The total length of the knife is 7.3 inches and it weighs 2.26 ounces.

OUTBOUNDER 180

The standard Outbounder was designed by Bill McHenry and Jason Williams. It is a traditional hunting knife with a wide, hollow ground droppoint blade with a long, false incision and ridges on the back for a stable grip.

Osborne Model 960 CFP

long, with a 3.65 inch long blade and a 4.2 inch long handle. Both knives are also available in stainless 154CM steel or M2 High Speed steel with a hardness of 60-62 HRC.

OSBORNE MODEL 960

The Osborne Model 940 is a robust working knife, as well as an ele-

The Benchmade Outbounder with a Damascus blade

The 3.75 inch long and 0.125 inch thick blade of this integral knife is made of stainless 440C steel and runs to the end of the handle. The handle plates are made of stabilized hardwood and attached with Allen screws. The total length of the knife is 7.45 inches. It weighs 3.3 ounces and comes in a leather sheath. The blade of the special Outbounder 180 DM is made of Damasteel. The bolster is made of stainless steel, with Amboyna burl wood handle plates fixed with mosa-

Rant Bowie by Mel Pardue

ted to the front and some to the back, allowing it to cut in both directions. The 3.42 inch long, 0.13 inch thick drop point blade is made of stainless 154 CM steel. The opened knife is 8.25 inches long and weighs 5.64 ounces. The detachable carry clip on the right side of the handle can be attached to the left side as well.

The Benchmade Mini-Pika (top) and the larger Pika (bottom)

ic pins. The leather sheath is handmade by the Chris Kravitt. The measurements are equal to those of the standard model, but it only weighs 3.75 ounces.

PIKA / MINI-PIKA

The Pika got its name from a small rabbit that lives in mountainous areas all over the world. This 2.7 ounce folding knife has a lockback mechanism. The clippoint blade is made of stainless N690 steel with 50-60 HRC hardness. It is 3.5 inches long and 0.115 inches thick. The opened knife is 8.25 inches long. The 4.8 inch handle is made of Zytel. The blade of the 1.8 ounce Mini-Pika is 2.9 inches long and the total length is 6.95 inches. Both knives have detachable carry clips that can be placed on the left or the right side.

PRESIDIO

The Presidio is a sturdy folding knife with the Axis locking system, designed by Mel Pardue. The handle is made of 6061-T-6 aluminum with wide ridges for a stable grip. Some of the ridges are poin-

RANT BOWIE / DPT

The Rant Bowie is a fixed knife, designed by Mel Pardue for Benchmade. The Bowie shaped blade is 4.0 inches long, and made of stainless N690 steel with a hardness of 58-60 HRC. The total

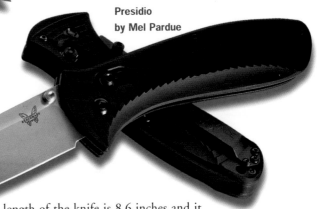

Presidio by Mel Pardue

length of the knife is 8.6 inches and it weighs 9.3 ounces with its leather sheath. The 4.6 inch handle is made of Kraton, a thermo plastic rubber with polymer developed by Shell from natural oil. The bolster and pommel are made of nickel steel. The 9.1 inch Rant DPT, also designed by Pardue, is made of the same material and has a spearpoint blade. The blade is 4.5 inches and the handle 4.6 inches long and it weighs 8.5 ounces with the sheath.

The Resistor

RESISTOR

Mike Snody designed this folding

The Benchmade Skirmish

knife with a unique blade – something between a clippoint and a droppoint, called a Gotham Swedged Clip-Point. The blade back runs up from the deeply ridged foot, then it tapers down in an arch, rises again and ends in a sharp point. This wide blade is made of 154 CM steel, tempered to 58-60 HRC. The blade length is 3.75 inches, the total length is 8 inches and it weighs 5.7 ounces. The handle is made of anodized aluminum with a decorative covering layer of G10. The Resistor also features the Axis locking system. The carry clip is detachable and can be placed on the other handle plate.

Benchmade Tanto Model 940 by Warren Osborne

SKIRMISH

The Skirmish folding knife was designed for Benchmade by Neil Blackwood, and it lives up to its name. The 4.3 inch skinner blade is made of stainless S30V steel with 58-60 HRC hardness and is locked with a linerlock system. The total length of the open knife is 9.4 inches. There are three holes in the blade. The back hole serves as a thumbhole to open the knife with easily. The 5.1 inch handle is made of titanium and decorated with a series of small holes on the inside of a colored ceramic layer and has a detachable stainless steel carry clip on the right-hand side.

STRYKER

The Benchmade Stryker was designed by Allen Elishewitz. It is a typical tactical knife with a Tanto-shaped blade made of stainless ATS-34 steel, or of 154CM steel in 58-60 HRC hardness or of M2 High Speed steel with 60-62 HRC hardness. The total length is 8.25 inches, the blade is 0.125 inches thick and 3.7 inches long, with a double-sided thumb bolt attached to the blade back and a linerlock system with a 6 AL-4V titanium bolt rod. The knife weighs 3.8 ounces. The blade comes with a double-sided smooth edge or with partial serration. The

The Stryker by Allen Elishewitz

4.68 inch handle is made of G-10 synthetic material. The 2.7 ounce, 7.1 inch long Mini-Stryker, of the same shape and material, has a 2.9 inch blade and a 4.1 inch handle.

TANTO 940

The Tanto Model 940 folding knife was designed Warren Osborne. The 3.4 inch long, 0.115 inch thick blade of stainless 154CM steel, tempered to 58-60 HRC has the typical

Tanto-shape, also referred to as Reverse Tanto. The handle plates are made of dark green or black anodized 6061-T6 aluminum on a casing of stainless 410 steel. The opened knife is 7.87 inches long and the length of the handle is 4.47 inches. The knife has a linerlock system and weighs 2.9 ounces. The blade comes with a smooth or partially serrated edge.

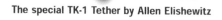

The special TK-1 Tether by Allen Elishewitz

TK-1 TETHER

The small TK-1 Tether, with a skeleton grip, designed by Allen Elishewitz from stainless GIN-1 steel or 440C steel, has a Kydex sheath and a chain or cord so that it can be worn around the neck. The handle is covered with a rough dark gray synthetic material for a firm grip. The knife is 5.75 inches long, the blade is 2.0 inches long and 0.125 inches thick with a smooth or partially serrated edge. The knife weighs 1.5 ounces and the sheath 1 ounce.

The emblem of Beretta

BERETTA

www.beretta.com; www.berettausa.com

The Italian company Pietro Beretta is well known for its pistols and shotguns. Less known is its excellent assortment of knives. Their daughter company Beretta-USA makes collectible knives mainly for the American market.

It is not known exactly when Beretta started making knives. The company has been handed down from one generation to the next since the fifteenth century, when the Beretta family started making weapons in Gardone. Old records show that Master Bartolemo Beretta received 296 ducats from the Arsenal of Venice in 1526 for delivering 185 harquebus barrels. At the beginning of the twentieth century, Beretta was producing hunting weapons, and knives were added as service articles. The S687 EEL, for example, had a casing and handle similar to the forearm plates of the double-barrel shotgun with the same model number. Today Beretta makes excellent hunting knives with additional blades that can be removed and used to clean venison. Beretta knives are currently made in Japan.

AIRLIGHT II

Beretta brought the Airlight II knife to the market in 2002. It has the same sleek shape as the bestselling Airlight. The blade is made of stainless AUS 6M steel and locks with a linerlock system. The handle plates are made of lightweight aluminum, with a carry clip mounted on right plate. The Airlight II comes in two sizes. The blade of the smaller, 7-inch, knife is 3.12 inches long and the handle is 3.9 inches in length. The bigger knife is 8 inches long with a 3.75 inch blade and a 4.25 inch handle. Both models come with smooth or partially serrated edges and black or white anodized handle plates.

ALUMINUM AIRLIGHT TANTO

The Beretta Aluminum Airlight Tanto is called a tactical folding knife due to its measurements and blade shape. The 8-inch knife is excellent for daily use by the police, hunters and those who love the outdoor life. The 3.75 inch blade, made of stainless AUS 6M steel, comes with a smooth of partially serrated edge. Beretta

Beretta Model Airlight II in Silver and Black

uses iron strong 6061-T6 aluminum with white or black detail. The handle is 4.25 inches long and has a frontlock system. This variation of the backlock system means that the lock is on the front, not the back. The short bolt rod hinges on an axis directly above the blade and latches on to the back.

ALUMINUM AIRLIGHT

The Aluminum Airlight has come in a black, anodized version since 2002. The knives are slim, with typical spearpoint blades with thumb studs attached on either

Beretta Aluminum Airlight

Aluminum Airlight series in Black & White

The trailing-point model has a blade of stainless AUS-8 steel, 2.87 or 3.37 inches in length. The total length is 7 and 8 inches respectively. The handle of both models is made of black Micarta, with plates mounted on stainless steel casings, attached with nickel steel pins.

side. The Airlight comes with a skeleton or a solid blade and a smooth or partially serrated edge. A detachable carry clip is mounted on the right handle blade. The Aluminum Airlight comes in three different lengths of eight, seven and five inches, with blades 3.75, 3.12 and 2.37 inches long, respectively. The smallest version does not have a carry clip.

Typical Beretta Avenger II

AVENGER II

Busfield Clippoint folder

The Avenger was designed by custom knife maker Warren Thomas. Its flat handle is made of dark gray to black fiberglass, which is particularly strong and exceptionally lightweight. With its stainless VG-10 Tanto steel, it is the perfect tactical folding knife, with a linerlock system. With two working thumb studs, it can be opened quickly with either the left or the right hand. The total length of the knife is 7 inches, the blade is 3.12 inches and the handle is 3.9 inches long. A detachable carry clip is on the right side of the handle.

BUSFIELD

This knife by master knife maker Jack Busfield comes with either a clippoint or a trailing-point blade and has a frontlock system. The clippoint model is available with a total length of 7 or 8 inches and comes with a black G-10 synthetic handle.

Beretta Busfield Trailing point

FIELDLIGHT

The Beretta Fieldlight is lightweight, small and made for use in the field or while hunting. The blade or multi-blades are made of stainless AUS-8 steel. The handle is made of durable Zytel synthetic material and has a deeply imprinted checkered motif for a stable grip. Every Fieldlight comes with a woven nylon belt sheath. There are two versions of this model, both eight inches long. The simplest version has a single 3.25 inch droppoint blade. The skinner model, with the same blade length, has a typical skinner blade at the top end of the blade point. Both have a simple frontlock system.

Simple Beretta hunting folder

The simple Fieldlight knife has a double blade with a droppoint as well as an additional sawing blade that is locked separately with a backlock system. The cutting blade has a front-lock

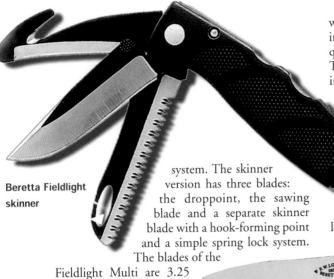

Beretta Fieldlight skinner

with long hollow grinds that end in razor-sharp incisions. The 2004 series includes a knife with a quince wood handle and one made of stag horn. The total length is 8 inches with a blade of 4 inches. The handle, somewhat on the long side, is in the characteristic Loveless shape.

system. The skinner version has three blades: the droppoint, the sawing blade and a separate skinner blade with a hook-forming point and a simple spring lock system. The blades of the Fieldlight Multi are 3.25 inches long and the total length is 8 inches.

LOVELESS ZYTEL HUNTER

The Zytel Hunter by Loveless is actually a series of two knives. One version has a 4-inch hollow ground droppoint blade made of AUS-8 steel. The second version has a skinner blade of the same length. Each knife is 8 inches long, is made of

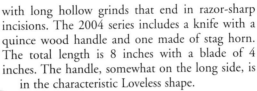

Beretta Hunter designed by Bob Loveless

LOVELESS WHITETAIL COLLECTOR

American knife maker Bob Loveless is a pioneer among custom knife makers. This special knife was issued in a limited, numbered edition of one thousand mostly handmade pieces. The handles are of exclusive quince wood, decorated with etched hoof prints of the whitetail deer. The blades are of stainless AUS-8 steel, engraved with a beautiful depiction of a whitetail, by Michael Collins. The hollow ground blade is 4 inches

shock resistant Zytel synthetic material and comes with a black leather sheath.

M9 AMERICA'S DEFENDER COLLECTION KNIFE

The special M9 'America's Defender' knife is only available in a limited, numbered edition of one thousand pieces. The model commemorates the fact that the Beretta M9 has been in use by the American military for fifteen years. The Tanto blade of AUS-8 steel has a protective layer of black Teflon and is 3.5 inches long. The total length

Whitetail Collector by Bob Loveless

long and the handle is also 4 inches long, for a total length of 8 inches. The knife comes in a special gift package.

LOVELESS HUNTER

Bob Loveless designed a few knives for Beretta for serial production: good news for Loveless knife collectors as the standard delivery time for a custom-made Loveless is more than one year. These fixed knives have droppoints of stainless AUS-8 steel

The Bob Loveless Zytel Hunter in droppoint version

of the knife is 8 inches. The handle is similar to the Model 92 knife and looks like the handle plates of the military pistol. This knife comes specially packaged.

The special 1 of 1000 Beretta M9 America's Defender knive

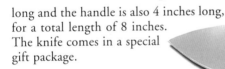

Tactical folder Model 92, refers to the Beretta Model 92 pistol

MODEL 92

The Beretta folding knife Model 92 was named after the well-known Model 92 pistol. This single hand-operated folding knife has the same casing as the pistol with similar handle plates and handle plate screws. The 8-inch knife has a typical Tanto blade made of stainless AUS-8 steel with the same markings on the blade as on the original Beretta Model 92 pistol. The 3.5 inch blade locks in place with a linerlock system. The handle plates are made of black Zytel. The knives come with smooth or partially serrated edges and a carry clip mounted on the right handle plate.

STAG BIG GAME

Except for the Fieldight series with Zytel handle plates, Beretta also offers a series of classic hunting folders, the Stag folders. The big Stag hunter has three blades. The biggest blade is skinner shaped, with a long, wide contour so that the knife can be opened with

The Beretta Bird Knife

the thumb or nail of one hand. The second blade is the cutting blade, meant for cleaning game. The third blade can be used as a bone saw. All three blades are made of stainless 440C steel and are 3 inches long. The bolster is made of nickel steel. Stag horn was used for the handles. Only the skinner blade has a backlock system.

STAG BIRD KNIFE

The so-called Bird Knife is in the same series as the Stag Hunting Folders and it was specifically developed for hunting birds. Along with the skinner blade, which is made of stainless 440C steel and is 3 inches long, the knife also has a "bird intestine hook" for pulling out the intestines of shot birds so that the game does not get spoilt while hunting. The bolster is made of nickel steel and the handle is made of stag horn with an inlaid Beretta logo. The skinner blade works on a backlock system.

TASCA SERIES

The Beretta Tasca is a series of small and compact folding knives. The

The Beretta Stag Big Game Skinner

Tasca is a typical pocketknife in that the big carry clip can also be used as a money clip. It comes with three different types of handle plates made either from white lightweight 6061 T6 aircraft aluminum with a hard protective layer against scratches, from stainless steel or from black Micarta. The Tasca has a droppoint blade made of stainless AUS-8 steel that is 2.25 inches long. The knife is 5.5 inches long in total. The blades of all three versions are partially serrated and locked with a frontlock system.

TRIDENT

The light Beretta Trident is the ideal pocketknife. The typical Sheepfoot blade, also called the Wharncliffe, is made of special VG-10 steel: a type of steel with relatively high carbon content

Small Tasca folder

The characteristically shaped Trident folder from Beretta

of 2.37 inches and a total length of 6 inches. This version only comes with skeleton blades with smooth or partially serrated edges, no carry clip and a black Zytel handle. The next largest, 7-inch model has a 3.12 inch blade and is 7 inches in total length. The blade is made of solid steel in an open skeleton shape with a smooth or partially serrated edge.

The biggest model is 8 inches long in total with a blade length of 3.75 inches. The knife has a solid steel or skeleton shaped

and a lot of chromium, molybdenum and nickel. The Electra model has handle plates made of a computer printer plate. The Trident has handle plates made of Cocobolo wood and G-10 synthetic material. The total length of both knives is 6 inches, the blades are 2.75 inches long and lock using the linerlock system.

Commemorative knife 'United We Stand'

'UNITED WE STAND' COMMEMORATIVE KNIFE

blade with a smooth or partially serrated edge. The handle comes in black or in camouflage. The two bigger versions have carry clips on the right handle sides. Their Zytel handles are covered with black camouflage or Zytel Camo.

The Zytel Airlight

This special Airlight folding knife is a commemorative model honoring all military units sent out in the name of the United States of America to all parts of the world. The knife has handle plates made of black anodized aluminum. The skeleton shaped blade has a spearpoint and is 3.75 inches long. The total length of the knife is 8.0 inches. The handle is decorated with a brass colored shield with the mark of Beretta, a depiction of the American flag and the inscription 'United We Stand.'

ZYTEL AIRLIGHT

The Zytel Airlight knife series was designed with a particularly firm grip with a rough surface to prevent slipping. Beretta makes them with a standard solid or skeleton-shaped spearpoint blade and a smooth or partially serrated edge. Each blade is made of stainless AUS-6 steel, ground razor sharp. The knives come in three different sizes. The smallest has a blade length

ZYTEL AIRLIGHT SKINNER

The Zytel Camo Airlight Skinner was specially designed for hunting. The typical skinner blade has a 'gut hook' at the top of the point. This big knife is 8 inches long in total. Its 3.75 inch blade comes with a smooth or partially serrated edge. The handle has

The Beretta Zytel Airlight Skinner

a carry clip on the right plate and a shackle for a carry cord on the back. This is handy as the knife is only available with a camouflage pattern: once you have laid it down in the forest it is very hard to find it again.

The Zytel Airlight Camo

BOEHLKE

www.boehlke-messer.de

Emblem of Günter Böhlke

At a field archery competition in 1985, Gunter Boehlke showed a few friends his self-made kni-ves. They were so enthusiastic that he had to make knives for them.

Ever since then he has been making about thirty hunting and collector's knives per year.

Even though he makes smaller knives as well, his heart is with the bigger work.

His knives are particularly strong, with blades at least 0.24 inches thick and handles that fill the enti-re hand. He cuts the blade himself with a band saw from a rough plate of unhardened steel and grinds it with a self-made belt grinder. After it is hardened by a specialist, Boehlke mounts the guard, the handle and the pommel. The accom-panying sheath is also handmade.

Boehlke spends around 30 – 50 hours on each knife. The television engineer currently working as a civil servant is self-taught and never had any training in working with metal. He can often be seen at markets and exhibitions of ancient crafts offering demonstrations in making knives and handle material.

DAMASCUS DAGGER

The Damascus Dagger has two ground blades of 'wild' Damasteel, a brass guard and pommel and a handle of dark ebony with a diagonal decorative strip of polished mammoth ivory through the middle for a beautiful contrast. The leather sheath was designed so that the dagger could be carried around the neck. The total length of the Damascus Dagger is 5.9 inches and the blade is 2 inches long and 0.14 inches thick.

Böhlke Dagger

Damascus Dagger

Damascus Hunter by Günter Böhlke

BOHLKE DAGGER

This is an integral dagger: drilled, filed and ground from one piece of stainless steel. The lovely wide blade was ground sharp on both sides with a flat edge that divides the blade into two halves. The handle is of carbon fiberglass. The total length is 8.7 inches, with a blade 4.72 inches long and 0.18 inches thick.

A beautiful Damascus Hunter

An example of beautiful Damascus steel

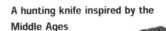

has finger grooves and is made of dark Palmyra palm, the Borassus flabelliformis from India. The total length of the Damascus Hunter is 10.1 inches, with a 4.7 inch long, 0.20 inch thick blade.

DAMASCUS HUNTER 1

The Damascus Hunter has a Damasteel blade ground into a long V-shape. The bolster is made of the same Damasteel, but this is hard to tell because it is polished differently. The light wood on the handle comes from the Amboyna burl. The dark patches are of alternating pieces of ironwood and mammoth ivory. The total length is 8.7 inches and the blade is 3.9 inches long and 0.14 inches thick. A handmade sheath goes with the knife.

A hunting knife inspired by the Middle Ages

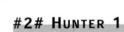

DAMASCUS HUNTER 2

This Damascus Hunter has a hollow ground Damasteel blade as well as a Damasteel bolster and pommel. The handle is of Amboyna burl with a strip of ironwood in the middle, flanked by strips of mammoth ivory. The knife is 8.1 inches long, with a 3.7 inch long, 0.18 inch thick blade.

DAMASCUS HUNTER 3

The blade of this lovely Damascus hunting knife is made of three layers of laminated steel. The inner layer is of stainless steel, sandwiched between a covering layer, consisting of six-way torsion Damascus. The guard and pommel are of nickel silver, finished with a dark red decorative edge. The handle

#2# HUNTER 1

This hunting knife is shaped like a primitive tool from the Middle Ages. The blade is made of Chrome Moly Steel 42 CrMo4. The handle is a piece of stag horn that looks like it has been attached to the blade with a leather thong. A round leather sheath with a braided seam goes with the knife. The total length of the knife is 11.8 inches with a 6.5 inch long, 0.20 inch thick blade.

BOJTOS
bojtos@stonline.sk

Arpad Bojtos from Lucenec in Slovakia, is a part of that country's Hungarian minority. His work is characterized by the unique engravings that run from the

A modern hunting knife

handle right on to the steel of the blade. He got his inspiration from books he read during the communist era, when it was difficult to travel. Educated as an economist, he only started to make knives after the fall of the regime in 1990. The mystic shapes of his creations, inspired by the Touareg nomads and ancient civilizations of the Middle East, quickly brought him renown. His first show was in 1991 in Bern, Switzerland with Lubomir Madaric and Julius Mojžíš, both knife makers and engravers. There he caught the attention of the Soppera family in Zurich and the Dutch knife makers Van Eldik and Van den Heuvel/Hill Knives. In 1996 he became a member of the prestigious American Knife Makers Guild.

The African Hunter is not a hunting knife, but a work of art

AFRICAN HUNTER

The Bojtos Buffalo Hunter

This integral knife, 7.5 inches in total length with a 3.4 inch blade made of stainless ATS-34 steel, is a work of art. The blade, the pommel and the steel in the 5.1 inch ironwood handle are all made of one piece of steel adorned with African warriors. The pommel is a crouched lion, ready to spring. The sheath is of bone, covered with stingray leather and decorated with carved water buffalo and Nile herons.

BUFFALO HUNTER

This 6-inch fixed knife has a Damasteel blade made by Devin Thomas and a Damasteel handle made by Stephen Schwarzer. Bojtos engraved a beautiful image of an Indian bison hunter on it. The top edge of the blade displays a herd of bison, cast in silver and gold.

FAIRY TALE

The Fairy Tale is actually a museum-quality Art-Nouveau statue with an exquisite depiction of a stainless

steel elf, inlaid with gold, silver and opal, resting on the mother-of-pearl handle. The Damasteel blade of this 5.5 inch folding knife was made by Fritz Schneider.

FLAMINGO

The Flamingo is a 6-inch long, integral folding knife with a linerlock system. The Damasteel blade, ground by Fritz Schneider, has an arch at the back. The handle plates are of tortoise shell, inlaid with silver. The image of a flamingo is offset in silver.

GAZELLE HUNTER

The Fairy Tale

His imaginary travels to Africa were Bojtos' inspiration for this knife. The fixed knife is 8.7 inches long, with a 4.5 inch long blade made of ATS-34 steel and a 4.2 inch long handle. The sheath and handle are made of ebony and palm wood. The bolster has a unique guard: a beautifully crafted gazelle that forms the transition between the handle and the blade. The pommel is shaped

Flamingo

The beautiful Gazelle Hunter

into a swan and gained her love. The goddess conceived and laid an egg which was found by a shepherd, who gave it to Leda. The child that hatched from the egg, Helen of Troy, was so beautiful Leda claimed her as her own daughter. This folding knife is 6.75 inches long with a Damasteel blade made by Fritz Schneider. The handle is silver, mother-of-pearl and gold-plated stainless steel.

LION HUNTER

Leda & Swan

like a jaguar cut into the palm wood. On the sheath are African warriors carved in ebony.

HUNTER 2

The Hunter is a practical hunting knife, with a blade of stainless 440C steel, a guard of nickel silver and a handle of Caucasian walnut. The

The Lion Hunter

The Lion Hunter is a beautiful integral knife made of ATS-34 steel. The steel of the pommel and the bolster are embellished with engravings of lions and antelope that extend halfway down the blade. The bone sheath, into which a herd of zebras is carved, is covered with stingray leather. The 7.5 inch knife has a 3.4 inch blade and a 5.1 inch handle with ironwood handleplates.

TUAREG FIGHTER

The Tuareg Fighter is a large, fixed 8.7 inch long hunting knife. The 4.5 inch, ATS-34 steel blade is engraved with a falcon in his natural habitat. The large bolster is engraved with a Tuareg horseman, inlaid with gold, silver and copper. The 4.2 inch long handle is made of snakewood, attached to the knife with silver pins. The artful sheath is also made of snakewood, embellished with a piece of ivory and rounded off with a band of silver.

total length is 9.3 inches, with a 4.6 inch long, 0.26 inch thick blade.

LEDA & SWAN

The entwined woman and swan on this knife stem from Greek mythology. Leda, the daughter of Thestios, the king of Aetolia and the wife of Tyndareus, the king of Sparta, was seduced by the god Zeus, in the guise of a swan. In another version of the tale, the goddess Nemesis changed herself into a goose to escape Zeus. But he turned himself

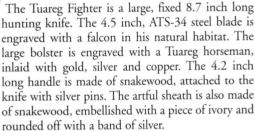

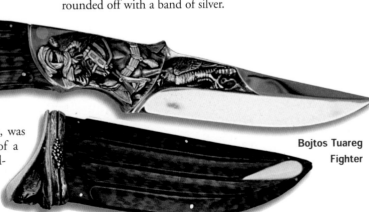

Bojtos Tuareg Fighter

Bojtos Tuareg

TUAREG

The Tuareg dagger is only 5.5 inches long. The blade is made of Damasteel, partially decorated with an ibex. The handle is made of stainless steel and plated with silver, gold, jasper and black coral. A depiction of a Tuareg, a nomad from the African Sahara, standing with his camel, is on the bolster. The pommel is shaped like a sculpted dromedary.

The emblem of Böker

BÖKER/MAGNUM
www.boker.de

The history of Böker starts in 1829 at a forge for hand tools in Remscheid, Germany where Hermann and Robert Böcker started making sabers. A year later, when production reached two thousand pieces, the brothers decided to divide their activities. Herman Böker started H Böker & Co in New York. Robert went to Canada, then Mexico and worked under the name Casa Böker. Heinrich – another member of the family – established Heinrich Böker & Co with knife manufacturer Hermann Heuser in 1896 in Solingen, where he started producing razors, scissors and pocketknives which proved to be best-sellers on both sides of the Atlantic. Because their American and Spanish clientele had problems pronouncing Böker, Heinrich suggested the old chestnut tree from the old forge in Remscheid and an arrow as brand images. After 1900, the lion's share of Böker's merchandise went to the United States in the form of pocketknives, which outstripped sales of razors, scissors and cutlery. Because the German company did not have sufficient capacity, the New York branch also started

producing pocketknives under the tree logo.

World War II upset this cooperation. The Solingen company was completely destroyed and America confiscated the tree logo. But after the war, John Böker Jr., the son of Heinrich, steered the company out of troubled waters. Solingen quickly restarted production and the American branch started placing orders. Soon Böker New York was once again Solingen's most prominent buyer.

At the start of the 1960's, Böker USA's ownership passed to Cooper Industries, a golden move for the German branch. Mutual ties were strengthened and the American market share soared. Böker Solingen was able to renew and modernize their entire production line and develop new products. In 1986 Cooper returned the logo rights to Böker Solingen, which established Böker USA, Inc. in Denver, Colorado. The old activities in South America were also given a new lease on life. Böker Arbolito SA in Argentina was established in 1983 with the Tree and Arbolito brands, among others.

Today, Böker Solingen is both a knife manufacturer and wholesaler, making knives of their own design or special order knives, designed by well-known knife makers, on site or at other factories. The Böker Arbolito knife, for example, was designed by Dietmar Pohl and produced in Argentina. The company also cooperates with well-known knife factories such as Frost Cutlery; Japanese knife makers Hatto-

The AK-47

ri, Moki and Tak Fukuta; and American Spyderco and Columbia River Knife & Tool (CRKT).

Every year Böker issues the *Magnum Knife Catalog* featuring their own knives plus well-known marks from all over the world and makes a special Knife of the Year for serious knife collectors in limited editions. The American, German and South American companies also trade through the Internet at www.boker.de or www.bokerusa.com

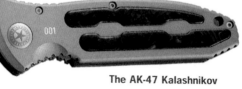

The AK-47 Kalashnikov Damascus knife by Böker

The lovely AK-74 Kalashnikov

AK-47 KALASHNIKOV SERIES

The name Kalashnikov is tied to the famous Russian AK-47 military weapon. Böker is allowed to use the name for a series of high quality folding knives, designed by German knife maker Dietmar Pohl. The casings are not made of cast iron, but are especially dry cut with a CNC machine. The grip plates are of 6061 airplane aluminum. These knives have a linerlock system with thumb studs on the blade for easy opening. The inlay pieces of the handle of G-10 synthetic material and, in the limited edition, from polished snake wood, have the exact shape and contours of the lower and upper grip plates of the AK-47 weapon.
On the right side is a carry clip.
The blade is made of 440C steel, shaped like the AK-47 leather bayonet and comes highly polished or with matte finishing. The AK-47 Limited was made in a limited edition of 2003 units. The total length of the 6-ounce knife is 9 inches and the blade length is 3.93 inches.
Böker also introduced the AK-47 knife in a

The Applegate-Fairbairn daggers

Damascus version, with a blade made of 180 layers of stainless Damasteel and colonel Kalashnikov's signature etched on the blade. The casing, like that of the standard AK-47 knives, is milled from a single piece of 6061-T9 aluminum by the computer driven CNC machines. The handle is inlayed with desert ironwood from New Mexico. The AK-47 Damascus knife, produced in a limited edition of only 500 hand-made copies, comes with a special collector's case and a certificate of authenticity. The knife is 8.86 inches long, with a 3.93 inch blade and weighs 5.96 ounces.

AK-74 KALASHNIKOV

The AK-47 folding knife, which hearkens back to the 5.45 x 39 mm caliber Russian AK-47 rifle, was designed by Dieter Pohl with a left linerlock system. The 4.73

inch handle is based on the original weapon's bayonet. The 3.35 inch stainless AUS-8 steel blade has a black Teflon protective layer and is partially serrated. The knife comes with an aluminum handle in black, matte or military green. The Knife is 7.87 inches long and weighs 4.23 ounces. There is a Kalashnikov logo on the axis of the blade.
Böker also makes a stiletto under the name AKS-74 Automatic. A button in the handle releases the locking system of the blade, which flips out under spring pressure. Stilettos with blades longer than 3.5 inches or narrower than 0.55 inches are subject to legal regulations in most countries. The AKS-74 Automatic is 8.87 inches long, with a 3.35 inch blade and weighs 4.6 ounces.

The AKS-74 Kalashnikov Automatic version

APPLEGATE-FAIRBAIRN

This knife was named after First Lieutenant Rex Appeletage of the OSS (a forerunner of the Special Forces) and William Advart Fairbairn, the inventor of Defendu a self-defense system used by the Britis S.A.S. (Special Air Services). The Applegate-Fairbairn Combat knife is made of stainless 440C steel, tempered to 58 HRC. The handle is of polyamide, reinforced with fiberglass. Small weights are worked into the handle for optimal balance. The guard is made of solid brass. The knife weighs 8.6 ounces and is 10.7 inches long, with a 5.9 inch blade and is issued with a Kydex Cordura sheath. A similar model, the Applegate-Fairbairn Desert dagger has a double-sided cutting edge. The Utility II knife only has one edge while the Combat II knife has two. The names Applegate and Fairbairn are etched into the blades.

The double sided Applegate-Fairbairn Mini-Smatchet dagger

APPLEGATE-FAIRBAIRN MINI SMATCHET

The Applegate-Fairbairn Mini Smatchet is a cross between a dagger and a machete. Its heavy blade is 0.185 inches thick and made of stainless 440C

The Böker Beluga
diving knife made from X-15 TN steel

steel. The unusual shape makes it ideal for cutting and cleaving. The hole in the blade serves as a reminder to use that edge for rough hacking and breaking work and the other side for more subtle cutting work. The knife comes with a Cordura holder on an adjustable belt sheath, so it attaches to an ordinary belt as well as a military one. This compact knife weighs 7.4 ounces, is 9 inches long with a 4.8 inch blade and a 4.2 inch handle, made of fiberglass reinforced polyamide, is 4.2 inches long.

Two examples from the Böker Gemini knife series
The Gemini Badger and the Gemini Tactical

BELUGA

This is an integral knife diving knife with a special skeleton grip. The blade and grip were made of one piece of metal. Holes in the steel reduce the weight considerably and ensure a stable grip. The knife is made of special stainless X-15 T.N steel, 0.24 inches thick and coated with a gray Teflon protective layer. The

knife comes with a Cordura sheath. Its total length of is 10.4 inches, with a blade length of 5.1 inches and a weight of 13.0 ounces.

BOA

This lovely traditional folding knife has a modern touch thanks to a thumb stud on the blade. Despite its conventional appearance, this is a high-tech knife with a blade of stainless CPM-S60V powder steel, a nickel silver bolster and handle plates of Micarta. Böker also makes it with a titani-

The Böker Boa folding knife made from special
CPM-S60V powder steel

um handle and Cocobolo or Amboyna plates. The Boa has a backlock system. The knife is 7.5 inches long with a 3.15 inch blade and a weight of 3.5 ounces.

GEMINI

The Böker Gemini comes in several styles. The blade is stainless X-15 T.N or 3034 steel. The handle is fiberglass reinforced polyamide, with a Kraton inlay, a carry clip on the right-hand side and a 3034 steel linerlock. The Gemini Badger has a blade made of X-15 T.N steel and the blade of the Tactical is of 3034 steel with a Teflon protective layer. Both blades are partially serrated. The total length of both knives is 8.27 inches, the blades are 3.54 inches long and the weight is 3.18 ounces.

NEALY SPECIALIST

Bud Nealy is the designer of the patented Kydex sheath that can be carried in many different and comfortable ways. He designed the Nealy Specialist especially for Böker. This integral knife is made of stainless 440C steel with a hardness of 58 HRC. The four holes drilled in the handle, a typical Nealy feature,

The Nealy Specialist integral knife

serve to reduce weight and improve the grip. The handle plates are made of G-10 synthetic material or of Cocobolo wood. The remarkable carrying system, called the MCS (Multi Concealment Sheath), has a small magnet which keeps the knife in the

The special Böker Orca diving knife (top) and the Orca II hunting knife (bottom)

sheath, so it can be carried upside down. The total length of the specialist is 7.24 inches with a blade 3.46 inches long. The knife weighs 2.82 ounces.

ORCA

The Orca was specially designed as a diving knife. The blade, of special X-15 T.N steel, has a very fine, partially serrated edge that easily cuts through nets and lines. The long axe on the back of the blade can chop through thin steel wire or tree roots. The pommel of this integral knife can be used as a hammer. The handle is of Hytrel synthetic material that is shock, acid and saltwater resistant. The blade has an additional dark gray protective Teflon layer. The knife comes with a synthetic sheath.

The special Submariner integral diving knife

The Orca II, has the same shape, but it is a hunting knife, with a smooth edge and a long, false incision running from the point halfway down the back of the blade. The knife comes with a Cordura sheath. Both knives are 10.4 inches long with 5.1 inch long ergonomically designed blades. The knife weighs 13 ounces.

SPEEDLOCK

This is a stiletto designed by Dietmar Pohl. With the push of a button, the blade pivot pushes out the blade at the side of the handle with spring pressure. The Speedlock, with aluminum handle plates inlaid with Kraton of different colors or thuya wood, is 7.9 inches long with a stainless 4034-steel blade of 3.4 inches and weighs 4.23 ounces. Boker also makes the smaller Speedlock II: 6.8 inches long with a 2.75 inch blade and weight of 2.82 ounces.

SUBMARINER

The Submariner is an integral diving knife specially designed by Dietmar Pohl and Jens Honer, a world-record holder in deep sea diving at 787.4 feet. The skeleton handle was specifically designed to prevent the buildup of salt crystals under the handle plates. The knife is of special Alpha-

The Böker Speedlock stiletto

Beta Titanium V steel and comes in two different designs: double sided with smooth edges or double sided with one edge, partially micro-serrated. The knife was designed short, so it could be carried on the lower arm. The handle can be gripped properly, even with thick, Neoprene diving gloves. The Submariner comes with a Kydex sheath and various arm and leg straps. The sheath also has a special Tek-Lok carry piece that clicks into place on a strap. The total length of the knife is 8.85 inches. The blade is 3.93 inches long and it weighs 6.35 ounces.

SUPER TITAN LINER

The Super Titan Liner is a unique one-handed knife with a linerlock system. The foot of the blade is kept in place by a steel ball so that the knife can-

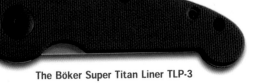

The Böker Super Titan Liner TLP-3

not flip open by itself, which could easily happen, as the blade is fitted with bearings. The Titan has a 440C steel, 2.75 inch long blade and a handle available in titanium, fiberglass carbon or G-10 synthetic material. The knife is 7.9 inches long and it weighs 3 to 3.8 ounces. Another version features

The emblem of Buck Knives

partial serration with a Teflon protective layer. There is a thumb stud on the blade for easy opening with one hand.

BUCK

www.buckknives.com

The Buck Woodsman hunting Knife

The name 'Buck' is so well known that the words 'Buck folding knife' have become synonymous with the article intelf. In the late 1890's Hoyt (Heath) Buck, an apprentice smith decided to find a way to keep farmers' hoes sharp longer. The simple hardening process, which he developed and tested on knives he made from old files, is the foundation of the company's current hardening system. In 1941, he and his son Alfred Charles Buck set up a smithy in Hoyt's church basement and started making Buck pocketknives for the military.

Hoyt died of cancer in 1949 at 59. Al and his family barely kept the company running until Howard Craig, a quality controller at Ryan Aeronautics, helped Al establish Buck Knives Inc. and acquire the necessary capital to expand the company by selling shares.

Nowadays, the company is working on a hardening process developed by Paul Bos an employee of Buck Knives Inc. The steel is first heated to 1950 degrees Fahrenheit and suddenly cooled. It is then frozen with liquid nitrogen to -120 degrees Fahrenheit, and slowly reheated to between 350 and 950 degrees Fahrenheit, depending

on the knife and the type of steel.

Buck also has a special technique for grinding the edge to obtain its trademark 'Edge 2X.' In the past, blades had always been ground to an angle of 35 to 50 degrees. The height of the cut was 0.03 inches. The new Edge 2X was developed by a team of engineers and experienced grinders under the leadership of Al's son Chuck Buck who changed the grinding angle to 26 to 32 degrees and increased the height to 0.04 inches. The result led to a sharper, wear resistant and easy to sharpen blade.

MODEL 102 BUCK WOODSMAN

Buck has been making the Model 102 Buck Woodsman hunting knife for a long time. The 4-inch long blade has a fine point for working on fish or small game. Made of 420 HC steel, tempered to 58 HRC, it has a high carbon and chromium content, which makes the blade wear resistant and the steel easier to grind. The total length is 7.75 inches. The handle is made of phenol synthetic material and weighs 2.5 ounces. The similar Model 102 BR has a handle made of Cocobolo wood, which weighs 3.6 ounces and a guard and pommel of nickel steel or brass. The knife comes with a leather sheath.

The Model 103 Skinner (top) and the 105 Pathfinder (bottom)

MODEL 103 SKINNER / PATHFINDER

The Buck Skinner is a typical skinning knife with a wide blade and a wide, round knifepoint. The 4-inch blade is made of stainless 420 HC steel, the total length of the knife is 8.25 inches and it weighs 4.3 ounces. It only comes with a synthetic handle

The Model 110 Folding Hunter

Model 112 Ranger

Model 110, it is made with a proper casing and a handle with finger grooves. The bolster and pommel are made of brass and the knife has a backlock system.

and a black leather sheath. The Model 105 Pathfinder is a good knife for general use, such as hunting, camping and fishing. It has a 5-inch long blade and is 9.13 inches long in total. The handle is made of synthetic material and therefore weighs only 4.5 ounces. The guard, pommel and rings in the handle are made of 420 HC steel as well.

MODEL 110 FOLDING HUNTER

Model 110 Folding Hunter was the first folding knife Buck Company made. In 1963, Al Buck decided to make a folding knife for the outdoorsman who needed a strong knife, but did not want to walk around with a long fixed knife. His instincts were right. Model 110 has been the cornerstone of the company ever since. After its introduction in 1964, the knife became a sensation, despite the ridiculously high price of US $16.00. Within two years it was the best selling sports knife in the world. It was also the most copied knife in the world, but Buck still sold fourteen million of them. The total length of Model 110 is 8.6 inches with a handle 4.88 inches long and a 3.75 inch long stainless 420 HRC steel blade, tempered to 58 HRC. The knife weighs

Model 172 Mayo TNT (top) and the Model 173 Mayo Northshore (bottom)

MODEL 119 SPECIAL

The first knife that Hoyt Buck made in 1902 from an old file was the model for this ideal working knife that, along with Model 110, is the basis of the success of this company. The original design has undergone a few evolutionary changes, especially in the hardening process. The blade is made of stainless 420 HC steel, tempered to 58 HRC. A horizontal groove, the 'blood

Model 119 Special hunting knife

7.2 ounces and has a backlock system. The traditional tight Buck-line handle has inlaid plates of birch wood and the bolster and pommel are brass. Model 110 FG has a handle with finger grooves.

MODEL 112 RANGER

Model 112 Ranger is a smaller version of Model 110 with a total length of 7.2 inches. The stainless 420 HC steel clippoint blade is 3 inches long and has a handle of 4.25 inches. The knife also features birch wood handle plates and weighs 5.6 ounces. Like the larger

groove,' is cut into the blade. Model 119 Special weighs 7.5 ounces, has a handle made of phenol synthetic material, and a guard and pommel made of polished aluminum. The 10.5 ounce Model 119 BR is the same, but has a Cocobolo handle and the guard and pommel are made of brass. Both knives are 10.5 inches long with 6-inch blades.

Model 177 Adrenaline-BK

Model 183 Alpha
Crosslock

MODEL 172 MAYO TNT / MODEL 173 MAYO NORTHSHORE

Tom Mayo is a custom knife maker and surfboard designer from the north coast of Hawaii. He got into knife making in 1981. His love of innovative materials and his unorthodox solutions make his knives popular, eventhough his delivery time is at least two years. Model 172 Mayo TNT is a modern folding knife with a framelock system. The blade is made of S30V steel with a high quantity of carbon, chromium, molyb-

The special Model 185 Tiburon
for water sports enthusiast

denum and vanadium. This type of steel, doubly tempered to 59.5 - 61 HRC, was specially developed for the knife industry by the American company Crucible Steel. Mayo stipulated that 6A1-4V titanium had to be used for the handle, with holes drilled into it to make it lighter. The right handle plate serves as a bolt for the blade and also contains a moveable carry clip. The handle of Model 172 TNT is 4.133 inches long and the total length is 7.2 inches. The length of the blade is 3.11 inches and the knife only weighs 2.7 ounces. Model 173 Mayo Northshore is a similar folding knife, except for its linerlock system. The handle is made of anodized aluminum and stainless 420 HC steel is used for the blade. The knife has the same dimensions as the TNT model.

MODEL 177 / 178 ADRENALINE

Buck wanted to expand the range of folding knives with the 177 and 178 models. Model 178 Adrenaline was designed for use with only one hand and a carry clip. The knife has a 3-inch blade made of ATS-34 steel, tempered with the Bos method to 61-62 HRC. The linerlock is made of anodized blue-purple titanium. Model 177 Adrenaline has a black anodized aluminum handle. 177 BK has a bead blasted blade with a linerlock made of stainless 420 HC steel. With 177 SPX, the blade and linerlock system are fitted with a Teflon protective layer. The total lengths of all three models is 7.13 inches. When closed, the knife is 4.13 inches long. Depending on the material used, it weighs between 2.4 and 2.6 ounces.

MODEL 183 ALPHA CROSSLOCK PBS

As a successor to the older models, Buck developed Model 183 Alpha Crosslock PBS. This award-winning system consists of a double blade with an innovative cross linerlocking system. It offers a choice of a gutting hook or a knife blade that flips out of the handle. Both blades are made of 420 HC steel and have integrated guards allowint the knife to be easily opened with one hand. The handle is made of anodized aluminum in dark gray or camouflage pattern. The blades are all 3 inches long, the handles are 4.65 inches long, the knives are 7.6 inches long when fully opened and weigh 4 ounces.

Model 191 Buck Zipper Guthook

MODEL 185 TIBURON

Tiburon is the Spanish word for shark. This knife is ideal for rafters, canoeists, divers and sailors. Buck cooperated with Ed Gillet, one of the best kayakers in the world, on the design. The asymmetric skeleton grip and stainless steel 17-7PH steel were tested for one

Model 192 / 692 Vanguard hunting knife

week on Tiburon Island in the sea of Cortez by specially selected water sports specialists. The skeleton grip was specifically designed for use with the gloves of a wetsuit and the finger grooves ensure an extra firm and stable grip. There is a safety hook on the blade for skinning or for pricking or cutting through a line or fishnet. The edge of the blade is partially serrated for cutting through rope or cable. There is a six-sided hole in the integrated guard for a carbine hook to attach the knife to equipment, which can also

The Alpha Hunter

be used to put in the 'tool bit.' The pointed hole in the blade reduces some of the weight and comes in handy when opening a hook lock. The length of the blade is 4 inches, the total length is 8.5 inches and the knife weighs 4.8 ounces. The sheath is made of fiberglass-reinforced nylon and has nylon rings attached to both ends for hooking onto a life jacket or other equipment.

MODEL 191 / 691 BUCK ZIPPER GUT HOOK

Model 191 and 691 Buck Zipper are typical hunting knives with special gutting hooks on top of the blade. The knife with the laminated wood handle is Model 191. Model 691 has a checkered rubber Kraton grip. Both knives have brass guards and pommels. The blade is of stainless 420 HC steel and is 4.13 inches long, the total length is 8.5 inches. They weigh 6.3 or 6.6 ounces respectively. The sheath for Model

The decorative Alpha Hunter Guthook

191 is made of brown leather. Model 691 has a sheath of black shock resistant nylon.

MODEL 192 / 692 VANGUARD

Vanguard is similar to the Buck Zipper but it does not have a gutting hook. The beautiful, broad blade is made of hollow-ground 420 HC steel, 4.13 inches long and the total length of the knife is 8.5 inches. It weighs between 6.3 to 6.6 ounces. Model 192 has a laminated grip with a polished brass guard and pommel. Model 692 has a black Kraton handle with a matte guard and pommel. Both versions come with sheaths.

MODEL 193 / 693 ALPHA HUNTER GUT HOOK

Models 193 and 693 Alpha Hunter Gut Hook is a strong, comfortable, ergonomic and highly functional hunting knife. Buck planned to release it in 2003, but, after extensive testing, hunters were so enthusiastic that production started immediately. This integral knife has a series of ridges on the blade back and on the back end for a more stable grip. The handle plates are rounded and

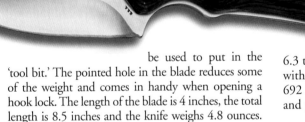

Model 196 Mini Alpha Hunter

arched so that it fills the hand. The blade has an integrated guard and on the back of the handle is a large shackle. Model 193 is made of Japanese ATS-34 steel, tempered with the Bos method to 61 HRC. Both models are made of stainless 420 HC steel. The blade

Custom Model 204 Koji Folder

is 3.74 inches long, the total length is 8.5 inches and it weighs 7.2 ounces. You can choose between synthetic resin, impregnated palisander wood, walnut wood or black Kraton rubber for the handle.

MODEL 194 / 694 ALPHA HUNTER

Model series 194 and 694 have the same shape, but with droppoint blades and without gutting hooks. Model 194 is made of ATS-34 steel, while the other version is made of 420 HC steel. The handle, just as with the 193/693 series, is made of palisander or walnut wood or black Kraton. One exception to this is Model 694, available in a limited, numbered series of only a thousand. This knife is 8.5 inches long and has a blade length of 3.25 inches. This integral knife is made of 420 HC steel and the handle is of a combination of palisander wood and stag horn.

MODEL 196 MINI ALPHA HUNTER

276 / 278 Folding Alpha Hunter Guthook

This smaller version of the Alpha Hunter is ideal for careful gutting work. The blade, of ATS-34 steel, is slightly more curved than the standard Alpha. The

handle plates are made of palisander wood with synthetically impregnated resin. The 3.6 ounce knife has a 2.5 inch integral blade, total length of 6.25 inches and weighs 3.6 ounces. Model 196 Mini Alpha Deer is a limited edition of only 2004 units, each numbered and supplied with a certificate of authenticity. Buck used stainless 420 HC steel for this knife and the silhouette of a deer on the blade. The handle is burl nut wood.

MODEL 204 KOJI FOLDER

Custom Model 208 Koji hunting knife (top) and Model 205 Koji Dagger (bottom)

Award-winning Japanese knife maker Koji Hara from Seki city, the center for Japanese sword and knife production, helped design this knife. He and Buck used polished ATS-34 steel, tempered to 60 HRC for the blades. The layered bolster is made of stainless 420 HC steel. A special type of burl wood called Karin wood is used for the handle. The 1.8 ounce knife is 5.35 inches long, with a 2.25 inch long, 0.085 inch thick blade.

MODEL 205 / 208 KOJI-SERIES

Buck developed the Model 205 Koji Dagger with Koji Hara, who only produces a few knives per year. This 6.38 inch integral dagger is made entirely of ATS-34 steel, tempered to 61 HRC. The blade is 3 inches long and the dagger weighs only 2.2 ounces. The integral guard and pommel feature the unique Koji layer pattern. The handle plates are maple burl wood. The 6.89 inch Model 208 hunting knife, of the same material as the dagger, has a 3-inch blade and weighs 2.7 ounces. The bolster also has the typical Koji Hara layered pattern.

Models 277 / 279 Folding Alpha Hunter

Model 281 / 282 NXT

Model 276 / 278 Folding Alpha Hunter Gut hook

The Alpha Folding Hunter is based on the fixed Alpha hunting knife and is the modern successor of

Model 290 / 291 Rush ASAP folder

the old Model 110. A thumb stud on the blade and the knife's linerlock system enables one-handed opening and closing. The casing of the folding knife can be carried horizontally or vertically. Unique is the gutting hook. The blade of Model 276 is made of special ATS-34 steel, tempered to 61 HRC. Both Model 278s have blades made of 42 HC steel. The casing is made of stainless steel and has an ergonomic shape with deep finger grooves that serve as a type of guard. Model 276 has handle plates made of impregnated palisander wood, while Model 278WA has walnut wood handle plates and 278BK has a handle made of Kraton. The 8-ounce, 8.5 inch knife has a blade 3.5 inches long, and a 5-inch handle.

The remarkable Model 421 Newt

Model 277 / 279 Folding Alpha Hunter

The measurements and weight of these folding knives are the same as the Alpha Hunter Gut Hook, but the blades are shaped somewhat differently.

Model 277 has blades of ATS-34 steel and palisander handle plates. The Alpha has a rubber Kraton handle, while a third version has a handle of walnut wood.

Model 281 / 282 NXT

This low-cost high-tech folding knife has a pressed casing with two parts: a hard nylon inner casing reinforced with fiberglass and a soft rubber outer layer for a comfortable, stable grip. The knife can be opened with one hand because of the triangular hole in the blade and the linerlock system. The total length is 6.8 inches and the blade is 2.75 inches long. Model 281 has a partially serrated edge and Model 282 has a smooth edge. The blade is of stainless 420 HC steel with a lovely grinding line running evenly to the cutting edge. The knife weighs between 2.0 to 2.1 ounces.

Model 290 / 291 Rush

These models were designed to outperform the spring pressure knifes and to create a safe and reliable opening mechanism. The patented ASAP (Advanced Spring Assisted Performance) system contains a double-sided spring pressure blade pivot, which makes opening the blade through spring pressure much easier. It is neither an automatic knife, nor a stiletto. The blade must still be opened with the one

Model 301 Stockman

hand thumb stud, but it does so very easily and smoothly. The separate fastening button can lock the knife better. The knife has the standard linerlock system for locking and releasing. The 2.4 ounce, 6.25 inch long knife has a 2.5 inch blade of 42 HC steel or ATS-34 steel such as with Model 291. The anodized aluminum skeleton handle comes in black, dark gray or dark blue. The knife weighs 2.4 ounces.

Model 301 / 309 Series

Buck has been making this series of classic pocketknives since the 1960's. The handle plates are made of black shock-resistant synthetic material with the old Buck logo. The smallest, Model 305

**Model 437 Revolution-XT
hybrid knife**

MODEL 437 REVOLUTION-XT

Model 437 Revolution XT comes of cooperation with mountaineer Peter Whittaker, who runs the largest guide network in the United States. The fixed knife's lightweight but strong aluminum handle can be revolved and fixed to serve as a sheath. The knife can easily be attached to equipment or a belt with an integral carbine hook. The partially serrated blade is especially good for cutting through lines and ropes. The locking button on the handle remains locked while open or closed. The 2.6 ounce, 7.5 inch knife is of stainless 420 HC steel, with a 3-inch blade. With the carbine hook on the outside, the length is 6.75 inches.

MODEL 442 / 444 BUCKLITE

Lancer, has two blades made of stainless 420 HC steel. When closed, it is 2.52 inches long and weighs 0.7 ounces. The larger Model 309 Companion is 2.99 inches long when closed, has two blades and weighs 1.2 ounces. Model 303 Buck Cadet has a clip blade, a spay blade and a sheepfoot blade. The handle is 3.27 inches long and the knife weighs 1.9 ounces. The largest is the 3.86 inch, 2.9 ounce Model 301 Stockman, with a clip blade, a spay blade and a sheepfoot blade. All models feature a simple feather pressure locking system.

**Model 442 Bucklite and 444 Bucklite II
(from top to bottom)**

MODEL 421 NEWT

Frequent requests for a small key ring knife with a pair of scissors prompted Buck to create the Model 421 Newt. The inner casing is of stainless steel and

Bucklite and Bucklite II weigh only 2.5 and 1.3 ounces respectively because thermoplastic is used for the handles. The larger Bucklite has a detachable carry clip on the right side of the handle. The 7.4 inch knife has a 3-inch blade. The Bucklite II is 6.5 inches long with a 2.75 inch blade. Both knives have backlock systems.

MODEL 450 PROTÉGÉ

This folding knife is a modern version of the Model 110. It is fiberglass reinforced, but on the outside it has a soft runner casing made of thermoplastic, which ensures considerable weight reduction. The 3-inch blade is made of stainless 420 HC steel, ground in the Edge2X style. The 450 FX Protégé is a one-hand knife with a thumb stud and a partially serrated edge. The total length of both knives is 7.2 inches and they weigh 3 ounces. The blade has a backlock system.

Model 450 Protege

the small blade and the pair of scissors are of 420 HRC steel. The blade is 1.5 inches long and the transparent acrylic handle is 2.64 inches long. The Newt weighs 0.8 ounces.

MODEL 471 / 476 DIAMONDBACK

This updatet model of the Mentor has a special nylon sheath. Testing showed that the larger model had to have two finger slots as opposed to one on

Model 476 Diamondback (top) and Model 471 Diamondback (bottom)

the smaller version. Thermoplastic shaped like snakeskin is used for the outer layer. To reduce costs, the Diamondback is made in Taiwan under strict quality regulations. Model 471 Diamondback is 9.5 inches long, with a 4.25 inch stainless 420 HC steel blade that is 0.120 inches thick and weighs 54 ounces. The smaller Model 476 Diamondback 3.25 is 7 inches long, the blade is 3.25 inches long and 0.092 inches thick and weighs 2.4 ounces.

MODEL 477 CAPING KNIFE

Buck worked closely with renowned gamekeepers and professional big game hunters on this model. Gamekeepers constantly face the problem of inexpertly skinned and often damaged animal hides. Because skinning shot game requires proper tools and most hunters

carry larger knives than necessary, Buck developed a small, light and easily manageable skinning knife. It has a rubber handle for a stable grip, a small gutting hook on the blade and finger slots on the top and bottom. The total length is 7.13 inches with a 3.5 inch blade, weighs is 2.4 ounces and comes in black or camouflage.

MODEL 501 SQUIRE / 503 PRINCE / 505 KNIGHT

Requests for a smaller, lighter and more luxurious knife with similar features led to the successful 500-Slimline Series. The biggest knife is Model 501 Squire which is 6.5 inches long, with a 2.75

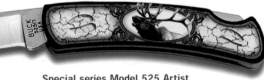

Model 477 Caping Knife

inch blade and weight of 3 ounces. The 5.9 inch 503 Prince has a 2.5 inch blade, a 3.35 inch handle and weighs 2 ounces. The smallest Model 505

Special series Model 525 Artist

Knight, is 4.6 inches in total length and has a 1.89 inch long blade and weighs 1.5 ounces. All three versions have handle plates of hardwood and nickel silver bolsters and a back-lock system.

MODEL 525 ARTIST

The limited edition 525 Artist series was made in cooperation with John Q Wright and various artists on the design. The total length of the knife is 4.25 inches with a blade of 1.89 inches and it weighs 1 ounce. The handles of the folding knives are adorned with depictions of animals by artists Bob Sch-

The luxury series: Model 505, Model 503 and Model 501

The Everyday series: Model 525 Gent, Model 526 Executive, Model 525 Lady Liberty and Model 525 American Eagle (from top to bottom)

MODEL 751 APPROACH

When Buck decided to design an all-purpose knife it sought out mountaineer Peter Whittaker, and when he and his team were satisfied, Model 751 Approach was taken to production. This knife has a linerlock system and features a big shackle behind the handle through which a large carbine hook can be attached. In this way the knife can easily be attached to a backpack, a climbing harness or a belt. The total length of Model 751 Approach is 7.5 inches. The blade is 3.11 inches long and it has a handle of 4.37 inches. The knife weighs 3.6 ounces. The handle is made of anodized aluminum in black or blue colors. The blade is made of stainless 420 HC steel and is partially serrated. There is a thumb stud for one hand closing.

MODEL 752 SHORT APPROACH

Model 752 Short Approach is a compact version of the larger Model 751, 6.3 inches in total length,

The smaller Model 752 Short Approach

midt, Cynthie Fisher and Philip Goodwin. This knife comes with a wooden box and a certificate of authenticity.

MODEL 525 / 526 EVERYDAY

Model 525 is an old Buck classic. Model 525 Gent has a stainless steel casing and a 420 HC steel blade, secured by the backlock system. The total length is 4.65 inches with a blade 1.89 inches long and weighs 1.0 ounce. The 525 AM American Eagle and Lady Liberty feature a depiction of the Statue of Liberty. Model 526 Executive has the

weighs 2.5 ounces and has a 2.75 inch long blade. It comes in blue, dark green, light green, orange, purple and black.

MODEL 759 METRO

The Model 759 Metro is a small, oval, high-tech pocketknife that can be opened and closed with one hand and doubles as a bottle opener. The blade is 1.14 inches long, the handle is 2.36 inches in diameter, it weighs 1.5 ounces and is produced in many different colors.

Model 751 Approach

same measurements, but a smoother and more luxurious finish. The edges of the casing are rounded and the blade is finished with high gloss.

Model 759 Metro

**Model 760
Summit**

MODEL 760 SUMMIT

The Model 760 Summit, designed in close coope-ration with mountaineer Peter Whittaker as an ergonomically shaped knife, comes with all the essential functions backpackers and campers need. The 2.5 inch blade is partially serrated to easily cut through lines and ropes. The total length of the open knife is 6.7 inches and it weighs 3.5 ounces. There is a separa-te bottle and can opener and screw-driver on the back of the handle and an expandable corkscrew in the top. On the back is a big steel eye, so it can be easily attached to a backpack. The larger blade and bottle and can opener have a linerlock system. The knife is made with an anodized aluminum casing in blue, green, red and black. The top edge of the casing is made of shock resistant thermoplastic.

MODEL 805 / 819 SIGNATURE SERIES

The Model 805 Signature and Model 819 Signatu-re were produced in limited numbers of 1,000 and issued with special cases and certificates of authen-ticity. Model 8035 Signature is based on the old Model 105, based in turn based on Hoyt Buck's first hunting knife from 1902. The total length is 9.13 inches, the blade is 5 inches long and the knife weighs 4 ounces. Model 819 Signature is based on the Model 119 hunting knife, with a total length of 10.75 inches, a 6-inch long blade and a

weight of 7.6 ounces. Chuck and C.J. Buck's sig-natures are on the blade of both knives and the handle plates are of beautiful walnut wood.

MODEL 880 STRI-DER / 881 MINI STRIDER SERIES

Mick Strider and Duane Dwyer, are famous for their high quality tactical fixed knives. Cost is not a factor for them. They never considered cooperating with a knife factory until Buck approa-ched them.

Extensive testing in the Buck laboratories showed that the Strider they designed was the strongest fol-ding knife Buck had ever produced. The handle is made of G10-synthetic material; the inner casing is made of titanium, part of which serves as a linerlock; the blade is of ATS-34 steel, tempered with the Paul

Model 880 / 881 Strider

Bos method to 60 HRC; the carry clip is interchan-geable and the handle has a shackle for a cord. The Strider comes with a spearpoint or a Tanto blade with a smooth or partially serrated edge and a thumb stud for one-handed opening. The total length is 9.25 inches, with a 3.86 inch blade and a weight of 7.3 ounces. The smaller Model 881 Mini Strider, of the same material, measures 6.9 inches with a blade length of 2.87 inches and a weight of 4.1 ounces.

Model 805 Signature (top) and Model 819 Signature (bottom

Model 886 Taclite from 2004

MODEL 882 STRIDER / 884 SBT POLICE UTILITY KNIFE

Model 882 SBT Police Utility Hunting Knife is the result of feedback from fifty different police corps from all over North America. Steve Tarani, a senior instructor and advisor at several military and police institutions, cooperated closely with the owners of Strider Knives on this knife.

Model 882 SBT Police Utility Knife

The 882 SBT is an extremely strong linerlock folding knife with a blade made of ATS-34 steel. The handle is made of fiberglass-reinforced nylon Tactical Composite (TACCOM) and ensures a stable grip, even in difficult conditions such as in grease, rain, snow and extreme cold. The total length of the knife is 8.15 inches and it has a 3.5 inch, partially serrated blade. The top half is rough on both sides, for safe opening and closing with two hands. The 4.7 ounce knife can also be opened with only one hand. Buck developed special blue knives with blunt points and cutting edges for training purposes. The weight and measurements are similar to those of Model 882.

MODEL 886 TACLITE

The criteria for the design of the Model 886 Taclite were strength, durability and light weight for outdoor use, plus the classical look of a knife meant for daily use. The handle has classical handle plates of lovely laminated wood, combined with a partially serrated modern spearpoint blade of stainless 420

HC steel. In order to reduce weight, the casing and handle plates have a number of round holes. This one-hand knife has a linerlock system. Its total length is 6.1 inches with 2.6 inch blade and a weight of only 2 ounces.

BUTOVSKY

www.rusartknife.urbannet.ru/gallery.html

Valery Butovsky was born in 1961 in Tula, known for its weapons industry since the Middle Ages.

After he finished art school, Valery became a graphic engraver at TWF, a large weapons factory in Tula. Eventually, he switched to handmade knives. In 1991 he started accepting personal orders to engrave hunting weapons. He has worked with knife makers such as Kurbatov, Danilin and Yury Harlamov and with famous master

Russian knife maker Valery Butovsky, with his emblem at the top right and below it, the logo of the Russian Knifemakers' Guild

knife maker Tatarnikov. Since 1996, Valery has had his own workshop and has been a member of the Russian Knife Makers' Guild since 2001. The knives shown here were photographed by Sergey Baranov and Valentin Overchenko.

The unique Butterflies hunting knife, named for the decorative butterflies on the container

BUTTERFLIES

Valery Butovsky got the inspiration for this knife in 2003, while walking through spring meadows full of colorful butterflies. This knife was not made to order and is currently in the collection of the maker. The 9.7 inch knife has a 5.5 inch long, 1.25 inch wide

Y12 and CT3, was forged by Alexander Kurbatov. The 10.4 inch knife has a 6-inch long, 1.38 inch wide blade. The handle is of Iranian nut wood, inlaid with gold and silver. The engravings on the guard, pommel and blade are also decorated with gold and silver. Valery was inspired by fairy tale "The Small Hunchbacked Horse" by the Russian writer Ershov. The knife is in a private collection.

Griffin knife by Valery Butovsky

blade of Damasteel hand-forged from Russian Y10, Y12 and CT 3 steel, by knife maker Egor Aseev and specially tempered to 60-63 HRC. The Iranian nut wood handle is inlaid with gold and silver butterflies and plant motifs. Viktor Kuznetsov made the case.

FAIRY TALE

This lovely knife has an inner power, beauty and mystery. As is usual with the Russian Guild, it was made by several artists. Butovsky made the knife itself with Kosta Tatarnikov in 2001, but the truly lovely Damascus blade, composed of Russian steel types Y10,

GRIFFIN

This knife was made by Valery Butovsky and Kosta Tatarnikov. The 5.9 inch long Damasteel blade was made of Y10, Y12 and CT3 steel types, tempered to 60-63 HRC by Alexander Kurbatov. The engravings on the blade, the guard and the pommel of the 10.8 inch knife are inlaid with 18kt gold and silver. Plants and fighting griffins twine gracefully around the blade and Iranian nut wood handle. This unique knife is currently in a private collection.

Fairy tale knife by Valery Butovsky

C

CAMILLUS

www.camillusknives.com

CAMILLUS
K N I V E S

The emblem of Camillus

The Camillus Cutlery Company is one of the oldest knife factories in the United States. Its history began with Adolf Kastor, a young German immigrant who established Adolf Kastor & Bros in New York City, for importing and distributing knives from Germany. But the Dingley Tariff of 1897, imposed to protect homeland industries against imports, made foreign knives too expensive, so Kastor started making knives himself.

In 1902 he and Charles Sherwood modernized the latter's small knife factory in Camillus, New York, adding the Clover and Sword Brand. Within eight years, the company had grown from 25 to 200 employees.

As production increased, Camillus modernized and brought German craftsmen to the United States and even built a German hotel, known as Germania Hall. Kastor started a sponsorship program for faithful employees, allowing entire families to emigrate from Germany to help him make knives.

During the First World War, the company shipped over 471 000 military kni-

ves to the battlefront. In the 1920's Camillus started importing a new 'stainless' steel. It made knives for trading houses, which sold them under their own trading names, including: Hibbart, Spencer, Bartlett & Co with the OVB (Our Very Best) label, Sears, Roebuck & Co with the trading name of Craftsman & Dunlap and Stay Sharp, Woolworth with the Kent mark, Simons Hardware Co with the Keen Kutter and Spahleigh Hardware Co with the Diamond Edge.

During the Second World War, Camillus made over fifty million knives for the Allied Forces. After the war, the company made knives under the Camillus and Camco labels. Camillus also issued special editions for young people, such as the Lone Ranger, the Dick Tracy, Davey Crocket and Daniel Boone knife. Camillus still produces an impressive series of models under the labels Camillus, Western, Becker Knife & Tool and Cuda.

AFTERMATH

This futuristic folding knife was introduced in 2003. The handle is made of strong titanium and the blade from stainless D2-steel. The knife has the new 'Robo' system, allowing the blade to be flipped quickly from the handle with the integrated 'flippers' that also serve as the guard. The blade is 5.5 inches long and the total length of the knife is 11.4

The Aftermath by Darrel Ralph

inches. Knives with a total length of 11.0 inches or more are forbidden in some countries.

ARCLITE

The lightweight Cuda Arclite is made of stainless 420-HC steel. Its narrow skeleton

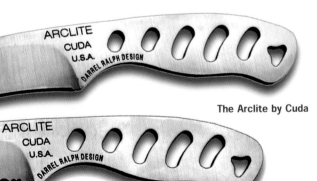

The Arclite by Cuda

handle folds firmly and easily, and has ergonomically designed holes for a stable grip. This knife comes with a Kydex sheath and a lanyard, so it can be carried around the neck. The 7.88 inch Arclite has a 3.13 inch blade with a smooth or partially serrated edge and it weighs 3.28 ounces.

It was designed by toolmaker and artist Darrel Ralph, one of the world's leading knife makers, who enhances his background as a maker of collectible knives with the most modern CAD computer technology. He is known for his hand-forged Damasteel and gives courses throughout North America.

BK10 CREWMAN UTILITY KNIFE

Becker Patrol Machete

This integral military survival knife, designed by Ethan Becker, is of special 0170-6C tool steel, tempered to 58-59 HRC. Its ergonomically shaped handle is made of patented Becker GV6H synthetic material. The sharp 5.5 inch blade is ground

flat, with a 0.188-inch thick spearpoint. The integral pommel is shaped like a hammerhead and can also be used as one. This knife comes with a woven nylon sheath, reinforced with Kydex and has an epoxy protective layer against corrosion and light reflection.

The Boy Scouts of America (BSA) official knife

BK6 PATROL MACHETE

After working with a Philippine parang, Ethan Becker was so impressed that he decided to make a

BK10 Crewman Utility Knife by Becker Knife & Tool

similar hacking knife. The result was an excellently balanced survival knife, meant for land surveyors, jungle soldiers or for primitive living. This 18.8 ounce machete is 19 inches long with a blade of stainless 0170-6C steel, covered with an epoxy protective layer. It is 14 inches long and 0.188 inches thick. The handle is made of Becker GV6H synthetic material.

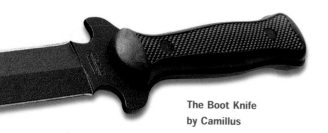

The Boot Knife by Camillus

BOOT KNIVES

Camillus produces Boot Knives in two sizes. The 7-inch Medium Boot Knife has a 3.25 inch blade, and the 8.62 inch knife has a blade 4.25 inches long. The blades of both models are made of 440C steel and have integrated guards. The daggers weigh 3.4 ounces and 4.8 ounces respectively. The handle is of Valox, a thermoplastic polyester synthetic resin, based on Polybuthylene Terephthalate (PBT), reinforced with fiberglass. It is resistant to heat, chemicals, oil and fat and is not a conveyor of electricity.

BOY SCOUT

Cuda EDC Talonite

Camillus was the first to produce a complete line of folding knives for the Boy Scouts of America (BSA). This 8-inch four-blade knife has a 2.5 inch long main blade with the BSA logo. The 3.75 inch handle is made of Delrin. There is also bottle opener with a screwdriver point, a can opener, a leather punch and a shackle. The Norman Rockwell Limited Edition emphasizes the Boy Scout oath of "One good deed every day," with a "good deed scene" depicted on the handle under transparent Lexan.

attack on the Twin Towers in New York in 2001. The handle is made of Delrin and it depicts flames. The 3.5 inch blade is made of stainless 420 HC steel. The bolsters are made of nickel steel.

The EDC 125th Anniversary knife in commemoration of the 125th year anniversary of Camillus

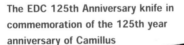

CUDA MAXX 5.5

The Cuda Maxx 5.5 inch Stiletto was also designed by Darrel Ralph. The massive 7 ounce knife is 11.6 inches long and has a 5.67 inch blade of 0.135 inch thick, special D2-tool steel. The handle is made of anodized aluminum. The right-hand side partially serves as the bolt rod for the framelock system and features a stainless steel carry clip on the handle plate. The term Stiletto

The Firefighter

EDC (EVERY DAY CARRY)

The EDC folding knife, designed by Darrel Ralph in 2001 to commemorate the 125-year anniversary of this knife, features a standard framelock system The total length of the 3-ounce knife is 6.85 inches. The stainless 420 HC steel handle is 3.81 inches long and the 2.95 inch blade is made of special 154 CM tool steel. Camillus introduced the EDC Talonite in 2001. The blade is of special Talonite steel: a layered combination of cobalt and chromium, used for the teeth of saws, heads for oil drills and high-speed milling heads. The thumb stud, screws and carry clip in both versions have a protective layer of matte gold Titanium Nitride.

FIRE FIGHTER

Camillus releases a new knife in the Firefighter series each year. A part of the profit is donated to the 9/11 fund, to support the families of the firefighters who lost their lives during the

means that the blade can quickly be released with two integrated switches, but technically this is not a stiletto as the blade is not operated by spring pressure. Folding knives more than 11 inches long are not allowed in some countries.

Cuda Maxx 5.5 Stiletto

CECH

vincent.czech@seznam.cz

**Emblem
of the Czech
BMAC Guild**

Jaroslav Cech comes from Nove Mesto in Moravia, located in the heart of the Czech-Moravian Carpathians. He started as an apprentice engraver during the 1960's and started working as an independent engraver in 1989, adorning hunting weapons with deeply engraved depictions in the butts and yokes. He also makes handmade knives. Cech is a member of the association of knife makers BMAC (Bohemiae et Moraviae Artes Cultellatores). The deep and open engraving work, inlaid with precious metals, exotic wood, semi-precious stones or mammoth ivory, makes his knives unique. Cech's engraving work is even known in the Vatican; one of his knives was donated to Pope John Paul II.

CHAMELEON

The Chameleon is an integral knife, made of a thick plate of steel with the excessive material carefully ground and cut away. A chameleon was shaped from the ultra hard ATS 34 steel. It stares at a beetle seated on the bolster among a mass of large leaves. The total length of this large knife is 10.1 inches. The length of the blade is 6.1 inches. The handle is 4 inches long and made of polished mammoth ivory.

HUNTER

Jaroslav Cech made this knife from stainless Damasteel. The total length is 9.25 inches with a blade 5.3 inches in length. The steel handle has an inlaid piece of stag horn. The roe pair, gilt in the steel, stands out beautifully.

ORIENTAL HUNTER

The Orient shaped blade of this knife was beautifully engraved. The pommel and bolster are made of gilded brass. The guard is made of silvered brass.

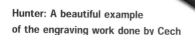

Chameleon

The 10-inch knife has a 5.8 inch skinner blade and a 4.3 inch long horn handle, beautifully engraved with hunting scenes.

HUNTING KNIFE

**Hunter: A beautiful example
of the engraving work done by Cech**

This traditional hunting knife was engraved and decorated with gems in the bolster of the guard. Flower motifs protrude from the blade. The total length of the knife is 10.2 inches the blade is 5.9 inches in length. Cech used a piece of crude stag horn for the handle.

**Oriental Hunter
by Cech**

The Gurkha Kukri

MACHETE SERIES

The Machete cuts, chops and hacks almost anything that is bothering you. You can kill fish or game with it and then cut it into pieces. The machete is a cheap tool and even the poorest

tem stands ready for problem-free deployment. The blade cuts with the speed of a chainsaw through the toughest materials, thanks to the wide, flat-ground surface and serrated edge. The sheepfoot blade of stainless AUS 8A steel is particularly well-suited to rescue activities as it will not wound victims when cutting loose safety belts or bothersome clothing. The heavy Zytel handle is 5.08 inches long, slightly contoured and deeply checkered to ensure an iron grip. At the back of the handle, a powerful pocket clip constantly keeps the knife within reach. The Land & Sea/Rescue is 9.06 inches long, with a 4.0 inch long, 0.118 inch thick blade and it weighs 3.5 ounces.

Cold Steel land & Sea/Rescue

farmer in South America or African tribal member owns one. The blade of the Cold Steel machete is made of SAE 1055 medium carbon steel with an anti-rust layer baked onto it. The comfortable handle is polypropylene. It is a maintenance free, extremely strong lifelong companion. The 20.5 inch long, 16-ounce Cold Steel Light Machete is

Laredo Bowie

LAREDO BOWIE

This traditional knife is large, wide and beautiful. The long, thick blade is made of Carbon-V steel, ground flat with a curved cutting edge that runs to the inside and ends in a dagger point. The false edge has a sharp cutting area 4.5 inches long, allowing the knife to cut in an upward direction as well. The coffin-shaped handle of exotic hard wood provides a firm grip while cutting, chopping or thrusting. The guard and bolster are enhanced with highly polished brass. The Laredo Bowie comes with a traditional sheath made of heavy, thick, brown leather. The knife is 15.67 inches long, has a 10.5 inch long, 0.313 inch thick blade, a 5.2 inch Cocobolo handle and weighs 17.4 ounces.

ideal for chopping grass, maize, creepers, shrubs and wood. It has a 14.88 inch long, 0.078 inch thick blade and comes with a Cordura sheath. The Heavy Machete is for difficult chopping. Thanks to its 24 ounces, little body weight is needed. The length is 20.25 inches, the blade is 14.61 inches long and 0.078 inches thick and the handle is 5.63 inches long. The 21.65 inch long Panga Machete, used on the African continent, is suited for chopping through thickets and small trees. The blade is 16.0 inches long, the handle is 5.63 inches long and the knife weighs 19.0 ounces. The Bolo Machete is popular in Asia and all over the Pacific Ocean with a wide point blade that shifts its weight forward for heavy chopping work, opening coconuts or chopping down a tree. The knife is 22.0 inches long with a 16.38 inch long blade and weighs 17.3 ounces.

The Cold Steel Machete

Master Hunter Plus

MASTER HUNTER

The standard Master Hunter has a wide, thick blade, ground flat with a distinct distal taper cutting edge for good cutting abilities and a wear-proof quality. The Kraton handle has a deep checkerboard motif. This modern hunting knife, tested extensively in Africa, Australia and Alaska, won the praise of Ross Seyfried from *Guns and Ammo Magazine*, one of the best hunters in

Three classic military knives: The Black Bear Classic, the OSS and the R1 Military Classic (from top to bottom)

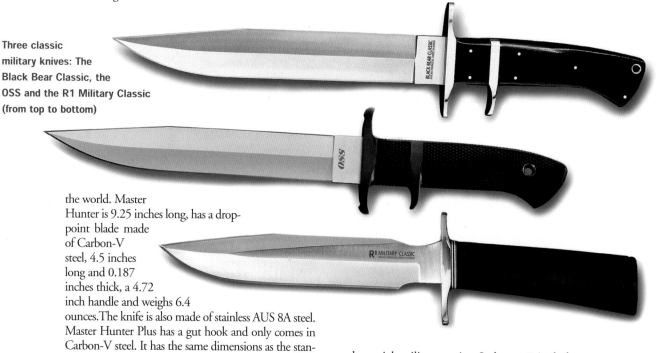

the world. Master Hunter is 9.25 inches long, has a drop-point blade made of Carbon-V steel, 4.5 inches long and 0.187 inches thick, a 4.72 inch handle and weighs 6.4 ounces. The knife is also made of stainless AUS 8A steel. Master Hunter Plus has a gut hook and only comes in Carbon-V steel. It has the same dimensions as the standard model, but is heavier, at 6.6 ounces.

MILITARY BLACK BEAR CLASSIC, OSS AND R1 MILITARY CLASSIC

The OSS, with its double guard, is a typical fighting knife. The double-sided stainless 420 steel blade is 8.25 inches long and 0.187 inches thick. It is tempered by freezing, which keeps the blade sharp longer. The 5.12 inch handle, guard and second guard are of one piece of Kraton. The 13.39 inch long knife weighs 8.2 ounces. It comes with a Secure-Ex sheath. The OSS, with a synthetic handle, is actually related to the Black Bear Classic described earlier.
The R1 Military Classic has been used in military

conflicts in Korea, Vietnam, Central America and the Persian Gulf and is an exact replica of the original military knife. The 9.25 ounce R1 is 11.61 inches long with a 7-inch long, 0.187 inch thick Bowie blade of stainless Aus 8A steel, with a thumb support on the back. The 4.6 inch black Micarta handle has a stainless steel guard and synthetic spacers. The knife comes with a leather sheath and a sharpening stone.

MILITARY RECON TANTO

The 11.75 inch long, Carbon-V steel Military Recon Tanto, based on a classic Japanese knife, is used by SWAT teams

and special military units. It has a 7-inch long, 0.187 inch thick blade with a black matte epoxy layer, a 4.75 inch long Kraton handle, weighs 9 ounces and comes with Concealex tactical sheath.

MILITARY SRK (SURVIVAL RESCUE KNIFE)

Cold Steel says the SRK (Survival Rescue Knife) is the best-selling non-official military knife in the conflict in Iraq. The typical clip-shaped hunting blade is resistant to just about every form of abuse. The 8.2-ounce SRK is 10.75 inches long, has a 6-inch long, 0.187 inch thick Carbon-V steel blade with an epoxy protective layer against

The Military Recon Tanto combat knife by Cold Steel

oxidation and light reflection, a 4.75 inch long Kraton handle and a Concealex sheath in military style.

MILITARY **ODA** AND **UWK** (UNIVERSAL WAR KNIFE)

The ODA is a low-cost version of the R1 Military Classic. The blade is bead blasted and the Kraton handle has an integrated guard. It is main-

The Cold Steel SRK (Survival Rescue Knife)

tenance free and resistant to heat and moisture. The 7.9 ounce ODA is 11.75 inches long, with a 7-inch long, 0.187 inch thick stainless 420 steel blade and a 4.75 inch handle.

The UWK or Universal War Knife is a lower-cost copy of the rare, costly Vietnam SOG fighting knife. The UWK is made of modern material: a 6.5 inch long, 0.187 inch thick, bead blasted, stainless 420 steel blade and a 4.88 inch Kraton handle with an integrated guard. The 7.1 ounce, 11.38 inch knife comes with a Secure-Ex military sheath resistant to tears and cuts.

MINI PAL

The half-ounce key ring hanger is also a push dagger or skinning knife and it performs like a heavyweight.

The razor-sharp edge easily and quickly cuts through most materials. It is ideal for opening boxes, envelopes or cutting through ropes. The 2.64 inch long knife with a 1 inch long, 0.079 inch thick stainless 400 steel blade has a Kraton transverse handle and a Zytel sheath. Push daggers and skinning knives are illegal in many European countries.

MINI TAC

The 7.5 inch long, 2.2 ounce Mini Tac has a 4-inch long, 0.059 inch thick, stainless, AUS 6A steel Tanto blade with a smooth or serrated edge and a 3.5 inch long, flat Kraton Handle with a deep checkered motif. The Concealex sheath has a bead lanyard, so the knife can safely be carried around the neck.

MINI CULLODEN

Kilted warriors used to conceal this small but deadly weapon at the top edge of their socks. The name Skean Dhu, or 'black knife' in Gaelic, refers to the famous Scottish battle of 16 April 1746. The 7-inch long, 2.3 ounce modern version has a 3.5 inch long, 0.118 inch thick blade of AUS 8A steel with a smooth or traditional serrated edge, and a 3.5 inch long Kraton handle with a checkered motif, a Concealex neck sheath and a bead lanyard.

Military UWK knife and the modern ODA Bowie

Mini Pal push dagger as a key ring

NIGHT FORCE

This tactical folding knife has an extra wide clip blade with a false incision, ending in a sharp point, ideal for cutting or stabbing through almost any type of material. The 4-inch long, 0.138 inch thick stainless 440 A steel blade has a black Teflon protective layer and a smooth or partially serrated edge, ground razor sharp so that it bites into the material with the slightest pressure. The 5 inch long, lightweight and almost unbreakable Zytel handle consists of two pressed halves joined and reinforced with a stainless steel plate. The 9-inch long, 5.1 ounce knife has a leafspring lock of Cold Steel's own design, that can withstand more than 100 lbs of pressure. Thumb studs on both sides of the blade allow fast, one-handed opening.

The Mini Culloden or Skean Dhu

OUTDOORSMAN

The Outdoorsman is an improved Cold Steel model with a covered serration on the back of the blade, giving the index finger and thumb more control. The new chopping edge or 'bone breaker' on the blade hacks through everything it comes up against, including heavy gauge steel wire. The 11-inch, 9.9 ounce knife has a 6-inch long, 0.187 inch thick AUS 8A steel blade, a 5-inch Kraton handle and a heavy leather sheath.

OYABUN

The name of this larger, heavier version of the Kobun Tanto is Japanese for 'undisputed leader.' It has a razor-sharp, 9-inch long, 0.187 inch thick, broad, double-sided, hollow ground blade of 420 Sub Zero tempered steel. The 5.08 inch Kraton handle is enforced internally with Zytel and has a deeply checkered motif. The knife is 14.06 inches long and weighs 8.3 ounces. Until 2000, 12.6 or 14.17 inch long versions were available.

PARA EDGE

This feather-light knife can be worn on a chain around the neck. The 5.7 inch long, 1.3 to 1.4

The Cold Steel Mini Tac

ounce knife weighs just 1.98 ounces with the Concealex sheath. The 3-inch long, 0.098 inch thick, stainless AUS 6A steel Tanto or dagger blade is ground to a paper thin, razor sharp edge. The handle is made of Kraton.

PEACE KEEPERS

The spearpoint blade of this double-edged dagger is designed not to bend or break, which tends to happen with boot daggers. The stainless 420 steel blade is tempered with a freezing process. Peace Keepers come in two sizes, along with a Secure-Ex military style sheath. The 5.6 ounce, 9.75 inch long Peace Keeper II has a 5.5 inch long, 0.187-inch thick blade and a 4.25

The Cold Steel Night Force

The beautiful Imperial Tai-Pan

TRIPLE ACTION

The Triple Action is a remarkable folding knife. The aircraft aluminum handle consists of two halves. To open the knife, one half of the handle must be folded aside and the blade can then be flipped open from the other half with a thumb stud. To close, the handle half is flipped back again. The Triple Action comes with a double-sided dagger blade or a Tanto blade. Both versions are 9.13 inches long with a 4 inch long, 0.118 inch thick blade of AUS 6A steel. The Tanto knife weighs 3.7 ounces, and the dagger knife weighs 3.6 ounces. The 5.118 inch handle, decorated with inlaid engravings, has a strong pocket clip on the back.

the larger knife and 0.093 inches for the smaller knife. The knife is made with a clippoint and drop point blade. The 5.0 or 3.62-inch handles consist of two parts of fiberglass reinforced Valox nylon with a deep checkered motif for a firm grip. The knife features a stainless steel pocket clip and a thumbhole in the blade for easy one-handed opening. The larger Trail Guide clippoint is 8.75 inches long with a 3.75 inch long blade and weighs 3.8 ounces. The smaller knife is 6.25 inches long,

The Cold Steel Tanto

has a 2.64 inch long blade and weighs 1.9 ounces. The Trail Guides with drop point blades are 6.25 inches and 8.75 inches in respective lengths as well. The blade lengths are 2.64 inches and 3.75 inches and the knives weigh 1.9 ounces and 3.8 ounces.

TRAIL MASTER CARBON V AND SAN MAI

This is a modern Bowie – a universal hunting knife that hooks and cuts with the best of them. The blade of the standard Trail master is of Carbon-V steel with a Teflon protective layer. The knife is 14.5 inches long with a 9.5 inch long blade. The steel is no less than 0.313 inches thick. The Kraton handle is 5 inches long. The 16.7 ounce knife comes with a black leather sheath. The San Mai Trail Master has a blade of triple layered San Mai III steel with the same measurements as the standard knife and weighs 17.5 ounces. The polished blade does not have a Teflon coating. This knife comes with a Cordura sheath. Both blade versions are razor sharp and ground somewhat round in a classic style. During testing it easily cut through a 4-inch thick cable.

URBAN PAL

The tiny push dagger was designed as a survival knife for self-defense in the concrete jungles of the big cities. It weighs only 0.7 ounces without its Secure-Ex mini sheath and can easily be carried in a purse or in a sheath around the neck. The Urban Pal is 3.11 inches long and the stainless 420 steel blade is 1.61 inches wide. The possession of a push dagger or skinning knife is illegal in many European countries.
(illustration page 75)

VAQUERO-SERIES

The Cold Steel Vaquero has a distinctive Nogales AUS 8A stainless steel clippoint blade with a long, shallow cross section, ideal for cutting thick fiber

The slim Cold Steel Ti-Lite, designed by Phil Boguszewski, with a blue anodized titanium handle, and a standard titanium handle

material such as rope, cables, pipes and belts. The serrated edges form a sinuous double curve, so that the object being cut is struck with the inward curving portion of the blade close to the hand, then with the middle and tip. The top-lock with its heavy spring has

Cold Steel Trail Guide with a clippoint

stayed intact in tests with a weight of more than 100 lbs. The ergonomically shaped Zytel handle has a deeply cut checkered motif for a stable grip. The double-sided thumb studs on the blade enable left handed and right handed users to easily open the knife. The small Vaquero is 6.61 inches long, with a 3-inch long, 0.118 inch thick clippoint blade. The Zytel handle is 3.39 inches long and the knife weighs 2.5 ounces. The large Vaquero is 9 inches long with a 4-inch blade, a 5-inch handle and weight of 3.3 ounces. The Vaquero Grande at 13.25 inches, with a 6-inch blade, weighs 6.4 ounces and has a 7.25 inch handle. Folding knives longer than 11.02 inches are forbidden in some European countries.

Trail Master

VOYAGER-SERIES

The Cold Steel Voyager is a handy single hand knife with a practical top-lock system and a lightweight Zytel handle. The wide blade has a long flat-ground cutting surface with a thin, razor sharp edge. The high carbon quality in the stainless AUS 8A steel ensures that the edge stays wear-proof and sharp. The knife comes in different sizes, with a smooth, partially-serrated or fully serrated edge. The serration has a new feature: small serrations, turned against the line direction of the blade

and alternated with a wider ground arc. This type of knife cuts easily through any type of material. The new Voyager series has an innovative oval handle, twenty percent thicker that the older model. This knife is handy when camping, hiking, hunting and working outdoors and for the police and rescue services. The Voyager Medium in the clip or Tanto shape is 6.89 inches long with a 3-inch long, 0.098 inch thick blade and a 3.86 inch reinforced Zytel handle. It weighs 1.8 ounces and includes a strong pocket clip on the right handle.

Trail Guide with a droppoint blade

The Voyager Large is 9.57 inches long, with a 4-inch blade and a 5.08 inch Zytel handle and weighs 3.6 ounces with the clippoint. The Tanto weighs 3.7 ounces. The Voyager Large comes with a smooth, partially serrated or completely serrated edge. The Voyager Extra Large is made with a clip and Tanto blade, is 11.14 inches long with a 5-inch long 0.138 inch thick blade. The knife weighs 5.1 ounces or 5.3 ounces depending on the type of blade. The X2 in the XXL Voyager is 13.25 inches long with a 6-inch long, 0.138 inch thick blade and a 7.2 inch long handle, but it only weighs 6.5 ounces. In factory tests the top lock system easily withstood more than 9,100 lbs.

Cold Steel Triple Action

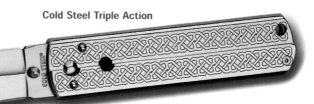

ALL TERRAIN HUNTER

This typical outdoor knife with a fixed, 4.5 inch, droppoint blade weighs only 4.4 ounces. The Carbon V steel blade has a black epoxy protective layer. The handle is of shock-reducing Kraton with finger slots and an eye at the back for a ring or a catch cord. The 9.5 inch knife comes with a black polycarbonate sheath.

ARC ANGEL

This super strong 1960's style butterfly knife was popular thanks to the movie West Side Story, until the Switch Blade Act of 1990 made importing stilettos and butterfly knives illegal. The 4.25 inch long, 0.125 inch thick blade, ground flat from a piece of Carbon-V steel comes with a clippoint and a spearpoint. The skeleton grip is of solid titanium, stock removed for optimal strength and lightness. Every knife is ground by

The small Urban Pal push dagger as a key hanger (see page 73)

KOBUN

Cold Steel Vaquero (see page 73)

hand and made to fit to ensure smooth opening and closing. The 9.69 inch Arc Angel of titanium has a 5.43 inch handle and weighs only 4.2 ounces.

BIRD & TROUT

This is a century-old classic. The secret of its popularity is its simplicity. The finger ring on the skeleton grip provides a firm grip for wet hands. The bead blast finished 6.3 inch knife, with a 2.25 inch long, 0.102 inch thick AUS 6A steel blade weighs 0.8 ounces.

The Kobun boot knife was designed around the Japanese word Kobun, or soldier. Most boot knives have paper-thin points that bend or break easily. The Kobun has a typical Tanto blade, however, with a wide blade back that runs nearly to the point. The slim handle offers a firm grip. The Kobun is made of Carbon-V steel with an Epoxy protective layer and bead blasted stainless 420 steel, tempered in a freezing process. The Kobun is 9.88 inches long, with a blade 5.5 inches long and 0.125 inches thick. The Kraton handle is 4.41 inches long and weighs 4.5 ounces. The Kobun knife was issued with a Kydex sheath until 2000, but now it comes with a Concealex sheath.

HAI HOCHO

The Japanese Hai Hocho knife, freely translated as the 'yes-knife,' can do almost anything. It is particularly well suited for camping, fishing or sailing and it is not out of

The Voyager Medium series with a clippoint and Tanto

place in the kitchen either, thanks to the thin and wide blade that is excellent for cutting and hacking. It comes with a sheath made of Secure-Ex. The 7.5 inch long knife, with a 4-inch long, 0.059 inch thick stainless AUS 6A steel blade and a 3.5 inch Kraton handle is 4 inches long and 0.059 inches thick and weighs only 2.2 ounces.

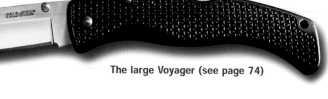

The large Voyager (see page 74)

SAFE KEEPER

This typical push dagger became popular during the California gold rush of 1859 because it was compact and simple to handle. It is easy to guess what it was used for at that time. Nowadays, the Safe Keeper is very popular among soldiers all over the world because, unlike firearms, it never refuses to work, breaks, malfunctions or runs out of ammunition. With the tactical Secure-Ex sheath it can easily be carried in combat gear. The 3.5 ounce, 5-inch long Safe Keeper

COLUMBIA RIVER KNIFE & TOOL (CRKT)

www.crkt.com

The emblem of Columbia River Knife & Tool (CRKT)

The American company Columbia River Knife & Tool (CRKT) is based in Wilsonville, Oregon. Established in 1994 by Paul Gillespie and Rod Bremer, it mostly manufactured tools at first, but quickly switched to knife production. CRKT focuses on producing top quality knifes at affordable prices, putting its money on high volume. It likes to call in the help of renowned knife makers and to reproduce their designer knives using cost saving production techniques, such as CNC machines.

**The Cold Steel Voyager Large series
(see page 74)**

has a 2.5 inch long, 0.187 inch thick, single-edged, stainless 420 steel, freeze-tempered, bead-blasted blade and a 2.05 inch long Kraton transverse handle. The 3.6 ounce, 6.38 inch Safe Keeper II has a 3.75 inch long, 0.187 inch thick double-sided blade and a 2.5 inch long Kraton handle. Push daggers and skinning knives are illegal in many European countries. (illustration page 72)

One of CRKT's first knives, the Wrangler folding knife, was designed by Gillespie and Bremer themselves. This robust stainless steel working knife is still being made and costs less than twenty dollars. CRKT is also very well known for its KISS (Keep It Super Simple) series. These knives, designed by Ed Halligan, and the M16 knives by Kit Carson, have long been the company's pivot of existence.

CRKT'S current assortment consists mainly of sport, working and pro-

**The Voyager in XXL format
(see page 74)**

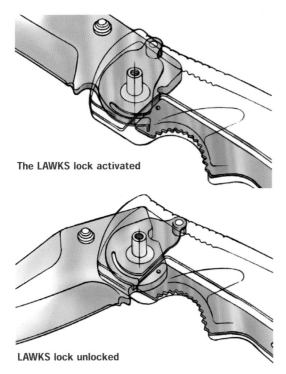

The LAWKS lock activated

LAWKS lock unlocked

fessional knives for the military, police, firefighters and other emergency services. CRKT uses stainless AUS 6M steel as a standard, due to its toughness and durability at 55-57 HRC (Rockwell). This company also produces various specialized knives of AUS 8 steel with a hardness of 57-58 HRC. A great number of its folding knives have the LAWKS locking system.

LAWKS stands for the patented Lake And Walker Knife Safety, referring to its designers, Ron Lake and Michael Walker. The LAWKS is a safety stud or an additional lock of the linerlock system. Working knives need a solid lock: the linerlock can accidentally come undone with vigorous use and a blade that suddenly snaps back can have nasty consequences. By moving a stud to the front with the thumb, the foot of the stud fixes the linerlock into place.

When the LAWKS is pushed back, the locking of the linerlock is lifted and can be pushed back again allowing the blade to fold back.

CARSON

Kit Carson from Vine Grove, Kentucky is a retired military sergeant-major. Growing up in the woods and trout streams in the mountains of North Carolina made him an enthusiastic hunter and fisherman. He has been making knives part time for

more than thirty years and full time since 1993. He is a member of the American Knifemakers' Guild. He is known for his solid working knives and for his fixed models and folding knives. His outdoor life as a boy and his career in the military, which took him all over the world, have had a clear influence on the shape of his knives, especially apparent in his M-16 series.

CARSON F4

Carson had been making this popular knife for a number of years himself, but could not keep up with the demand, so CKRT started producing it in 2004, along wih a special Zytel sheath which allows it to be carried on a belt or at the top of the pants or around the neck on a lanyard. The integral knife is 5.5 inches long, of stainless, 0.10 inch thick AUS 6M steel, tempered to 55-57 HRC. The 2.5 inch blade is available with a smooth or partially serrated edge with a special design called 'Triple Point' – a series of two small serrations and one long and deeply ground serration. The Zytel handle plates have a deep checkered motif which, along with the serrated finishing on the handle, contributes to a stable grip.

CARSON M16 / M16-Z

Carson F4

The original M16 knife by Kit Carson has a handle of special 6061 T6 aircraft aluminum. The blade is made of stainless AUS 8 steel, bead blasted for a matte finish. The M16 features the "Carson Flipper," a blade-integrated additional button that eases the opening and closing of the knife and ser-

The Carson M16

ves as a guard. The knife has a liner-lock secured with the LAWKS system and can easily and smo-othly be opened with one hand thanks to a Teflon layer. The second thumb button has a chec-kered surface for servicing the blade safely.

The standard M16 series is made in three different versions. The largest knife has a Tanto 3.94-inch long 0.14-inch thick steel blade, a 5.31-inch long handle and weighs 4.9 ounces. It is made with a smooth or partially serrated edge in the Triple-Point style. The medium knife has a 3.56-inch long, 0.10-inch thick spearpoint blade, a 4.63-inch long handle and weighs 2.9 ounces.

The M16 Spearpoint has a 3.38-inch long blade that comes with a smooth or partially serrated Triple Point edge. The smallest knife is 7.36 inches long with a 3.13 inch long, 0.10 inch thick Tanto blade. This model also comes with a smooth or partially serrated edge and a strong steel carry clip on the back of the Teflon-coated handle. The knives of the M16-Z series are virtually the same, except for their Zytel handles but they are heavier at 3.7 and 6.2 ounces respectively.

Carson M16 EDC (Every Day Carry)

CARSON M16 FD

The shield with "1*" on the Carson M16 FD refers to a pun on the word asterisk: policemen, marines and fire fighters only have 'one-ass-to-risk.' The logo was designed long ago by the police chief of the Shaker Heights Police Department, Gary Paul Johnson. His SWAT (Special Weapons and Tactics) unit was very successful in operational circumstances but during training there were always injuries. To make his men more alert, Johnson told this joke:

"An American History teacher asks students if they can make a sentence with an asterisk in it. One of the students raises his hand and says: 'Patriot Nathan Hale called out, "I'm sorry that I have only one 'ass-to-risk' for my homeland.""'

Johnson decided to add an asterisk to the shield shape of the large '1' used by the American military. He granted CRKT per-mission to use his idea on the profes-sional knife series. The M16 FD knife for firefighters, from 2002, bears the logo. The letters FD stand for Fire Department. The red G10 handles with epoxy resin reinforced fiberglass handles are not good heat-conductors and the stain-less AUS 8 steel of the blade and the steel of the liner-lock system have a titanium nitrate protective layer. The M16 FD comes in three sizes: the smallest Tanto has a partially-serrated 3.13 inch blade with a 4.25-inch long handle and weighs 2.9 ounces. The knife next in size has a 3.56-inch long spearpoint blade and a 4.63-inch long handle and weighs 2.9 ounces. The largest Tanto is 9.25 inches long, has a blade 3.94 inches in length and 0.14 inches thick and a handle that is 5.31 inches long and weighs 4.9 ounces.

Carson M16 FD series

CARSON M16 COMPACT EDC

CRKT brought these compact versions of the M16, the EDC (Every Day Carry) to market in January 2003 after buyers called for a smaller and more com-pact model. The 4-inch long, dark-green, 6061 T6 airplane aluminum handle is very strong relative to the blade length. This ensures a good grip. The stain-less AUS 8 steel blade has a black matte protective layer of titanium nitride and a linerlock system with the LAWKS security system. The M16 EDC is made with a Tanto and a spearpoint blade. The 2-ounce Tanto is 7.1 inches long, with a 3.06 inch long, 0.08 inch thick blade with a 3-inch cutting edge, available with a smooth or partially serrated Triple Point blade. The 1.9 ounce spearpoint blade model has the same dimensions and is also made with a smooth or partially serrated edge. Both knives have the 'Carson Flipper' guard and a Teflon layer.

The Carson M16 LE-Law Enforcement

The military version of the
Carson M16 folder

CARSON M16 LE

The M16 LE knife looks similar to the FD series,
but has a handle, made of 6061 T6 aluminum. The
knives in this series
have the same
features as the
other M16s. The
abbreviation 'SRT'
on the blade stands
for 'Search and Rescue Team.' The 1*
logo also has a superscription HIGH RISK
ENVIRONMENT. All other the technical specifications are the same as the M16 FD.

CARSON M16 M

The M16 M is the military version of the M16 series and the knives have the same technical specifications as the M16 FD and the M16 LE. The 6061 T6
aluminum handle has an olive green protective layer.

Two M16 knives from the titanium series

The blade and linerlock
are both covered with
titanium nitrate. The
M16 M features the
typical 'Carson Flipper'
that opens and closes the knife while also serving as
the guard

CARSON M16 SF

This knife was developed
by Kit Carson for the coaliti-
on troops from the United Nati-
ons. The soldiers in the Middle East and Afghanistan needed a robust knife that could
cut well, stay sharp for a long
time and resist the harsh desert climate. The M16
SF or Special Forces knife has a heavy set frame
with a stainless J2 steel casing, a stainless steel drum
and Zytel handle plates. The blade is of 0.14 inch
thick stainless AUS 6M steel with a titanium nitra-

The M16 Special Forces with the
double Carson Flipper

te protective layer. The double 'Carson Flipper'
makes it a real dagger, with a 5.31 inch handle, a
3.94 inch blade and a 3.88 inch long edge with a
partial Triple Point serration. The knife weighs 6.2
ounces and comes in black, green, desert yellow
and camouflage.

CARSON M16 TI (TITANIUM)

CRKT introduced the M16 knives
with a titanium finish in
2003. The handle is
made by a computeri-
zed CFC milling
machine from 6AL4V
titanium. The blade is
of stainless AUS 8 steel, bead
blasted for a non-reflective finish. Both knives come
with a partial Triple Point serration. A double-sided
thumb stud on the blade makes for effortless opening
of the Teflon-coated blade. The stainless steel linerlock system is secured by the LAWKS system. The
larger knife has a 0.14 inch thick, 3.94 inch long
Tanto blade with a 3.88 inch cutting edge. The tita-

The Carson M18 Black

nium handle is 5.31 inches in length and the knife weighs 5.9 ounces. A smaller version has a 3.56 inch spearpoint blade, 0.10 inches thick, a 4.63 inch long handle and weighs 3.4 ounces.

CARSON M18

Due to the huge success of the M16 series, CRKT asked Carson to design a lightweight version. The blade features the 'Carson Flipper.' The 6061 T6

The complete Carson M18 Blue series

aluminum handle is inlaid with a G-10 surface for a firm grip. The blade, of matted stainless AUS 8 steel tempered to 57-58 HRC, is somewhere between a dagger and a spearpoint, but it is not ground on two sides.

The linerlock system of the stainless 420J2 steel features the LAWKS security system. Carson designed this knife in different colors, but the knife actually comes in four different versions and in three colors. The larger knife is 8.7 inches in total length. The blade of it is 3.63 inches long and the steel is 0.14 inches thick. The handle is 5.06 inches long and the knife weighs 5.1 ounces. The knife comes with a smooth edge of 3.5 inches or with a partial Triple Point serration. The M18 knife is made with G10 inlaid layers in black,

blue or red. The somewhat smaller knife has the same shape and the total length is 7.63 inches. The handle is relatively wide and 4.38 inches long and the blade is 3.25 inches long and 0.12 inches thick. The knife weighs 3.5 ounces. The smaller knife is also made in black, blue or red by CRKT and comes with a smooth or partially serrated edge.

CORKUM

Steve Corkum is a custom knife maker from Littletown, Pennsylvania. His designs are inspired by traditional Japanese shapes. Corkum had been involved with Kung Fu for a while and made his first knife on the advice of his wife. He became a professional knife maker in 1996 and knife makers Don Fogg, Bill Moran and Bob Engnath showed him the ropes. Steve Corkum is a member of the American Bladesmith Society. His work can often be seen in knife magazines such as *Knives Illustrated* and he is known for his unique grinding method: he grinds a new knife design mostly complete, looking for a weak point. He is always on the lookout for the perfect combination of longevity, flexibility, functionality and the perfect balance.

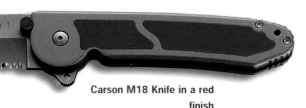

Carson M18 Knife in a red finish

CORKUM FIRST STRIKE

Corkum First Strike Tanto is based on the art of Japanese sword forging, which goes back to 645 BC. The blade is shaped like an ancient Chokuto sword and the classic double-sided Mohorazukuri Tanto. The transverse cut of the blade forms a curve that can be compared

Corkum First Strike Tanto

The Crawford Falcon

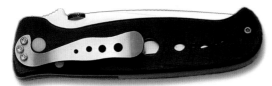

to the pip of an apple. This results in a stronger cut than from a tapped or hollow ground blade. The blade of this massive integral knife is 0.19 inches thick. The stainless AUS 6M steel runs right through to the pommel. The handle is traditionally covered with black stingray hide and then wound by hand with a Japanese cord in the ancient tradition. CRKT designed a pressed Zytel military sheath to carry the knife comfortably in many different ways. Despite its ceremonial character and Eastern origin, this heavy knife is suitable for daily use. The total length of the First Strike is 9.25 inches with a blade 4.5 inches in length. The knife weighs 6.4 ounces and the sheath weighs 2.4 ounces.

CRAWFORD

Pat Crawford and his son, Wes, are leading figures in the art of knife making. Crawford Knives, in West Memphis, Arkansas, specializes in high-tech folding knives and when it comes to fighting folding knives, Pat is a pioneer. A member of the American Knife Maker's Guild since 1973, his skeleton knives with their top lock system are known throughout the knife world. His technique, stock removal of material from a block of steel, differs from that of other knife makers who forge the knife from point to pommel. Pat makes folding knives in all sorts of shapes and handles from rare woods, mammoth ivory, stag horn, Micarta and a variety

of synthetic materials. Due to their success, the Crawfords could not keep up with demand and so they decided to create some designs for CRKT.

CRAWFORD FALCON

Crawford is famous for his minimalist designs, nonetheless the Falcon has a traditional flowing, bound line with a firm grip, emphasized by the forefinger saver, a continuous pommel and an ergonomic thumb rest. The frame is of a heavy casing with two stainless 420J2 steel plates. Holes are drilled into the handle plates and casing of the pressed Zytel handle to reduce weight and there is a stainless steel carry clip on the right plate. The blade pivot has a Teflon layer for smooth motion. The AUS 6M steel drop

The Crawford Fixed Falcon as a fixed knife

point blade curves slightly towards the point, and is finished to a satin shine. It comes with a smooth or partially serrated edge with a Triple Point serration. The flat thumb slide for one-handed opening is a typical Crawford feature. The knife has a linerlock with the LAWKS security system. It comes in two sizes, with a smooth or partially serrated edge. The larger, 8.87 inch, knife has a 5-inch long handle and a 3.87 inch long, 0.14 inch thick blade and weighs 5.5 ounces. The smaller knife is 7 inches long with a 4-inch handle and a 3 inch long, 0.12 inch thick blade and weighs 3.3 ounces.

CRAWFORD KASPER

The Crawford Kasper folding knife is based on a design by Bob Kasper the former marine and chairman of the Gung-Ho Chuan association, a society for instructors of close contact fighting for the American Marines. He worked with with Pat Crawford to design the ultimate folding knife for self-protection. This

The Crawford Kasper

The LAWKS
safety system
built into
the Crawford Kasper

robust knife, intended for very hard work, has an inner casing of stainless 420J12 steel with a double plate for extra hardness. The casing plates are attached to each other at the back with a hard anodized 6061 T6 aluminum spacer. The blade pivot turns on a Teflon layer and the carry clip on the right handle plate also has a Teflon coating.

This knife's extra heavy inter lock is protected with the LAWKS system and features the classic Kasper profile, with an extra deep slot for the index finger. The roughened Zytel handle plates are flat so that the knife does not show through a pocket. A thumb scallop on the left handle part makes it easier to open the knife

The Crawford Kasper Tactical model from the
'For Those Who Serve'

quickly and there is a thumb stud on both sides of the blade for left and right handed use. The blade is made of stainless AUS 6M steel with an adjusted clippoint, ground hollow on both sides and bead blasted to prevent reflection. The 9.2 inch larger knife has a 0.16 inch thick, 3.87 inch long blade, a 5.37 inch handle and weighs 7.4 ounces. The smaller 7-inch knife has a 4.25 inch handle, a 3-inch long, 0.12 inch thick blade and weighs 4 ounces. Both versions are available with smooth, full or partial CRKT Triple Point serrations.

CRAWFORD KASPER PROFESSIONAL

The popular Crawford Kasper folding knife is one of the most well thought-out knives that CRKT has ever produced, but it is somewhat heavy for professionals who have to carry knives all the time. Therefore CRKT developed the Crawford Kasper Professional for the police, emergency services and the military. The shape is roughly similar to the standard model, but the handle is made of hard anodized 6061 T6 aluminum and has a variety of holes to save weight, yet not compromise the strength. The stainless AUS 8 steel blade comes with a smooth or partially serrated edge. The liner-lock system of stainless 420J2 steel is protected with the LAWKS system. This knife comes in two

The Crawford Kasper
Professional

sizes: the larger, 9.2 inch knife has a 0.16 inch thick, 3.87 inch long blade a 5.37 inch long handle and weighs 6 ounces – considerably less than the 7.4 ounces of the standard model. The smaller knife is 7.2 inches long with a 0.12 inch thick, 3-inch long blade and weighs 3.6 ounces.

CRAWFORD KASPER TACTICAL

The Crawford Kasper Tactical is a standard folding knife but the blade has an anti-reflective Teflon protective layer. This knife comes in two sizes, with or without the partial serration of the blade.

CRAWFORD POINT GUARD

Crawford made this tactical folding knife as a custom series for special units of the American military and other law enforcement agencies. It has a heavy set frame with a casing of double stainless 420J2 steel plates and a spacer of anodized 6061

The Crawford Point Guard

T6 aluminum, special Torx screws, a Teflon layer and Zytel handle parts. The linerlock features the LAWKS security system. The modern Point-Guard design is slim, long and no-frills. Holes in the handle save weight, but do not compromise the strength of the frame. The back of the handle is rounded to maintain its minimal profile and, with the ribbed top edge of the handle, it provides a firm grip for every hand size. The Crawford thumb slide allows it to be easily opened with one hand. The large Point Guard is 8.3 inches long with a 4.75 inch handle and a 3.5 inch long, 0.14 inch thick stainless AUS 6M steel blade and it weighs 4.1 ounces. The smaller knife is 6.5 inches long, with a 2.75 inch long, 0.10 inch thick blade and a 3.75 inch handle and weighs 2.3 ounces. Both knives come with a smooth or partially serrated edge and a Teflon-coated carry clip.

The 14K Summit Pike's Peak

14K SUMMIT SERIES

In mountaineering, your life depends on your tools. This goes for pitons, ice axes, crampons and, of course, knives. American mountaineers consider

The Mo'Skeeter

reaching the 14,000 foot summits of North American mountains to be the highlights of their careers, so these knives are called 14K Summit. They are made with a strong InterFrame linerlock system, left open for easy cleaning. The casing and linerlock secured with the LAWKS security system are of stainless 420J2 steel. The zinc alloy handle has a chromium nickel protective layer in an open skeleton shape, which saves weight without compromising strength. The rough handle and the holes ensure a firm grip in wet and freezing conditions. The stainless AUS 6M steel blade is based on the drop point model, but is somewhat cut away. All versions of the 14K Summit feature double-sided thumb studs on the blade, with a Teflon

layered blade pivot. The casing can be adjusted with a Torx screw after a few years of intensive use. The 14K Summit Mount Whitney and the Denali knives have 3.5 inch long, 0.12 inch thick steel blades, 4.75 inch handles and weigh 6.4 ounces. The Denali knife also has a partially serrated Triple Point edge. The Long Peak and Mount Rainier knives have 2.94 inch long, 0.12 inch thick blades and 4 inch handles and weigh 4.1 ounces. Mount Rainier has a serrated edge. The smaller Pike's Peak, with a smooth edge, and Mount Shasta, with a partially serrated edge, have 2.5 inch long. 0.10 inch thick blades and 3.31 inch handles and weigh 2.7 ounces. The knife has a Teflon coated carry clip.

MO'SKEETER

This conventional folding knife with a backlock is large enough for heavy work, yet is still slim and light in weight. The Mo'Skeeter knife is a fraction larger than the popular Wrangler knives. It is 6.5 inches long and the handle, of one piece of Zytel, is 3.75 inches long, and it weighs only 2.1 ounces. The 0.10 inch thick, 2.75 inch long stainless AUS 6M steel blade comes with a smooth or partially serrated edge and a thumb stud on both sides for easy opening with the left or the right hand. Even the carry clip can be placed on the left or right hand side. The Mo'Skeeter knife features a built-in safety when opening and closing. As soon as the blade reaches a 90 degree angle, there is a hitch in the movement, giving the user enough time to get his/her fingers out of the way. The blade pivot has an adjustable Torx pivot.

WRANGLER

The Wrangler is not a shining example of design, but with a retail price of around twenty dollars it is the strongest and most advantageous working knife

The Wrangler working knife

The Rollock by Elishewitz

on the market today. Its handle is made of fiberglass reinforced nylon, pressed into an ergonomic shape. This slim folding knife with a simple backlock system has a taper ground drop point blade and opens easily. The blade pivot can easily be adjusted with Allen screws. The 6.25 inch knife has a 0.10 inch thick, 2.75 inch long stainless AUS 6M steel blade, a 3.5 inch handle and weighs 1.4 ounces.

ELISHEWITZ

Allen Elishewitz is a young knife maker from New Braunfels, Texas. He has a degree in criminal law and he lived in the Far East for a period of time. In 1988, his knowledge of the Eastern fighting arts and time in the Marine Corps led to his decision to devote himself to making knives. He also designs clocks and jewelry. In 1994 he became the youngest member of the American Knife Maker's Guild. He is also a member of the Italian Knife Maker's Guild and the American Bladesmith Society. He has won many local and international awards for his knives.

ELISHEWITZ ROLLOCK

The original Rolox from 1975 was a custom sliding knife. Its production was severely limited by the American company Benchmark, but CRKT got the rights to the design. Allen Elishewitz redesigned it into the smoothest Rolox mechanism of all time with a completely new exterior, available for about forty dollars. He changed the blade shape to a droppoint, improved the handle and added a stainless steel carry clip. The handle plates are translucent, so

you can see the mechanisms of the sliding knife. The casing is decorated with a small waffle motif. The handle is available in white, blue, red and black. The knife also got a new name: Rollock. The trick behind the transformation was exceptional quality control. Thanks to computerized CNC machines, this was possible and Bill Adams, the director of Rolox Corporation, was impressed: he found that the Rollock knife was the smoothest working sliding knife he had ever held. Rollock is an extremely sharp tool. The stainless steel casing is made of 420J2 steel and 0.10 inch thick AUS 6M steel is used for the highly polished blade, with a long V-section and a smooth edge or partial CRKT Triple Point serration. The 420J2 steel carry clip can also be used as a money clip. To open the knife, the blade must be pushed forward at the base by the thumb and will click into a rock-solid locking system. In order to close it, the locking system at the bottom of the knife must be pushed in and the blade can be moved back with the thumb and index finger. The total length of the 2.3 ounce opened knife is 5.75 inches. The handle is 3.5 inches long and the blade is 2.25 inches long.

FRANKLIN

Mike Franklin, a former music teacher from Maysville, Kentucky, is an enthusiastic archer and often hunted with a bow and arrow in his youth, when he made himself a number of different hunting knives. When he saw a copy of the *Gun Digest Book of Knives* for the first time, he decided to start making knives for others. In 1973, he went with Jimmy Lile to the Knifemakers' Guild Show in Kansas City. He took twelve of his self-made knives with him and sold everything. That's when he decided to make knives on a

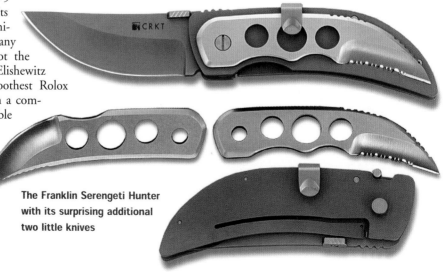

The Franklin Serengeti Hunter with its surprising additional two little knives

full-time basis. He also became a member of the American Knifemakers' Guild that year. At first he only made fixed knives, and had a hard time selling them. Times were tough until 1980, when he started to produce folding knives, with the help of fellow knife maker A.G. Russel. He compiled all of his designs and sent them to well known knife dealers in North America, who liked what they saw. His logo is 'Knives with an attitude.'

K.I.S.S. and K.I.S.S. In the Dark

FRANKLIN SERENGETI HUNTER

Seen for the first time, the Franklin Serengeti Hunter, which won the prize for innovation in 2001 at the Knifemakers' Guild Show makes one wonder: "What is this?" It looks like a good folding knife with beautiful decorations, but it is actually three knives in one. A small skinning knife is attached to the one side of the handle. Another small, serrated knife, shaped like a bird claw, or "hawksbill," is on the other side. This combination makes skinning

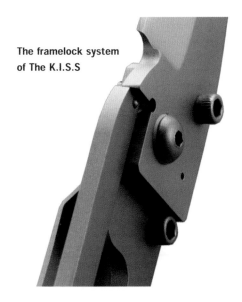

The framelock system of The K.I.S.S

easier. The Serengeti folding knife is the heart of the system. The casing, of two stainless 420J2 steel plates, kept apart with two spacers, is easy to clean. The blade locks with a framelock system, with the right casing plate latching onto the foot of the blade. It looks like a linerlock, but lacks the separate locking rod. The LAWKS system is attached for additional protection. The blade is made of 0.12 inch thick, 3.5 inch long AUS 6M steel. A thumb pal on the blade ensures lightning quick opening with one hand. The Teflon layer around the axis ensures that the mechanisms of the knife operate

very quietly and easily. The 8.5 inch Serengeti knife has a 5-inch handle and weighs 5.8 ounces on its own and 8.3 ounces as a complete system with both skinning knives. The two small knives, of stainless AUS 6M steel, are rounded at the corners by a CFC machine for a firm grip and holes are drilled into them to reduce weight. They click into the handle with stainless steel saddle clips and are held in position at the back of the knife by the excellent blade pivot. The so-called caping knife has a mostly serrated blade in the shape of a bird of prey claw. The 4.62 inch handle holds the 1.75 inch long, 0.12 inch thick blades and the knife weighs 1.3 ounces. The 2-inch long blade of the Detail Skinner goes upwards in an arching skinner shape. The 4.62 inch long knife is made of 0.12 inch thick AUS 6M steel and weighs 1.2 ounces. The Serengeti Hunter comes with a Cordura sheath.

HALLIGAN

Ed Halligan is a technician by heart. After 37 years of working on aircrafts at Delta Airlines, he started his own company called Halligan Knives in Sharpsburg, Georgia. He had started learning the scrimshaw technique earlier on and his leatherwork had attracted some attention. In 1996, Ed was awarded the title 'Master Smith' by the American Bladesmith Society and he also won the B.R. Hughes prize for the best knife. He prefers to use the stock removal system and works on the knives himself, from the shaping to the hardening process. He also makes his own Damasteel. In addition to art knives, Halligan also makes military and tactical knives and is the inventor of the K.I.S.S. knife series that stands for 'Keep It Super Simple.'

The K.I.S.S.

HALLIGAN K.I.S.S. / K.I.S.S. IN THE DARK

The original K.I.S.S. design dates to 1998. This folding knife, the size of the palm of one's hand, only has two parts: the blade and the handle with a very simple casing lock system. This consists of the lower handle part that latches on to the lower part of the blade after it is opened and keeps it locked. In order to close this knife again, the handle has to be pushed back so that the blade can unlock. This is actually a derived linerlock, without the separate locking rod. The uniqueness of the casing lock lies in its simplicity, safety and strength. The knife can easily be opened with one hand because of the thumb stud on the blade.

The K.I.S.S. knife has a Tanto shaped blade with a chisel shaped point. When closed, the razor sharp

The Halligan P.E.C.K.

edge sits right against the handle so that it cannot cause any damage. The blade and skeleton casing are made of stainless AUS 6M steel, bead blasted to a matte finish. A strong carry clip at the back also serves as a money clip. One year after the introduction of K.I.S.S., CRKT brought K.I.S.S. In the Dark to the market. This is like the standard model, except for its non-reflective black Teflon protective layer which also prevents corrosion, even though the knife is made of stainless AUS 6M steel. Both knives are 5.75 inches long, with a 3.5 inch handle and a 2.25 inch long, 0.12 inch thick blade and weigh 2.2 ounces. The blade comes with a smooth edge or a partial CRKT Triple Point serration.

The K.I.S.S. and K.I.S.S. In the Dark knives are made with 24kt gild adornments including the thumb stud, blade screws, blade pivot as well as the carry clip. This is why it is classified as a luxury knife at the incredibly low price of only $50 (in 2003).

HALLIGAN P.E.C.K.

P.E.C.K. is the abbreviation for Precision Engineered Compact Knife. This is actually a smaller S.S.T.

The even simpler K.I.S.S. S.S.T.

knife, shaped like the Wharncliffe or sheepfoot blade. The 0.9 ounce, 4.62 inch P.E.C.K. can serve as a money clip or a key ring but it also has a very sharp 1.88 inch long, 0.10 inch thick blade and a 2.63 inch handle, both of stainless AUS 6M steel. The locking system is similar to the K.I.S.S. and the S.S.T. knives. Like its bigger brothers, P.E.C.K. is also available in the Dark edition, with a black Teflon coating and only comes with a smooth edge.

Two luxurious knives are the P.E.C.K. Gold and the Black Gold. The Peck 24K Gold is of white stainless AUS 6M steel and the thumb stud, blade stopping screw, the blade pivot and the carry clip are all gilded with 24kt gold. The P.E.C.K. Black Gold has a black Teflon protective layer on the stainless AUS 6M steel.

The luxury P.E.C.K. Gold and Black Gold

HAMMOND

Jim Hammond was the first custom knife maker to work for CRKT in 1994. His designs set the standards for machine produced folding knives. In 1977, right out of school, Hammond started working as an independent knife maker and soon became known for his extraordinary work. A member of the American Knifemakers' Guild, when he is not busy spending his time designing and making knives, he can be found fishing on the seashore or skiing in the mountains. He is also a certified hang glider. Fundamental to Hammond's work are: excellence, flair and functionality. He strives for a perfect style and design, with a sharp eye on usefulness. His company, Jim Hammond Knives, is in Arab, Alabama. The ABC and the Cascade knives he designed for CRKT are simple, strong, stylish and extremely useful.

HAMMOND ABC

The name of this fixed knife stands for 'All Bases Covered.' It is made with two designs: the Aqua, a water knife for divers, canoeists, rafters and fisher-

The Hammond Cascade folding knife

men and the Operator's Model for campers, climbers, parachutists and military personnel. The Aqua has a blade with a blunt point, suited for taking underwater: if it should fall, it cannot accidentally make a hole in a rubber boat or diving suit. The cutting edge is ground hollow for specialist jobs. The other side of the blade has a Triple Point serration for cutting through lines, nets, seaweed or other obstacles. ABC Aqua is indispensable for rescue services, paramedics and police or security services. The sharp pointed Operator's Model has a droppoint shaped Tanto blade, ground sharp on both sides of the cutting edge. A false incision runs into a razor sharp Triple Point serration. Both knives are integral, of 0.16 inch thick stainless

AUS 8 steel with a black titanium nitrate layer to protect them against aggressive salt water. They are 8.38 inches long, with a 3.25 inch blade and weigh 4.6 ounces, or 8 ounces with its sheath. Large holes drilled into the skeleton handle reduce weight and

Hammond ABC

provide a firm grip. The handle has Zytel plates with a deep checkered motif on either side, attached with stainless steel Torx screws. The knife comes with a Zytel ABC sheath with a detachable and moveable carry clip made of feather steel. The lock holding the knife in the 3.4 ounce sheath can be adjusted with Chicago screws.

HAMMOND CASCADE LOCK BACK

This series by Jim Hammond is an excellent design basis for a cost effective folding knife. Jim transformed his original design into a working knife that can be produced easily and relatively cheaply. The blade of the Cascade is made of 0.13 inch thick, 3.5 inch long stainless AUS 6M steel and it has a somewhat changed clippoint. It is ground hollow and bead blasted to a matte finish and comes with a smooth or partially serrated edge. For optimal comfort, the frame is made of fused and pressed hook free polycarbonate. The arched Kraton handle has a checkered motif for a firm and stable grip. A deep finger slot is in the handle for the index finger. The base of the blade is notched to keep the thumb from sliding when applying pressure. Thumb studs on both sides of the blade allow easy opening with the left or right hand. It has a back-lock system called 'lock back' in which the blade is kept in place with a steel rod when opened. As soon as the visible part of this rod is pushed in on the top

Hawk D.O.G. (Deadbolt Over Grabstep)

of the handle, the blade unlocks and can be folded back. CRKT also built in an extra safety feature to allow one-handed closing. As soon as the blade reaches an angle of 90 degrees in relation to the handle, there is a clear stoppage point through which the blade has to be pushed to keep fingers out of the way of the razor-sharp edge. The knife comes with a Cor-

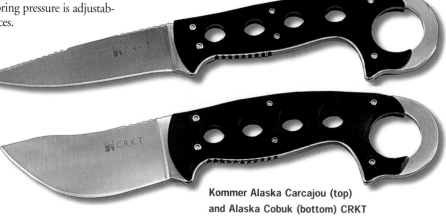

Kommer Alaska Bwana

dura sheath that can be attached to a belt. The Cascade is 8.6 inches long with a blade 3.5 inches long, a handle 5.12 inches long and weighs 4.7 ounces.

HAWK

Grant Hawk a former maker of mining tools, and his son Gavin started making knives in Idaho City, Idaho in 1994. Their first project, to design the 'perfect folding knife,' resulted in the D.O.G.

HAWK D.O.G.

This knife's unique locking system, the 'Deadbolt Over Grabstep,' or D.O.G., consists of a sliding locking pin that shoots out under spring pressure to the front. The spring is isolated in the casing and this protects it against sand or dirt. Thanks to the grabstep, a blade periphery that runs diagonally, the blade starts to lock even before it has been fully opened. The deadbolt is on both sides of the frame for left or right-handed use. The rugged knife has an open casing of hard anodized 6061 T6 aircraft aluminum; a 0.15 inch thick, 3.5 inch long modified clippoint blade of AUS 8 steel with an oval thumb slot for one-hand opening and a smooth or partially serrated Triple Point blade; a Teflon-covered blade pivot; and a casing with a deep finger slot for the index finger and an angled back. The knife comes with 4.62 inch long checkered or diagonally-slotted handle plates, attached with Torx screws and a short carry clip. The spring pressure is adjustable. The knife weighs 4.9 ounces.

KOMMER

Rus Kommer from Anchorage, Alaska has been a professional hunting guide since 1980. He became interested in making knives when one of his clients showed him that he could skin an entire moose without having to sharpen his knife once. Well known knife maker John Shore taught him to grind a blade. Kommer started producing his own designs in 1997. Knife catalogs are filled with his series of fixed knives, including Bowie hunting knives, skinning knives and fighting and boot knives made of exotic wood and with engravings. Kommer is the designer of Bear Claw, Big Eddy and a growing number of hunting knives, such as the Pro Hunter series. His knives are very functional and easy to use.

KOMMER ALASKA BWANA

Kommer designed this folding knife for skinning the game that his clients shot. Skinning a 1,600-pound caribou or moose calls for a very strong knife that maintains a sharp edge, is easy to handle and can be easily cleaned at the end. CRKT turned Kommer's design into a production model that it could manufacture at a reasonable price. This knife won the Outdoor Knives Award in 2002 at the international weapon trade show (IWA) in Nuremberg. It is a very comfortable knife with an arched handle with finger slots for a firm grip and four large holes to reduce the weight without influencing the strength of the knife. The stainless steel carry clip is detachable because Kommer is no great enthusiast of such clips. The long, hollow ground, arched skinner blade is of stainless and rugged AUS 6M steel, and serrated on the back for a firm grip on the base during slippery gutting work. The knife has a linerlock system, secured with the LAWKS. The casing is of two stainless 420J2 steel plates covered with molded Zytel handle plates. The knife is 8.5 inches long, with a 4.87 inch handle and a 3.62 inch long, 0.12 inch thick blade with a sharp, smooth 3.37 inch cutting edge, and weighs 3.4 ounces.

Kommer Alaska Carcajou (top)
and Alaska Cobuk (bottom) CRKT

The Alaska Pro Hunter by Russ Kommer

KOMMER ALASKA CARCAJOU & COBUK

In the north of Alaska, the Inuit word for wolverine is Carcajou and the word for moose is Cobuk. Both of these special hunting and skinning knives are integral: the 0.12 inch thick blade and the flat horn extending up through the pommel are all made of one piece of AUS 6M steel. The slim Carcajou can easily be used to clean slippery fish, poultry and for other precision jobs. The ridges on the back of the blade at the handle and at the point ensure comfortable skinning work around ears and feet. Kommer says this knife is the best for removing blood grooves from salmon. It is 7.0 inches in total length, has a 2.88 inch cutting edge and weighs 2.4 ounces.

The Cobuk knife is based on a knife Kommer made for himself to skin game his clients shot. The proportions make it ideal for stags, roedeer, and even moose. The blade is hollow ground and 2.75 inches long – about like the index finger so that one can work intuitively inside the game. The finger ring at the back of this integral knife makes it easy to grip properly. The knife can even hang on the pinky when the skinner needs his/her other fingers to grasp something. The total length of the Cobuk knife is 6.63 inches and it weighs 3.0 ounces. Both knives have very hard sheaths made of shock resistant polycarbonate and feature special belt clips. The handle plates are made of Zytel and four large holes drilled into them lead to a significant weight reduction and provide a comfortable grip. The handle plates are fixed with Torx screws and can be taken off to clean the knife.

KOMMER BEAR CLAW

Russ Kommer designed the Bear Claw to be an extension of the hand. it is easy to grip, difficult to lose and very well suited for the bleak conditions in Alaska.

Initially, Kommer designed this knife as a lightweight self-defense weapon for women, but it seemed as if every parachutist, bush pilot and professional fisherman wanted one as well. His Custom Bear Claw, made of ATS 34 steel, was such a huge success that he could not keep up with demand. CRKT recognized its commercial possibility and decided to produce the knife. Thanks to its large finger hole, it is an exact extension of the hand, ideal for cutting lines, webbing or nets, especially in an emergency. The Bear Claw is made with three blade shapes: a razor-sharp, smooth cutting edge with a sharp point; an almost completely serrated edge with the special CRKT Triple Point serration; and a completely serrated edge with a blunt point. The last is well suited for emergency services that often need to

The remarkable Kommer Bear Claw

cut through something quickly without running the risk of punching a hole into it.

The blade runs through into the tang of the knife. It is made of 0.13 inch thick, hollow ground stainless AUS 6M steel. Ridges are at the top, under the finger hole and close to the point. The round shaped Zytel grip fills the palm of the hand properly. The total length of the knife is 5.63 inches. The length of the edge is 2 inches and it weighs 3.2 ounces. Its Zytel sheath has a Teflon-covered belt ring that can be attached to either side of the body.

LAKE

Ron Lake is a custom knife maker from Eugene, Oregon. A member of the American Knife Maker's Guild since 1971, Ron has won many prizes and

Lake Signature

Lightfoot M1

LIGHTFOOT

Greg Lightfoot, from Lloydminster in Alberta, is the chairman of the Canadian Knifemakers' Guild. In 1985, while he was still managing a gymnasium he bought a book about knives and a grinding machine and started making hunting knives. When he made a series, he toured the Western states on his Harley Davidson motorcycle and sold his knives along the way. He quickly fell for the charm of tactical folding knives, however. According to the knife magazine *Blade*, Lightfoot is one of the top ten tactical knife makers in the world.

LIGHTFOOT M1

The people at Columbia River Knife & Tool (CRKT) like to work with knife makers who are never satisfied – designers who always strive for perfection and try to make the next design better than the one before. But with the M1, Greg Lightfoot outperformed himself. The unique blade is taken from the Tanto shape and is specially hollow ground to form a slight arch and a curve that runs back into a drop point. Greg calls it the 'Millennium Tanto.' The false incision on the blade back makes the blade extra strong. The 0.13 inch thick stainless AUS 8 steel blade has a black titanium nitrate protective layer and a smooth or partially serrated edge. There are ridges on the back of the foot of the blade and fine teeth on the 'Mako Flipper.' Double-sided thumb studs and the flipper ensure quick opening and, when the blade is opened, also serve as the guard. The asymmetrically shaped handle has deep finger slots and Zytel handle plates. The knife has a heavy InterFrame casing with black 420J2 steel liners, one of which serves as the linerlock and also features the LAWKS security system. The M1 is held together with black stainless steel spacers and Torx screws. The blade turns on a Teflon layer. The unusually large 'paddle clip' carry clip is heavy for use on belts, straps or climbing gear and can be attached to the handle in four different ways. The M1 is a remarkable knife with an unusual shape; as Lightfoot says, "Grab it and it fits well." It is 7.5 inches long with a 3.12 inch long blade, a 4.37 inch long handle and weighs 5.7 ounces.

his knives are displayed in national and international magazines about knives, the outdoors and hunting. He is also the co-author of a book published in 1988 titled *How To Make Folding Knives*. He was inducted into the 'Cutlery Hall of Fame' in 1998 and labeled "The Father of the Modern Folding Knife" by sports reporter B.R. Hughes. Lake is a partner in Lake & Walker Bullfrog knives, which feature the patented LAWKS security system for folding knives. LAWKS stand for 'Lake And Walker Knife Safety.' A number of his knives are displayed in the Smithsonian Institute Museum, the National Metal Museum and the Randall Knife museum.

LAKE SIGNATURE

Ron Lake designed the Signature especially for CRKT. It is a folding knife with a linerlock, additionally secured with the patented LAWKS system. Instead of the well known thumb stud, this system is activated by pushing the carry clip down to lock the linerlock. To fold the knife back again, push the carry clip up so that the linerlock can be pushed back in. The open casing is made of anodized 6061 T6 aluminum. The bolt rod of the linerlock is made of 420J2 steel. The inlaid synthetic material plates are made of Zytel. The 0.12 inch blade, of stainless AUS 8 steel, ground to a classic clippoint, comes with a smooth or partially serrated edge. Large grooves are ground into the top of the blade for opening. The knife opens smoothly thanks to a Teflon layer hidden under the large blade pivot – a typical Lake feature, along with the leather fob at the shackle. The knife is 7.5 inches long, with a 4.25 inch handle and a 3.25 inch blade and weighs 3.8 ounces.

The Marzitelli Prowler folder

MARZITELLI

Peter Marzitelli, from Langley in British Columbia, has been making custom knives since 1982. He also draws, paints, sculpts and carves. When he found a book in the library about making knives, he wanted to try it himself. Known for his remarkable angular designs, he uses many types of blade steel and more than fifty types of handle material. More than seven hundred designs carry his name, ranging from Bowies to art knives. Although they look like works of art, their functionality as working tools matters most to Marzitelli.

MARZITELLI PROWLER

CRKT had to produce a special casing for this folding 7.6 inch long knife, their heaviest design until then. This 14.5 ounce working knife has a 3.25 inch long stainless AUS 6M steel blade 0.16 inches thick and 0.06 inch thick casing plates. Stainless 420J2 steel rods are in the casing of the linerlock system. This knife features the LAWKS security system as well. The casing is held together with four stainless steel spacers and Torx screws. The black Zytel handle plates have a deep checkered motif for a superior grip. The 4.37 inch handle is resistant to scratches, chemicals and acids and will stay good for life. The Marzitelli blade has a protruding thumb grid with transverse ridges against the grain and deep grooves on both sides of the back, so that it can be opened with the left or right hand. The blade comes with a smooth or partially serrated Triple Point edge and a Teflon layer to ensure smooth opening and closing. The detatchable stainless steel carry clip is covered with a gray Teflon protective layer.

Nealy Pesh-Kabz

NEALY PESH-KABZ

This folding knife by Bob Nealy is based on a Persian design from the fifteenth century. It has an open casing with stainless steel spacers, held together with Torx screws, and two stainless 420J2 steel inner plates, one of which serves as a linerlock, secured with the LAWKS system. The handle plates are of checkered Zytel. Both sides of the blade have thumb studs for left or right-handed opening and also serve as blade stops. The 'flipper' under the blade opens the knife quickly and serves as the guard along with a deep finger slot for the index finger. The special 0.12 inch thick blade point is made of stainless AUS 6M steel, ground to a particularly strong point for greater penetration ability – the knife was originally designed to penetrate chain mail – which says something about its construction. The knife turns on a Teflon layer. The 3.9 ounce, 7.4 inch long knife has a smooth or a partially serrated Triple Point edge on a 3.12 inch long blade and a 4.25 inch long handle with an extraordinary carry clip based on a rolling Eastern motif.

POLKOWSKI

Al Polkowski of Chester, New Jersey, known as the ultimate designer of knives for self-defense, makes custom knives alone or with Bob Kasper. His philosophy is simple: make and design knives with a carry system that are functional, of high quality and reasonably priced.

The Polkowski Kasper is for serious work

POLKOWSKI KASPER COMPANION

This is a rugged tactical knife, egual to the heaviest work. The Zytel sheath can be carried comfortably in different positions. The robust handle has a deep slot for the index finger that turns into a sort of guard in the blade. A widening on the back of the handle, just behind the little finger, ensures a stable grip. The injection molded handle plates are of polyoxymethylene acetal (POM) and fit well in the palm of the hand, thanks to a good roughened surface. This 6.5 ounce, 8.56 inch long integral knife is very strong, as it has a 3.56 inch long, 0.14 inch thick steel blade that extends to the end of the handle, with a smooth or partially serrated edge. The specially designed, 1.6 ounce, shock-proof Zytel sheath is resistant to scratches, chemicals, acids and extremely high or low temperatures.

RYAN

Steve Ryan from California and has been making knives since he was fourteen years old. He developed a wide range of tactical folding knives by hand in his workshop. He is inspired by Eastern martial arts, such as Go Gyo from Okinawa, and is studying the history of the knifemaking trade. His indi-

The Ryan Model Plan B looks like
a completely new weapon system

vidualistic designs are characterized by a muscular and broad shape and handles that have typically grooved handle plates.

RYAN MODEL SEVEN

Steve Ryan was inspired by the Philippine Barong for this model. The CKRT version is somewhat smaller and lighter than the original custom model. The deep slot for the index finger forms a type of guard and ensures a very powerful grip.

The Ryan Model Seven

The wide, long ground, 0.12 inch thick stainless AUS 6M steel blade has excellent cutting abilities. When grinding the blade, the thickness of the material was preserved as far as possible for extra strength.

The 3.5 inch long blade, which turns on a Teflon layer, comes with a smooth or partially serrated edge and thick ridges on the back to keep the thumb from slipping when applying a lot of pressure. The knife has a linerlock system made of stainless 420J2 steel, protected with the LAWKS system. The dark gray Zytel handle plates have a typical-Ryan skeleton shape, wide ridges to reduce weight and an extremely stable grip. This knife is also made with a blade with a black Teflon protective layer in the 'For those who serve' series. The 5.7 ounce knife is 8 inches long and has a 4.5 inch long handle.

RYAN PLAN B

Ryan's beautifully shaped compact knife, based on the larger Model Seven folding knife, is not the folding knife it seems at first glance, but a fixed integral knife. The 3-inch long, 0.14 inch thick stainless AUS 6M steel blade runs straight through to the back of the handle. It has a spear-point, is matte bead blasted and comes with a smooth or partially serrated edge, with a protective black Teflon layer in the tactical series. The Zytel skeleton shaped handle plates have zigzag black textured scales, curved slightly to ensure a firm grip. The Zytel sheath has a detachable belt clip that can be carried around the neck with a lanyard and several holes so that it can be attached anywhere. The sheath alone weighs only 0.9 ounces. The 6.75 inch long knife weighs 3.5 ounces.

Tighe Tac

The streamlined Wasp by Viele

show him how to do it. He learned through trial and error, which meant he was not influenced by the style of any trade master. He has been a member of the Knifemakers Guild and its German sister organization since 1976.

TIGHE

Brian Tighe, a jack-of-all-trades from Ridgeville, Ontario, is not only an instrument and matrix maker, but also a photographer, an industrial designer and he makes his own custom-designed knives.

TIGHE TAC

Tighe's graceful Tac knife is a traditional gentleman's folding knife. It comes in two sizes, both with smooth or partially serrated edges, and a special CRKT InterFrame casing with a 420J2 linerlock system. The bolster is made of matte bead blasted stainless steel with an arched back for a firm grip. The Zytel handle plates are attached with Torx screws. The stainless AUS 6M steel spearpoint blade with a false incision on the top opens on a Teflon layer. There is a unique right angled thumb slide for opening the knife and a Teflon covered stainless steel carry clip is on the right bolster plate into which the tie logo of Tighe is cut. This beautifully balanced folding knife can be carried in the pocket of formal pants or jeans. The larger knife is 7.4 inches long with a 4.13 inch long handle, a 0.12 inch thick and 3.25 inch long blade weighs 3.4 ounces. The smaller knife is 6.02 inches long, with a 3.38 inch long handle and a 0.10 inch thick, 2.63 inch long blade and weighs 2.0 ounces.

VIELE

Howard Viele makes beautiful and modern linerlock knives by hand at his workshop in Westwood, New Jersey. He became a knife maker in 1973 when he reached his third Dan – the 'Sandan' – in karate and became interested in the weapons of the East. He decided to make something in that line by himself, but nobody could

VIELE WASP

The Wasp knife is a production version of the custom knife made by Howard Viele. The 0.12 inch thick, 3.13 inch long blade is made of 0.12 inch thick stainless AUS 118 steel with a preferable hardness of 59-60 HRC. The casing is made of titanium, stock removed in CNC machines to make space for the stainless steel bolt rod and linerlock. The handle plates are of G10 in a specially designed laminated structure of blue and black fiberglass. Howard is known for his innovations, such as the axis screws, turned with layers, and the soft Kraton cap on the thumb stud on the left side of the blade. The detachable long carry clip with its gray Teflon coating and the blade have Viele's trademark three holes. The Wasp comes in two different sizes, with smooth or partially serrated edges. The larger Wasp has a 4.38 inch handle and weighs 3.4 ounces. The smaller knife is 6.9 inches long with a 4 inch handle and a 0.12 inch thick, 2.87 inches long blade and weighs 2.5 ounces.

WALKER

Michael Walker, from Taos, New Mexico is not only the designer of the BladeLOCK, but another twenty locking systems, including the LAWKS security system which he designed with Ron Lake for linerlock knives. His knives and other technical innovations have won more than twenty awards in the United States and beyond. His work of the past twenty years is clear proof of his mastership in the field of design, technical expertise and innovative

Walker BladeLOCK

Walker BladeLOCK 2

use of material. Articles about his knives are published in a great number of weapon and hunting magazines.

WALKER BLADELOCK

CRKT introduced Walker's BladeLOCK in 2001. He got the idea for this new locking system in the 1980's, but he could not find a manufacturer capable of making it. The machine work required was too complicated and the small tolerances could not be made for an acceptable price. But around 2000 CRKT invested in a machine park that could do such precision work. The result was a superior knife that won the "Knife of the Year" award at the 2001 Blade Show.

The BladeLOCK is an incredibly strong folding knife with a blade that is totally locked whether open or closed. Pressing the thumb stud locks the blade. To open it, the thumb stud has to be pushed again. The blade turns to the outside, and when it opens completely, a clear click locks it in place. To unlock the knife, press the thumb stud again, and the blade 'clicks' back and will not open accidentally in the pants' pocket.

The elegant knife has a beautiful handle and unique balance. The 0.14 inch thick, 3.44 inch long blade, of stainless AUS 6M steel with a typical matte blasted Walker clippoint, turns on special bronze layers and comes with a smooth or partially serrated edge. The handle casing is of bead blasted 420J2 steel. The 4.5 inch checkered Zytel handle is attached with Torx screws. The 4.6 ounce knife has a beautiful ergonomic design with a slot for the index finger and a serrated lifted base. The lid of the locking and the blade pivot is typical Walker style.

WALKER BLADELOCK 2

The 2001 BladeLOCK was a sensation, due to its beautifully elegant line and unique and innovative lock system. The BladeLOCK2 features the same system, combined with a 0.14 inch thick, 3-inch

long Walker drop point blade made of stainless AUS 6M steel with a smooth or partially serrated edge. Unlike the BladeLOCK, this knife's handle is rough at the bottom. It is 4 inches long and the entire knife weighs 3.8 ounces. This lightweight knife is small enough to carry in your pocket, yet strong enough for serious work.

DON COWLES CUSTOM KNIVES

The emblem of
Don Cowles

COWLES
www.cowlesknives.com

Don Cowles of Royal Oak, Michigan, made his first knife in 1963. He focuses mainly on long, thin, elegant alternatives to folding knives. He is a member of the Miniature Knifemakers' Society and the American Knife and Tool Institute. Don can make everything by hand and is against the use of gimmicks and novelties. He offers life long guarantees on his handmade knives.

PEARL

Cowles' Pearl knife is made of ATS-34 steel handle plates of mother-of-pearl attached with 14kt gold pins. The precious stone on the blade is a ruby. The bolster is made of stainless 416 steel and is inlaid with mother-of-pearl circles. The knife is 5.5 inches in total length. This photo was taken by Weyer International.

Cowles Pearl

**Pearl Gent-
Damascus knife**

the steel does not have time to separate. Later the powder is compressed in vacuum conditions under high temperature into homogeneous steel. This process is indicated as HIP (Hot Isostatically Pressed).

PEARL GENT

Mike Norris made the stainless Damasteel blade of this knife. The mother-of-pearl handle attached with 14kt gold pins has a so-called Crazy Lace pattern. Like the Pearl knife, this knife has a ruby in the blade. The bolster is made of stainless 416 steel. The total length is 5.5 inches. This knife was photographed by Hoffman.

SILVER BULLET

The Silver Bullet is a slim and elegant knife. The mother-of-pearl handle is fixed with silver pins. The bolster is made of stainless 416 steel and the total length of the knife is 7 inches. The blade with the set ruby is made of stainless CPM-S30V steel, which includes four percent vanadium and two percent molybdenum.

CPM stands for Crucible Particle Metallurgy, a patented process used to produce steels that can resist high speeds such as drilling or milling. The advantage of CPM steel is that the alloys segregate

The emblem of the Spanish firm Cudeman

CUDEMAN
www.cudemanamerica.com

The old Spanish knife company Cudeman is located in Albacere, in the district of Mancha, known for its excellent swords and knives. Cudeman's models consist of a wide assortment of hunting and sporting knives, traditional Spanish knives and a small series of luxury knives issued in limited editions. The blade of every Cudeman knife is cut from steel with a laser, polished by hand and hollow ground. Noble Spanish woods, such as olive, thuya, birch and walnut or other materials, such as moose and buffalo horn, are used for the handles. Cudeman steel is tempered in a special process to 68 HRC.

Silver Bullet knife by Cowles

non-uniformly. First, the manufacturers smelt the regular steel in large ovens, then they refine it by reducing the carbon quality by means of argon and oxygen, then they cast it in rods for further processing. During the casting process it slowly divides into the separate layered components forming a non-uniform microstructure.

The smelted steel is then sent through a small tube instead of being cast in a casting mold. This results in a number of small round drops, actually micro balls, cooling very quickly in a sort of powder. With direct cooling,

The Abanico Butterfly

The Abanico
Wood series

ANILLA-FOLDING KNIFE

The Anilla folding knife features a simple spring mechanism and a strong leaf spring that ensures the blade will stay firmly open or closed, but does not lock it in the way a back or top lock would. The blade is made of stainless 440 steel. The bolster is made of 304 steel. Cudeman uses buffalo horn, stag horn, olive or stamina wood for the handle.

BOLSILLO BACKLOCK

FOLDING KNIFE

The Bolsillo Backlock is a beautifully shaped, slim folding knife. The clippoint blade is made of stainless 440 steel with a backlock system. The bolster is made of matte 304 steel. The Bolsillo model is produced in three different dimensions: 5 inches long, with a 2.4 inch blade and 2,5 ounce weight; 7 inches long with a 3.2 inch blade and 4 ounces in weight;

ABANICO WOOD BUTTERFLY KNIFE

The Abanico Wood series has the same dimensions as the standard model described on page 101, but its weight ranges from 4.6 to 4.8 ounces. Cudeman uses stainless 420 steel for the blades. The bolster and pommel are of galvanized nickel or brass. The handles are made of olive or stamina wood: veneer plates of hard wood, impregnated with synthetic resin and pressed into a solid wooden block under high temperature. This is also known as diamond wood.

Anilla folder

and 7.87 inches long with a 3.5 inch blade and weight of 4.76 ounces. Cudeman uses olive wood, stamina wood and holly oak for the handles.

BOLSILLO TOPLOCK FOLDING KNIFE

The Bolsillo Toplock folding knife is shaped like the French Laguiole knives. Its toplock system is located just to the top of the blade pivot. The spring locking system grabs the opened blade with a coping in the back. To open it, the locking key has

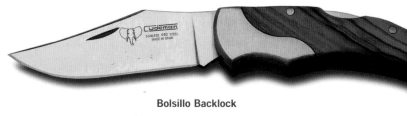

Bolsillo Backlock

The slim Bolsillo Toplock folding knife

to be tilted somewhat to unlock the blade. The Bolsillo is made in three different dimensions. The largest knife is 8.5 inches long. The blade is made of stainless 440 steel and is 3.93 inches long. It weighs 2.5 ounces. The medium knife is 7.7 inches in total length, has a blade that is 3.5 inches long and it weighs 2.1 ounces. The smallest knife is 7.3 inches long. Its blade is 3.15 inches long and the knife weighs only 1.76 ounces. The handle is made of bull horn, olive or pearl wood.

and weighs, depending on the handle material, between 6.0 to 7.0 ounces. Stag horn, stamina or thuya wood are used for the handle. The bolster is made of polished or matte nickel silver.

CAZA CLIPPOINT HUNTING KNIFE

The Caza Clippoint also has the same dimensions, but different handles. The total length of the hunting knife is 8.85 inches. The blade is made of stainless 440 steel and is 4.1 inches

The Bowie

BOWIE

The larger Cudeman Bowie knives are 15 inches long, weigh from 14.1 to 18.3 ounces and can truly be called large. The smaller Bowie, the top knife depicted, is 13.2 inches in total length and weighs 16.2 ounces. The blades and guards of these Bowies are made of stainless 440 steel. The blade of the larger knife is 9.8 inches long and the smaller knife has a 7.87 inch blade. The handle comes in stag horn, thuya or stamina wood.

long. The knife weighs between 6.2 to 6.9 ounces, depending on the handle material: stag horn, stamina or thuya wood.

CAZA SKINNER

The Caza Skinner hunting knife comes in two different sizes. The Skinner 142 is 7.7 inches in total length, has a blade that is 3.3 inches long and weighs between 6.9 to 7.2 ounces. Skinner 143 has the same length, but the blade is 3.5 inches long. The weight varies from 6 to 6.7 ounces. The blade

The Caza Droppoint hunting

CAZA DROPPOINT HUNTING KNIFE

The Caza Droppoint hunting knife series is in fact the same model as the Bowie, with a different handle. The knife is 8.7 inches in total length. The stainless 440 steel blade is 4.35 inches long

Caza Clippoint

is made of stainless 440 steel. The handle is made of stag horn, stamina, olive or thuya wood. The bottom two knives have handles made of stamina, combined with what Cudeman refers to as amourette wood that looks like snake wood.

The Caza Skinner

CAZA TOPLOCK FOLDING KNIFE

The Caza Toplock is a traditionally shaped folding knife. Its locking system consists of a top lock plate attached with a bolt rod, serviced by a backlock system – a unique feature in itself. This knife comes in two different lengths: 7.3 or 8.5 inches. The blade is made of 3.3 or 3.7 inch long stainless 440 steel and the weight varies between 3.35 to 4.6 ounces. The bolster is

Caza folder with a nickel steel bolster

made of highly polished or matte aluminum and there is a choice of cow horn, olive, stamina or pearl wood for the handle.

CAZA FOLDING KNIFE

The standard Caza folding knife has a clippoint blade made of stainless 440 steel. The bolster is made of A-304 steel. This knife is produced in lengths of 7.1 or 7.8 inches, with a 3.15 or 3.5 inch

blade, respectively. The weight varies from 4.1 to 4.9 ounces. Cudeman makes the handle from cow horn, olive or stamina wood.

CAZA LUXURY FOLDING KNIFE

The luxury Caza folding knife comes in three different dimensions. The smallest knife is 7.1 inches long with a blade length of 3.15 inches and it weighs 2.82 ounces. The medium sized knife is 7.7 inches long, with a 3.5 inch long blade and weighs 5.5 ounces. The largest model is 8.7 inches long with a 4.3 inch long blade and weighs 6.35 ounces. The blade of this knife is made of stainless 440

Caza Toplock folder

steel and the bolster and pommel are made of beautifully polished brass. Cudeman offers a choice of cow or imitation horn and stamina wood for the handle.

DAGAS HUNTING DAGGER

The Dagas hunting dagger is especially meant for hunting large game such as wild boar and mouflon. The largest is 16.9 inches in total length with an 11.8 inch long blade and weighs 15.2 ounces, the

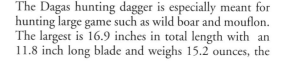

A luxury version of the Caza folder

medim knife is 14.6 inches long and the blade is 9.1 inches, the smallest weighs 12.7 ounces. The blade of this dagger, as well as the guard, is made of 440 steel. Cudeman use cow horn, olive, stamina or thuya wood for the handles.

The less luxurious version does not have a bolster, but the blade forms a guard. This model comes in two different dimensions. The smaller knife is 7.1 inches in

Dagas hunting dagger

total length with a blade length of 3.5 inches. The larger version is 8.5 inches long with a blade length of 4.1 inches. The knives weigh between 3.7 and 6.9 ounces, depending on the handle material and size. The handle is made of cow horn, stamina, olive or thuya wood or a combination of stamina and snake wood.

Desolladores 'Guthook'

DESOLLADORES GUTHOOK

The Desolladores Gut Hook is a typical gutting knife with characteristic cutting teeth on the blade, designed for skinning the hide of shot game. Rough work can be done with the wide and thick edge of the blade.
The total length of the knife is 7.1 inches and the length of the blade is 2.95 inches. Depending on the handle material, the knife weighs between 5.6 and 7.4 ounces. The handle is made of cow horn, stamina, olive or thuya wood or a combination of stamina and snake wood.

Desolladores hunting knives

DESOLLADORES HUNTING KNIFE

The blade of the Desolladores hunting knife runs partly from the bolster into the guard. The bolster is made of A-304 steel and the blade is of the usual stainless 440 steel. The knife is 8.5 inches long and the blade length is 3.93 inches. The knife weighs 7.4 or 7.8 ounces. The handle is made of stag horn, stamina or thuya wood.

LARGE DESOLLADORES HUNTING KNIFE

The Desolladores hunting knife series consists of one model with different handle types. The total length of the knife is 9.25 inches and the blade is

**Large Desolladores
hunting knife**

4.3 inches long. Either they are finished with beautiful brass bolsters or do not have bolsters at all. This reduces their weight to 9.2 ounces, instead of 10.9 ounces. The handle is made of stamina, olive or thuya wood. The blade is made of stainless 440 steel.

The Desolladores skinner

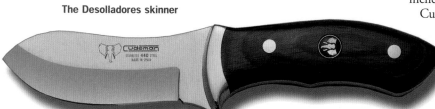

ESTILETES FOLDING KNIFE

Estiletes are typical subtle Spanish folding knives with spring pressure locking systems in five diffe-

MACHETAS COMBO

The Machetas is a combination set of hacking and skinning knives. The largest hacking knife is 10.4 inches in total length, has a blade length of 5.9 inches and it weighs 13.05 ounces. The small knife is 6.7 inches in total length, its blade length is 3.15 inches and it weighs 2.8 ounces. Cudeman uses olive or stamina wood for the handles. This combo set comes with a two-part sheath.

MONTERIA HUNTING DAGGER

This typical hunting dagger is for hunting wild boar and mouflon. The three larger daggers are 16.3 inches long with blades 11 inches long. The weight varies from 20.8 to 22.6 ounces. The smaller hunting dagger shown on the right is 15.6

Traditional Spanish Estiletes folder

rent dimensions. The smallest knife is 4.7 inches long with a blade length of 2.2 inches and only weighs 0.71 ounces. The next largest knife is 5.9 inches long, with a blade length of 2.75 inches and weighs 1.05 ounces. The third knife is 7.1 inches long with a blade of 3.3 inches and weighs 1.23 ounces. The next knife is 8.5 inches long, the blade is 3.9 inches long and it weighs 1.76 ounces. The largest knife is 9.6 inches in length with a blade length of 4.3 inches and it weighs 2.5 ounces. The blades are made of stainless 420 steel. The bolsters and pommels are made of brass. The handle is available in imitation buffalo horn or stamina.

inches in total length and has a blade 10.4 inches long. The handle is made of stamina or pearl wood and the bolster is made of A-304 steel or brass.

Machetas Combo

Montero hunting knife

The Montero series only comes in one size, but with different handle material and different

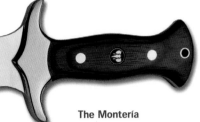

The Montería

color variations. The two top knives have bolsters made of brass. The guard is actually worked into the blade. The total length of the knife is 13.6

inches with an 8.3 inch long blade. The knife with its bolster weighs 16.6 ounces and 14.5 ounces without.

Abanico Butterfly knife

The Abanico Butterfly knife is a simple version of the luxurious Wood model described on page 96. The blade of the Abanico is made of stainless 420 steel.
The handle is made of a combination of a light metal alloy, Zamak, and shock resistant synthetic material. This Butterfly knife is produced in two different lengths. The Abanico 506 is 8.3 inches long in total, has a blade that is 3.3 inches long and weighs 4.6 ounces. The somewhat larger Abanico 505 is 8.7 inches long. The length of the blade is 4.1 inches and it weighs the same.

Montero hunting knives

D

DANILIN
www.rusartknife.urbannet.ru/gallery.html

Sergey Ivanovich Danilin with his master sign, top right, and below, the logo of the Russian Knifemakers' Guild

Sergey Ivanovich Danilin was born in 1959 in a small town in Russia, close to the city of Tula, south of Moscow. Trained as an engraver at the school for weapon technicians in Tula he graduated to the Central Design and Developing Commission for Sport and Hunting Weapons where he worked with the best engravers in the weapons factory. Gradually he got to work on expensive and exclusive weapons.

He taught himself to engrave freely without fixed patterns. Danilin especially likes hunting scenes of animals and birds. Depicted in their natural habitat, they seem more lively and fuller, yet the surface cuts are never deeper than 0.039 inches.

In 1989, he left the Commission to work for himself. His knives are original, functional, reliable, perfectly balanced, have comfortable grips and are made of the best materials . He prefers to work alone, from the initial idea, through the crafting, of the accompanying sheath. To this end, he taught himself to forge Damasteel as well as ordinary blade steel. His knives are on display at the Weapons Museum of the Kremlin. He has been a member of the Union of Russian Artists since 1998, a member of the association for weapons historians, and a member of the Russian Guild of Knifemakers since 1999. He received an award for cultural achievement in 2000. The knives shown here were photographed by Sergey Baranov and/or Valentin Overchenko.

POINTERS

Danilin made this beautiful hunting knife in 2003. The brilliant Damasteel blade was forged by Victor Soskov, a smith in Moscow from Russian steel types: VG(BI), U8A(Y8A) and 5JNM (5XHM). The guard/bolster attachment of the blade is engraved with gold inlays. The bolster is realistically engraved on both sides with the heads

The extraordinary Wild Boar hunting knife

of Pointer hunting dogs. The handle, with beautiful finger slots, was made of hard Wenge wood. The 9.72 inch long knife has a 4.88 inch long blade. Danilin spent four months working on this knife, currently in a private collection in Russia.

WILD BOAR

Almost the entire surface of this knife is engraved with animal figures. The top of the pommel is a vicious wild boar jumping from a golden bush. On the ebony handle is another wild boar surrounded by artfully crafted leaves. Plant

The Pointers knife by Sergey Danilin with an oversized engraving on both sides of the bolster

The Wild Cats knife by Danilov

DELL
www.dell-knives.de

Wolfgang Dell got involved in the art of making knives by pure chance when he gave himself a birthday present of a holiday to Alaska in 1992. He wanted to buy a good knife for this trip, preferably a Bowie. Unfortunately, he could not find anything suitable and decided to make one himself. Upon his

Left, the emblem of Wolfgang Dell with the weapon shield of the DMG (German Knifemakers' Guild) on the right

return, his friends in Schwäbisch Hall, Germany saw his new knife and soon he had to make six more of them. Gradually, demand increased and soon Dell was constantly making knives in his free time. The turning point came when he visited the knife show, Real German Products, in 1995. He was so impressed by the work of others that he wanted to give up knife making completely until he met Peter Herbst and Jockl Greiss who endorsed him as a member of the German Knifemakers' Guild in 1996. Wolfgang Dell is also a member of the Corporazio Italiana Coltellinai, the Italian Knifemakers' Guild, after being endorsed by Francesco Pacchi and Alfredo Botecchia. Since 2000 his work has been discovered by many knife collectors.

motifs twine around the ebony sheath. Its metal foot is beautifully engraved with the head of a phoenix on the left side and a sabre-toothed tiger on the right and inlaid with gold. The knife is 10.8 inches long with a 6.14 inch long Damasteel blade by Victor Sosov. The total height, including the sheath, is 11.7 inches. Sergey Danilin made this knife in 2002 and he is still in possession of it.

WILD CATS

Danilin made this beautiful hunting knife in 2001. He forged the Damasteel blade himself from Turkish Damascus. Flower motifs inlaid with gold adorn the blade. The engravings on the guard and the tiger standing alone are gilded. The handle and the sheath are made of walnut wood. The engravings on the guard were made by engraver E. Generalov from Tula. The knife is 10.7 inches long alone and 11.8 inches long with the sheath, and the blade is 5.7 inches long. Danilin used Russian steel types U12 ((У12)), ST30 (СТ30) and SHJ15 (ШХ15). This knife is currently in a private collection in Russia.

DAMASCUS HUNTER

The Dell Hunter is an integral hunting knife made of Damasteel. The beautifully shaped handle fits the line of the palm precisely. The inlaid pieces in the handle are made of mammoth ivory. The blade is 4 inches long and is made of special stainless Damasteel that had been folded one hundred times to produce the unique Damascus structure. The length of the knife is 9 inches.

The extraordinary integral Damascus hunting knife

DAMASCUS HUNTER II

This piece concerns two integral hunting knives, each made of a single piece of steel. The blade of the top knife is made of the beautiful contrast Damascus and is 4.3 inches long. Its total length is 8.5 inches and the knife weighs 4.2 ounces. The handle plates are made of dark patented mammoth ivory. The bottom knife is made of Elmax Superclean steel.

Integral Hunter by Dell

INTEGRAL HUNTER

Dell made this integral Hunter from one thick plate of Elmax Superclean steel. The blade runs out thin, but is still 0.178 inches thick at the back. The total length is 8.85 inches and the length of the blade is 4 inches. The inlaid pieces in the handle are polished mammoth ivory. The beautiful engravings are by Ralph Salzmann from Zella Mehlis.

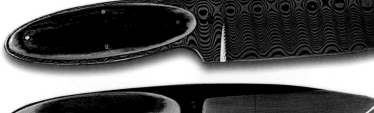

The lovely shaped integral hunting knives by Dell

MAMMOTH BOWIE

This large Bowie knife by Dell is made of stainless D-2-steel, tempered to 59 HRC by a freezing process. The total length is 13.0 inches and the massive blade is 9.6 inches long and 0.22 inches thick at the back. It is an integral knife, meaning that the blade, guard, and tang in the handle and the pommel are all made of one piece of steel. Dell chose a matte finish for the entire steel structure to ensure an even finish. The handle plates are made of mammoth ivory. This large knife weighs 21.2 ounces.

INTEGRAL DROPPOINT HUNTER

This Integral Hunter by Dell is made of one piece of thick steel from which the shape was ground, cut and drilled. The guard and pommel form a complete unit and were not attached to the blade later on. In order to reduce some weight in the tang, five big holes were drilled into the handle. The handle plates are made of Cocobolo wood and the blade from stainless Elmax Superclean steel. The total length of this integral knife is 8.9 inches and the blade is 4 inches long.

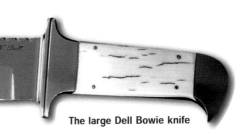

The large Dell Bowie knife

Integral Hunter with a droppoint blade

men had knives with long handles, while the women used short skinning knives, handed down from one generation to the next. The perfect shape of the handle and edge evolved through centuries of experience.

She returned to Moscow in 1976 where she worked at the Scientific Institute for Industrial Art. She devised an art form using fur and leather for settlements in Chukchi Peninsula and other northern areas. She received a diploma from the Exhibition of Achievements of National Economy for a piece of bone and leather, entitled The Day at the Pole at the Bering Straits.

Efimova is a member of the Russian Artists' Guild and of the Russian Knifemakers' Guild. Her knife called "Life is Short, Art is Eternal," is currently in the possession of the national Weapons Museum.

At the moment Efimova is working on a project entitled Jortie Borzois, named after the Borzoi hunting dogs, which she breeds and hunts with. The beauty of hunting along the endless plains gives her creative energy. The knives shown here were photographed by Sergey Baranov and/or Valentin Overchenko.

AN UNEXPECTED MEETING

This knife dates back to 1999. Elena Efimova designed it in cooperation with Damasteel smith Alexander Kurbatov, using a mixture of the Russian steel types U10(Y10), U12(Y12) and ST3(CT3). The handle is shaped like a walrus with a youngster on its back and the holder is a polar bear made of mammoth ivory and walrus tusk. The knife is 9.8 inches in total length and has a blade 4.7 inches long. As soon as the knife is pla-

EFIMOVA

www.rusartknife.urbannet.ru/gallery.html

Elena Efimova with her hunting dogs. On the right is her logo and below it is the logo of the Russian Knifemakers' Guild

Elena Ivanovna Efimova inherited her love of knives from her father, who loved hunting, owned brilliant hunting knives and always had a hunting dog or two around the house.

After graduating from the Abramtsevo Art and Industrial school in Basnetsov, Elena, went to the Uelei settlement on the Chukchi Peninsula, the most northern point in the Bering Straits. There she went on a traditional whale hunting expedition, witnessed hunts for walruses and sea lions, and hunted reindeer in the tundra on dog sleds. The Chukchis used special knives: the

An Unexpected Meeting in the real sense of the word

ced in its holder, a dramatic meeting between both animals takes place: the walrus comes dangerously close to the polar bear.

Efimova found the walrus tooth on a beach in the Bering Straits, close to a small town called Uelen in Chukotka. The mammoth ivory tusk comes from the steppes of Yakutia and was given to her by a friend. While she was living in Chukotka she saw polar

An Unexpected Meeting

The art knife 'Life for Life'

bears, reindeer and polar foxes almost every day. Whales, walruses and sea lions swam in the ocean and she often came eye to eye with these wild animals. Such a meeting brought this knife to life. It was displayed at the exhibition 'Blades of Russia' held by the Kremlin in 2000. She spent six months working on it. It is currently in a private collection.

LIFE FOR LIFE

Elena Efimova created this letter opener with Alexander Kurbatov who forged the Damasteel blade in 2003. It is 11.2 inches long, including the stand. The knife itself is 9 inches long. The 3.9 inch blade has a beautiful Damascus structure. The handle, shaped like a leopard, the stand and both of the antelopes are of mammoth ivory from the steppes of Yakutia and walrus tusks from Chukotka on the Bering Sea. Efimova was inspired by her passion for the quick Borzoi hunting dogs and the leopard, king of sprinters. She tried to depict the beauty of the extreme sprinter and the fight for existence on the sharpest point of the cut. This knife was made for an exhibition about Elena Efimova, held in April 2004 in the Kremlin in Moscow.

SNOW AMAZON

Efimova made the Snow Amazon in 1998 for an international jewelry exhibition: 'Jewelers and the Weapons Art in Russia on the Border of Two Centuries.' The Damasteel blade was forged by Valery Koptek and Valentin Timofeev. The arty chignon serves as a sheath for two daggers. The entire piece of art, with the penetrating daggers is 8.4 inches long. The chignon is 7.5 inches long. The hairpin daggers are 5.1 inches long, with 0.51 inch wide blades. The mammoth ivory comes from Yakutia. Valentin Timofeev gave Efimova that idea for this piece when he showed her a large cylinder of mammoth ivory, 5.9 inches in diameter. He wanted to make a chest from it, but Efimova wanted to make smaller hairpins so Timofeev designed the unique

The emblem of Eickhorn

twisting end of the hairpin daggers and the Snow Amazon dagger-hairpin came about. This knife is currently in a private Russian collection.

EICKHORN-SOLINGEN

www.eickhorn-solingen.com

Records show that the Eickhorn family has been involved in the knife making trade since 1356, when mention is made of a metal hardener called Eykorne. The name of Johan de Eycor-

The chignon with a hairpin dagger in mammoth ivory

PRT-I т/м PRT-V

PRT stands for Pocket Rescue Tool, or rather, a protection knife with the measurements and handiness of a pocketknife. All PRT's have a partially serrated cutting surface on the back of the handle, a safety belt cutter, an extra large thumb area and a handy carrying clip. The blade swings to the outside through spring pressure on a button on the handle, making this knife a virtual stiletto. All of the knives in this series are 8.1 inches long and weigh 4.9 ounces. The blade is made of stainless 440A steel and the handle is of anodized aluminum. The length of the blade is 3.3 inches and the steel is 0.118 inches thick. The PRT-I has a drop-point blade and a silver colored handle. The PRT-II knife has a wavy blade and a red handle. The PRT-III knife has a black Tanto blade. The PRT-IV knife has a separately finished blade and a black handle. The PRT-V has a clippoint blade and a black handle.

The PRT-I t/m PRT-V

The PRT-VI t/m PRT-X

The PRT-VI knife has the same clip blade, but it is completely black and has an inlaid piece of anti-slip rubber in the handle. The PRT-VII knife has the same handle as the VI and the blade is the same as the II. The PRT-VIII is the same as the VII, but it is completely black. The PRT-IX knife also has a handle with rubber inlays, but with a Tanto blade. The PRT-X is the same as IX, but it is completely black with a SmoothLock system.

RT-I

The RT-I as a Rescue Tool is a variation of the military LL80-snare knife that Eickhorn-Solingen sells in more than fifty countries around the world. The RT-I has a hooked blade, a glass-breaker and a partially serrated cutting edge. It is available in black, red and green. Its total length is 7.7 inches and the knife weighs 7 ounces. The blade is made of stainless 440A-steel and is 3.4 inches long. The handle is made of polyamide, reinforced with thirty percent fiberglass. The handle of the military version is green/black. A Cordura sheath, a punch/screwdriver in the handle and a strap come as standard accessories with this military knife, which is available with or without a partially serrated cutting surface.

The RT-I in black and red

RT-I GDF

The RT-I GDF of the Italian police

RT-I GDF stands for Rescue Tool I Guardia di Finanza, which means that it is the official knife of the Italian police force. This folding knife is 8.7 inches long when opened and weighs 7.7 ounces. The separate blade is made of 440A. The handle is made of polyamide, reinforced with thirty percent fiberglass. A hole punch, a cord, a link and a Cordura holder are all standard accessories.

RT-II AND RT-III

The RT-II and RT-III knives were developed in cooperation with professional law enforcement agencies, fire brigades and other rescue teams from Europe and the United States. This knife is equipped with a punch/screwdriver, a seat belt cutter, a (safe) glass cutter, a partially serrated blade and a glass-breaker. This knife is 10.7 inches long and weighs 11.3 ounces. The special 440A blade is exactly half the total length of the knife, at 5.3 inches. The handle is made of polyamide, reinforced with thirty percent fiberglass. The sheath is made of Cordura. An instruction video is available at the request of law enforcement agencies.

RT-IV

The RT-IV is equipped with a hooked blade, a screwdriver, strips on the handle that can be lifted, a partially serrated edge, a glass-breaker and a Cordura sheath. This black knife is 10.5 inches long and weighs 13.4 ounces. The specially shaped blade is made of stainless 440A steel and is 5.2 inches long. The handle is made of polyamide, reinforced with thirty percent fiberglass. The sheath is made of Cordura. The RT-IV-S is almost the same in every aspect as the standard RT-IV, except that it

RT-II

was developed for divers. This is why the handle has a sharp yellow color and comes with a special sheath that divers can attach to various parts of their bodies or breathing equipment.

SKIPPER

The Skipper folding knife is very striking, not least because of the fluorescent inlaid piece in the handle which makes it easy to find it in the dark. The handle is 4.56 inches long, the length of the blade is 3.15 inches and it weighs 6 ounces. The knife has two blades made of stainless 440A steel and a handle made from anodized aluminum. The Skipper has a partially serrated droppoint blade and a marlin spike. The knife has a linerlock system with liners that are 0.053 inches thick.

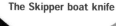

RT-IV

The Skipper boat knife

Slimcut

SLIMCUT

The Slimcut folding knife comes with a choice of eight different handles: silver colored anodized aluminum with Matrona inlays, gray anodized aluminum with carbon inlays, carbon fiberglass and Kydex in black, silver-gray, green, red or blue. This knife is 7.41 inches long when opened and weighs 3.15 ounces. The spearpoint blade is 3.03 inches long and about 0.098 inches thick. It is made of stainless 440A steel and has a separate, laser cut serrated edge for which no special sharpening tool is necessary.

STRYKER

The Stryker is a folding knife, available in two variations: with a black handle and inlaid bocote wood and with a silver colored handle, inlaid with G-10. The casing of the handle is made of aluminum. This knife is 7.93 inches long and

Stryker

weighs 4.9 ounces. The blade is made of 440A steel and has an adjusted droppoint shape. It is 3.17 inches long and 0.138 inches thick. The Stryker has a linerlock system.

THRUST

The Thrust folding knife is available in two handle colors: black and silver. Both of these are made of anodized aluminum. This knife is 7.4 inches long when opened and weighs 4.2 ounces. The spearpoint blade is made of stainless 440A-steel. It is 3.2 inches long and 0.138 inches thick, with a linerlock system.

WOLVERINE

The Wolverine is a robust fixed hunting and outdoor knife. Its design was based on the new knife used by the German infantry, the KM2000. This

The elegant Speedy

SPEEDY

The Speedy Automatic models are 'spring-loaded' stilettos with the patented SmoothLock system, which ensures that the blade can never jump open by itself. This knife is 7.63 inches long and weighs 4 ounces. The droppoint blade is made of 440A-steel. It is 3.22 inches long and 0.118 inches thick. This knife is available with or without a partially serrated cutting surface. The handle is made of anodized aluminum in silver or gray.

**The Thrust folder with
its striking spearpoint blade**

knife is 6.9 inches long and weighs 10.5 ounces. The Bowie clip blade, made of polished 440A-steel, is 5.04 inches long and 0.198 inches thick. The handle is made of polyamide, reinforced with thirty percent fiberglass. A glass-breaking point is at the end of the handle. A black, double-stitched sheath goes with the Wolverine.

of one strip of metal. All of the excess material around the blade and the handle plates is ground away and stock is removed.

Wolverine

ELSEN

vdelsen1@zonnet.nl

Gert van den Elsen from the Netherlands started his career as an independent knife smith in Tilburg in 1978. He made knives from his own designs, as well as custom knives for his clients. His knives are mostly sold at European knife fairs and are known among

Lately, Van den Elsen has been focusing more on forging his own steel for the blades. All of his knives are made by hand and are delivered with handmade leather pouches or in elegant wooden chests. Crucial to him is the use of the best materials, coupled with an uncompromising attitude to the trade. Van den Elsen gives life-long guarantees with his knives.

DRIVA HUNTER

The Driva Hunter hunting knife has a beautifully shaped blade, made of so-called raindrop Damascus, forged with a combination of ATS-34 steel and Sandvik 12C27 steel. The guard is made of stainless Damasteel. The handle has a short ring made of buffalo horn and a large piece of Indian Sambar stag horn. The knife is 8.45 inches in total length, has a blade 3.75 inches long and a handle 4.7 inches long. A nice leather sheath comes with it.

FINE HANDMADE KNIVES

The emblem of Gert van den Elsen

collectors from Belgium, Canada, Germany, England, France, Italy, Norway, Saudi Arabia, the United States, South Africa, Sweden and Switzerland, and in his own country.

Van den Elsen makes pocketknives with linerlocks, as well as hunting, outdoor, combat and tactical knives.

NUECES BOWIE

The Nueces Bowie has a typical heavy and large Bowie blade, made of stainless ATS-34 steel. The guard and pommel are made of hand ground stainless steel. The handle is made of Indian Sambar stag horn. The total length of this knife

The Driva Hunter with a blade made from raindrop Damascus

He also makes Katanas, Tantos and historical knives such as daggers, Bowies and fantasy knives. He uses ATS-34, D2 and powder steel such as CPM 420V and Böhler K190. The important parts of his knives are made of stainless and carbon Damasteel. Most of his models are made by the stock removal method. This means that an integral knife is made, including the guard and pommel,

Nueces Bowie

FULCRUM II D

The Fulcrum II D folder

The Fulcrum II D is a folding knife with a backlock system. This is a multi-purpose knife and can therefore be used by private individuals, as well as by tactical police and military forces. The Fulcrum II D has a Tanto shaped blade with a smooth edge. The total length of the knife is 8.7 inches and it weighs 7.1 ounces. The clippoint blade is made of stainless cobalt steel N690 and is 3.7 inches long and 0.23 inches thick. The handle is made of anodized black Anticorodal, a type of aluminum alloy that is particularly resistant to corrosion. The extreme point of the handle can be used as a glassbreaker or as a stabbing weapon in close combat. The knife has a matte black Testudo coating against damage, oxidation and light reflection.

Fulcrum II T with a serrated edge

FULCRUM II T

The Fulcrum II T folding knife is similar to the Fulcrum II D. The difference between these two knives is the T version's partially serrated edge.

This knife is 8.7 inches in total length when opened and weighs 7.1 ounces. The clippoint blade is made of stainless cobalt steel N690 and is 3.7 inches long and 0.23 inches thick. The other features are identical to the Fulcrum II D.

In 2004, Extrema Ratio introduced a special version, the Fulcrum II T G.I.S., commissioned by the Special Invention Group of the Italian carabinieri, a type of anti-terror unit.

Fulcrum II T G.I.S.

MPC

The abbreviation MPC stands for Multi Purpose Coltello. This multi-purpose folding knife with a backlock system is 10.2 inches long when opened and weighs 8.6 ounces. The long clip blade is 4.5 inches long and 0.23 inches thick. It is made of stainless cobalt steel N690 and the handle is made of black anodized Anticorodal, an aluminum that is resistant to corrosion. The entire knife has a Testudo coating to protect it against minor damage and oxidation and to keep it from reflecting light.

The MPC knife

NEMESIS

The Nemesis is a multi-purpose folding knife with a backlock system. This heavy knife is 10.2 inches long and weighs 7.9 ounces.

Nemesis by Extrema Ratio

The handle is made of Anticorodal and the blade of stainless cobalt steel N690. The drop-point blade is 4.5 inches long and 0.23 inches thick. The Nemesis has a Testudo coating against scratches, oxidation and light reflection. This large folding knife is used by many different law enforcement agencies.

Shrapnel

SHRAPNEL

The Shrapnel is a multi purpose knife. It is 8.3 inches long and weighs 7.1 inches. The droppoint blade is made of stainless cobalt N690 steel and the

handle is made of Forprene synthetic material. The blade is 4.3 inches long and 0.25 inches thick. This knife is available with two different protective layers: a black Testudo or a camouflage coating. The sheath is the same as the Fulcrum Compact and can be carried horizontally on the lower back or vertically on the hip.

T.F. RESCUE

The T.F. Rescue is a survival tool, especially designed for parachutists, pilots, vehicle occupants, anti-terror units and mountain troops of the Italian military. The length of the knife is 7.5 inches and it weighs 7.8 ounces. It consists of a central hand grip made of Anticorodal aluminum, to which two blades of stainless cobalt N690 steel, are attached. The first knife, shaped like a beak, opens at an angle of 55 degrees, where an additional cutting edge appears. These cutting edges form a V-shape. A thumb stud on the handle opens the blades. The purpose of the blunt-ended side of the blade is to select and cut cables, ropes and straps. The large second blade is less specialized, making this part of the knife a standard folding knife. This blade has a partially serrated edge and can be opened with one

T.F. Rescue

hand. A steel point on the same side of the handle serves as a glass breaker. A nylon sheath comes with the T.F. Rescue knife.

T.F.S. PILOT

The T.F.S. Pilot is a survival tool as well. It was especially designed for aircraft and helicopter pilots. Its total length is 7.5 inches and the knife weighs 8.5 ounces. The central handle is made of

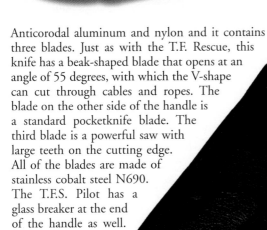

The T.F.S.
Pilot survival knife

Anticorodal aluminum and nylon and it contains three blades. Just as with the T.F. Rescue, this knife has a beak-shaped blade that opens at an angle of 55 degrees, with which the V-shape can cut through cables and ropes. The blade on the other side of the handle is a standard pocketknife blade. The third blade is a powerful saw with large teeth on the cutting edge. All of the blades are made of stainless cobalt steel N690. The T.F.S. Pilot has a glass breaker at the end of the handle as well. This knife has a dark finish.

T.F.V. D.L.

Extrema Ratio designed this emergency knife for paratroopers and loadmasters. Its total length is 7.5 inches and the knife weighs 10.2 ounces. It consists of a central hand grip made of titanium to which two blades made of stainless cobalt steel N690 are attached. The first blade, just like the previous two, is a V-shaped survival tool used for cutting through cables, ropes and straps. The second blade is less specialized and makes for a standard folding knife. This part of the tool can also be opened with one hand. A glass breaking point is located on the side of the handle. An ABS and a Cordura sheath come with the knife.

The T.F.V. D.L.
survival tool

F

FÄLLKNIVEN
www.Fällkniven.com

The emblem of the Swedish company Fällkniven

Fällkniven is a typical family company, run by father, mother and son. The knife factory was established in 1984 in Boden, in the north-east of Sweden on the Gulf of Bothnia. Initially Fällkniven specialized in military knives. But in 1987 they also started producing hunting and survival knives. It took ten years of testing to develop the A1 and F1 knives, as the sub polar climate asks a lot of military tools. These knives satisfy international military quality requirements and have been used by the Swedish Air Force since 1995. Model A1 has a tang that runs straight through to the back of the handle. This makes it ideal to hack and tap with, without causing damage to the handle. The black versions of the F1 and S1 have been approved for use by American Military aircraft crews since November 2000. The knives are tested by the company and by the technical University of Lulea, where special attention is paid to the breaking point, which makes Fällkniven knives

dependable even in the most extreme situations. All Fällkniven knives are made with cores of special stainless VG10 steel. The outer layer consists of stainless 420J2 steel, which is particularly hard and keeps the edge razor sharp for a much longer period. The company uses Damasteel, made of VG10-steel, combined with Cowry-X-powder steel. Each knife comes with its own sheath, available in leather or Kydex.

Fällkniven also sells knives without handles. The client can provide the handle him/herself, or order one from Fällkniven. This way the knife can be made to order. This company also offers a unique service: each Fällkniven knife can be sent back to the company for resharpening.

A1

The A1 survival knife is a favorite with soldiers and civilians who need a reliable companion on their belt during a week in the woods. Despite its size, the A1 has a wide variety of uses and good balance. The blade is 0.24 inches thick and is made of VG10 laminated steel, which makes it particularly strong. As this knife has a long curved blade it is excellent for cutting wood. The black A1 has layer of Cera-

Integral knives half produced for clients to finish themselves

The Fällkniven A1 survival knife

after extensive testing in the summer heat, as well as in the icy polar nights, it became part of the survival kit of the Swedish Air Force. The F1 hunter is 8.3 inches long with a blade length of 3.8 inches and it weighs 5.3 ounces. Both the standard and Teflon versions come with a handle made of a new type of synthetic material called Thermorun. This knife is available with a Kydex or leather sheath.

coat 8H that protects it against rust and reflection. The length of the A1 integral knife is 11 inches, with a 6.3 inch blade. The 4.7 inch long handle is made of Kraton. The knife weighs 12 ounces and is delivered with a Kydex or leather sheath.

A2

This large A2 expedition knife was designed for extreme circumstances. It is equally at home in Antarctica and in the Brazilian jungle. It is a very strong knife that can be used in just about every conceivable situation. The

The large A2-expedition knife

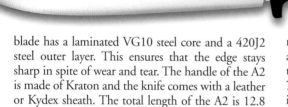

blade has a laminated VG10 steel core and a 420J2 steel outer layer. This ensures that the edge stays sharp in spite of wear and tear. The handle of the A2 is made of Kraton and the knife comes with a leather or Kydex sheath. The total length of the A2 is 12.8 inches and the blade is 8 inches long. The knife weighs 13 ounces.

F1 HUNTER

The Fällkniven F1 Hunter is actually a small series in itself. It is an integral knife with the blade and the core of the handle made of one piece of stainless VG-10 laminated steel. The F1 Hunter was the first model produced by Fällkniven in 1984 and,

FG1 (MILITARY)

The Fällkniven G1 dagger

This dagger is called G1 and was developed for special units of the Swedish military. It is a short weapon that can easily be carried without getting noticed. It is made of VG10 laminated steel. The blade has a black layer of Ceracoat 8H, to protect it from rust and light reflection.

The symmetrical handle with the cast guard is made of Thermorun. The G1 comes with a Kydex sheath that can be carried in many different ways: around the neck or horizontally on a cross belt. The dagger is 7.5 inches in total length. The length of the blade is 3.5 inches and it weighs 3.53 ounces.

**The Fällkniven F1 Hunter
in various versions**

H1

The H1 hunting knife is based on a traditional Scandinavian knife. The long curved line of the cut with the wide ground point was speci-

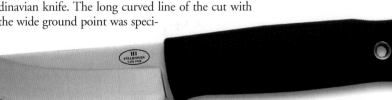

The H1-hunting knife

ally designed for large game hunters. This knife is made of strong, stainless VG10 laminated steel. The blade is 0.20 inches thick. The handle is made of Kraton and provides a stable and comfortable grip for its size. When using the knife, one has to be careful, as there is no guard. This knife comes with a leather or Kydex sheath. The total length of the H1 is 8.3 inches, the blade is 4 inches in length and it weighs 6.3 ounces.

The large MC1 (Mine Clearance) knife by Fällkniven

MC1

The large MC1 knife was designed on the request of several NATO countries. Since the spring of 2002, it has been used at many clearing operations. The blade undergoes a unique method of grinding. A long strip of VG10 steel 0.24 inches thick is ground on a belt grinder with an extra large diameter. The resulting hollow grind is then finished by hand and ground to a ball-round edge. The result is a razor sharp and very robust cut. The handle is made of Kraton that is resistant to solvents, oil and acids. The tang runs through to the outside of the handle and is visible as a pommel at the end of the handle. The MC1 knife is 14.3 inches long with a blade length of 9.5 inches and weighs 12.7 ounces without the Kydex sheath.

Northern Light (NL)

The Northern Light series have a traditional shape, right down to the handle with its polished leather rings. Less traditional is the VG10 laminated steel tempered to 59 HRC that Fällkniven uses. The guard is made of stainless 420J2 steel and the pommel is aluminum. The smallest knife is the Frey, named after the Norse god of peace, fertility and prosperity. Frey was also the king of Trolls and Elves that played an important role in Scandinavian farmers' superstitions. The Frey knife is 9.6 inches long with a blade length of 5.1 inches and it weighs 6.7 ounces. The somewhat larger knife is the Njord, named after the god of fertility, the head of the Vanir Clan, the protector of the sailors and fishermen and the ruler of the coast and its waters. The Njord is a beautifully balanced knife that is particularly strong because of its VG10 laminated steel. The Njord's total length is 10.5 inches, the blade is 6 inches long and the knife weighs 10 ounces. A larger knife is the Odin, named after the one-eyed Wodan, the highest god according in the Norse pantheon. Wodan was the father of all the other gods and humans. He rode on his eight-legged horse Sleipner and was followed by his two servants, Hugin and Munin. He was the undisputed leader of Valhalla. The Odin is a powerful and multi-functional knife, with a wide blade that is excellent for hacking. Its total length is 12.7 inches, with a blade that is 7.8 inches long and it weighs 13.4 ounces. The largest knife is the Thor,

The Fällkniven Northern Light series

named after the thunder god. Its massive blade gives the clear impression that it is meant for specialists.

The special Northern Light Idun version

This tool is meant for the hardest possible work. The total length of the Thor is 15.2 inches, the blade is 10 inches long and it weighs 18.3 ounces.

NORTHERN LIGHT IDUN (NL)

The Idun knife has a different shape compared to the Northern Light series. This knife was named after the Norse goddess of fertility and love, who was also responsible for protecting the apples of eternal youth. The Idun knife is made with Cowry X Damascus laminated steel, consisting of 120 layered Damasteel plates, forged on either side of a core of special powder steel with a hardness of 64 HRC. This steel is not only particularly hard, but also very strong and tough. The pommel and guard are made of nickel silver. This knife is made in a limited edition. The

The Fällkniven Model P folder

Damasteel Idun is 8.5 inches long, with a 4 inch blade and a weight of 6.3 ounces. It comes with a brown leather sheath. A somewhat simpler version is the standard Idun, made of VG10 laminated steel. The guard is made of stainless 420J2 steel and the pommel of aluminum. It has the same measurements and weight as the Damasteel knife.

P FOLDER

Model P was the first folding knife that Fällkniven ever made. It has a simple and classic design and is

suitable for both hunters and fishermen thanks to its dimensions. The P is simple to clean, as the casing is open on the top. The blade can easily be opened and closed with one hand because of the thumb stud. When fully opened, the knife is locked in place with a linerlock. The droppoint blade is made of VG10 steel. The casing itself is made of stainless 420J2 steel and is inlaid with black Micarta. The Model P knife is 7.2 inches in total length, with a 4.2 inch long handle and a 3.3 inch blade. The knife weighs 2.82 ounces.

S1 FORESTER

The Fällkniven S1 Forester is the best choice for pathfinders and mountain hikers who want a high-quality lightweight knife. It is also particularly well

The S1 Forester knife

suited to hunting and fishing. With the excellent tang that serves as the pommel, pike can easily be killed and the razor-sharp blade makes short work of the thickest moose hide. The VG10 steel is 0.20 inches thick and specially tempered for hard work. The standard knife has a matte blade and the black version has a protective layer of Ceracoat 8H. The total length of the S1 is 9.7 inches, with a blade that is 5.1 inches long and a weight of 6.7 ounces.

U2 FOLDER

The U2 was the first folding knife with a blade made of Super Gold Powder Steel or SGPS. Powder steel is of particularly high quality, but it is very expensive and hard to work with. It requires ultramodern tools and the hand of a very experienced knife maker. Its advantage is in the durability of the edge, which cannot be equaled by any other steel ava-

The U2 folder

The Fällkniven WM1 Hunters

patterns of the forged mosaic Damascus are Antonio Fogarizzu's trade marks. By applying various chemicals to the steel, he achieves a unique blue-white color. Fogarizzu learned this technique while visiting American knife maker Steve Schwarzer from California.

HOT BLUE NO. 003
HUNTING KNIFE

This beautiful fixed knife has a Scandinavian blade made of hot blue mosaic Damascus as are the guard and pommel. Fogarizzu used a piece of walrus ivory for the handle. The total length of the knife is 8.7 inches. The

ilable to us today. The U2's slim handle, made of Zytel, reduces the weight so that it can easily and comfortably be carried as a pocketknife. The traditional backlock system prevents unpleasant surprises and it always works. The total length of the U2 is 6 inches, the blade is 2.5 inches long and the knife weighs only 1.5 ounces.

The Hot Blue-hunting knife No. 003

WM 1

The Fällkniven WM1 hunting knife may be small in size, but it is very handy. The total length is 6.9 inches. The blade is made of VG10 steel, 0.12 inches thick and 2.8 inches long. The handle is made of Thermorun and is 4.1 inches long. This knife comes with a special Kydex sheath that can be carried in many different ways. The WM1 is very popular among mountaineers, canoeists, mountain bikers and hikers. It is also one of the few knives that were especially developed to fit in the smaller hands of women.

blade has a remarkable long and deeply ground false incision.

HOT BLUE NO. 006

This beautiful folding knife has a backlock system and it is a part of the hot blue series. The smith work on the Damasteel of the blade and the bolster is remarkable. The handle is made of first class mot-

Extraordinary inlay work in Fogarizzu knives

FOGARIZZU
a.fogarizzu@tiscali.it

Fogarizzu knives come from Sardinia, Italy. Antonio Fogarizzu's entire family works with metal. It was Fogarizzu's father Salvatore who taught him the trade of making knives. Fogarizzu has been working for himself since 1997 and concentrates on innovative designs and unusual materials. The unique and remarkable

her-of-pearl and the screws are made of 18kt gold. The total length of the knife is 7.1 inches.

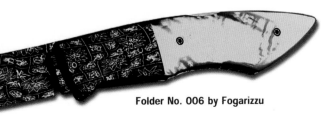

Folder No. 006 by Fogarizzu

HOT BLUE NO. 010

This folding knife is made of a different material. The 3.1 inch long spearpoint blade is made of stainless RWL-34 steel. The bolsters are made of hot

Folder No. 010

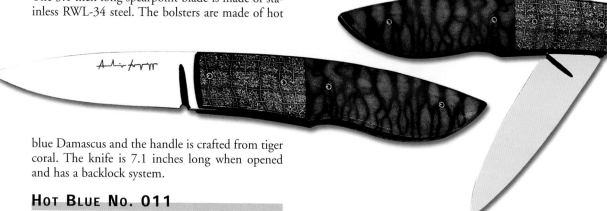

blue Damascus and the handle is crafted from tiger coral. The knife is 7.1 inches long when opened and has a backlock system.

HOT BLUE NO. 011

This folding knife has a blade and bolster made of hot blue mosaic Damascus. The handle is made of mammoth ivory colored by floor acids. The Allen screws are made of 18kt gold. The total length of the knife, which has a backlock system, is 7.1 inches.

PATTADA NO. 015

These knives were named after the Pattada region in Sardinia, where Antonio Fogarizzu comes from. The 14.7 inch spearpointblade of the Pattada is also made of the beautiful hot blue mosaic Damasteel. The bolsters and rivets are made of silver. Fogarizzu used mouflon horn as handle material.

Hot Blue No. 011

MOSAIC 2

This folding knife is also made of mosaic Damascus with a special oval pattern worked into the Damasteel. The blade and handle are made of

Pattada No. 015 knife

Damascus, which makes this a completely unique knife. The knife is 7.1 inches long and has a backlock system. The inner casing is made of titanium.

Extraordinary Folder No. 023

WALRUS DAGGER

This dagger is 9.4 inches in total length. The blade is made of stainless RWL-34 steel and the bolsters and pommels are made of mosaic Damascus. The handle is made of walrus ivory.

Walrus dagger No. 018

FOX

www.foxcutlery.com

FOX KNIVES®
MANIAGO   MADE IN ITALY

The emblem of the Italian knife factory Fox

Coltellerie Fox was established in the Italian Maniago in the foothills of the Carnian Alps, close to the Austrian border in 1977. Fox is run by the Oreste family and makes a wide assortment of military and survival knives, hunting knives, folding knives and miniature knives. Fox has always had its own way of putting their knives together and over the last few years has made a number of innovative knives in its line. Fox uses stainless 440 C steel, tempered to 57-59 HRC, for most of their knives. Stainless 430 steel and brass is used for bolsters and guards. Fox is also a supplier for different producers and makes Browning knives, among others.

FOLDER 472/473/474 SERIES

This new Folder series consist of several models. The blades of two of these knives are covered with Teflon protective layers. The third knife has a bead blasted blade. The handle is made of anodized 6061-T6 aluminum in black, dark gray or camouflage colors with inlaid pieces of G-10 synthetic material. Both 473 OL models have inlaid pieces of olive wood and are 8.6 inches long. The blade is made of stainless 440C steel and is 3.7 inches long, the handle is 4.9 inches long and the knife weighs 3.2 ounces. At the back of the handle a part of the inner casing protrudes from the contour of the handle plates. This makes the knife seem like it has a backlock system. In fact, it has a linerlock system.

FOLDER 475/476/477 SERIES

This is the second series made in 2004/2005. The knives have Tanto blades with the characteristic contour at the top of the blade. This provides

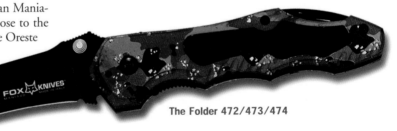

The Folder 472/473/474

good support for the index or other fingers when extra pressure is applied to the cutting surface. The blade is made of stainless 440C steel tempered to 57-59 HRC. The handle is 3.5 inches long and is bead blasted or covered with a black Teflon protective layer. The total length of this folding knife is 8.8 inches and the handle is 4.3 inches long. The handle is made of anodized 6061-T6 aluminum in black, dark gray or camouflage colors. The knife weighs 3.5 ounces. Inlaid pieces of G-10 synthetic material or olive wood adorn

The Folder 475/476/477
with Tanto blade

Folder from the 481/482/483 series with spearpoint blade

the handle. What looks like a bolt rod for the backlock system protruding from the back of its handle is a really a sort of shackle, as the knife really has a linerlock system.

481/482/483 SERIES

The folding knife in the 481/482/483 series is very nicely shaped, thanks to of the spearpoint blade. A few slots have been cut into the blade with a laser on the top of the blade, in front of the thumb stud. The blade has a protective layer of Teflon in black, dark gray and even in camouflage print. The blade of the upper knife is bead blasted. The total length of this knife is 8.0 inches and the blade is 3.3 inches long. This folding knife is 4.7 inches long and it weighs 3.2 ounces. The handle is made of anodized 6061-T6 aluminum with inlaid plates of G-10 synthetic material or Cocobolo

Folder from the Fox 487/488 series

wood. The steel inner casing protrudes through an angular shackle at the back. The knife has a linerlock system.

FOLDER 487/488 SERIES

The knives from the Fox 487/488 series are actually very graceful and look like pocketknives or gentleman's knives. This hand knife has a linerlock system. The handle is especially gracefully shaped with a partly visible aluminum handle that flows around the large handle plates depicted at the top and lower down. These inlaid plates are made of G-10 synthetic material, but have a metallic sheen. The other handle plates are made of olive burl, Cocobolo wood and thuya burl. This beautifully shaped blade is hollow ground and forms an

arch. The total length of the knife is 6.6 inches and the blade is 2.7 inches long. The handle is 3.9 inches long and the knife weighs 3 or 3.1 ounces.

FOLDER 489 SERIES

This series is a variation of the 487/488 series. The knife has a casing made of anodized 6061-T6 aluminum as well, but the protective layer is done in dark red, orange, blue or black. The inlaid plates are dark gray and made of G-10 synthetic material. The spearpoint blade has a Teflon layer or is bead blasted. It has a false incision and the point looks like a dag-

The Fox 489

ger. The thumb stud on the blade is the same color as the casing, with the exception that the silver stud on the black knife. The knife has a linerlock system. The total length of the 489 is 7.6 inches and the blade is 3.3 inches long. This handle is 4.3 inches long and weighs 3 ounces.

FOLDER HAWK 478/479/480 SERIES

The name of this knife is guite apt, as it is roughly the same shape as the head of a bird of prey or its claw. This knife was a prototype in 2004 and was on display at the IWA in Nuremberg. The knife has a 6061-T6 aluminum casing in black, dark gray or in camouflage print, a large ring at the back of the handle and ergonomic finger slots. The Hawk has a linerlock system. At the back of the blade is a

Hawk

unique tuft-like protrusion with ridges cut into it to provide a stable grip and to help open the blade quickly. The curved blade is 3.1 inches long and the handle is 4.7 inches in length, excluding the large ring.

colors. The second knife from the top has a bead blasted blade. The total length of the Invader is 8.8 inches and the blade is 3.5 inches long. This handle is 4.3 inches long and it weighs 3.5 ounces. The Invader has a linerlock system.

FOLDER 487/488 WALLIGATOR SERIES

The name Walligator sounds like an alligator and this is also what the blade looks like. The oval shaped thumbhole even looks like the eye of the reptile. The Walligator's casing is made of anodized 6061-T6-aluminum and the handle plates from Micarta or

Fox Hunter

FOLDER HUNTER 431/432-SERIES

The Fox Hunter series has a casing made of anodized 6061-T6 aluminum in black or dark gray and handle plates made of stag horn, laminated wood, thuya burl wood or black G-10 synthetic material. The blade is in the well-known skinner shape and has a noticeable notch at the back. The handle is ergonomically shaped and

The Invader

G-10 synthetic material in red, black, blue and the swirling colors depicted. The knife has a blade length of 3.3 inches, a handle of 4.5 inches and is 8.8 inches long. The knife has a linerlock and weighs 3.5 ounces.

Walligator

begs to be picked up, as it is clear that it will lie well in the hand. The handle is 4.9 inches long, the blade is 3.7 inches long and the entire knife is 8.6 inches long. The knife without its handle material weighs 3.1 to 4.4 ounces. The Hunter has a linerlock system.

LEATHER HUNTER-SERIES

The knives from this series are more traditionally shaped than the previous ones. The Leather Hunters have droppoints, gut

FOLDER INVADER SERIES

The Fox Invader has a typical hollow shaped edge, and the blade literally clings to the material it is cutting. The casing of the knife is made of anodized 6061-T6 aluminum and protrudes at the back to form a shackle. The handle comes in different colors and has inlaid plates of G-10 synthetic material or thuya burl wood. The blade has a Teflon protective layer in black or camouflage

The Leather Hunter series by Fox

Military 1668/1669/1670

hooks or skinner blades and are made in different sizes. The blades come in lengths of 3.5, 4.3 and 4.9 inches. The handles are 3.5 or 4.3 inches long. The total knife-lengths are 7.1, 8.7 or 9.4 inches and they weigh between 3.5 and 5.1 ounces. The blade of the hunting knife is made of stainless 420C steel, tempered to 54-56 HRC. The handle is made of impregnated leather rings between the steel guard and pommel. Fox had made these knives before, but on the 2004 model, they added a deep finger slot to the handle.

MILITARY 1668/1669/1670 SERIES

The Military knife from the 1668/1669/1670 series is a beautiful integral knife with an extraordinary blade. The blade and handle are made of one piece of stainless 440C

The special Kydex sheath for the Fox military knives

steel. Three long slots are milled like cooling plates of the ventilating edge of a revolver. A cord can be attached to two slots are at the back of the pommel. The total length of the knife is 10.1 inches and the blade is 5.1 inches long. This handle is 12.7 cm long and the knife weighs 13.7 ounces. The handle plates are made of G-10 synthetic material inlaid with soft rubber pieces. The knife does not have a loose guard, but two deep finger slots are cut into the handle and blade. The blade has a Teflon protective layer in black or camouflage colors.

MILITARY 1671/1672/1673 SERIES

The Military 1671/1672/1673

This military knife looks like the previous model, but has a Tanto blade and no 'cool slots' in it. Other than that, they look alike. The total length is 10.0 inches, the blade and the handle are 5 inches long. This knife comes with a so-called tactical sheath made of thermoplastic Kydex with a carry cord. This type of sheath is suitable for all military knives from Fox.

T-1-SERIES

The T-1 linerlock folding knife is a new Fox model for 2004/2005. The knife has a well-known 6061-T6 aluminum casing in different colors and inlaid plates of laminated or thuya burl wood. The blade of the top knife has a protective layer of black Teflon and the lower knife is bead blasted. The knife is 8.6 inches long in total. Its elegantly undulating blade is 3.7 inches long and the handle is 4.9 inches in length. The knife weighs 3.2 ounces.

The Fox T-1 knife

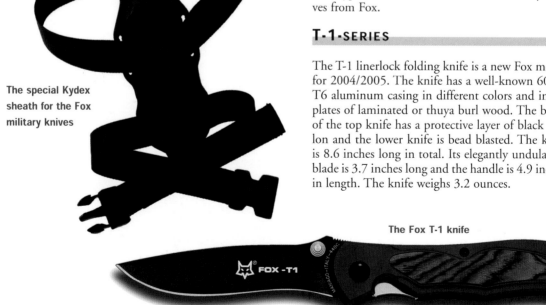

The special Techno Reef knife

a linerlock system clearly visible in the depiction. The varnished wood finish of the top edge of the handle is very nice, as is the ring of the blade pivot. There is a choice of Cocobolo wood, olive wood, briar burl wood or G-10 synthetic material depicted on the lower knife. The Trendy comes in a nice steel tin.

TECHO REEF

The Techno Reef was designed as a diving knife, but can also serve excellently as a military knife. It is an integral knife, made of one piece of stainless 440B steel with a black Teflon protective layer. It is interesting to note that the smooth or partially serrated edge on the blade back is protected with a layer of titanium nitrate. The handle is made of G-10 synthetic material and is rounded off at the ends for a better grip. Four holes are drilled into the handle to reduce the weight. The knife is 9 inches in total length and has a handle and blade of 4.5 inches each. The knife weighs 7.5 ounces and is delivered with a woven Cordura sheath and leg straps.

The Trendy gift box

TRENDY SERIES

The Trendy is a very trendy pocketknife of pure beauty. It can be carried as a key holder knife, but this would actually be a sin. The

The Trendy by Fox

handle was cut by laser from one plate of stainless 420 steel and then perfectly finished. The blade is made of stainless 440C steel and is bead blasted or covered with a Teflon layer. The skeleton blade has

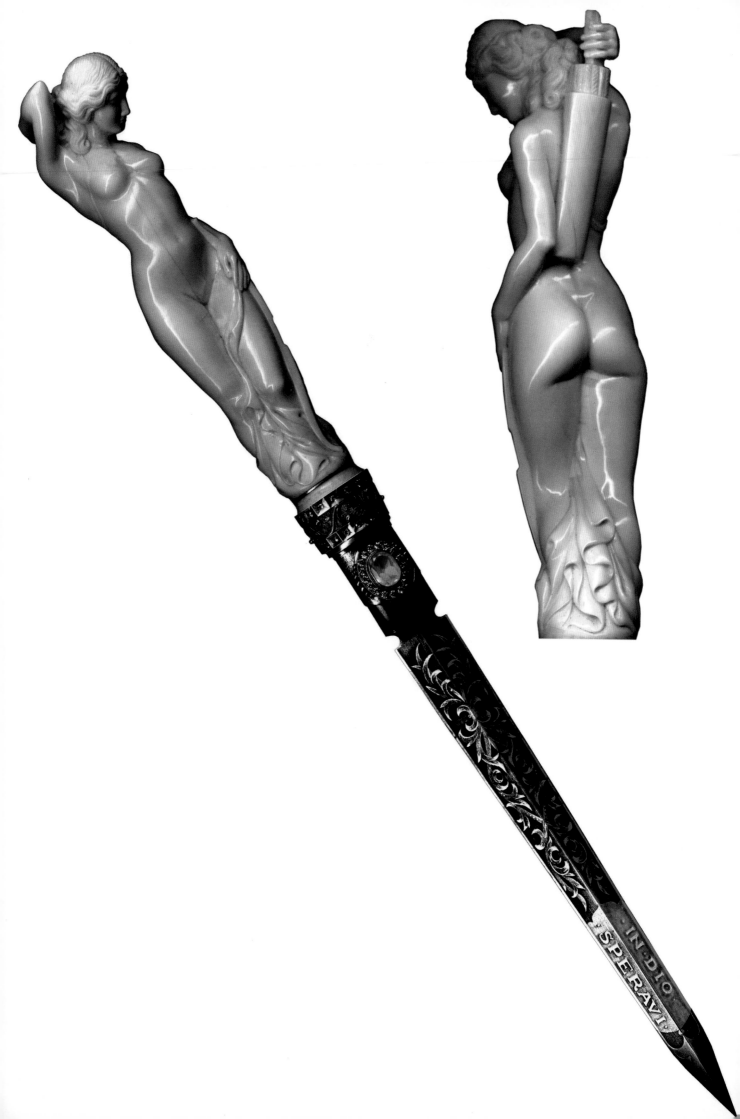

GATHERWOOD

www.gatherwood.nl

The logo of Gatherwood

Gatherwood Knives is a Dutch company that trades in handmade and factory produced knives and sells steel types and handle material for handymen. The company is run by Rob and Denise Sprokholt. Rob could never resist buying a knife when he went on holiday. A few years ago, while discussing mokumé gané with American knife maker Steve Hulett from West Yellowstone, they got the idea of making knives themselves.

Rob produces the handmade knives, and Denise finishes them. As Buckx is Rob's pseudonym on the Internet, the name "Buckx Gatherwood" is often used. Rob and Denise do almost everything by hand. The knives are not stock-removed from the steel, but cut and ground. This is why a

The Gatherwood MSC knife with the special Damascus blade

knife typically takes around forty working hours to produce and the process takes on a sort of mysticism. They do all of the work themselves, including the hardening and Rockwell testing.

In the process of making knives, Rob met novices to the field. He spent hours every day advising less-experienced knife makers. Finally he decided to tell his tale in an on-line handbook called 'How to Make Knives.' They later decided to publish a paper version and the Buckx Gatherwood handgemaakte messen (Buckx Gatherwood Handmade Knives) guide came about. Rob and Denise do not make knives on commission, but they do welcome inspiration from knife enthusiasts.

Gatherwood works exclusively with top quality material such as ATS-34, 440, powder steel and Damascus from powder steel. They prefer to use the same beautiful wood that is used for musical instruments or the butts of rifles, well crafted and oiled in the authentic way. Rob does not like gimmicks. He is preoccupied with making robust "manly" knives with something extra: a beautiful shape, good balance, but most of all he strives for the ideal blade shape and edge.

BOWIE

The 11.4 inch long Gatherwood Bowie is a considerable knife to carry with you. The heavy stainless ATS-34 steel blade is 0.22 inches thick and tempered to 59 HRC, then polished to a slight sheen. The guard is made of stainless steel. The linen Micarta handle has a tang that runs straight through and is attached with ten pins. A black leather sheath, finished with horse-hair bristles, comes with the knife.

The Bowie hunting knife by Gatherwood

MSC

The abbreviation MSC stands for 'Men's Survival Companion.' The Damascus powder steel blade was worked into a type of fantasy fishbone pattern with a hardness of 58 HRC. A part on the back of the knife was flattened off for hacking work. The blade runs integrally through to the protruding tang and is worked into a shackle. The MSC knife is 11.4 inches long. The blade has a maximum width of 1.3 inches and is 0.165 inches thick. The guard is made of the unique mokumé gané

Damascus of nickel silver and copper. The mammoth ivory handle and the handle parts are attached with silver colored rivets of 925/1000 quality.

The Sneaky Hunter with a handle made from snake wood

SNEAKY

Sneaky is a robust, 8.8 inch long working knife with nothing sly about it. The stainless ATS-34 steel blade, tempered to 59 HRC, is 0.16 inches thick and finished to a high gloss. Ridges cut into the back provide a stable grip. The stainless steel bolster is put together with rivets, then welded together. The snake wood handle is atta-ched with solid silver rivets.

SPIRIT OF THE HAWK

The name goes well with this big, beautiful knife. The blade of stainless 440-B steel, tempered to 58 HRC, is 9.25 inches long and 0.165 inches thick. It was hollow ground (convex) and finished to a high gloss. The guard of alpaca nickel silver has a garnet on each side. The snake wood handle is attached with hollow silver rivets.

ULTIMATE THUYA

The Damascus powder steel blade of the Ultimate Thuya has a wild pattern and was etched dark. It is 0.197 inches thick and has a hardness of 58 HRC. The blade back was polished to a high gloss and the guard was made of stainless steel. The unique thuya burl handle is attached with beautifully contrasting silver rivets.

The portrait of Alexander Georgiev with his master sign, top right, and the logo of the Russian Knifema-kers' Guild, below

GEORGIEV
www.rusartknife.urbannet.ru/gallery.html

The Gatherwood Spirit of the Hawk

Alexander Georgievich Georgiev was born on 11 April 1958 and grew up in the Druzhnaya Gorka settlement near Leningrad, where he became interes-ted in hunting and fishing. Fellow hunters told him about special hunting knives so sharp that they could skin an entire elk without having to be sharpened

The Ultimate Thuya

once. A forced laborer had made a similar knife as a token of gratitude to his father during the Stalin dic-tatorship, and his father was very attached to it.

After graduating from the military topographical officer's school in Leningrad, he was transferred to Moscow, where he was selected for special work, such as carpentry, engraving and processing preci-ous stones into jewelry.

In 1982 he was inspired by the book *Russian Gold and Silver Filigree*. For the next ten years he studi-ed Old Russian jewelry work, such as filigree and enameling. From 1988 to 1991 he worked on res-toring the works of the Old Masters. His first pay-ing project was a special filigree of the icon of the Holy Mother. Within two years he was fully boo-ked with orders.

Georgiev started making art knifes in 1992, where his knowledge of jewelry stood him in good stead. The knives shown here were photographed by Ser-gey Baranov and Valentin Overchenko.

LAD

This unique hunting set was exhibited at the Russian knife show, "Blades," at the Central Art Museum in Moscow in 2003. It is used for an old Russian hunting ritual in which the liver of shot game is baked in a pan, divided among the hunters and eaten, accompanied by vodka, of course. Around one hundred years ago such hunting sets were very popular among aristocratic circles in Russia and Europe, but as hunting is no longer an elite sport, it has been largely forgotten. This set consists of a hunting knife 14.4 inches long with an 8.5 inch blade, a fork and knife, a mug for the vodka, a jack

for making mustard and a salt and pepper shaker-set. The Damasteel blades were forged from a combination of Y10, SH-J15, 65G and ST0 steels and tempered to 58 HRC by the young knife makers S. Epishkin and R. Okushko from Tula. Burl wood from the wild olive tree was used for the handle of the larger knives. The handles of the rest are of roe horn from the Ukraine. The ornaments on the handle and the spares of all the objects were made of 711 grams of 925 quality silver.

el blade, forged by the knife smiths Lunev and Koptev. The filigree sheath contains 8.96 ounces of 925 quality, forged silver. On the back of the pommel is a large garnet from the mines of Karelia. The wood for the handle and sheath comes from a branch of a pear tree that blew off during a storm in Georgiev's backyard.

A beautifully done traditional
Russian hunting set: Lad

LEGEND

This beautiful knife was made in 2000 and displayed that year at the "Blades" knife show in Moscow. The knive is 11 inches long, with a 7.1 inch long Damaste-

Georgiev got the idea for the hunting knife while holding a freshly forged piece of Damasteel in his hands. Damasteel is a unique material: a piece of of 35-40 HRC hardness can easily carve holes in glass. Damascus is like water, whose properties change when it cry-

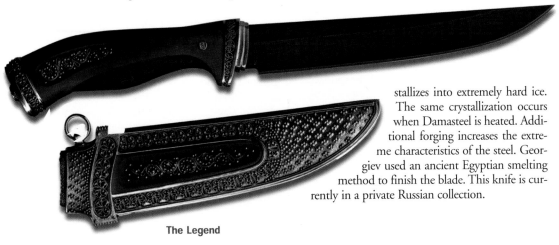

stallizes into extremely hard ice. The same crystallization occurs when Damasteel is heated. Additional forging increases the extreme characteristics of the steel. Georgiev used an ancient Egyptian smelting method to finish the blade. This knife is currently in a private Russian collection.

The Legend

SVATOSLAV

This decorative dagger was made for the "Blades 2001" knife exhibition held at the Weapons Museum at the Kremlin. Svatoslav, an ancestor of the Scandinavian Rurik clan, was a great Russian warlord from the tenth century. With only ten thousand men, he defeated a Greek army of one hundred thousand soldiers. His soldiers worshipped him because he slept next to the fire with his sandals as pillows and ate dried horsemeat, just like them.

Svatoslav

The stand of the dagger is shaped like a a Viking ship. The dagger in the sheath looks like the sail. At the end of the sheath is a round Viking battle shield, Svatoslav's own emblem. The dagger, with its powerful blade and inspiring handle, is made according to the fashion of the time. Smith Egar Aseev from Tula forged the blade. The central part came from an old battle tank and the cutting edge was made of Damasteel forged to it at a later stage. The steel has a hardness of 58 HRC. Svatoslav's motto, "I'm joining the battle," is engraved in the blade in old Slavic. The etchings are by one of the greatest masters of the craft in Russia, Andrey Koreshkov.

The dagger and sheath are richly decorated with Scandinavian and traditional Russian decorations and filigree work. In the handle and the sheath are tourmaline and amethyst from the Ural, garnets from Karelia and pearls from China. The handle is crafted of birch burl wood and the stand is oak. Carved into the foot of the stand and inlaid with silver, are the words Svatoslav said to his soldiers

before they joined battle against the Greek army: "Do not shame the Russian country. Better to lay our bones to rest here, as the dead know nothing of shame." The dagger with the stand is 17.7 inches long. The dagger alone is 15.35 inches long, with a nine inch blade, 2.36 inches wide at the guard. 908 grams of 925 quality silver was used in the artwork. This knife is currently in a private collection.

GERBER LEGENDARY BLADES
www.gerberblades.com

The Gerber logo

In 1939 Joseph Gerber hired a local knife smith to make 25 sets of kitchen knives as Christmas presents. These knives turned out to be so good that he had more sets made and eventually, he decided to leave a career in advertising to found Gerber Legendary Blades in Portland, Oregon. Initially he only produced kitchen knives, but in 1958 his son Pete started making sporting knives. They were so successful that the program expanded to hunting, fishing and pocketknives.

Gerber was the first American company to bring special lightweight knives to the market, with the Gator and the Gator Mate series. The handles of these knives were made of fiberglass-reinforced nylon with a Kryton outer layer. Later, Gerber started using other handle material such as Zytel and DuPont. Gerber also makes military and survival knives. In fact, Gerber is the only cutlery on display at the Museum of Modern Art in New York. From the beginning, Gerber worked with known knife designers such as 'Blackie' Collins, Ernest Emerson, William Harsey Jr., Bob Loveless, Al Mar and Paul Poehlmann. Even though Gerber was taken over by the Finnish company Fiskars in 1987, these methods are still used today. In 2003, Gerber introduced a number of Multi-Tools and the new Recoil Plier MP500 to the market. The lifelong guarantee for all Gerber products attests to their high quality.

The Svatoslav dagger without its sheath

En Rond the Chien

COUVEE HIVERNAL

The creation entitled Couvee Hivernal or 'Winter Hatchling' from 2000 is wonderfully shaped. It reminds one of a type of insect or an imaginary animal. The blade is 9 inches long, made of Damasteel and the handle has a type of lancet shape with a serrated blade back. The handle is made of mammoth ivory from sterling silver, rhodolite and small pearls. The stand is made of sterling silver wire. Gilbert made a similar knife which she entitled Bihoreau. This knife is made of 18kt gold and silver.

EN ROND DE CHIEN

With the En Rond de Chien 'Turning Dogs' knives, Chantal Gilbert indeed depicted two dogs that are turning around each other. These knives are roughly similar and are 11.8 inches in length. The blades of both knives were made of Damasteel. The handles were made of sterling silver and bronze with inlaid pieces of ebony. Chantal Gilbert created this work of art in 2001.

LA GROSSE BALERINE

La Grosse Balerine or 'The Fat ballerina' looks like an insect. With its high feet it looks like a mosquito that has drunk more than

Les Âme Soeurs

enough. This object is 5.9 inches in total length. The blade is made of Damasteel and the handle from sterling silver. Chantal made this knife in 2000.

LES ÂME SOEURS

Les Âme Soeurs or 'Soul Sisters' are twin knives that form a complete unit. Each knife is 11.8 inches long and the blades are

La Grosse Balerine

made of Damasteel. The handle is made of silver and the rump from bronze. The knife in the foreground is made entirely from sterling silver.

L'OIE BLANCHE

L'Oie Blanche 'The White Goose' was made in 2001. The knife is 14.6 inches long. The blade is made of Damasteel and the handle from sterling

L'Oie Blanche

silver. The support, or rather 'paws' of this imaginary animal are made of sterling silver.

Strates

STRATES

The name Strates is probably a combination of the Stratosphere and Straights. This set consists of three real knives with different blade shapes made of Damasteel. The bottom knife is very interesting. The blade of this knife creates the impression that it was made of chopped stone.

The handles are made of mammoth ivory, combined with silver, 18kt gold and meteorite stone. The total length of the knives is 9.4 inches. This set was made in 2002.

GOBEC
www.gobec.at

The emblem of Stefan Gobec

Stefan Gobec was born in Pochlarn, Austria in 1962. He had a technical education at the famous rifle school of Ferlach and has been making rifles and handmade knives since 1984. He took part in the IMA knife exhibition in Munich in 1987 with the Austrian sculptor Johannes Markus Weselka. He was also one of the founding members of the Austrian Knifemakers' Guild in 1994. Gobec also organized the first Austrian knife exhibition in Vienna in 1996. For this event he made, among other things, a special dagger for the commemoration of the one thousandth year of his country's existence. Gobec mostly works on commission. He

Modern Damascus shotgun barrel in .270 Win

also holds regular courses for beginner knife makers and gives lessons in making Damasteel. These photos, were taken by PointSeven Studios.

The Africa hunting knife with beautifully engraved bolster

The Africa knife in detail

AFRICA

The Africa hunting knife is an integral knife made of stainless RWL-34 steel. This special steel consists of carbon, silicone, manganese, chromium, molybdenum and vanadium, tempered to 60-62 HRC.

The handle plates are made of white mammoth ivory. A beautiful jaguar resting on a tree branch on the bolster was engraved by Armin Bundschuh. The Africa hunting knife is 8.5 inches in total length. The total length of the blade is 3.93 inches and the handle is 4.5 inches long. A nice leather sheath comes with the knife.

AMBOINDA

This large hunting knife looks like an integral knife, but it is not. The large and wide blade with a beautiful V-shape is made of stainless CPM-420V powder steel, known as CPM-S90V steel. The bolster is made of a piece of polished nickel steel. The handle is 4.5 inches in length and has plates of flattened Amboyna wood. The ball shaped burl wood of the Indian padouk or Amboyna tree (Pterocarpus indicus), belongs to the butterfly flower family that comes from Indonesia and Malaysia. The total length of the Amboinda is 8.9 inches. The blade is 4.3 inches long. This knife fits well in a beautiful medium brown leather sheath.

BIG HUNTER

At 9 inches in total length, this knife is not so large, but it does seem enormous because of its sturdy blade and large nickel steel bolster. The droppoint blade of the Big Hunter is made of stainless CPM-S90V steel that was tempered to 58-61 HRC. The length of the blade is 4.1 inches. The handle is 4.9

The large Amboinda hunting knife

Big Hunter

inches long and is made of stag horn with a beautiful rough structure that ensures a stable grip. The bolster has a nice arch that serves as a finger grip and doubles as a guard as well.

LEOPARD

The Leopard folding knife has a steel casing sculpted with a depiction of a naked lady being 'protected' by a spotted panther. These engravings were done by Jan Slezak. Stefan Gobec used stainless 440 BTS steel for the blade tempered to 58-60 HRC and consistsing of a mixture of carbon, silicone, manganese, chromium, molybdenum, vanadium and cobalt. The V-shape and the etching cre-

The Leopard folder

ates a beautiful contrast to the white steel. The casing is made of stainless 440C steel. The total length of the Leopard knife is 6.9 inches. The total length of the blade is 2.95 inches and the handle is 4.2 inches long. The knife has a linerlock system.

OREX

The Orex is another folding knife with a linerlock. The blade is made of Damascus, made of powder Damasteel with a motif that is indicated as 'hakkapella.' The total length of the Orex is 7 inches. The blade is 3.93 inches in length and has a handle of 4.5 inches. The casing has handle plates made of oryx horn. The bolster is made of nickel steel and decorated with creepers.

Andrey Golovin with his master sign right, and the logo of the Guild of Russian Knifemakers, below

The Liner Orex with a linerlock

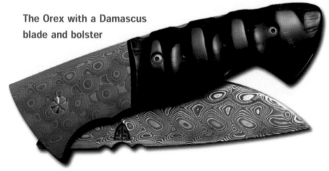

Another version of the Orex linerlock folding knife has a bolster made of Damasteel. The handle is made of oryx horn, attached with deep screws.

The Orex with a Damascus blade and bolster

GOLOVIN

www.rusartknife.urbannet.ru/gallery.html

Andrey Vladimirovich Golovin grew up in Tula, where he worked in thermal work shops in the TS weapons factory where he learned to smelt, temper and process steel. From there it was only a short step to hardening, filing and putting together his

first knife. In the engraving department, where the best and most beautiful weapons in the country were being engraved, he was trained by the best experts.

He subsequently went to work in the Revival weapons factory in Tula and within four years he became a professional engraver. He then took a post at Russian Chambers in Moscow where he is still employed. He has also rediscovered many old and complicated techniques, such as processing gold sheets and inlaying engravings with gold. Theses knives were photographed by the gallery at the Russian Palace in Moscow.

EAST PATTERNS

The East Pattern hunting knife is based on a traditional knife from the south east of Russia and Turkey. The blade of Damasteel was forged by Egor Aseev. The engravings on the bone handle were done by Vladimir Kostenko. The handle is made of walrus bones attached to the metal with pins, finished on the surface with mother-of-pearl. Verses from the Koran are engraved in the blade in the Old Turkish alphabet, inlaid with gold. On the right is: 'Enemies will be broken with one stab from this knife.' The left side says: 'This hand needs a sword and this heart a song of praise for the Almighty.' The total length of the knife is 10.6 inches and the blade is 6.3 inches long and 1.38 inches wide at the widest point. The Damasteel blade was forged with a combination of

The East Patterns hunting knife

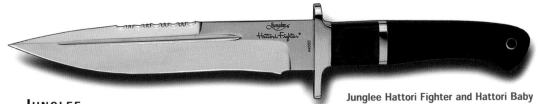

Junglee Hattori Fighter and Hattori Baby

JUNGLEE
EXTREME FORCES

The new Junglee Extreme Forces knife was designed for the extreme circumstances of military missions. The blade of this knife is made of stainless ATS-34 steel and is

The Junglee JF2 knife in two blade versions

covered with a black Teflon layer as additional protection against corrosion. The handle is ergonomically shaped and is made of shock resistant synthetic material with inlaid pieces of Kraton to ensure a stable grip. The skinner blade has a false incision on the back. Its total length is 8.75 inches, the blade is 3.94 inches long and the knife weighs 4.7 ounces. Due to the large thumb stud on the blade, the knife can even be opened with one hand while wearing a glove. The Extreme Forces knives have linerlock systems.

JUNGLEE HATTORI FIGHTER

The Hattori is a very well balanced knife and it is, despite its luxurious exterior, a solid and tough survival knife. The blade is made of stainless 440C steel and has a heavy saw serration on the blade back. In the direction of the point, the false incision is relatively sharp and the actual cutting edge of the blade is

razor sharp. The Hattori Fighter and the Hattori Baby have handles made of polished hard wood, combined with a Kraton grip and a nickel silver guard. This knife comes with a leather sheath. The Hattori Fighter is 13.25 inches in length with a blade length of 7.75 inches and it weighs 11.7 ounces. The Baby Hattori is 11 inches long, has a blade of 6.06 inches and weighs 9.2 ounces.

JUNGLEE JF2

The Junglee JF2 folding knife from the Armed Forces series has a linerlock system. Like the Extreme Forces knife the blade of the JF2 is made of special stainless ATS-

The Marshall Junior knives

34 steel. The blade has a protective Teflon layer against corrosion and light reflection. The blade is 3.93 inches long and has a spearpoint that comes with a smooth or partially serrated edge. Its total length is 8.86 inches and the knife weighs 4.7 ounces. The synthetic material handle has inlaid pieces of Kraton.

JUNGLEE MARSHALL-SERIES

The Marshall series was designed as a police knife for daily use in the patrol vehicle or on the police horse. The clip-point blade is pointed, sharp and durable

Junglee Marshall

enough for police work. This knife is made in Seki, Japan for Gutmann from AUS-10 or ATS-34 steel. The ergonomic handle is made of stainless steel or lightweight Zytel synthetic material. On the right handle plate is a large detachable carrying clip and

AUS-10 steel and is 2.64 inches long with a handle 3.5 inches in length. The stainless steel version weighs 3.1 ounces and the Zytel version 1.7 ounces. The Marshall Junior has a carrying clip on the right handle plate.

JUNGLEE SHENZI

The Junglee Shenzi folding knife has a beautiful clippoint blade with a high back, which makes the knife easy to handle. The high-ridged blade back with a double-sided thumb stud on the blade provides good support for the thumb or forefinger. The blade is made of stainless 440A steel and has a handle 2.36 inches long

Junglee Shenzi

the knife can be carried with the point facing up or down. Gutmann provides an extra large and heavy carrying clip. The Marshall has a linerlock system and is produced with a smooth, partially serrated or completely serrated edge. The total length of the Marshall knife is 8 inches. The handle is 4.88 inches long and the blade is 3.07 inches in length. The version with the stainless steel handle weighs 4.9 ounces and the version with the Zytel handle weighs 2.8 ounces.

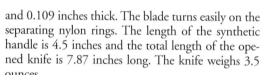

Tri Force

and 0.109 inches thick. The blade turns easily on the separating nylon rings. The length of the synthetic handle is 4.5 inches and the total length of the opened knife is 7.87 inches long. The knife weighs 3.5 ounces.

The Special Forces combat knife

JUNGLEE SPECIAL FORCES

The new Junglee Special Forces fighting knife is a well-balanced knife with a heavy sheath made of woven Nylon with a carry strap so that it can be carried out of sight. The blade is made of AUS-8 steel, tempered to 57 HRC and has a black Teflon coating against corrosion and light reflection. The edge is partially serrated and the top of the blade back runs with an arch. The arched Kraton handle ensures an optimal grip.

JUNGLEE MARSHALL JUNIOR SERIES

The Marshall Junior series is a smaller version of the Marshall. The Junior also has a linerlock system and is made with a stainless steel or Zytel handle. The blade is made of stainless

The Venom folder

The total length of the Special Forces knife is 9.37 inches, the blade is 4.75 inches long and the knife weighs 5.2 ounces.

JUNGLEE TRI FORCE

The most typical feature of the new Tri Force is the thumb-hole in the blade, patented by Spyderco. A second recognizable feature is the angular Tanto point. The blade is made of stainless ATS-34 steel covered with a black Teflon protective layer. The handle is made of shock resistant material and has Kraton inlaid plates. The knife is 8.75 inches long with a blade length of 3.07 inches and it weighs 4.7 ounces. The Tri Force has a linerlock system.

JUNGLEE VENOM

The Venom is a part of the Junglee Armed Forces series. There is a heart-shaped thumb-hole in the pointed spearpoint blade which is 3.94 inches in length with a smooth or partially serrated edge. It is made of stainless ATS-34 steel, covered with a black Teflon protective layer. Its total length is 8.86 inches and the knife weighs 4.7 ounces. The handle is made of shock resistant material and has Kraton inlaid plates. A detachable and changeable carrying clip is on the right of the handle. The Venom has a linerlock system.

JUNGLEE Z KNIFE

The ancient art of scrimshaw originated with the old whale hunters who made everything from the tooth ivory of the sperm whale and walrus. Today it is forbidden to use these materials and they have been replaced with modern synthetic material or mammoth ivory. This Z Knife of the Junglee series is made in Seki, Japan. The skeleton blade is made of stainless AUS 6 steel in which the letter 'Z' is

The Z Knife by Junglee

clearly visible. The handle is made of lightweight Zytel. The Z Knife series are adorned with a great number of scrimshaw depictions of fish, hunting scenes, wild animals and sailing ships. The knife has an extremely sharp edge and makes a nice key holder or it can be used as a money clip because of its large carrying clip. The Z Knife has a backlock system. The total length is 5.25 inches, the blade is 2.25 inches long, the handle is 2.99 inches and it weighs 1.3 ounces.

H

ly uses stainless 440C steel and stainless Udeholm UHB steel. He hardens the steel himself in a special oven. He started experimenting with forging Damasteel in 1982, mostly using a combination of 1095 and 15N20 carbon steel. This type of steel is well suited for grinding and it keeps its sharp edge longer. He guarantees that his forged knives cannot be broken. The photos below of the Hagen knives were taken by Bob Glassman from privé-collectieknifegallery.com.

BUCKHORN

The Buckhorn folding knife has a blade and bolster made of beautiful wild Damascus. This is also called random Damascus because it can be folded and forged with various resulting patterns. The handle is made of nut burl. This knife has a spring pressure locking system and it can be furnished with a bolster locking system, which makes it necessary to turn the bolster plate in order to unlock the knife. The total length of the knife is 6.5 inches and the blade is 2.75 inches long. The blade back is beautifully decorated.

CUTLASS NO. 61

This short hunting knife or Cutlass is made of stainless ATS-34 steel. The total length is 11.6 inches and it weighs 10.9 inches. The blade is 6.2 inches in

HAGEN

www.dochagen.com
www.privé-collectieknifegallery.com

The emblem of Doc Hagen

Doc Hagen has been making custom knives since 1973 and has been a voting member of the American Knifemakers' Guild since 1976. All of his knives are made by hand. He has produced many hunting knives, but his specialty is folding knives. He prefers natural materials – the more exotic and beautiful, the better. He most-

The Mammoth Damascus knife

length. The handle plates are made of polished mammoth ivory and attached with engraved screws. The Renaissance-style engravings were done by Geoffroy Delahaut.

MAMMOTH

The Mammoth got its name from the piece of patented mammoth ivory used to decorate the handle. The

The Buckhorn folder by Doc Hagen

blade and casing were made of beautiful ladder Damascus that Doc Hagen forged himself. The handle is 8.62 inches long and the blade is 3.75 inches in length.

MAPLE

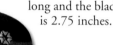

The Maple folder

The maple is a tree with beautiful wood which Doc Hagen used as handle plates for this folding knife, attaching them with decorated pins. The blade was made of stainless Udeholm UHB steel and the bolster from stainless 440C steel. The knife locks with spring pressure, but it can also be furnished with a bolster lock. The knife is 6.5 inches in total length and has a blade of 2.75 inches.

SCRIMSHAW DAGGER

The Scrimshaw Dagger is a double-sided folding dagger with a beautiful Damascus blade and a bolster made of random Damascus. The handle plates

The Tiger Coral folder with handle plates made from tiger coral

are made of white mammoth ivory inscribed with the scrimshaw technique. The dagger itself is 7.25 inches in length and has a blade of 3.25 inches.

TIGER CORAL

The Tiger Coral folding knife has handle plates made of the material for which it was named. It looks beautiful, but is forbidden in most countries. The blade and bolster were made of wild Damascus. The knife is 6.61 inches long and the blade length is 2.75 inches.

HEAVIN
www.africut.co.za
www.bladegallery.com en
www.privé-collectieknifegallerly.com

Kevin and Heather Harvey live in Belfast, South Africa. Both of them had been making knives before they got married and both are members of the South Afri-

The Scrimshaw folder dagger

can Knifemakers' Guild and the South African Blade-Smith Association (SABA). They are also the only Master Smith couple of the American Bladesmith Society (ABS). Their knives are on offer through the Internet under the name Heavin Knives, a combination of Heather and Kevin and also a wordplay on the word 'heaven.' Kevin has been making knives since the age of twelve under the influence of his grandfather. He currently makes hand-forged Bowies and historical knives with his own Damascus or Damascus made by his wife. Kevin specializes in this technique and in fresh designs with special attention given to the finish and materials. Heather started forging Damasteel in 1995. When she met Kevin in 1996, he taught her how she could make knives from her own steel. Heather produces Damasteel under the

The Crown Dagger that Heather and Kevin Harvey made together

The traditional African Dagger by
Heather Harvey

HEATHER IMPALA HORN UTILITY

name, Damsel Damascus, and she makes traditional African weapons from her own Damasteel. In 2003, Heather recieved the honor of becoming the second ever female member to receive the title ABS Master Smith from the American Bladesmith Society. The photos here were taken by Blade Gallery and Custom Knife Gallery.

HEATHER AFRICAN DAGGER

This traditional African knife bears witness to Heather's cultural inheritance. The dagger blade was hand forged from Damascus with copper and is 8.45 inches long, 0.13 inches thick and 1 inch wide. The handle is made of African black wood, cut and processed by hand with twisted copper and iron wire. The pommel is inlaid with two coins: a 'ticky' from South Rhodesia and a coin from Botswana. This African Dagger is 14.5 inches long and weighs 13 ounces. The sheath is made of hollow gemsbok horn with copper details and a Rhodesian coin at the bottom.

The Impala Horn Utility hunting knife weighs 4.8 ounces and is 9.75 inches long. The hand-forged, spearpoint blade made of 5160 carbon steel is 5.5 inches long, 0.14 inches thick and 1 inch wide. The bolster is made of copper and the handle of impala horn with spacers from the fangs of a warthog. This knife is one of the five 'journeyman' knives that got Heather accepted as a member or 'journeyman' of the American Bladesmith Society in June 2001.

The Flame Bowie with its particular
fantastical Damascus

HEATHER MOUNTAIN MAN FOLDER

This folding knife weighs 4.4 ounces and is 7.75 inches long when folded. The clip blade is 3.4 inches long and made of carbon steel in mosaic Damascus and forged with a flame pattern. The blade is 0.11 inches thick and 1.04 inches wide. The handle is made of antelope antlers. The Damascus spring of the toplock system is decorated with a nickel silver saddle in the shape of a lily and copper flowers. The iron rings that release the toplock can be used to hang the knife as well.

The Impala Horn Utility
hunting knife

HEATHER FLAME BOWIE

This fixed knife was one of Heather's first submissions for the title of Master Smith. This Bowie knife is 10.5 inches long and weighs 8 ounces. The clip blade is made of Damascus that Heather forged herself from carbon steel. The two colors, tinted gray and sharp silver, form a flame pattern. The blade is 0.15 inches thick and 1.21 inches wide. The bolster and guard are made of copper and have an antique exterior. The handle is made from African acacia wood.

The Mountain
Man Folder
with the toplock

The Recurve Utility by Heather Harvey

A 1942 Rhodesian penny was worked into the end of the knife. South Rhodesian 'tickies' from 1947 are on either side of the bolster.

HEATHER RECURVE UTILITY

This knife is 8.25 inches long and weighs 5.5 ounces. The arched droppoint blade is 4.5 inches long, 0.18 inches thick and 1.09 inches wide. It is made of Damascus with a random pattern. The bolster is a nickel silver mounting ring and the handle is made of tiger maple wood with a mosaic pin. A brown leather sheath goes with the knife.

The Giraffe Shin folder

KEVIN AZURITE/ MALACHITE LINERLOCK FOLDER

This linerlock folding knife is 6 inches in total length and weighs 2.2 ounces. The 2.5 inch long blade is made of blued damsel Damascus, forged by Heather. The droppoint blade is 0.102 inches thick and 0.713 inches wide. The bolsters are made of the same Damascus as the blades, but were blued under a higher temperature, which creates a sharper color. The handle is

made of compounded azurite and malachite stone with 6AL4V-titanium liners. Malachite and azurite are soft materials that can easily chip or break, which is why the stones were recomposed and pressed into shape, making the material more durable, but just as beautiful as the original stones. A handwoven grass sheath goes with the knife.

KEVIN GIRAFFE SHIN FOLDER

This linerlock folding knife was one of the first folding knives Kevin had ever made. It is 6 inches long. The clip blade is 2.63 inches long and made from damsel Damascus, forged by Heather with a polished and baked layer of varnish. The blade is 0.09 inches long

The fantastically beautiful Azurite/ Malachite Linerlock folder

0.09 inches thick and 10.7 inches wide. The bolster is made of the same material as the knife. The handle was made of the shinbone of a giraffe and has 6AL4V titanium liners. A handwoven grass sheath goes with the knife.

KEVIN PEARL IN HIPPO FOLDER

This folding knife is 6.75 inches long and weighs 2.16 ounces. The droppoint blade is 2.87 inches long, 0.12 inches thick and 0.8 inches wide. The carbon steel Damascus was forged by Kevin himself and blued with a gas burner in a mosaic pattern of pheasant feathers. The handle is made from an hippopotamus tooth worked with mother-of-pearl. The knife has a linerlock system with liners made of blued titanium.

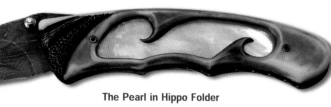

The Pearl in Hippo Folder

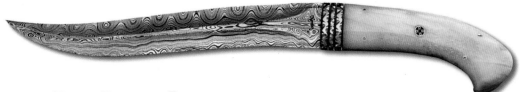

The Persian
Fighter by
Kevin Harvey

KEVIN PERSIAN FIGHTER

This knife, made in a traditional Persian design, weighs 13 ounces and is 13 inches long. The drop-point blade is 8.38 inches long, 0.16 inches thick and 1.13 inches wide. It is made of Damascus that Kevin forged into the desired shape himself. The handle is made of giraffe bones and attached with mosaic pins. The bolsters are of nickel silver into which a motif was filed. The end is decorated with copper. The sheath is made of iguana leather with a nickel silver tip and a motley edge at the top.

KEVIN SEARLES STYLE BLACKWOOD BOWIE

Kevin won the Antique Bowie Assignment Award with this knife. It weighs a whopping 24 ounces, is 14.38 inches in total length with a blade length of 9.38 inches. The blade is made of Damascus and was 'hot gun-blued Heart Beat pattern,' forged by Kevin. The handle is made of checkered African black wood with copper pins and shield plates. Spacers made of nickel silver and stainless steel are

Searles Style Blackwood Bowie

attached to the handle. The guard and pommel are made of the same Damascus as the blade. The sheath is made of buffalo leather worked open on wood and accented with nickel silver.

HERBERTZ

www.herbertz-messerclub.de

German wholesale company, C. Julius Herbertz GmbH, was established in 1956 in the city of Solingen, famous for its knife industry. In addition to Solingen and its regions, Herbertz also represents manufacturers from all over the world, including Spain, the United States and Taiwan. With fifty employees, this company arranges the export of knives for representatives in Germany, Luxemburg, Norway, Denmark, the Netherlands, Belgium, France, Austria, Switzerland and Italy. Herbertz imports knives from American producers Al-Mar,

Benchmade, Buck, Gerber, Kershaw and SOG for these countries. They are involved with French producers Laguiole Opinel, with the beautiful knives of Nieto in Spain and in Scandinavian countries with the products of Marttiini, Helle and Eka. Herbertz also produces a great number of knives themselves.

The emblem of Herbertz

The company also sells swords, bows and arrows for archery, billiard accessories, darts and fishing tackle. The Herbertz Knife Club has an on-line shop and provides extensive technical information about knives, blade shapes, steel types and handle material. This club also features an on-line workshop on grinding knives. Below are a few knives that were brought together under the mark of Herbertz knives as well as knives by various designers produced by or on behalf of Herbertz.

The Herbertz logo as a belt-fastener

The Carter Adventurer folder
by Herbertz

CARTER ADVENTURER

Dr. Fred Carter is one of the most productive designers in the knife industry. He first encountered hand-made knives in 1970. Since then he has twice been chosen as the president of the Knifema-kers' Guild. His designs are made in Taiwan by Gigand Company, one of the largest knife manufacturers in the country. Gigand makes more than 1 million knives per year for household marks of different producers and wholesalers. Since 1995, Gigand has also been making knives under its own name, in cooperation with Fred Carter. Herbertz is in charge of distribution for Western Europe and distribution for North America is done by United Cutlery. The Adventurer knife is remar-

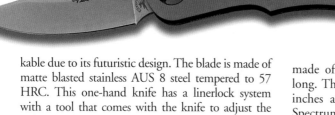

Carter Gigand

kable due to its futuristic design. The blade is made of matte blasted stainless AUS 8 steel tempered to 57 HRC. This one-hand knife has a linerlock system with a tool that comes with the knife to adjust the tightness of the blade pivot. The handle, made of aluminum with inlaid pieces of G-10 synthetic material, is 4.7 inches long. The knife is 7.95 inches in total length, with a 3.25 inch blade. On the right of the handle is a stainless steel carrying clip.

CARTER DESIGN

The Carter Design knife has handle plates made of aluminum, in metallic colors or anodized in a dark gray anthracite color. This knife has a linerlock and is 7.3 inches in total length. The handle is 4.3 inches long and has a three-inch blade made of stainless steel.

CARTER GIGAND

This knife has the typical Carter shape, characterized by the special screw on the blade pivot. The handle of the Gigand is made of 6061-T6 aircraft

aluminum, anodized in many different colors. The Gigand has a liner-lock system. The blade is 2.8 inches long, made of stainless AUS-8 steel and is matte blasted. The length of the knife is 7.1 inches. The handle is 4.3 inches long and has two long, curved finger slots at the bottom.

The Carter Design

CARTER SPECTRUM

The Spectrum looks very much like the Gigand model, but does not have the finger slots. The handle is made of 6061-T6 aluminum and comes in many different colors. The tightness of the blade can be adjusted with a screw on the blade pivot. The blade is made of stainless AUS-8 steel and is 2.9 inches long. The total length of the opened knife is 7.2 inches and the handle is 4.3 inches long. The Spectrum has a linerlock system for the blade.

CARTER TITAN

The Carter Spectrum folder

This Fred Carter knife, designed exclusively for Herbertz, is unique with decorative blue stripes. The blades of both knives are made of ATS-34 steel and are 2.8 inches long. The handle is made of titanium and is 4.3 inches long. The total length is 7.1 inches. The Titan has a linerlock and a detachable carrying clip on the right side of the blade.

Carter Titan

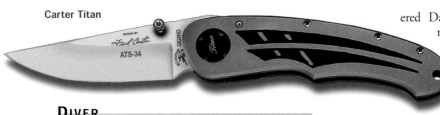

DIVER

This series of diving knives is made by various producers in Italy and Spain. The blades are made of stainless 440C steel. Characteristic for this knife is the saw serration on the back of the blade, with which lines or nets can be cut if a diver gets caught in them. The handles are all made of synthetic materials. The guard and pommel, if there is one, are made of stainless steel as well. (Still, after a plunge in seawater, knives always have to be cleaned well in fresh water, since in the long run no type of steel is resistant to salt.) The total lengths of these diving knives vary between 11 to 14.6 inches and the blade between 4.7 and 7 inches. In general

ered Damasteel and the handle is made of Amboyna wood. The Diamond series have a Damasteel blade forged from 49 layers of steel with a casing of nickel silver and handle plates from specially selected nut burl wood. The bottom knife actually does not belong in this series, but it was added for comparison. This knife has the so-called 'Damascus look.' The blade is not made of real Damascus, but a Damascus

The Diver

effect is etched into it. The bolster is not engraved, but etched as well. The handle plates are made of laminated wood. The total lengths of these knives vary between 7 and 7.7 inches and the handles are 4.3 inches long each.

FOLDER 2

The total length of backlock knives made of Damasteel varies from 7.7 to 8.3 inches, the handles from 4.3 to 4.7 inches and the blades from 3.3 to 3.9 inches. The knife below has a blade made of seventeen-layer Damasteel with a core of stainless 440C steel. The knife from the Collector's series has a blade of forty-nine-layered Damascus, an engraved bolster made of nickel silver and a handle made of nut burl wood. A third knife has a blade made of forty-nine-layer Damascus, with the bolster made of Damascus as well. The handle looks like it is made of rough wood, but the plates are actually made of tagayasan wood, which is the Japanese name for Bombay black wood from the Indian shisham tree (Dalbergia). This wood has a fine, dark grain and a beautiful natural gloss. A fouth version has a blade made of forty-nine-layer Damascus as well, with stainless steel bol-

The linerlock Damascus

the handles are extra long to ensure a good grip, even when wearing gloves. These knives come with synthetic material sheaths.

FOLDER 1

The Damascus linerlock folding knives from Herbertz actually fall in the custom made category, as they are made in very small series, mostly by hand. One blade model features a seventeen-layer Damasteel with a core of stainless 440C steel. The handle is made of burl wood and the bolster from nickel steel. Another version has a blade made of 512 lay-

The backlock folder in Damasteel

The special luxury model

sters and handle plates made of pakka wood. The fifth knife has dark pakka wood handle plates, an engraved bolster made of nickel silver and a forty-nine-layer Damascus blade. The dark Damascus blade is achieved by mixing carbon-deficient steel with hard, carbon-rich steel. The hard steel turns light after it is etched and the softer, carbon-deficient steel turns dark gray or black.

FOLDER 3

This luxurious backlock knife has a blade made of stainless 440C steel with a golden etched Herbertz logo. The bolster is made of nickel silver, polished and engraved. The handle is made of nut burl wood with strips of malachite, demarcated with nickel silver. The knife is 7.7 inches in total length, has a blade of 3.4 inches and a handle of 4.3 inches.

Backlock folder with walnut wood

FOLDER 4

This linerlock knife has a beautiful, tight shape and luxurious inlaid plates in the handle. These knives have spearpoint blades made of stainless AISI 420 steel and handles made of nickel steel. The inlaid plates are made of nut burl wood, combined with mother-of-pearl. The two bottom knives have inlaid plates of green marble and mother-of-pearl. The total lengths of these knives vary between 6.1 to 6.3 inches. The handles are between 3.5 to 3.9 inches long respectively.

FOLDER 5

This backlock series features traditional shapes with clippoint or spearpoint blades. The knives have handle plates made of nut burl wood, combined with mother-of-pearl. The blade and bolsters are made of stainless AISI 420 steel. The total lengths vary between 6.1 to 8.15 inches. The blades are from 2.6 to 3.4 inches long.

The luxury linerlock folder with Mother of Pearl

FOLDER 6

This luxurious series of backlock knives come from various collectors' series. The knife below, the 'Hound,' depicts a hunting scene etched in gold with a fetching hound on the blade. The bolster is made of engraved nickel silver and the handle plates of nut burl wood. The engraving also features: the Pony Express, General Custer's Last Stand and the shoot-out at the OK Corral.

Special version with etched blade

A small folder

FOLDER 7

This knife series has a classic design with a bead blasted handle and bolsters made of stainless 440C steel set off beautifully by handle plates made of nut burl wood. The series consists of five knives, ranging from 5.4 to 8.9 inches in length. The handles range from 3.1 to 5.1 inches in length.

FOLDER 8

These linerlock folding knives have particularly beautiful handles. The knife has a blade and bolster made of AISI 420 steel and handle plates made of nut burl wood, combined with inlaid pieces of different types of malachite. The knife is 8.15 inches in

FOLDER 9

The knives from the Wildlife series have birds or hunting scenes decorated with gold etched into the stainless 440C steel blade and handle plates made of pakka wood. A flying eagle is depicted on the blade of the top knife. The knife second from the top has a

Special linerlock folder with malachite

brass bolster and an 'American Eagle' on the blade. The bolsters of the other knives are all made of engraved nickel silver or nickel steel. The third knife from the top is decorated with an etching of a soaring eagle. The blade of the bottom knife is decorated with a wild pig. The knives are from 7.9 to 8.5 inches long. The handles are 4.3 to 4.7 inches in length, respectively.

FOLDER 10

These linerlock knives are a must for right-minded computer fanatics. The blades are made of matte blasted, stainless 440C steel with a partially serrated edge. The handle plates are in the shape of a computer printing plate, complete with a CPU and complicated patterns of resistors and other small loitering objects. The knives are 6.5, 7.4 and 8.2 inches in total length and have handles made of black synthetic material.

Wildlife series: Folder 7

total length and has a blade of 4.7 inches. The knife also comes with handle plates made of pakka wood with inlaid pieces of green marble and is 8.5 inches in total length.

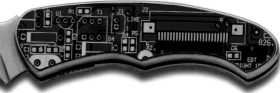

The 'IT Board' folder

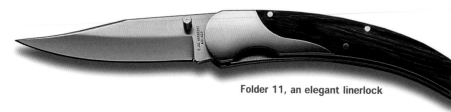

Folder 11, an elegant linerlock

FOLDER 11

This particularly elegant linerlock knife falls into the category of 'Gentleman's Knives.' The blade and the bolster of this knife are made of AISI 420 steel with handle plates made of pakka wood or burl wood. Some models have inlaid pieces of green marble. The total lengths vary from 6.7 to 8.9 inches. The blades are from 3.9 to 5.1 inches long.

FOLDER 12 TACTICAL

Folder 13, modern Herbertz linerlocks

The Tactical Folder from Herbertz comes in two variations. The model with the black Teflon blade is 6.8 inches in total length, has a handle 3.9 inches long and a blade made of stainless 440C steel 2.8 inches long. The other variation is 8.2 inches long and has a handle of 4.7 inches. The handles of both knives are stock removed from 6061-T6-aluminum and are provided with a fine ridge structure on the outside. The slot in the left handle plate is for easy operation of the thumb stud and linerlock.

FOLDER 13

These linerlock knives of modern design and execution have spearpoint blades that allow long, sloping grinds and false incisions. The standard edge is smooth or partially serrated. The blade is made of stainless 420 steel that is matte bead blasted. The handle is a lightweight alloy with an aluminum basis. The handle

Folder 12, Herbertz Tactical

plates in natural or black colors are made of the same material and have a scale-like motif for a firm grip. A steel carrying clip is on the right of the handle. The total length of the knife is 8.3 inches, the handle is 4.7 inches long and the length of the blade is 3.5 inches.

FOLDER 14

These backlock folding knives are also part of this special series and are decorated with marble and malachite. The blade and bolsters of these knives are made of stainless AISI 420 steel with handle plates made of pakka wood with inlaid pieces of green marble or nut burl wood, combined with malachite. The knives are from 7 to 8.3 inches long.

A special marble and malachite Folder 14

A heavy Folder 15 linerlock working knife

FOLDER 17

This tactical linerlock knife has a Tanto blade with similar measurements, but with a different handle, made of aluminum alloys. The handle plates have injection molded ridges and inlaid pieces of carbon fiberglass. The total length is 7.8 inches, the partially serrated blade is 3.1 inches long and the handle is 4.7 inches in length.

FOLDER 15

This series of robust knives has very strained shapes. The blade and casing are made of bead blasted stainless 440C steel. The total length of these knives is 7.5 inches. The handle is 4.3 inches in length and has a blade 3.15 inches long. The handle plates are made of G-10 synthetic hardwood.

Elegant Folder 16 Gentleman's Knife

FOLDER 16

Folder 17 Tactical Tanto linerlock

FOLDER 18

This series looks very similar to the previous one, except that, instead of being Tanto-shaped, the blades have a spearpoint shape. I associate it with the beak of a bird. The third knife from the top is a more luxurious version, with inlaid plates of hardwood and the second from the top has inlaid pieces of carbon fiberglass.

This small pocketknife has a very beautifully shaped linerlock system, reinforced with oval holes in the blade that look like the eyes of a bird. The blade is shaped like a beak. A peculiarity of this knife is the fact that the blade is not opened with these holes but with a thumb stud on the blade. It is no illusion that this knife looks like another, Spyderco-patented, one. The knife is 5.5 inches long and the blade is 2.3 inches long. Aluminum of different colors is used for the handles, inlaid with pieces of stained maple or white mother-of-pearl.

The Folder 18 series with its typical beak blades

**A lovely linerlock folder
with adjustable blade axis**

FOLDER 19

This linerlock series has blades made of stainless Sandvik 12C27 steel
in a spearpoint or Tanto
shape. The knives are
7.4 or 8 inches in total
length, have blades 3.1 or
3.3 inches long and weigh 15.2
ounces each. The handle plates are
made of anodized aluminum. The handle of the
black knife with the Teflon blade is made of carbon
fiberglass. The other knives have handle plates
made of nut burl wood.

The Herbertz Future

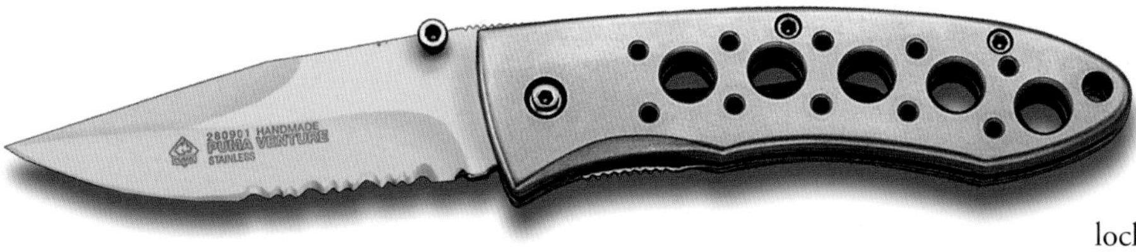

FOLDER 20

This model folding
knife has a linerlock
system with a central
push button for un-
locking. The blade is
then folded out with the
thumb stud. It is shaped like a
dagger with a large, wide false
incision on the back. The
handle is made of alumi-
num with holes in it to
reduce the weight. These
holes are closed off on the
inside with a piece of CD. The
knife is 7.7 inches in total length. The handle is 4.7
inches long and the stainless 420 steel blade is three
inches long.

FOLDER 21

The Future linerlock
series has lightweight
handle plates made of
light metal with a series of
holes for additional weight reduction. The knives
have Tanto blades made of stainless 420 steel and
the other models have clippoint blades with smooth or partially serrated edges and are matte bead

The Folder 20 with push button lock

blasted. The handles come with the original
metal color or is black anodized. The knife is 8.2
inches in total length. The handle is 4.7 inches in
length and the blade is 3.3
inches long.

FOLDER 22

This lightweight fol-
ding knife with a frame-
lock system has lightweight
metal handles and lengthwise slots instead of holes.
The blade comes either in a Tanto shape or with a

Lightweight linerlock folders

clippoint that has a smooth or partially serrated
edge. A wide steel carrying clip is on the right
handle plate. The bottom of the right handle plate
serves as a bolt rod. The blade is made of matte

The Dart

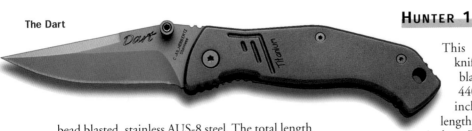

bead blasted, stainless AUS-8 steel. The total length of the knife is 8.2 inches and the handle is 4.7 inches long.

FOLDER DART

The Dart is a slim linerlock knife with an aluminum casing, and handle plates made of snake wood or of G-10 synthetic material. The bottom knife has a handle made of titanium. There is a steel carrying clip is on the right side. This knife is 6.7 inches in total length. The handle is 3.9 inches long and the blade length is 2.8 inches. The blade is made of stainless 440C steel.

FRANKLIN DESIGNER

The American knife maker Mike Franklin, alias 'HAWG! The Hawg Man,' designed this series. He has his own knife company called HAWG! in Aberdeen, Ohio where he makes 'knives with character.' He became a member of the Knifemakers' Guild in 1973 and initially

The Hunter in Macho style

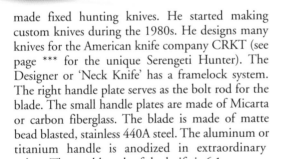

made fixed hunting knives. He started making custom knives during the 1980s. He designs many knives for the American knife company CRKT (see page *** for the unique Serengeti Hunter). The Designer or 'Neck Knife' has a framelock system. The right handle plate serves as the bolt rod for the blade. The small handle plates are made of Micarta or carbon fiberglass. The blade is made of matte bead blasted, stainless 440A steel. The aluminum or titanium handle is anodized in extraordinary colors. The total length of the knife is 6.1 inches. The blade is 3 inches long and the handle is 3.1 inches long. A cord with a carbine hook comes with the knife.

HUNTER 1

This large, heavy Bowie knife by Herbertz has a blade made of stainless 440A steel and is 10.6 inches long. The total length of the knife is 15.8 inches. The heavy guard and pommel are made of stainless steel. The pakka

The extraordinary Franklin Designer

wood handle is 5.2 inches long and is large enough to ensure a comfortable grip. The basic is extremely functional, while the featured knife has a more macho image with an over-proportioned and unusable saw on the blade back. The series of holes in the blade serves to reduce the weight.

HUNTER 2

This fixed integral hunting knife has a 'back to basics' shape. It is made of one piece of stainless 420 steel with a skeleton-shaped handle wound with a leather lace to ensure a better grip. The blade comes in a spearpoint or Tanto shape and is matte bead blasted or matte black. The knife is 12.2 inches in total length and has a blade of 5.1 inches.

The skeleton-shaped Herbertz Hunter

173

The Master Ranger model

HUNTER 3

The knife on this picture is the Junior Ranger with a blade made of stainless 440A steel and is 7.1 inches long and 12.1 inches in total length. The handle is made of pakka wood and the guard and pommel from solid brass. The 'Outlaw' looks the part. The large blade is 11 inches long and the total length of the knife is 16.8 inches. The largest Bowie knife from the Herbertz collection is the Master Ranger. This is actually a short sword, 16.8 inches long in total, with a blade length of 11.8 inches.

HUNTER 4

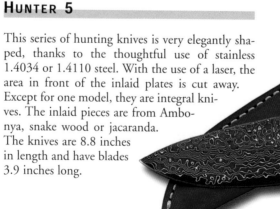

The graceful Hunter

These Hunters are more humble in dimension, but are beautifully decorated with nut burl wood or inlaid pieces of turquoise or malachite. The blade and the guard are made of stainless 440A steel. The knives are 7.3, 7.9, and 8.5 and 10.4 inches in total length. The blades are 3.15 to 3.5 inches long.

HUNTER 5

This series of hunting knives is very elegantly shaped, thanks to the thoughtful use of stainless 1.4034 or 1.4110 steel. With the use of a laser, the area in front of the inlaid plates is cut away. Except for one model, they are integral knives. The inlaid pieces are from Ambonya, snake wood or jacaranda. The knives are 8.8 inches in length and have blades 3.9 inches long.

HUNTER DAMASCUS

The Hunter knife is part of a special series made of particularly nice, 512-layer Damascus. The nut burl wood handle was selected because of the uni-

The special luxury Hunter

que wooden structure. The guard and slots around the rivets are made of nickel silver. The pins and cord slot are made of brass. The knife is 7.4 inches in total length and has a blade 3.15 inches long. The lower knife was made in a limited edition of only 99 pieces. The blade is 0.16 inches thick and made of 31-layer Damascus. The handle is made of Brazilian rose wood and the guards from nickel silver. The knife is 10.2 inches in total length. The blade is 4.7 inches long. Both knives come with a leather sheath and the bottom knife comes with a certificate of authenticity and a wooden chest as well.

Damascus Hunter

The unique skinner
by Herbertz

either of aluminum in a white or anodized black color, or with inlaid plates of hard wood. The Tanto blade only comes with a smooth edge. The Spectac is 7.7 inches in total length, has a stainless steel 440A steel blade three inches long and a handle 4.7 inches long.

HUNTER VILLER

This special skinning knife from Herbertz has a distinctive blade, designed for the task. Skinning shot game with such a blade is much easier than with an ordinary knife. The length of this knife is 8.15 inches and the blade is 3.5 inches long. A part of the back of the blade is ribbed to ensure that the thumb or index finger will not slip. The handle is made of nut burl or stag horn.

The Spectac by Jermer

JERMER FRAMETAC

Helmut Jermer is a well-known German knife designer who has designed various models for Herbertz, Puma and other knife manufacturers. The Frametac knife has, as its name would suggest, a framelock system. The right handle plate serves as the bolt rod for the blade. The skeleton handle, just as with the Tanto blade, is made of stainless 440A steel. The smooth or partially serrated edge is matte bead blasted. A carrying clip is attached to the right handle plate. The diagonal slots in the handle serve to reduce the weight. The knife is 7.7 inches in total length and has a blade three inches long.

JERMER SPECTAC

The Spectac was designed by Helmut Jermer as well and has a linerlock system with an unbolting stud in the left handle plate. The handle is made

MILITARY 1

The Jermer Frametac

Herbertz sells various military knives in different sizes. The knife in this picture is an original Glock field knife. The blade is 6.7 inches in length and the saw serration on the blade back is 3.5 inches long. The total length of the knife is 11.9 inches. The handle is made of shock resistant synthetic material, as is the accompanying sheath. The second model, the new ACK (Advanced Combat Knife), has a special synthetic handle for voltage isolation so that it can cut electric cables without any problems. This is the purpose of the false incision on the top of the blade. A wire cutter can be improvised using the hole in the blade and the notch in the sheath. The total length of the ACK is 12 inches and the blade is 6.9 inches long. The width of the blade is 1.18 inches and it weighs 7.76 ounces. The knife weighs 15.17 ounces with its sheath. The third military combat knife, the Combat, has a matte black handle and blade. The special Cordura sheath has two closable front parts. The total length of the knife is 12.6 inches and the blade is 7.5 inches long.

Military knife from
the Herbertz collection

The heavy military combat knife by Herbertz

MILITARY 2

This large military combat and survival knife has a blade 7.9 inches long and 0.20 inches thick. The total length of the knife is 13 inches. A wire cutter can be made with the hole in the blade and the notch in the foot of the sheath. Attaching the sheath is easy thanks to a quick-lock that can be disconnected from the belt. The Cordura sheath has a large, closeable front part. The hollow handle is made of aluminum.

SAILOR

The Sailor is an extremely practical knife for use on board a sailboat or yacht. The knife has a ergonomic handle and a blade with a partial serration with which ropes can easily be cut. The long slot

A skeleton Knife by Herbertz

in the blade can easily loosen a stuck slip hook. The marlin spike on the back of the handle is well suited for slashing and weaving clusters and lines. The blade is made of stainless 440A-steel and is 2.8 inches long. The total length of the Sailor is 6.9 inches and the light metal handle is 4.1 inches long. This knife comes with a brightly colored cord.

SKELETON KNIFE 1

The skeleton knives from Herbertz consist of a hollow handle made of stainless steel in which notches or holes are drilled and stock remo-

ved in order to reduce the weight. The knives have top-serving framelock systems, so that a separate linerlock rod is not necessary. The blade is made of AISI 420 steel. The skeleton series knife is 7 inches in total length and has a blade 3.9 inches long.

Herbertz Sailor

SKELETON KNIFE 2

The skeleton series consists of somewhat larger knives with handle lengths of 4.3 inches and total lengths of 7.2 inches. This series also has a framelock system, especially visible at the bottom of the knife. The blade as well as the handle is made of bead blasted stainless 440A steel.

STILETTO 1

This stiletto series has stainless spearpoint blades with smooth or partially, serrated edges. The handles of the stilettos are of ergonomically shaped light metal. The blade can be opened to the side with spring pressure through the thumb stud right behind the blade pivot. The total lengths of these stilettos are 7.75 inches. The handles are 4.7 inches in length and the blades are 3.03 inches long. Stilettos are prohibited completely in some countries. In some European countries stilettos are only prohibited if the blade is a certain length or width.

Skeleton Knife

The Stiletto Spearpoint

STILETTO 2

This similar series of stilettos has spearpoint blades. The handles are made of aluminum with lengthwise slots to reduce the weight. These knives also have thumb studs in order to open the blade sideways with spring pressure. These knives are 8.1 inches in total length and have blades 3.35 inches long.

SURVIVAL KNIFE

This large survival knife is world famous thanks to the Rambo movies. Sylvester Stallone defe-

TOOL 1

This Herbertz Multi-Tool is a mini tool-box. It incorporates combination needle nose pliers and a wire-cutter and a cross point screwdriver in the right leg of the tool, a can opener, an Allen key for the bit set and a flat screwdriver. A combination file is in the left leg, as well as a fish de-hooker, a saw blade, a clippoint blade, a large screwdriver, a mini screwdriver and a small blade. The Multi-Tool comes with a Cordura sheath.

The Stiletto 2

The large survival knife

ated complete armies with only this knife between his teeth. The blade is made of stainless steel and is 7.5 inches long. The top of the blade back is furnished with a wavy saw edge and in the middle of the blade back is a series of dangerous saw teeth standing upright. The total length of the knife is 12.5 inches. Two removable pins in the guard can be used in many different ways. There is space for matches, fishhooks, nylon cords, a wire saw and other survival gear in the hollow handle. There are two closable front parts in the Cordura sheath, one of which contains a compass.

Multi-Tool 109000 by Herbertz

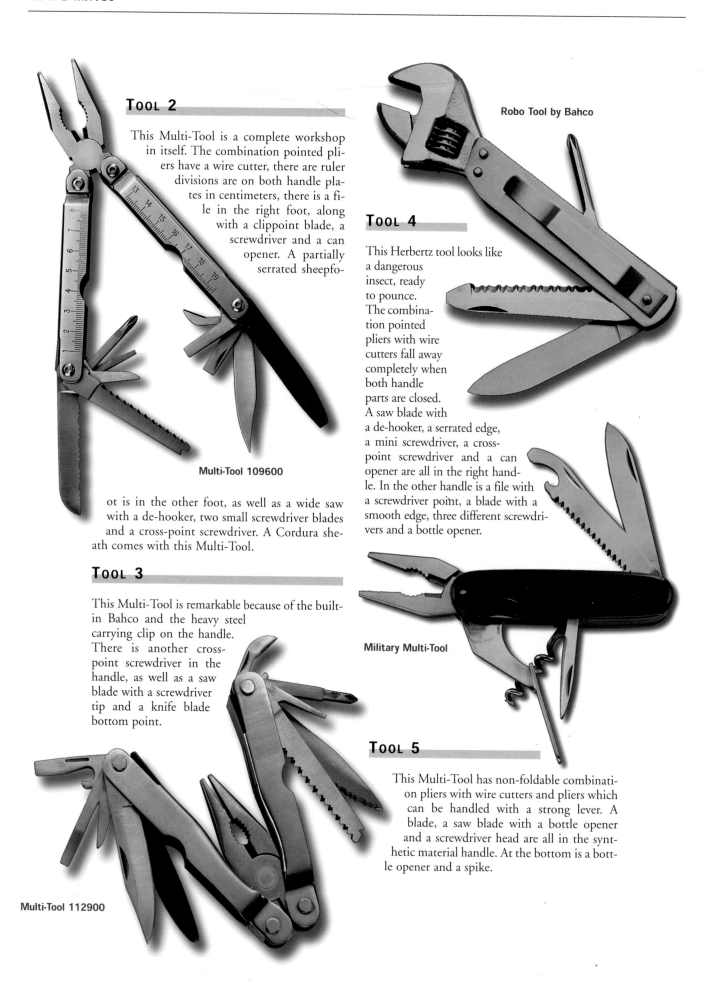

Tool 2

This Multi-Tool is a complete workshop in itself. The combination pointed pliers have a wire cutter, there are ruler divisions are on both handle plates in centimeters, there is a file in the right foot, along with a clippoint blade, a screwdriver and a can opener. A partially serrated sheepfo-

Multi-Tool 109600

ot is in the other foot, as well as a wide saw with a de-hooker, two small screwdriver blades and a cross-point screwdriver. A Cordura sheath comes with this Multi-Tool.

Tool 3

This Multi-Tool is remarkable because of the built-in Bahco and the heavy steel carrying clip on the handle. There is another cross-point screwdriver in the handle, as well as a saw blade with a screwdriver tip and a knife blade bottom point.

Multi-Tool 112900

Robo Tool by Bahco

Tool 4

This Herbertz tool looks like a dangerous insect, ready to pounce. The combination pointed pliers with wire cutters fall away completely when both handle parts are closed. A saw blade with a de-hooker, a serrated edge, a mini screwdriver, a cross-point screwdriver and a can opener are all in the right handle. In the other handle is a file with a screwdriver point, a blade with a smooth edge, three different screwdrivers and a bottle opener.

Military Multi-Tool

Tool 5

This Multi-Tool has non-foldable combination pliers with wire cutters and pliers which can be handled with a strong lever. A blade, a saw blade with a bottle opener and a screwdriver head are all in the synthetic material handle. At the bottom is a bottle opener and a spike.

Throwing Knife by Herbertz

THROWING KNIFE

Herbertz also has an assortment of throwing knives for professional use and a Blitz bear killer stainless steel series consists of a small throwing knife 5.9 inches in length. The larger knife at 8.7 inches and the largest, 9.4 inches. These specially balanced knives come with a handy sheath. Throwing knives are completely forbidden in some countries and in others, such as the Netherlands, they are only allowed with special permission.

HILL KNIVES
www.hillknives.com

The finest handmade knives

The emblem of Hill Knives

Hill Knives was established in 1980 by father and son Van den Heuvel from Rotterdam. The English translation of the surname 'Heuwel' is Hill. Both had technical educations as toolmakers. Father and son initially only made a few knives for their own use. Over time, however, this hobby expanded to making knives for friends and acquaintances. The orders continued to increase until they decided to switch over to fulltime knife pro-

duction. Albert van den Heuvel Junior took over the business side a few years later and started specializing in folding knives.

Not only does this company provide superior work, but their etching department can pass the test of critics. Hill knife advocates can by found at a number of well-known and prominent companies such as Browning weapons, the luxury outlets of Asprey in London and New York as well as the SIG weapons factory in

A beautiful hunting knife in a semi-integral version

Switzerland. Hill Knives manufactures a special commemorative model of the SIG P210 pistol with a matching and even numbered folding knife. The engraving work on this knife is done by Belgian weapon engravers Alain Lovenberg, Eduard Vos and Geoffroy Delahaut. Father and son have reason to be proud of the beautiful hunting and folding knife that they custom-made for Prince Bernhard, the husband of the former Dutch Queen Juliana.

Hill Knives makes military knives as well. This is the KCT knife (KCT is the Nederlandse Korps Commando Troepen; Dutch Corps Commando Troops) and its forerunner, the Break-Out knife, for the helicopter crew of the Royal Dutch Air Force. Hill Knives will have been in business for 25 years in 2005 and will produce a special anniversary knife or a special numbered anniversary set. Hill Knives only uses valuable Hitachi ATS-34 steel and special Damascus steel. Clients can have virtually any knife made here. The photos of Hill Knives that follow were made by the Dutch photographer, Bob van Tienhoven.

The No. 44 Dagger in a half-integrated version

A beautiful 'Gentleman's folder'

DAGGER NO. 44

This is a boot dagger. A 24kt gold lion head was engraved on the guard by Geoffroy Delahaut. The 4.96 inch blade is made of stainless ATS-34 steel and ground on both sides. Its total

The No. 3 Hunter by Hill Knives

length is 9.65 inches and the dagger weighs 7.4 ounces. The handle plates are made of mammoth ivory and attached with screws engraved in the same style as the bolster.

A lovely engraved hunting knife

GENTLEMAN NO. 32

This graceful folding knife has a backlock system. The blade, as well as the casing, is made of ATS-34 steel. The total length of the knife is 6.4 inches, the blade is 2.6 inches long, the handle is 3.8 inches long and it weighs 2.6 ounces. The handle plates are made of Cocobolo wood. The graceful, flowing bolster was engraved in the English style by Eduard Vos.

HUNTER NO. 3

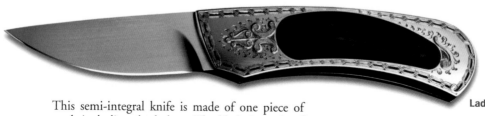

This semi-integral knife is made of one piece of steel, including the bolster. The blade is made of ATS-34 steel and is 3.82 inches long. The handle is

4.25 inches long and is made of desert ironwood. The handle plates are attached with decorated pins. The knife's total length is 8.07 inches and it weighs 4.9 ounces. The Birmingham-arabesque engraving on the bolster is made by Eduard Vos.

HUNTER NO. 46

This Hunter is a fully integral knife, made of one strip of stainless ATS-34 steel with the surplus material stock removed. The blade is 4 inches long and the knife is 8.5 inches in total length. The handle is 4.4 inches long and is made of desert iron

wood. The guard, pommel and handle screws are all engraved in the Old English style by Alain Lovenberg.

INTERFRAME HK-A02

This folding knife has a blade and casing made of stainless ATS-34 steel. The blade length is 1.85 inches. It is locked with a backlock system. The length of the casing is 2.87 inches. The total length of the opened knife is 4.72 inches. The engravings on the handle were done by Geoffroy Delahaut and the fantasy figures are made of 18kt gold. The inlaid piece in the handle is fossilized mammoth ivory more than 20,000 years old.

A beautifully done Lady Interframe folder

A 5th Pocket model HK-66 with 38 Top Wesselton diamonds

Alain Loveberg. The engravings on both of the handle plates were inlaid with 32 diamonds of Top Wesselton VVSI quality and ground with 58 facets.

This version of the 5th Pocket Knife was beautifully engraved with stylish plant motifs. The inlaid plates on the casing are made of mother-of-pearl.

The 5th Pocket Knife model has strained engravings, alternated with an exuberantly styled rose on the blade pivot. Nineteen Top Wesselton diamonds were placed in the both sides of the casing in the middle of the engraved rose gold.

THE SCORPION & THE COBRA NO. 49

This lovely hunting knife has a blade made of stainless ATS 34 steel, 5.51 inches long. The total length is 11.02 inches. The guard was engraved on both sides by Geoffroy Delahaut. An 18kt gold Cobra is depicted on the right side. A golden scorpion is on the left side. The handle is made of snakewood, attached with beautifully engraved screws. Snakewood comes from the wig tree from South America, Suriname and French-Guinea. The tree is called Hububalli there

and the Latin name is Loxopterygium Sogotii. The color changes from yellow to red-brown. It is a very hard type of wood that has a texture ressembling snake skin.

A beautiful gold engraved hunting knife

VIRGIN NO. 37

This folding knife has an astrological decoration. The bolster has a relief engraving with a golden frame and a golden depiction of the Virgo symbol, adorned with an emerald. On the right side of the bolster is a monogram of the owner, inlaid in gold with an inset ruby. These engravings were done by Alain Lovenberg. The blade and casing are of ATS-34 steel. The blade is 2.6 inches long, the total length of the knife is 6.38 inches and it weighs 2.6 ounces. The handle is 3.78 inches long and the handle plates are made of mammoth ivory. The blade is locked with a backlock system.

The No. 37 Virgin folder

Richard van Dijk of Hoiho Knives

When he bought a book about making knives in 1980 he realized he could make a living at it, and he has been making several knives every year in his free time. In 1996, he started forging Damasteel by himself.

More than thirty-two years of making and repairing jewels gave him a head start. Initially, he forged his knives from old saw blades and files, but he slowly moved on to stainless 440C steel. Over the last eight years, he has mostly been using Damasteel he forged himself from packets of L6-, 1095, O1 and 5160-steel, combined with old chainsaws, motorbike chains and steel cables. He hardens all of his Damasteel and stainless steel blades himself. He hardens the different parts of the blade separately, making the edge harder than the blade back. He makes the knives entirely by himself, with the exception of the Celtic wood carvings. The leather sheaths are shaped while wet and then impregnated with wax to make them harder and waterproof.

Damask Bowie

HOIHO KNIVES

www.hoihoknives.com

Hoiho is not the name of the knife maker, but it is what the yellow-eyed-penguin is called in Maori in New Zealand. The knife maker's name is Richard van Dijk. He was born and grew up in the Netherlands, but immigrated to New Zealand in 1979 where he established himself in Harwood, close to the Otago harbor.

He had been fascinated with knives since an early age.

BOWIE

The edge and blade back of this large knife are made of two pieces of 135-layer forced Damascus. This means that one rod is turned clockwise and the other counterclockwise. The middle part of the blade consists of two strips of cable Damascus with crude pieces of saw blades sandwiched between them and smelted together. The blade is tempered so that the edge is harder than the blade back, which ensures a more flexible blade. The total length of the knife is 14.8 inches and the blade is 10.4 inches long. The handle is made of stag horn from New Zealand deer and is attached to the bolster and sterling silver pommel. The sheath is made of leather and painted with natural plant extracts.

Mediterranean Dirk

The Persian Knife by Richard van Dijk

MEDITERRANEAN DIRK

This dagger was forged from 144-layer Damasteel and finished by filing. The handle is made of ebony with sterling silver for the bolster and the pommel. The knife is 13 inches in total length. Its leather sheath is decorated with sterling silver.

PERSIAN KNIFE

sists of two rods of nine layers each smelted using the same technique, which was then repeated with four rods. The blade is 10 inches long and the knife's total length is 15.9 inches. The New Zealand walnut wood handle was impregnated under vacuum with linseed oil, glue and turpentine. The bolster and pommel are made of subuichi, which consists of 75 percent copper and 25 percent silver. The sheath is made of 0.14 inch thick leather, tanned and painted with plant extracts.

Sax Knife

This Persian knife has a Damasteel blade, forged from 520-layer steel. The blade back was finished by filing. The length of the blade is 5 inches and the total length of the knife 9.4 inches. The handle is made of rata wood, an tree indigenous to New Zealand. It is impregnated with linseed oil and has a bolster made of sterling silver. The sheath is made of leather.

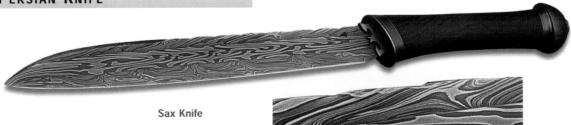

SAX KNIFE OR SCRAMASAX

The blade of this large knife was forged from four rods of Damasteel. The edge and blade back are made of forced Damasteel. The center piece con-

SCOTTISH DIRK

The 17.7 inch Scottish dagger has a 11.8 inch blade of 136-layer Damasteel, finished with filing. The ebony handle is carved in a Celtic motif. The

Scottish dagger

bolster, pommel and adornments on the leather sheath are made of sterling silver. At the top of the pommel is a large citrine, a yellowish variety of quartz. The sheath is made of wood. A boot dagger, or Sgian Dubh, goes with it.

SGIAN DUBH

Like the Scottish Dirk, this boot dagger has a blade of 40-layer Damasteel, adorned on one side by filing work. The blade is 4.1 inches long and the total length is 8.5 inches. The handle is made of

Details of the Scottish Dirk and, the Sgian Dubh

stag horn from New Zealand deer. The guard, bolster and pommel, made of sterling silver, are reminiscent of Van Dijk's previous occupation as a silver smith. The sheath is made of 0.14 inch thick leather, tanned and painted with plant extracts. The adornments on the sheath are made of sterling silver as well.

A lovely example of a Sgian Dubh, or boot dagger

HONS

www.knife.cz/noziri/hons/

The logo of the Bohemian knife makers, left and the logo of Karel Hons as it is on his knives, right

Karel Hons has actually always been a full time knife maker since 1990. He has his own workshop and owns two shops. He is also a member of Bohemia Cutallatores, the association of the Czech and Moravian knife makers. Karel has been to many knife exhibitions in Europe with his knives and have won many prizes through the years, including Knife Maker of the Year in 1999. He makes the swords for the honor guard of former Czech President Václav Havel. Hons makes his custom knives from stainless RWL-34-, AK-5 and AK-9 steel. He prefers to use stag horn, hard wood types, burl wood and Micarta as handle material. For the sheaths he always uses first class material. Other than making handmade knives he also provides a sharpening service for knives, scissors, kitchen knives and chisels.

HUNTER

The Hunter has a main blade and separate folding blade made of stainless 440C steel. A large section of the blade back was decorated with filing work. The saw blade can be used as a wood saw, but it is actually meant for cutting

**The Hunter with
a folder saw blade**

horns off shot game. The handle is made of stag horn and the bolster is of 440C steel. The blade is 3.9 inches long and the total length of the knife is 8.6 inches.

POCKET KNIFE

Karel Hons made the blade of this folding knife from stainless RWL-34 steel. It is 3.5 inches long and locks with a linerlock system. The handle is 5.1 inches long and the total length of the opened knife is 8.6 inches. Hons used stag horn for the handle,

Pocket Knife by Karel Hons

engraved beautifully in the shape of a wild boar with plant motifs on the sides. The bolster of this knife is made of Damasteel.

POCKET KNIFE

This folding knife has a linerlock system on the blade as well as a folding wood saw blade. The blade is made of RWL-34 steel and is 3.9 inches in total length. The handle is 4.7 inches long and the total length of the knife is 8.6 inches. Karel Hons made the handle from stag horn and the bolster from stainless steel.

HORN
deshorn@usa.net

Des Horn is a custom knife maker from Newlands in Cape Town, South Africa. He was originally a dentist, but has been making handmade knives since 1965. He is also an active marksman. He prefers working with Damasteel and special ATS-34 steel

DES HORN
CUSTOM KNIFES

5 Wenlock Road
Newlands 770(
Cape Town, South Africa
Tel/Fax: +27 21 671 579!
E-mail: deshorn@usa.ne

Des Horn business card

which he gets tempered in liquid nitrogen by a specialist to a hardness of about 61 HRC. In the beginning, he focused on hunting knives, but in the last twenty years he has been specializing in folding knives. He uses linerlock and backlock systems for his folding knives, but he has used the ball Lock system on a few knives as well. Des Horn takes part in knife exhibitions in South Africa, Australia, France, Germany and Italy. He is a member of the South African Knifemakers' Guild, the German Knifemakers' Guild (DMG) and is a Maestro in the Italian Guild of Knifemakers.

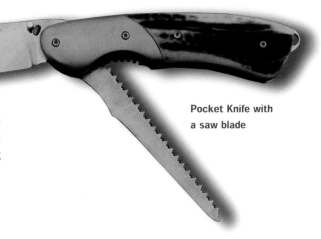

**Pocket Knife with
a saw blade**

MODEL 450

Model 450 is a folding knife with a linerlock system. The blade and handle plates are made of

Model 450 Damascus folder

stainless Damasteel with a particularly beautiful drop structure. The length of the opened knife is 6.5 inches, the blade is 3 inches and the handle is 3.6 inches long. The screw of the blade pivot has a particularly beautiful rose motif. A shackle is at the back of the handle.

The beautiful, colorful Model Alphen 450

MODEL ALPHEN 450

The handle of Model Alphen 450 has a very beautiful color pattern in different metallic tints. Very unique are the handle plates made of nickel Damascus and colored with deep etching liquid. The blade is made of stainless Damasteel with a unique fan structure. The Alpha 450 has a linerlock

Model Goldinlay backlock Damascus knife

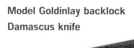

system. The opened knife is 6.5 inches long and the blade is 2.9 inches in length with a handle of 3.6 inches.

GOLDINLAY BACKLOCK

This folding knife has, as its name indicates, a backlock system. The blade is 2.5 inches long and is made of Damasteel. The handle is made of titanium, decorated with a gold motif. The inlaid piece in the handle is a 4.6 million year old plate of Gideon Meteorite. The total length of the opened knife is 5.25 inches and the handle is 2.9 inches long.

HBP

When looking at it for the first time, the HBP seems to have a strange shape: the angles of its slim and trim stain-

less Damasteel were ground on a slant, the stainless Damasteel blade has a very sharp spearpoint, and there is a large shackle at the back of the handle. The length of the opened knife is 5.4 inches. The blade is 2.4 inches long and the handle is 3 inches in length. The knife has a linerlock made of titanium Grade V. The least visible, but most unique feature of this knife is its lack of a blade pivot hole. The blade turns on an axis which is fully integrated into the inside of the handle. The blind hole on the inside is extremely difficult to make, as it must be fitted to within a hundredth of a millimeter on both sides of the handle so that both indentations lie directly in opposition to each other. This special concept is very difficult, but extraordinarily strong.

SMALLBALL GOLDINLAY

The Smallball Goldinlay is a unique variation on the linerlock shape. A round spring ball is on the right handle plate. When this is depressed, the linerlock rod in the casing shifts to the inside, so that the blade can be released and folded in. The blade is made of

The pointy Model HBP knife

stainless Damasteel and has a beautiful structure, somewhere between drop and ladder Damascus. The bolster is made of titanium with a complicated line structure, inlaid with gold. The handle is made of mother-of-pearl. The ball of the locking system is made of silicone nitride, a material used in space with 91 HRC, which is almost as hard as a diamond. The total length of the opened knife is 6.5 inches, the blade length is 2.9 inches and the handle is 3.6 inches long.

SMALLBALL THIERS BLUE

Thiers Blue is a beautiful, slim folding knife, 7.7 inches in total length. The length of the blade is 3.3 inches and the handle is 4.4 inches long. The blade is made of stainless Damasteel and colored with different colored etching liquid. The handle plates are made of mammoth ivory

Logo of Flip Horvat

career as a knife maker. His designs are based on the ancient Damascus technique, combined with flowing forms and natural materials. Every Horvath knife is a unique design with its own original character.

Smallball Goldinlay

that is more than fifteen thousand years old. The bolster is unique: made of a piece of Gideon Meteorite that is 4.6 million years old. Is this really a new knife?

HORVATH
fh.filip@azet.sk

ALL STEEL KNIFE

This is a classic example of an integral knife. It is a single strip of Damasteel, made of pieces of chainsaw. The handle is shaped like a long, folded pair of tongs with a deep contour serving as a guard. The blade is 3.9 inches in length and the handle is 3.7 inches long. The sheath is made of wood and covered with leather.

Thiers Blue Damascus knife

Flip Horvath was born in Bratislava, Slovakia in 1970, where he got his training as an ornamental blacksmith. Through his work as a renovator of historical art, he became interested in the art of forging knives and swords. He was especially interested in historical assembling and manufacturing techniques. By making replicas for museums and exhibitions, he was able to develop his own forging techniques. In 1997, he took part in a knife fair for the first time and this was the start of his fulltime

ANTELOPE KNIFE

A distinctive feature of this knife is the beautiful structure of the Damascus blade. Forging a blade with this type of motif is an exceptional achievement. The handle is made of antelope horn and is 4.7 inches in length. The blade is 4.65 inches long and the total length of the knife is 9.4 inches. The cow leather sheath has a wooden lining and a pressed motif of an antelope at the end.

The All Steel Knife made from Damasteel

Antelope Knife with
a wonderful Damascus blade

ANTELOPE KNIFE

The handle of this knife is made of the horn of a sabre antelope and the bolster is made of a piece of Amboyna wood. The length of the handle is 4.8 inches and the blade, of wild Damascus, is 5.4 inches long. A deep contour in the blade serves as a type of guard. A leather sheath with a wooden lining comes with the knife.

BUMPKIN KNIFE

Bumpkin means 'awkward' or 'oaf,' but this is not the case with this knife. It has a graceful arch shape and the solid

Bumpkin Knife

handle does not spoil this effect. The Damascus steel for this integral knife was forged from pieces of chainsaw. The handle has the typical Horvath groove that serves as the guard. The small handle is made of owangol wood. The

The pommel of the Hyeronimus Bosch Knife

blade is 3.425 inches long and the total length of the knife is 7.3 inches.

HYERONIMUS KNIFE

This knife was dedicated to the famous Dutch medieval painter, Hieronymus Bosch. The blade is 3.9 inches long and was forged from beautiful Damasteel. The handle is made of an engraved walrus tusk and is 4.5 inches long. The pommel is

Another example of
a knife with a handle made from antelope horn

in the shape of a satyr's head being swallowed by a large predator fish. The knife is 8.4 inches in total length and it lies, with its beautifully decorated sheath, in a cherrywood case.

MULBERRY KNIFE

This knife got its name from the mulberry tree (Morus alba or Morus rubra) wood from which its handle is made. This integral knife is 7.75 inches long and was forged from pieces of a chainsaw. It has Horvath's characteristic finger

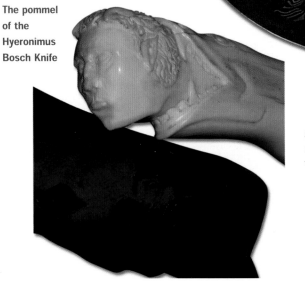

Hyeronimus Bosch Knife

slots. The blade is 3.9 inches long. The accompanying sheath is made of painted cow leather with a wooden lining.

I

absolutely childproof and cannot be opened by accident. A carry clip can be attached to the shackle at the end of the handle.

In order to open the knife, push the safety slideback with the thumb. Then, with the same thumb, push up the bolt rod at the front end. Then push the blade out from the handle sideways. Then hook the

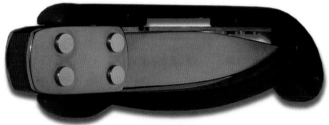

ID 2000 Flip Knife

IMAGICAL
www.flipknives.com

The emblem of Imagical

index finger around the hinge block and swing the blade out 180 degrees until it latches into the lock. In order to close the blade again, push the safety slide back to the front. To lock the knife: first push the safety slide to the back, then lift the bolt rod with the thumb. The blade will swing back inside with a click. The safety slide must then be pushed forward to lock the knife again.

The blade of the Flip Knife is 3 inches long and is made of C70-Sheffield carbon steel, hollow ground and tempered to 58 HRC. It turns around a hinge block made of Zytel and stainless steel bolster plates.

The Sheffield ID 2000 Flip Knife, designed by Imagical Design, is made in Sheffield, England, the center of the knife industry until the end of the nineteenth century. Stainless steel is said to have been developed in Sheffield. The unique Flip Knife can be opened and closed with one hand, regardless of whether the user is left or right handed. The knife has an extremely simple construction and no internal locking mechanism. Because of this, it cannot get stuck due to excessive dirt or sand. Also, the closed knife is easy to clean: it can be washed as it is or with the dishes. The handle is made of Zytel or carbon fiberglass and thus is strong and lightweight. Thanks to the bolt rod in the handle, the harder you push, the firmer the blade stays locked. When the blade is closed and the safety slide is in position, the knife is

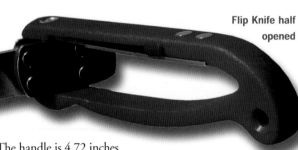

Flip Knife half opened

The handle is 4.72 inches long and the total length of the open knife is 7.8 inches. The Flip Knife weighs 2.9 ounces. The bolt rod is made of stainless 420 steel and the name and patent numbers are printed on it. The vertical running blade pivot is 0.157 inches thick and turns in a stainless steel casing with a brass mantle. The rivets of

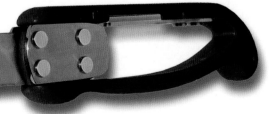

Opened and locked Flip Knife

the hinge block and the bolt rod are made of brass. The Flip Knife is patented in Europe, Japan, the United States and South Africa.

ISMAYLOV

www.rusartknife.urbannet.ru/gallery.html

Yashar Ismaylov was born in 1967 in a small town in Georgia but soon after, his family moved to Moscow, where he was influenced by his grandfather, an applied arts teacher, and by his father, an architect. While still in primary school, he made pen knives which he sold to his fellow students and teachers.

Yashar Ismaylov with his son. His master sign is shown here on the top right and below is that the emblem of the Russian Knifemakers' Guild

After completing his education at the Arts Academy he went to the Technical Aviation School in Moscow. Remarkably enough, he then took up the jewelry trade and learned the techniques and skills that would be so useful to him later on. Yashar Ismaylov eventually became a knife maker. A sixteen minute documentary entitled, *Nugget,* about his work was broadcast in Russia. The knives shown here were photographed by Sergey Baranov and/or Valentin Overchenko.

FAREWELL, THE WEAPON

This knife is one of Ismaylov's favorites. He compares it with the work of the Old Masters. It has different names or nicknames, such as 'The Thinker,' 'The Beginning of a New Civilization' or

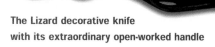

The Lizard decorative knife with its extraordinary open-worked handle

An extraordinary dagger

'The First Weapon of Mankind.' Ismaylov made it in 2003. The blade was forged by Alexander Kurbatov and processed by Andrey Koreshkov from ST3/CT3 steel and 925. The sculpted male gorilla is a particularly beautiful piece of art.

Detail of the Lizard

LIZARD

This knife was made for the exhibition at the Kremlin in 2001. The blade is made of Damasteel forged from 252 layers by smith and knife maker Alexander Kurbatov from Tula. The turned handle is made of solid 925 silver. Ismaylov modeled the handle on a similar one he started work on years earlier, while visiting his friend, Vladimir Tyut, in France. A few years later, Ismaylov tackled it again and this is the result. The total length of this knife is 8.3 inches and the blade is 4.1 inches long. Ismaylov spent three months working on this knife, which is currently in a private collection.

OPEN, THE SPECIAL SUB-GROUP'

Ismaylov's knives make people stop and ask themselves, 'What does he mean with this?' This is the case with the knife shown here. Ismaylov is said to have been inspired by athe film *Open! The Police!* The knife displays a dark, characteristically Russian humor, artfully playing upon fears of the secret police and paramilitaries which have haunted Russian history from Tsarist days until more recently when police vans or 'Black Marias' rolled through the streets after dark. The irony is, of course, that the 'Open, the Special Sub-group' knife is actually bottle opener, suitable for festive, happy occasions. What is Ismaylov trying to say with his knife? "Eat, drink and be merry while you can because you never know when they will come for you. So, let's open another bottle and toast to your health!" The blade was forged of 252-layer Damascus by Alexander Kurbatov. The engraving work was done by Sergey Danilin; Yashar Ismaylov made the sculpture. The figure on the pommel is made of 925 silver, oxidized to make it look old. A jasper and a tiger's eye were worked into the fittings. The total length of the knife is 7.4 inches and the blade is 2.4 inches long.

The remarkable 'Open, the Special Sub-group' knife

nian eucalyptus, Norwegian birch wood and different types of horn. He also uses legal ivory, mammoth ivory, mother-of-pearl, stingray and shark skin for his sheaths. Decorations, pommels and guards are often made of alpaca, silver, Damasteel or stainless steel. His sheaths are made of leather, stingray, shark, snake, lizard and crocodile hide.

AFRICA

This beautiful hunting knife has a blade of 300-layer stainless, wavy Damasteel forged by Lubos Smidrkal. The length of the blade is 3.5 inches. The handle is made of thuya wood, set off with a bolster and a pommel made of mammoth ivory. The total length is 7.7

JANČA

www.knife.cz/noziri/janca

Zdeněk Janča has been preoccupied with knives ever since he was young. He was a trained carpenter, but it was soon clear to him that his heart was not in it. He wanted to do something creative and switched to restoration. He found that working with steel was much more interesting than working with wood and he decided to take the plunge. Initially, he occupied himself with sheath-making and worked leather on a daily basis. Over time, he progressed to forging steel and assembling and finishing knives.

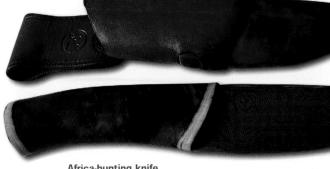

Hunter of the Woods

inches. The bottom part of the accompanying sheath is made of thuya wood as well and the top part is leather.

HUNTER OF THE WOODS

This knife has an interesting blade that was forged from pieces of cable. Its structure can clearly be seen in the steel. The length of the blade is 4.7 inches. Janča used horn from the Indian sambar deer for the handle and alpaca for the bolster and pommel. The sheath is made of cow leather.

PRE-HISTORIC

This knife has a blade made of Swedish stainless Damasteel with a fine torsion structure length of 3.3 inches. The handle is made from the fossilized horn of a European

Africa-hunting knife

All of his knives consist of three parts: the blade, the handle and the sheath. Only special material is used and he is prepared to go to considerable effort to find it. Stainless steel such as 440C, D2, ATS34 and RWL-34 or modern powder steel is always used. He uses tropical wood types such as Ceylon ebony wood, grenadille wood, zebra wood, Tree of Life wood, Tasma-

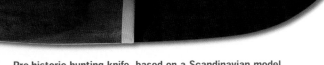

Pre-historic hunting knife, based on a Scandinavian model

**The Bat knife looks
a bit like a bat**

deer. The bolsters and pommels are made of white polished mammoth ivory. The total length of the knife is 6.7 inches. The accompanying sheath has a bottom piece made of the same fossilized horn and mammoth ivory and a top part made of leather.

THE BAT

The knife 'The Bat' has a blade made of carbon steel forged in the ancient Japanese style. The length of the blade is 4.1 inches and the total length of the knife 8.3 inches. Janča used the hide of a stingray for the handle. The ring-shaped guard is made of stainless Damasteel. The sheath is made of leather and gives, because of its shape and stitching, the illusion of a bat wing.

THE TOOTH

This hunting knife with the appropriate name of The Tooth, has a handle made of the horn of an Indian water buffalo with the fossilized canine tooth of a prehistoric cave bear. The blade is made of carbon steel and forged in the Japanese style. The length of the blade is 3.7 inches. A piece of water buffalo horn was worked into the bottom of the accompanying sheath and the rest is made of cow leather. The knife is 6.7 inches in total length.

JOBIN, JACQUES
http://pages.globetrotter.net/jjobin

Jacques Jobin was born in 1951 and lives in Levis, a town south of the beautiful Saint Lawrence River and

Photo: Louise Bilodeau

The Canadian knife maker Jacques Jobin

opposite Quebec City in Canada. He started making knives in 1985. He has always loved working jewels, cut and ground stones and has tried many other techniques. This experience with jewels comes in very handy when making his knives, but he only uses simple tools and raw material. Each knife he makes is unique. His designs are based on his feelings at the time. No mold is used, not even for his folding knives, which means he has to

Can you guess why this knife is called the Tooth?

The Battlestar fantasy knife

BATTLESTAR

The Battlestar knife looks like something out of a science fiction movie. In fact, it looks like a spaceship. Jacques let his imagination run free here with the theme 'knife and outer space.' This knife has a few remarkable features: two miniature rocket launchers, complete with the rockets and a 635 nm laser diode. The blade is made of stainless ATS-34 steel. The handle and the 'command control' built around it are made of anodized aluminum. The total length of the knife is 18 inches, large enough for it to serve as a mini-space ship.

CAMP KNIFE

The beautiful Camp Knife has a more earthly design, with a unique blade back in a long, tight, flowing line. Jacques chose a laminate of CPM 10V powder steel for this integral knife with nickel Damascus on both sides, for high contrast. The blade was made by his friend Darryl Meier. The handle is made of the long tooth or horn of a narwhal.

FANCY DAMASCUS

This knife looks futuristic because of the shape of the handle. The blade is of nickel Damascus with a drop pattern and can be taken out of the anodized titanium handle, covered with plate of mammoth ivory from Siberia. The length of the knife is 11 inches.

FANCY HUNTER BOWIE

improvise often. Many of his knives are slim, but not extravagant. His hi-tech knives, look more like spaceships than cutting tools. Jacques Jobin makes 10 to 30 knives per year, ranging from miniature knives to swords. He does all the work on the knives himself, but

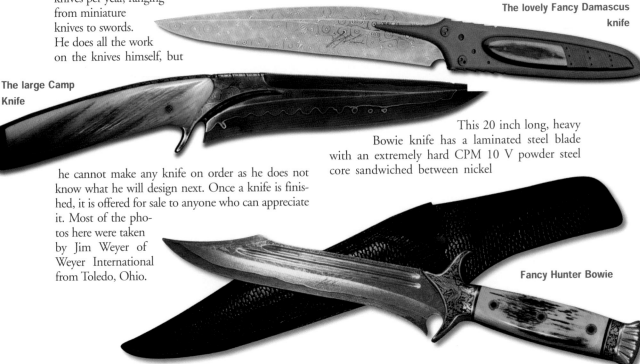

The lovely Fancy Damascus knife

The large Camp Knife

he cannot make any knife on order as he does not know what he will design next. Once a knife is finished, it is offered for sale to anyone who can appreciate it. Most of the photos here were taken by Jim Weyer of Weyer International from Toledo, Ohio.

This 20 inch long, heavy Bowie knife has a laminated steel blade with an extremely hard CPM 10 V powder steel core sandwiched between nickel

Fancy Hunter Bowie

203

The futuristic Pegasus with laser fireballs and .22 LR weapon on board

Damasteel, made by Darryl Meier. The guard and pommel are made of special layers of brass and nickel. The guard is beautifully engraved in the relief technique: the metal around the depiction is removed so that the depiction itself seems to burst out of the material. The handle of this Bowie is made of mammoth ivory.

PEGASUS

This 19 inch knife was based on space exploration, with a few added features. As far as is known, this was the first knife ever to have a laser aiming device, handy for shooting down projectiles. Two catapults under the knife, which look like the motor rockets of a spaceship, can actually shoot mini fireballs. With an adaptor, it can even shoot .22 Long Rifle bullets.

SPACE BOWIE

The 20 inch Space Bowie is another futuristic knife. The blade is of stainless ATS-34 steel with a row of holes drilled into it and filled with anodized titanium. The handle and guard, or actually the parry rod, are made of anodized titanium with a mother-of-pearl covered layer.

Space Bowie by Jobin

JORDAN
www.jordanknives.com

Andrew Jordan busy working on his logo on the right

Andrew Jordan comes from a family of smiths. His great-grandfather left Ireland and settled in London as a smith. There he taught his son, Andrew's grandfather, the trade. Grandfather Jordan inspired Andrew's interest in knife forging by allowing him to play regularly with steel by the forging fire. Jordan decided to become a fully trained knife smith in 1994 and to work in the traditional ways of his forefathers.

He got a job in Japan and studied there under the guidance of a Japanese Mukansa, a knife smith. Andrew is one of the few Europeans who have witnessed the full process of the medieval forging technique, currently used in Japan.

After his learning period in Japan, he went to the United States and worked under the leadership of Rob Hudson and Daryl Meier and shared his knowledge about European

An example of a Bowie by Andrew Jordan

Saxon Saex

Andrew Jordan won the prize, 'Best of the Show,' with this large knife at

forging techniques and forging Damassteel while he was there. When forging his knives, Andrew uses his knowledge of modern metallurgy, in combination with ancient techniques. The specialized magazines, *La Passion des Couteaux, Hephaistos, Messermagazin* and various hunting magazines have all published extensive articles about Jordan's work. Jordan has many weapon collections in Europe and

Anglo Saxon Saex

the IMA 2003 exhibition. The 11.8 inch Damascus blade, forged with complicated patterns, consists of a number of Damascus rods and strips. The handle is made of mammoth ivory, set in Micarta rings. The Damascus pattern with its large shark teeth has not been made for about 1,300 years and is a reconstruction of an original weapon from the seventh century. It

constantly studies European weapons, but he still uses his own judgement when making his knives. The focus is on functionality as well as harmony. The shape of the blade, the guard and the handle must flow into each other, but the main focus is on the blades. He uses ancient hardening techniques for the edges of his blades. If one looks very well the hardening lines can be seen. They are not only lovely, but also form an important part of the high quality, hand forged blade. Jordan makes his knives for experts and enthusiasts who understand the need for a high quality, handmade tool.

took Andrew three years to study and forge the original pattern. He failed three times to reconstruct the original handwork, but eventually succeeded, and thus gained the deepest respect for the smiths from the Anglo-Saxon period while making this deceptively simple blade.

Profile of the Anglo Saxon Saex

Bowie

This large Bowie has a hand-forged 'Sanmai' Damascus blade with a core of 1059 steel. Sanmai is a technique in which the steel is sandwiched between Damascus layers. The blade is 11.4 inches long and runs into the tang, which occupies three quarters of the blade width. The guard and decorated pommel are made of blued steel and the handle is from marbled maple wood.

Small Knife

This knife has a short blade of 2.8 inches length and is made of 1.2842 steel. The handle is made of desert ironwood and French walnut wood. A leather sheath, made by Kenny Rowe, comes with the knife.

A small hunting knife or utility knife

JURKIJEVIC

knives@austarnet.com.au

Simeon Jurkijevic busy forging at his workplace

Simeon Jurkijevic is truly a world citizen. He is of Russian-Hungarian descent, but grew up in Serbia where he studied with Bela Bernad, the dean of the Guild of Knifemakers and Renovators. Simeon worked on the restoration of castles, churches and palaces until he immigrated to Australia in 1966. As an immigrant, he had to take any work that came his way and he spent about twenty years working as a plumber and welder. In 1986, he started a mango nursery in Palmerston, located next to the big No 1 Stuart Highway, southeast of Darwin in the Northern Territories.

In his free time, he started forging knives and eventually switched to fulltime production. Jurkijevic has won many prizes with his knives and he regularly displays them at galleries. His knives are forged by hand from old iron from cars, tools and machines. He mostly uses Australian wood types and indigenous precious and semi-precious stones. Sometimes he receives requests to make knives out of old family pieces or other unique objects, such as the knife he made of the rear axis of a police motorbike that was totalled during a pursuit. He also had to make a knife from the engine block of a Ferrari, which had been blown up during the Australian Cannonball Race. Jurkijevic custom makes the sheaths for his knives. His wife Paulina does the etching of the Damasteel as well as the decorations on the knives. Karl, his second oldest son, works with his father in the smithy and does all of the engraving work.

AUSTRALIAN BOWIE

This Australian Bowie is a large and heavy utility knife. The total length of the knife is 15.2 inches and the length of the blade is 8.9 inches. The blade is made of 5160 carbon steel from a leaf spring, which comes from an old pickup truck. The text 'Australian Bowie' was etched onto the blade by hand. The guard is made of brass and nickel silver. Jurkijevic made the handle from iron wood (Erythrophleum chlorostachys) with finger slots in the Marakai style. This style was named after the African Marakai tribe in Nigeria. The pommel on the handle is made of brass and nickel silver with an azurite cap. This knife comes with a leather sheath.

BREAD KNIFE

Australian Bowie

Jurkijevic made this bread knife from the leaf spring of an old car. The blade is 7.87 inches long and the total length of the knife is 13 inches. The knife does not have a guard, but a type of bolster, made of brass and nickel silver. Jurkijevic made the handle from the wood of the black Darwin acacia (Acacia auriculiformis) that grows mostly in the Australian Northern territories. The pommel at the top of the handle are made of brass and nickel silver with a cap of rose agate from Queensland. The knife has a leather sheath.

**Decorated bread knife
by Simeon Jurkijevic**

DAMASCUS CARVING KNIFE

This decorative long knife is a traditional knife from Asia, used during ceremonies. The standard version is for daily use. Jurkijevic made this knife

Damascus Carving Knife

with a Damasteel blade that he had forged himself from layered steel. This long blade is 12.6 inches in total length. The guard, or better yet, the bolster, is made of sterling silver. Jurkijevic made the handle from the wood of an indigenous myrtle bush. The pommel was cut out in the shape of a dragon's head. The sheath was handmade of leather.

DAMASCUS DAGGER

This decorative dagger was designed as a letter opener with a blade 4.7 inches long and is made of layered carbon steel that had come from the parts of various leaf springs of an old vehicle. The steel

Damascus Dagger

in itself is of an excellent quality. Jurkijevic made the guard from brass and sterling silver. The handle is made of the bone of a dugong, the Australian version of a hippopotamus, found the coast around Darwin. The pommel is made of brass and sterling silver with a cap of jade from Papua New Guinea. The sheath is made of barramundi leather. Barramundi is a large perch found in the coastal waters and river deltas of the Australian Northern Territories. This predatory fish can grow as large as 6 feet and weighs up to 130 lbs. It is favored among sport fishermen.

DOUBLE EDGED PIGSTICKER

The Double Edged Pigsticker is a dagger with a blade 7.4 inches in length. The hand-forged blade is made of 9260 carbon steel, taken

from a leaf spring of an old vehicle. The grip is made of horse bone. Jurkijevic made the guard from brass and the bolster from nickel silver. The pommel is made of the same nickel silver with a brass knob. A handmade leather sheath comes with the knife.

JAMBIYA

Double Edged Pigsticker

The Jambiya is a traditional curved dagger carried by every man in Yemen. Jurkijevic forged the blade for this Jambiya from 260 carbon steel that had come from the leaf spring of an old scrapped vehicle. The length of the blade is 6.3 inches and the total length of the knife is 10.6 inches. The guard is made of brass and sterling silver. The handle is made of iron wood and horse bone, set with

Jambiya hunting knife

spacers of sterling silver. The pommel is made of brass, sterling silver and jade. The sheath is made from the of the Australian giant perch or barramundi.

KA-BAR KNIVES

www.ka-bar.com

The emblem of Ka-Bar

A group of 38 men in Titidoute, Pennsylvania decided in 1898 to start a company for the production and sales of knives. When Titidoute Cutlery Company ran into financial troubles in 1900 and was disbanded, the estate was bought by Wallace R. Brown who started a new knife factory called Union Razor Company. As the emphasis shifted increasingly from razors to pocket and hunting knives, the factory name was changed again in 1909 to the Union Cutlery Company. In 1910 it company moved to Olean, New York, encouraged by the city council of this area to do so.

The name Ka-Bar was the result of a letter received from a trapper written in the 1920's. While he had been out hunting he was attacked by a rushing bear. His rifle failed, but he managed to kill the bear with his Union hunting knife. In the hardly legible letter, he thanked the company as his knife had 'k a bar,' which was derived from 'killed a bear.' The company's owners saw the opportunity for promotion and changed its name to Ka-Bar. Other trademarks from this time are Olcut and Keenwell.

The name of Ka-Bar got such a good reputation during World War Two that the owner Danforth Brown decided to incorporate in 1952. In 1961 the family company was sold to a few local businessmen who drove it to bankruptcy shortly thereafter. The company changed hands several times until Atlas Corporation of Olean, New York took it over in 1996 and moved Ka-Bar back to the town where it had started.

BLACK FIGHTER & KBD1

The Black Fighter was introduced in 2004. This knife has an extra wide blade of 1.5 inches and it is made of 109 carbon steel with a baked-on epoxy protective layer. The guard is made of carbon steel as well and Ka-Bar uses Kraton thermoplastic for the handle. The Black Fighter is 12.87 inches in total length, has a blade of 8 inches and the handle is 4.9 inches long. The knife weighs 12.9 ounces and comes with a Cordura sheath. The new KBD1 combat knife from 2004 has the same features as the Black Fighter. The knife has a droppoint blade that is 7 inches long, is 11.75 inches in total length and weighs 11.3 ounces. The KBD1 comes with a Kydex sheath.

The new KBD1 and the Black Fighter from 2004

BLACK KA-BAR

The Black Ka-Bar is based on the USMC military knife. The 1095 carbon steel blade has a smooth or partially serrated edge, an epoxy protective layer and is 7 inches long. The Kraton handle is 4.7 inches in length. The total length of the knife is 11.75 inches and it weighs 11.3 ounces. The knife comes with a choice of a Cordura or Kydex sheath.

The Black Ka-Bar

The Black Recurve

BLACK RECURVE & BLACK TANTO

This short Black Ka-Bar knife has a blade of 5.25 inches and is 9.25 inches in total length. It is a smaller version of the large Black Ka-Bar combat knife and it weighs 6.2 ounces. The Black Tanto has a Tanto blade of 5.25 inches. The handle of this Tanto is 4.1 inches long and the total length of the knife is 9.37 inches. The Black Tanto weighs 6.35 ounces and come with a Kydex sheath. The Black Recurve, with its typical round blade point, is 9.25 inches in total length. The blade has an epoxy protective layer, is 5.12 inches long and has a Kraton handle that measures 4.1 inches. The Recurve knife weighs 6.2 ounces.

COMMEMORATIVES

Folder designed by Bob Dozier

Ka-Bar Knives Inc. is known for issuing special commemorative knives. The first Commemorative was brought out in 1998 in honor of the 100-year existence of Ka-Bar. In 2002, Ka-Bar brought out the Pearl Harbor Commemorative. The blade of 1095 carbon steel has a black epoxy protective layer in which the following text is etched: A Date Which Will Live in Infamy. The second knife from 2002 commemorated the war in Korea with 'Lest we forget' on the blade. The third knife, introduced in 2004, is in commemoration of Operation Iraqi Freedom. The fifth knife is the luxurious version of the USMC. All have blades of 6.89 inches and are 11.89 inches in total length. The handles are made of impregnated leather.

DOZIER FOLDER

The Dozier Folder from 2004 was designed by Bob Dozier. The blade of stainless AUS-8A steel has, depending on the shape, a length of 4 to 4.5 inches.

Commemorative

Its total length is 7.25 to 7.5 inches. The knife weighs 2.24 ounces. It is made in Hunter, Clippoint and Skinner versions. The newest model from 2004, the Thumb Notch, has a thumbhole in the blade. The handle is made of Zytel synthetic material, reinforced with fiberglass, developed by DuPont de Nemours.

FIGHTING KNIFE
USMC

This is the famous USMC (United States Marine Corps) combat knife. Ka-Bar brought this knife to the market in USMC, US Army and US Navy versionin 1945. It was initially only made with a total length of 11.89 inches, with a blade of 6.69 inches. It comes with or without serration and with blade lengths of 7 or 5.25 inches. The total length of the new model is 11.89 inches or 9.25 inches for the smaller models.

American marine knife

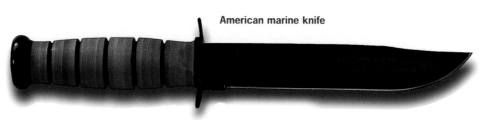

Little Fin

HUNTER 1

This traditional hunting knife has a blade made of stainless AUS-6 steel and a handle of impregnated leather pieces. The guard and pommel are made of aluminum and brass. These hunting knives are made for Ka-Bar in Japan in three different models. The small Little Fin has a blade of 3.62 inches and is 7 inches in total length. The large Hunter has a blade 4 inches long and it is 8.11 inches in total length. The blade of the large Skinner is 4.37 inches and it is 8.25 inches in total length. The knives weigh 7.1, 5.6 or 4.2 ounces, respectively.

The Small Hunter

Skinnerpoint Hunter

HUNTER 3

Ka-Bar introduced two new versions of the 2002 models in 2004, with orange colored Kraton handles. These models are Skinners with blades that taper to a point or a Droppoint that runs down with the blade point. The total length of the Skinner is 7.25 inches and the blade is 3.39 inches long. The Droppoint is 6.75 inches in total length and has a blade of 3.11 inches.

HUNTER 4

Versions of the Hunter Gamehook and Classic were introduced with orange Kraton handles in 2004 as well. The Gamehook is 6.75 inches in total length and has a blade of 3.31 inches. The Classic is 7 inches in total length and has a blade of 3.58 inches.

HUNTER 2

The Ka-Bar Hunter series appeared on the market in 2002 with a number of small models with specialized blades. The small versions have droppoint, game hook or skinner blades and are 5.87 or 6.14 inches in total length. The blades are made of stainless 440A steel and tempered to 55-56 HRC. The length of the blade is 2.13 inches and the blade with the gutting hook is 2.36 inches long. The knives weigh 1.28 ounces each, which is mostly due to its lightweight Kraton handles.

**The Hunter
with the Gamehook**

The Impact Warthog by Ka-Bar

IMPACT

The Impact series came to market in 2002. This tactical knife has a blade made of 1095 carbon steel, protected by a baked-on black epoxy layer. The handles of the three knives at the top are made of Zytel. These models are: the Small Warthog, the Spear and the Tanto. Both the Large Spear and the Combat, have handles made of gray Micarta and blades made of D2 tool steel. The steel is tempered to 59-60 HRC. The total lengths of the knives vary from 8.25 to 9.5 inches, while the extra large Combat knife has a length of 11.14 inches. The blade length is between 3.6 to 4.49 inches and on the Combat it is 6 inches. The special Cordura sheaths are from Eagle Industries from Fenton, Missouri.

LONG HUNTER

The claw shaped Maserin Hawk

The Long Hunter is made with a set blade that is ground to half the length of the blade width or with a flexible blade, ground over the entire width. The so-called Firm Point has a rigid blade that is 7.64 inches in total length and a flexible blade of 4.21 inches. The total length of the Flex Point is 7.5 inches and the flexible blade is 4.0 inches long. The knives weigh 2.6 ounces each. Stainless 440A steel was used for the blade and the handle is made of Kraton.

MASERIN HAWK

The 2003 Hawk, made by Italian knife factory Maserin, has a handle made of 6061-T6 aircraft aluminum that comes in two different versions. The blade is ground shallow and is made of stainless 440A steel. It is 2.75 inches long and bead blasted or provided with a black epoxy protective layer. The triangular thumb hole allows the knife to be opened with one hand. The handle is 4 inches long and the total length of the opened knife is 6.75 inches. The knife weighs 3.2 ounces. The Hawk has a linerlock system indicated by Ka-Bar as a sidelock system.

Long Hunter

MASERIN SPEAR

These two knives have pointed blades of 3.39 inches and are 8 or 8.11 inches in total length respectively. The blade, with a thumbhole or thumbholes, is made of stainless 440A steel and the handles are made of aluminum. Both knives have linerlock systems and weigh 4.48 ounces each. A detachable carrying clip is on the right of the handle.

The Maserin Spearpoint folder

The large Wild Kat hunting Knife

He almost always uses Damasteel that he forges from three up to even one thousand layers. He uses only natural materials for the handles. He does the engraving on the blades and handles as well. His unique approach is evident in the broad array of materials he uses for the sheaths.

KAUFMANN

www.cuttingart.net

Robert Kaufmann got involved in knife making while living in Lapland in his twenties. His distinctive knives express a certain lifestyle. Knife making is not simply work for him, but a form of meditation. He allows his feelings, intuiti-

Archetyp Barb

Robert Kaufmann at the anvil

on and spontaneity to guide him. Kaufmann likes to find out about the client's personality, work, hobbies and interests. In this way, the knife becomes a living object that fits seamlessly with the personality of its owner. Robert does everything by himself.

ARCHETYPE BARB

The Archetype Barb is a beautiful knife with a Damascus blade of 4 inches. The knife is 8.3 inches in total length. The handle and sheath are made of grenadilla wood, combined with mammoth ivory, decorated with scrimshaw in the style of cave drawings from the Stone Age.

DAMASCUS LINER

This knife has a Damasteel blade and a bolster Kaufman calls puff pastry steel. The blade is 5.5 inches long and is locked with a linerlock system. The inner casing is made of puff pastry Damascus as well. The pins with which the handle plates are attached and the end of the blade pivot are made of gold. The handle plates are of mammoth ivory and red satin wood.

Damascus Liner with mammoth ivory

DAGGER

This Dagger has a wonderful blade made of torsion Damascus, etched with different acids to bring out its

The Dagger with an extraordinary Damascus blade

lovely colors. The bolster and pommel are made of blackened steel. The handle is made of mammoth ivory and attached with silver pins. The accompanying sheath is made of cow leather.

ELVIN DAGGER

The double-sided Damasteel blade, made of more than sixty steel layers, is beautifully ground. The handle is a combination of mammoth ivory, palisander and pock wood. The sheath is a work of art in itself. It is made of birch, mammoth ivory, pock wood and leather.

The Integral knife with the solid Damascus grip

FLAORE

It is not clear where the Flaore name comes from, but it has to do with the flowing wavy lines of the Damasteel blade. A series of five size-sequential holes were drilled in the blade. A rough diamond was placed in the first hole. The handle is

The Elvin dagger by Robert Kaufmann

made of Cocobolo wood, combined with mammoth ivory in which a golden pin is barely visible. The sheath is made of Cocobolo wood, mammoth ivory and beautifully treated leather.

INTEGRAL KNIFE

This large integral knife was forged from one piece of Damasteel. The handle is solid and the palisander wood, pock

The Flaore fantasy knife

wood and mammoth ivory grip literally wraps around it. It comes with a piece of steel for sharpening the blade.

HUNTING KNIFE WITH ADDITIONAL KNIFE

The large hunting knife with a small knife in the handle

This large hunting knife has a large and wide forged Damasteel blade of 7.4 inches. The entire knife is 12.6 inches long.
The handle is made of red satin wood with a cover of mammoth ivory. The skeleton sheath is made of reindeer bone, mammoth ivory and leather.

OLD SNAIL

The unique protruding blade is made of beautiful Damasteel in the shape of a snail. The snail shell is made of mammoth ivory and gold. The antennas that stick out of the snail shell are made of snake wood. This object is a decorative piece.

The small knife, hidden in the handle

A small dagger is hidden in the handle. This dagger has a Damasteel blade as well and a handle made of mammoth ivory.

The Damascus folder with a Damascus saw blade

KLAPMES

This folding knife not only has a blade made of Damasteel, but a folding and sawing blade as well as a bolster made of the same material. The bolster and handle plates are fixed with golden pins. The handle plates are made of mammoth ivory and palisander wood, which are separated by a silver edge.

OPINELVERSCHLUSS

The folding knife shown here has a bolster with a twist lock system, like on the Opinel knives, but that is the only similarity between them. The layered blade is made of beautifully forged 60- layered Damasteel with a core of carbon steel. The bolster is made of Damasteel as well. The handle is made of a complicated combination of bruyere wood, stag horn, granadilla wood and mammoth ivory. The handle plates are attached with silver pins. The blade pivot turns on a bronze bearing ring.

The folder with an Opinel locking system

An extraordinary object

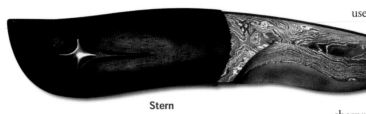

Stern

STERN

The Stern is a short hunting knife with a blade made of 100 layered Damasteel. The blade is 3.8 inches long and the total length of the knife is 7.8 inches. The handle is made of pockwood and has a subtle decoration accentuated by a silver star.

used is unique or exotic. When finishing such a knife there must be no marks on it. It must be carried in a safe and reliable way for normal usage. Hardening is of fundamental importance and has great influence on the wear resistance of the steel and the sharpness of the edge. Kehiayan's knives are tempered to 60 HRC. These utility knives come with leather sheaths. Standard models displayed on his website can be ordered with any finish imaginable.

DIRK IN THE BOX

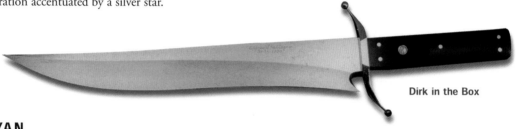

Dirk in the Box

KEHIAYAN

www.kehiayan.com.ar

Alfredo Kehiayan, a metals industrialist until 1980, made his first knife, a classic Bowie, at the age of fifteen of a twelve-inch strip of Nicolson steel.
He is a member of the Trade Industry in San Isidro, the Trade Industry of Buenos Aires and the Argentinean Center for Trade Members.
His first article about knives was published in the

The large Hunter

This large Bowie style knife has a 9.1 inch long blade made of stainless 440B steel. The blade is ground hollow and has an upturned skinner point. The knife is 13.0 inches in total length. The gracefully arched guard is made of stainless 304 steel. The handle is made of Cocobolo wood and attached with brass pins. This knife comes with a unique presentation chest made of a piece of burl wood that was carefully split and hollowed out.

HUNTER

This large hunting knife has a blade made of stainless 420 steel. This is ground in a particularly decorative way with a wavy pattern. The length of the blade is 9.1 inches. The bolster is made of nickel steel and engraved with plant motifs. The handle plates are made of thuya wood and attached with mosaic pins.

magazine *Aventura & Co* in 1990. He also writes columns for the Argentinean magazine *Aire & Sol*. A great deal has been written in a several international magazines about the knives of Alfredo Kehiayan. The American knife yearbook, *Knives 2000*, featured his knives on its cover. A documentary about him was shown on Argentinean television in 2001.
Kehiayan has very specific ideas when it comes to his collector's knives: they must be functional, even when the material

Small Hunter

The special Whirlwind RMEF version

The Whirlwind RMEF is a special version by Kershaw to support the Rocky Mountains Elk Foundation which receives a part of the sales profit.

SCALLION

The Scallion, designed by Ken Onion, is made in a number of lively colors and comes with a smooth or partially serrated edge, as shown here. The handle of the colored version is made of anodized aluminum, but the black knife has a handle made of polyamide 3.5 inches long. The blade is made of stainless

rewed from the handle after a saltwater dive to rinse in fresh water or to mount a different blade. There are currently two types of blades available, both made of stainless 420J2 steel and with a spearpoint or a flattened point. The blades are 3.75 and 3.5 inches in length and the total length of the knife is 7.75 or 7.625

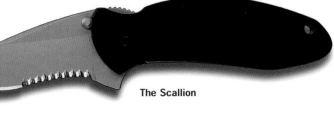

The Scallion

inches respectively. Because of the polymer handle, the knife weighs only 3 ounces. The blades of both versions have grooves that serve as cord cutters and are partially serrated. A diving sheath with a leg strap comes with the knife.

SEAGAL

This linerlock folding knife was designed by Ken Onion with Hollywood actor Steven Segal, whose signature is etched into the beautiful blade made of AUS8A steel in the shape of a beak. It is made with or without partial serration of the cutting edge. The blade is 3.6 inches in length. The handle is 5 inches long and is made of anodized aluminum. Inlaid pieces of polymer are in the handle with the rough structure of the skin of a stingray. The knife weighs 5.5 ounces.

Sea Hunter diving knife

420HC steel, is 2.25 inches long and is locked with a linerlock system. The knife weighs 2.3 ounces.

SEA HUNTER

The Sea Hunter model is a special diving knife with an ingenious blade switching system. A long screw in the synthetic material handle screws the blade into the handle. The blade can be unsc-

The folder by Steven Seagal

Vapor

VAPOR / VAPOR II

Vapor has a droppoint blade made of AUS6A steel and is 3 inches long. The handle is made of stainless 410 steel and is 4 inches long. The Vapor weighs 3.25 ounces. The somewhat larger Vapor II has a blade that is 3.5 inches long and a handle 4.5 inches long. It is similar to the smaller Vapor, but it weighs 4.5 ounces. Both models come with smooth or partially serrated edges. Both knives have framelock systems for the blade where a part of the outer casing of the handle serves as

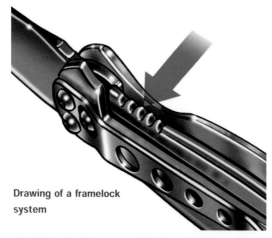

Drawing of a framelock
system

the bolt rod of the opened blade. Other than that, it works and is loosened in a similar fashion to the liner-lock. The principle of the framelock can clearly be seen in the accompanying drawing by Kershaw.

KIZLYAR
www.kizlyar.ru

Dagestan, which means 'mountain land,' was occupied by the Tartars and suffered during the military campaigns of Tamerlane and Alexander the Great. It survived the Arabic and Khazar wars, and invasions of the Iranians, Turks and Russians. Yet this unique country has more than thirty indigenous nationalities that live in peace.

The mountain town of Amuzgi used to serve as the center for excellent daggers and swords. The ornamental patterns such as 'tutta' and 'markharai' were not only used for engraving work, but were also used in forging Damasteel in Amuzgi.

The emblem of Kizlyar

Today, this industry is one of the leading producers of special blade steel in the Russian Federation and Kizlyar sells to all of the Russian states as well as to the United States, Germany, Austria, the Czech Republic and Australia.

Kizlyar uses the traditional methods of the old Caucasian weapon masters, combined with the latest technology and modern materials. Caucasian walnut wood is often used as handle material, stainless steel or carbon steel, or special Damasteel made on the spot for the blades, which are often adorned with traditional decorative patterns or depictions of hunting or nature scenes.

GYRZA

The blade of the Gyrza integral hunting knife is made of Russian stainless steel. It is 4.92 inches long and 0.17 inches thick. The total length of the blade is 9.65 inches. The blade steel runs through to the back of the handle, where a shackle is attached. The handle is made of Caucasian walnut wood and attached with two large brass pins. The two finger slots in the handle and blade serve as the guard. A threatening snake is etched on the blade as decoration.

The Gyrza hunting knife with
extraordinary decorations

green. The total length of the large dagger is 16.9 inches and the blade is 8.7 inches long. The smaller dagger, which represents Europa, is 15.4 inches in total length with a blade of 7.9 inches.

The Love Story knife by Igor Kochetov

LOVE STORY

These knives, made in 2003, are letter openers. They have blades made of mosaic Damascus, forged by Dmitry Zhukov, a student from the fourth class of V. Muyina, a lecturer at the art academy of St Petersburg, whose enameling course Kochetov attended. The enameling technique from ancient Egypt is growing popular again. Metal filings mixed with enamel powder are baked at a temperature of more than 1560 degrees Fahrenheit. The letter openers are 11 inches in length and the blades are 6.3 inches long each. In addition to the Damasteel, copper, enamel, steel and artificial diamonds were used.

WITH LENIN IN HEART

Russian ideological medals from the 1950's, bought at a garage sale, were worked into this knive. For this series of daggers, made in 2001, Kochetov used stainless 95X18 steel for the double-sided blade of the dagger. Cupronickel, copper and bronze were used for the handle. The total lengths of the daggers are 11.8 inches and the blades are 7.1 inches long.

With Lenin in heart

KOLESNIKOV

www.rusartknife.urbannet.ru/gallery.html

Alexander Kolesnikov was born in the fall of 1960 in a small city south of Moscow in Ryazan province. He has been making knives for as long as he can remember. He met a group of knife makers in 1992

Alexander Kolesnikov, with his emblem, top right, and below, the logo of the Russian Knifemakers' Guild

and then decided to dedicate himself to making knives. He experimented with shaping blades, decorations and using different types of material. In his shapes he always tries to follow his own style. A trademark of his work is the use of animal heads in the handles and pommels. Through this, his knives achieve a certain personality. His cooperation with the well-known smith Vasily Krivoshein, a student of the legendary master Basov, led to a revival of the production techniques of Damasteel. His working tools consist mainly of a workbench and jewelers and dentist tools. His creativity is inexhaustible. He says the best knife for any knife maker is he next one. The knives shown here were photographed by Sergey Baranov and/or Valentin Overchenko.

DRAGON

This knife is a mixture of a North European fantasy and decorative weapons carried during Eastern ceremonies. It is also a work of art. Its original and wonderful blade is shaped like a flying dragon. The blade was forged from Damasteel by the knife smith Alexander Bychkov. The handle looks like the body of an amfitipter, a legendary dragon without legs. It is slightly curled at the end so that it supports the hand when using the knife. Other than Damasteel, gold, silver and burl wood were also used. The burl wood from a birch tree is excellent material and it reflects the Russian soul, according to Kolesnikov. Three uninterrupted months

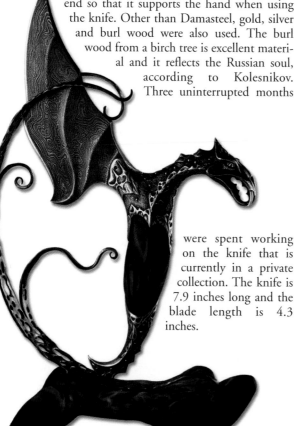

were spent working on the knife that is currently in a private collection. The knife is 7.9 inches long and the blade length is 4.3 inches.

Dragon

FRIEND

This is a traditional Russian knife with a thick, strong blade and a comfortable grip. The shape refers to an ancient dilemma: which is the hunter's best friend? His dog or his knife? Kolesnikov tried to convey this with the significant title of Friend. The pommel of the knife is shaped like a Russian spaniel's head. The handle is made of Russian birch wood. The Damasteel blade was forged by his friend, Vladimir Vasily Krivoshein. Kolesnikov spent half a year working on this knife in 2001, after which it was displayed at the knife fair, Blades of

The hunting knife Friend with the dog head on the pommel

Russia, in 2001. The knife is currently in a private collection. The length of the knife is 10.6 inches. The blade is 5.3 inches long.

STING

The Sting is a fantasy dagger in the shape of a long insect. It is the collective shape of all dangerous, stingy, poisonous and flying beasts. It nevertheless has something decorative, dynamic and even elfish about it. The blade was forged by the well-known smith Egor Aseev from Tula, a member of the Russian Knifemakers' Guild. The handle is made of snake wood. The other materials used are silver, hematite, chrysolite and enamel. The guard is in the shape of two insect wings with a pair of legs visible. The pommel was done in the shape of an insect head. Kolesnikov spent a year working on this knife. It was put on display at the knife fair in the Kremlin in 2004. The total length is 13 inches and the blade is 8.3 inches long.

The Sting, shaped like an insect

Detail of the Sting

238

KOPYLOV

www.rusartknife.urbannet.ru/gallery.html

Gennady Kopylov with his master sign, top right, and the logo of the Russian Knifemakers' Guild, below

Gennady Kopylov was born in Moscow in 1963. From the time he held a short dagger and a sword at the age of five, he was fascinated with knives. From his

His part-time job as a fitter at a garage, where hard to find parts often had to be made by hand, stood him in good stead. Not every knife maker is capable of becoming an artistic knife maker. But Kopylov has the necessary flair for design, philosophical impact, inspiration and an original style. As long as he is working on a knife, he loves it intensely. When it is finished, it goes off to lead its own life and Kopylov goes on to his next idea. In this way all of his favorite pieces of work are constantly ahead of him.

TESAK

The Tesak is an ultimate survival object, made by Kopylov in 2003. The blade of the hunting sword is made of Damasteel forged by Kost`a Dalmatov. The idea behind the design was the nostalgia for the old-style hunting days, before the time of the firearm. The sword with all of its attributes consists of 348 parts. The steel parts, such as the locks, needles, screwdrivers, drills, prods, blowpipes and arrows are all made of VT14-titanium. The sheath is of oak from Kopylov's garden, palisander, ebony and leather.

The short Tesak sword

VAKIDZASI

father, a part-time cobbler, he learned to work with leather and to grind leather knives.

He started making knives when his brother Sergey made a skinning knife and asked Gennady: "Can you do better?" The two knives he made were displayed at the Moscow knife fair. Next to the most beautiful work by Russia's best knife makers, his creations looked very humble, but this motivated him to devote himself to the craft. He sought out renowned knife makers like Andrey Aksenov, Valentin Timofeev, Alexander Kurbatov, Andrey Koreshkov, Gennady Sokolov and Sergey Danilin.

Kopylov made this Japanese style sword in 2002. He had been involved in the restoration of old Japanese swords and he spent a lot of time studying the history, the technology and the material used in previous centuries. In this Russian version of the Japanese sword, he used Damasteel forged by the master smith Kost`a Dalmatov from the ancient town of Kolomna. Dalmatov's famous Damasteel is elastic, flexible and has a particularly wear resistant edge. He is also the only Russian smith who can make beautiful wild Damascus from three packets of Russian steel types U8 (Y8), U10 (Y10), R14 (P14)and R18 (P180), combined with old files. All parts, such as the traditional tsuba, futi, kasira, minuki and kuchi-gane are made of the so-called black steel. Gennady

The Japanese sword Vakidzasi by Kopylov

Back view of the Tsuba

makes the kurigata and the kaechi-zuno from mammoth ivory from Yakutia. The handle is covered with the hide of a stingray, wrapped with an original Japanese cord.

The tsuba or guard is the separation between the handle and the blade. At the front end, it is engraved with a depiction of a pond surface with a water lily and

water plants. At the other end, under the water, two carps are chasing each other's tails in a circle. The carp is a symbol of wisdom in Japan. This Crucian carp, a Russian carp, is a particularly cunning ani-

Audrey Koreshkov. Top right, his emblem and below that, the logo of The Russian Knifemakers' Guild

mal that is difficult to catch. The sword is 31.8 inches in total length and is 35.2 inches in length with its sheath. The length of the blade is 23.1 inches and it is 1.1 inches wide. The sword weighs around 52.9 ounces.

KORESHKOV

www.rusartknife.urbannet.ru/gallery.html

Audrey Aleksandrovich Koreshkov was born in 1958 into a family of doctors of medicine and philosophy. He completed his education at a technical automobile school and got an academic degree there. Then he got involved with scientific work. In 1985 he held a piece of Damasteel forged by the Russian masker smith Basov in his hands for the first time, and he made his first knife. Three years later Koreshkov was a professional knife maker.

He is an individualist who does everything himself. His serious scientific

The hunting knife Kariis from 2002

and technical development as well as his perseverance and practical orientation help him create concise and functional, but still decorative designs. The techniques he developed in the multi-layered etching of steel are unique. With this he creates complete landscapes in his blades, varying a chillingly cold night, a thunderstorm, springtide against rocks, a tranquil fall or a warm summer evening.

Audrey Koreshkov is a member of the Russian Artists' Guild, and of the Russian Knifemakers' Guild. He held a personal exhibition at the knife show Blades of Russia in 2000 at the Weapons Museum of the Kremlin. His work has been purchased by the military museum and can be found in private collections. He has won numerous awards and has been decorated by the Russian Ministry of culture. His work is in demand at large museums and among collectors.

KARIIS

The sturdy Kariis was designed in 2002. It appears to be a very simple hunting knife, but appearances are deceiving. The blade is made of stainless 440C steel, indicated in Russia as 95X18. The actual cutting edge is made of Damasteel forged onto the blade. This Damascus trace was forged from joint stainless electrodes. The blade was etched with an intriguing depiction; Audrey leaves the interpretation to the beholder.

The hunting knife, Rustle above Water, from 2001

The handle is made of light ebony wood that Koreshkov bought from a guitar maker. The knife is 7.7 inches in total length and the blade is 3.9 inches long. This knife is currently in a private collection.

RUSTLE ABOVE WATER

This knife was shaped and finished as a hunting knife. The depiction on the blade, which was etched into multi layers, is that of a wolf staring at its potential prey from the edge of a pond bordered with reeds, marsh grass and other water plants, with the wind calmly rustling through it. A stag is reflected in the water. This depiction is made of 72 etched layers. This complicated knife comes in a matching chest in the shape of a

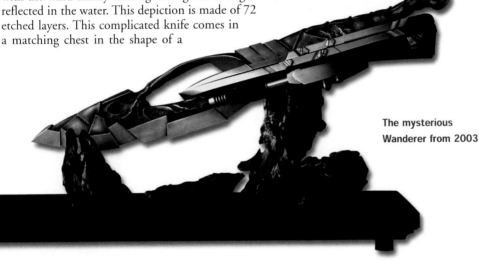

Detail of the blade of Rustle above Water

inches long. The trestle is made of ebony wood from the Soshalsky Islands. This knife is currently in a private collection.

The mysterious Wanderer from 2003

traditional Russian ornament. This knife was displayed in a personal exhibition that formed a part of the knife exhibition Blades of Russia 2001 in the Weapons Museum of the Kremlin in Moscow. The knife is 9.4 inches in total length and the blade is 4.7 inches long, of stainless 95X18 (440C) steel that was tempered to 59 HRC.

The chest and the handle are made of ebony from the Soshalsky Islands. The decorative edge that frames the blade is demarcated with golden ornaments. The gold came from his grandmother's wedding ring. This knife is currently in a private collection.

WANDERER

Koreshkov let himself get carried away with the design of this knife. 'The horizon of the imagination is only limited by the lack of imagination,' is his scarce commentary. He shows us a world with a techno civilization, capable of space travel. The Wanderer could set off for a long space journey in this way. The knife is made of 95X18 (440C) steel. It was built up from overlapping layers. The total length of the knife is 9.8 inches and the blade is 5.1

KOSTENKO

www.rusartknife.urbannet.ru/gallery.html

Kostenko is a hunter. He prefers to hunt with hounds, which chase the animal to exhaustion, bring it to a standstill and await his arrival. Hunting requires physical effort and a Spartan lifestyle, but it provides a lot

Vladislav Kostenko with his master sign and the emblem of the Russian Guild of Knifemakers

of excitement. Kostenko lives with his mother in her country house in the picturesque town of Stoyanovo, forty-four miles from Moscow. Here he can indulge in his passion for falcon hunting – one of the most authentic forms of the hunt. All of the knives made by Kostenko are linked to hunting in some way.

diamond needle for the pupil. The pattern in the Damascus increases the impression of concentration and readiness of the panther for a skilful bound. Kostenko made the feet of the stand in the shape of buffalo heads, thus combining gracefully the power of the black panther and the wild bull. This knife is currently in his posession.

The Black Eagle knife on a display-stand

Falcon knife alone and the knife on the stand

BLACK EAGLE

Kostenko made the sturdy Black Eagle knife in 2002. The blade is made of stainless torsion Damascus, forged by Egor Aseev, a good friend and hunting partner. The materials used for the knife are Damasteel, ebony, black agate and steel. The knife is 17.7 inches long and the blade is 11.8 inches long. Kostenko used macasar for the foot of the stand and ebony for the stand itself and the handle. The eye of the black eagle is a black agate in a thin, golden frame. This knife can be used for hunting. It is currently in a private collection.

BLACK PANTHER

The Black Panther was made in 2003. The 6.7 inch Damasteel blade was made by Egor Aseev. Macasar ebony, cat's eye and white metal were also used on the 8.7 inch knife. Kostenko was inspired by a book about Brazilian hunters, which describes the dangerous art of hunting jaguars (the black panther is a type of jaguar) in the Amazon. He imagined the large, beautiful black panther sitting peacefully and comfortably in a tree, just like a cat, but ready to spring once it senses danger. The eyes of the panther are of tiger's eye and with a hole drilled with a

FALCON

Kostenko made the Falcon knife in 2001. It is a sturdy knife with an artful sheath on a stand. The blade was forged by Egor Aseev and the etching was done by Oleg Gushchin. The materials used for the knife are Damasteel, ebony, black obsidian, part of a stag horn and the thigh bone of a deer. The knife is 11.8 inches long with a 7.9 inch blade. The height, including the stand, is 15 inches. The knife was inspired by the falcon. For his black eyes, without any white, obsidian from Kamchatka was used. The foot of the stand is made of ebony and the stand itself is the thigh bone of a deer. This knife is currently in a private collection.

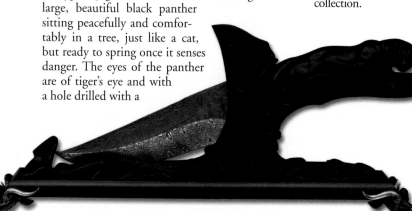

The Black Panther decorative knife

KURBATOV
www.rusartknife.urbannet.ru/gallery.html

Portrait of Kurbatov with his old logo on the top right, in the middle his current master sign and bottom right the logo of the Russian Knifemakers' Guild

Alexander Mihaylovich Kurbatov was born in Tula in 1955. He concluded his education in 1980 at the Abramtsevo School of Art and Industry in the metal works department, led by A.A. Drozdovskij for artists. Years of working and studying at a national applied arts project in Tula taught Kurbatov how to work with metals. He made gates, railings and open fireplace railings. At the end of the 1980's he took up knife making.

He is primarily interested in the relationship between design and development. Until recently, painted objects and material work were based on design functionality. A great breakthrough came with the arrival of the computer, which opened up endless possibilities in design. The lack of gravity, unreal combination of different materials, strange reflections and atmospheric effects created a new reality which could be applied to shape materials in virtual design. An example of this is the Cain knife. Kurbatov creates new objects that would have been impossible without the aid of computers and he has since developed into a master forger of blades which he does in the workshops of the Joint-Stock Company Diana. Kurbatov takes part in many Russian exhibitions, including the knife exhibition in the Wea-

The Aurum fantasy dagger

pons Museum of the Kremlin in Moscow and the Weapons museum in Tula. He has been a member of the Society of Weapons Historians and a member of the Russian Knifemakers' Guild since 1997. The knives shown here were photographed by Sergey Baranov and/or Valentin Overchenko.

AURUM

This fantasy dagger, entitled Aurum, was meant to be an artistic image. Alexander Kurbatov designed it by computer and then made it from iron and gold. He does not consider gold to be more noble than iron – he says gold is only precious because we have less of it. His second remark about this piece is that 'classifying metals according to their value is the same as classifying people according to their vices.' This object is still in Kurbatov's possession.

CAIN

The Cain knife is another artistic object that Kurbatov made with the aid of a computer. This knife is made of steel and decorated, or better yet, dressed, in a unique way. Kurbatov describes this work of art as: 'Cain lived, Cain is alive, Cain will live.' This object is still in Kurbatov's possession.

Cain

UZEL

The Uzel, or translated as 'The Knot' is meant to be an anti-weapon. This can clearly be seen on the enormous knot on the sword blade. Alexander designed this work of art by computer and made it with Russian steel types U10 (Y10), U12 (Y12) and ST3 (CT3). The maker's motto for this knife is: 'It is not com-

Uzel

pulsory to be a weapon enthusiast.' The sword is currently in the possession of the Weapons Museum of the Kremlin in Moscow.

KUSNETSOV

www.rusartknife.urbannet.ru/gallery.html
dormantdragon@mtu-net.ru

Victor Vasilevich Kusnetsov was born in February 1958 in a mine worker's camp south of Tula at the edge of a large forest. The love of the forest which Victor gained there, as well as hunting expeditions with his father, have influenced him throughout his life. When his father passed away in 1972, Kusnetsov's passion for nature and hunting intensified. After primary school he pursued a technical education. He was also successful at sports and achieved his

Victor Vasilevich Kusnetsov. Top right his logo, below that the emblem of the Russian Knifemakers' Guild

master's title in freestyle wrestling. After his military service he went to work in a factory and became the breadwinner in his fatherless family. In 1980 he started with evening classes at the technical school in Tula and graduated in 1985 with excellent results.

In the meantime he had found a job as a tool maker at a machine factory in Tula, married and started a family. Kusnetsov made hunting as well as kitchen knives in his free time. In 1991 he received an unexpected offer to work at a company in Rivival, which belonged to an old friend of his, as a furniture maker. This company specialized, among other things, in wood processing for guns and knives. Initially he did not know anything about working with wood but he learned fast, guided by a number of old craftsmen in the company. When the com-

pany was taken over a few years later, Kusnetsov decided that it was time for him to work for himself. In 2002 he was accepted into the Russian Knifemakers' Guild. The public does not really know his creations as almost all of his knives are snapped up by private collectors. Only one of his

The Bindweed hunting knife by Kusnetsov

daggers was displayed in 2003 at the Weapons museum in Tula. The knives shown here were photographed by Sergey Baranov and/or Valentin Overchenko.

BINDWEED

Victor Kusnetsov made the Bindweed knife in Tula in 2003. The blade was forged from 250 layered Damascus, made by Alexander Kurbatov and tempered to 56-58 HRC. The beautiful engraving work was done by Vladimir Gubarev and the inlaid work in the wood was done by Konstantin Filatov. The handle of the knife is made of Caucasian walnut wood. The inlaid work of flowers and plants are made of gold and silver in the traditional Vsechka technique from Tula. This knife did not make it to the exhibition as it had disappeared into a private collection before then. The knife is 9.7 inches in total length and has a blade of 5.1 inches. The steel thickness of the blade is 0.157 inches. This knife came with a handmade presentation chest of carved walnut.

HUNTER WITHOUT A NAME

The blade of this knife was forged from four different sheets of mosaic Damascus by the famous knife smith Vsevolod Soskov from Moscow. The cutting edge of the knife is of torsion Damascus,

A beautiful hunting knife without a name

The hand carved chest for the hunting knife without a name

RUSSIAN HUNTER

Many wars took place in Russia during the Middle Ages, so every man had to have a reliable weapon to defend himself with as well as a good knife for everyday use. New knives were first tested while hunting. A good, richly decorated knife was a symbol of prestige. This dagger is a reminder of those times. Kusnetsov designed it and the blade was forged by Natalia Zabelina. Vladimir Gubarev engraved the steel and the wood carving was done by the artist Anatoly Smokty. Ebony and nut wood were worked into the handle. The piece of bone in the handle was adorned with scrimshaw by Natalia Sergeevna Bobrovskaya. The master signs of the artists who had worked on this knife are all engraved on the dagger. This knife was displayed in 2003 in the Weapons museum in Tula and in 2004 in the Kremlin in Moscow. The total length of the dagger is 12.7 inches and the blade is 7.9 inches in length. The steel is 0.236 inches thick.

made of tool steel. The blade was tempered to 60 HRC. The engraving work was done by Vladimir Dmitrievich Gubarev, an engraver at the weapons factory in Tula. This knife comes in a handmade walnut chest that is decorated with a depiction of a wolf devouring a deer. The knife is 8.7 inches in total length and has a blade of 4.3 inches. The thickness of the blade is 0.157 inches. This knife is currently in a private collection.

The Russian Hunter

The chest of the Russian Hunter

PST (POCKET SURVIVAL TOOL)

The PST or Pocket Survival Tool is a somewhat older model from 1983. It underwent a few changes in 2001. The PST is now also available in a matte black version and with an extra rounding in the needle nose pliers in order to reclose bottle caps. Closed, the PST is 4 inches long and weighs only 5

The PST: Pocket Survival Tool

ounces. This Multi Tool has needle nose pliers with a gripping surface, wire cutters, steel wire cutters and, if desired, the earlier mentioned bottle cap closer, a knife with a clippoint blade, a metal and wood file, a small screwdriver, a medium sized screwdriver, a large screwdriver, a Phillips screwdriver, a ruler, a can and bottle opener and a prong. The old version the PST had a shackle, but this is not there anymore. All of the large bits are locked after they are opened. In order to fold these back in again the push button in the handle must be released.

The PST-II with a few more options

The successor of the Pocket Survival Tool, the PST II, dates back to 1996. The handle is 4 inches long as well and the length of the blade with its partial serration is 3.7 inches. The PST II weighs 5 ounces. The PST II was specifically designed for fishermen and water sports enthusiasts with the following features: needle nose pliers with a gripping surface, wire cutters and extra tempered steel wire cutters, the earlier mentioned blade with partial serration, a diamond file with an extra filing edge, scissors, a small screwdriver, a medium sized screwdriver, a large screwdriver, a Phillips screwdriver, a ruler and a can and bottle opener. The shackle and a ridge in the file blade for hook points were omitted in 2001. All of the large bits are locked after they are opened. In order to fold these back in, the push button in the handle must be released.

**Pulse
Multi Tool**

PULSE

The Pulse is a 2000 model. The unique features of this Multi Tool are the release buttons in each handle part that are operated with the side of the thumb. The Pulse was specifically designed for users who use the Multi Tool with one hand while holding on to something else with the other hand. This can be a ladder, a railing or the edge of a boat. The Pulse is 4 inches long and weighs 5 ounces. It has needle nose pliers with a gripping surface plus wire cutters and extra tempered steel wire cutters, a droppoint blade, a diamond file with an extra filing edge, scissors, a small screwdriver, a medium screwdriver, a large screwdriver, a Phillips screwdriver, a ruler, a can and bottle opener and a shackle. All of the large bits are locked after they are opened. In order to fold these back in again the push button in the handle must be released.

SIDECLIP

The Sideclip came onto the market in 1998. As its name indicates, this Multi Tool has a handy carrying clip. When closed, the Sideclip is 4 inches long and weighs 5 ounces. All of the large bits are locked after they are opened. In order to fold these back in again, the push button in the

The Sideclip model

handle must be released. The Sideclip features the following: needle nose pliers with a gripping surface plus wire cutters with extra tempered steel, a droppoint blade, a small screwdriver, a medium screwdriver, a large screwdriver, a Phillips screwdriver, a ruler, a can and bottle opener and the carrying clip that was mentioned earlier on.

The Squirt S4 with large scissors

SQUIRT

The Squirt P4 dates back to 2002 and was designed as a key holder. The length of the folded handle is only 2.25 inches and the Squirt P4 weighs 2 ounces. The handle parts are made of anodized aluminum in gray (Storm), blue (Glacier) and red (Inferno). The Squirt P4 features the following: needle nose pliers with wire cutters, a knife blade, a small screwdriver, a medium sized screwdriver, a flat Phillips screwdriver, a wood and metal file, a bottle opener, an awl punch and a key ring.

The second Squirt model, the Squirt S4, was introduced in 2002. For this model the handle parts are made of anodized aluminum in gray (Storm), blue (Glacier) and red (Inferno) as well. The S4 has the same dimensions and weighs the same as the P4 and it has powerful scissors, a blade, a small screwdriver, a medium sized screwdriver, a flat Phillips screwdriver, a nail file with a nail cleaner, a bottle opener, a ruler, demountable tweezers and a key ring.

The Squirt P4 from 2002

ST (SUPER TOOL) / SUPER TOOL 200

The old model Super Tool dates back to 1994. This large Multi Tool is 4.5 inches in total length. The large blade is 3.9 inches long and when opened fully the stainless steel Super Tool is 7 inches long. The tool weighs 9 ounces. The Super Tool underwent a comprehensive renovation and has been called the Super Tool 200 since then. The most distinctive detail is the release button on both of the handle plates. The large blades are locked after they are opened. They can all be folded back again with this release button. The old as well as

ST: Super Tool

the new Super Tool 200 model has the following pieces: needle nose pliers with an extra gripping surface, wire cutters and steel wire cutters, a blade, a serrated edge, a wood saw, a metal and wood file, a ruler, a can and bottle opener, a small screwdriver, a medium sized screwdriver, a large screwdriver, a Phillips screwdriver, a wire grip, wire strippers, an awl punch and a shackle. The new Super Tool 200 is also made with an additional rounding in the needlenose pliers in order to reclose bottle caps. Both types are available in matte black versions as well.

The large and extensive Wave Multi Tool

WAVE

The Wave dates back to 1998 and is a large Multi Tool with a great number of pieces. The stainless steel tool has a handle 4 inches long and weighs 8 ounces. What strikes one immediately are the large round hinge points for the long knife and saw blades. These blades are locked separately. The Wave has needle nose pliers with an extra grip surface, wire cutters and steel wire cutters, a clippoint blade, a serrated edge, a wood saw, a diamond file with an extra filing edge, scissors, a small screwdriver, a medium sized screwdriver, a large screwdriver, a Phillips screwdriver, a can and bottle opener, wire strippers and a shackle.

The New Wave appeared on the market in 2004 as a renovated product. The new model has a locking system that is fifty percent stronger than the old mechanism. A new type of diamond file was introduced as well. The needle nose pliers underwent a few changes as well and can now grip even tighter. The steel wire cutters are extra hard and enlarged. The saw blade

The new New Wave from 2004

has a new type of saw teeth and the saw can now be used without filling with sawdust. The New Wave also has two bit holders and two double sided screw bits. This is why at 8.5 ounces it is heavier than the older model.

WAVE 20TH ANNIVERSARY

This Wave was introduced in 2003 in commemoration of the twentieth anniversary of Leatherman. This Wave has dark handle parts, but other than that it is identical to the older model. It has the

same pieces as well: needle nose pliers with an extra grip surface, wire cutters and steel wire cutters, a clippoint blade, a serrated edge, a wood saw, a diamond file with an extra

The Wave jubilee edition from 2003

filing edge, scissors, a small screwdriver, a medium sized screwdriver, a large screwdriver, a Phillips screwdriver, a can and bottle opener, wire strippers and a shackle.

LEITNER

www.69nord.at

The emblem 69°Nord of Norbert Leitner

The Austrian knife maker Norbert Leitner has been making professional knives under the mark 69°Nord since 2000. He often wrote about the 69° latitude line, where the name was derived, during his travels through North Scandinavia. He is a mountaineer and nature hiker and has occupied himself for many years with the theme of survival.

The bright light of the North and his experience with the life outdoors recurs in his knife designs. Leitner focuses on harmonious design, durable construction and comfortable compactness. He prefers working with special 1.2379-D2 steel, which he finishes into a style he developed himself called 'facefinish,' because of the way it is washed with acids. The blades are etched with chloride and then polished by hand. This treatment is usually repeated from six to ten times. The polishing agent gets finer in structure every time until it is finally done with nothing more than oil. With this method, the steel is optimally protected and acquires a beautiful, deep gloss. Norbert Leitner currently has nine different models available that can be finished in a number of different ways. These models can be seen on his website. The photos here were taken by Norbert Leitner himself.

AGENT

Agent

The Agent is a fixed hunting knife with a blade made of 1.2379-D2 steel, tempered to 60 HRC. The length of the blade is 2.4 inches and the total length of the knife is 5.5 inches. The bolster is made of nickel steel and the handle from elderberry wood. Norbert describes this as a 'city knife' for daily use.

AKTO

The Akto is a medium sized knife that is 6.7 inches in length. The blade is made of 1.2379-D2 steel, tempered to 60 HRC, and is 3.1 inches

The wide Akto

long. The knife is ground very deep and long. Its ergonomic handle is made of desert ironwood and fixed with mosaic pins.

The Akto Sheet skeleton knife

AKTO SHEET

The Akto Sheet is an integral knife with a skeleton handle, in other words it does not have handle plates. A label to which only the name and blood type of the carrier should be entered is engraved on the handle. The knife is 6.7 inches in total length and has a blade of 3.1 inches. The knife is made of stainless 1.2379-D2 steel.

The strangely shaped Mygg

HAJ

The Haj hunting knife is 6.7 inches in total length. The blade is made of laminated steel, which consists of three layers of 1.2842 steel tempered to 62 HRC. The length of the blade is 2.95 inches. The long and slim handle is made of pear wood.

The Nicka hunting knife

MYGG

The Mygg looks like a very short skinning knife with an extremely short handle. The total length of the Mygg is 3.3 inches and the blade is made of 1.2379-D2 steel, which is only 1.7 inches long. The handle is made of layered fiberglass. The handle pin with which the handle is attached as well as the shackle is made of carbon fiberglass.

NANOOK

The large Nanook hunting knife is 9.1 inches in total length. The blade is 3.9 inches long and is made of 1.2379-D2 steel, tempered to 60 HRC.

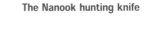

The Nanook hunting knife

Norbert makes the bolster from nickel steel. The handle is made of beautiful venous elderberry wood. It is a typical hunting and outdoor knife.

NICKA

The Nicka hunting knife has a typical pointed blade made of 1.2379-D2 steel with a large finger slot as an integrated guard. The total length of the Nicka is 8.9 inches and the blade is 3.5 inches in length. The handle is made of desert ironwood.

Haj

259

The remarkable Unna

UNNA

This short and compact Unna looks like a dagger, but the blade is ground only on one side. The total length of the Unna knife is 6.1 inches. The blade is

**The African
Art knife**

made of 1.2379-D2 steel and is 2.95 inches long. The handle is made of palissander wood and the bolster from mosaic Damascus.

LINDER
www.linder.de

**The emblem
of Linder**

This company was founded around 1870 by Carl Wihelm Linder, a knife maker from Bech, in Solingen, Germany. When he passed away in 1890, his youngest son Carl took over. In 1908 Linder was registered as a commercial entity. In May 1918, right before the First World War, Carl Linder purchased a premise in Solingen. After the war, business picked up and within a short time exports were back on target. The economic crisis of 1929 hit the company very hard. Sales decreased drastically and they had just started to recover in 1936, when

Carl passed away at the age of 66. His only child, a daughter, did not have any interest in the company. His widow sold the company to Paul Rosenkaimer, a knife maker from Solingen. Ever since this time the company was known as Carl Linder Nachf. (Nachf. stands for 'successor').

With the outbreak of the Second World War in 1939, production at Linder came to a virtual standstill. Rosenkaimer's co-workers all had to serve in the military or were put to work in weapons production. He had to do military service himself in 1943; even his fifteen-year-old son was called up by the Nazis. The factory was bombarded on 31 December 1944 and stayed in ruins until the end of 1948 when Rosenkaimer received a grant to rebuild. In 1949, after a break of ten years, production was resumed. In the beginning only father and son worked there, but after a few months the business expanded. By 1976, Paul had relinquished management of the company to his son Siegfried. In January 1980 the company was strengthened with the employment of grandson Stephan and a year later with the employment of another grandson Peter. Paul Rosenkaimer passed away at the age of 85 in 1985.

Linder is known for its excellent knives: hunting knives, Bowie knives, daggers and recreation knives. Another aspect of their range is a number of specific traditional products, the so-called Trachtenmessen. This type of knife usually has handles made of stag horn and decorated with hunting motifs. This company also represents the knives of various Scandinavian and Spanish factories.

AFRICAN ART

The knife called African Art has a long stretched skinner blade of 5.9 inches, made of stainless 420 steel. The handle is made of antelope horn with a guard and bolster made of nickel silver. A black leather sheath comes with the knife.

Big Eagle Bowie

BIG EAGLE

Boot Knife

This Classic Bowie goes by the model name Big Eagle due to the pommel in the shape of a large eagle head. The pommel and guard have protruding dog heads on either end, made of nickel silver. The large and heavy blade is made of stainless 440C steel and is 9.8 inches in length. The handle is made of Cocobola wood. The Big Eagle knife comes with a leather sheath.

Boot Knife

CLASSIC DAGGER

This dagger is 9.4 inches in total length. Its stainless 440C steel blade is 5.1 inches long and it weighs 7.1 ounces. The handle is 4.3 inches long and made of

The large Crocodile Hunter

BOOT

The Boot knife shown here is actually called Slirekniv and has a Scandinavian design. During earlier times, similar knives were often carried by sailors in their boots. The ergonomic handle is made of Cocobola wood and has a deep finger slot that serves as a guard. The blade is made of 440C steel and is 4.7 inches long. The Sailor's Tool is a typical traditional

ebony wood. This dagger is also made with a white perlex, Cocobola wood or a stag horn handle. The decorative dagger with a keris blade is made of stainless 420 steel and is 5.1 inches in length. The total length of this dagger is 9 inches. The handle is made of polished stag horn and the guard and sculptured pommel are made of silver. The dagger weighs 7.8 ounces. The last dagger is a traditional decorative weapon as well. The total length

sailor's knife. Ropes are cut with it, but one can also use it to peel potatoes and carve simple objects from wood or ivory. The blade is made of 440C steel and is 5.1 inches long. The handle is made of Cocobola wood as well. Leather sheaths come with both of the knives.

Classic dagger from the Linder collection

CROCODILE HUNTER

The Crocodile Hunter is a type of outdoor Bowie model that is 14.7 inches in total length. The blade is made of carbon steel, is 9.8 inches long and has a wide blood groove. The handle is made of Cocobola or pakka wood and is 4.9 inches in length. The guard and large pommel are both made of nickel silver. This knife weighs a whopping 16.2 ounces. It gained fame through the famous movie Crocodile Dundee.

is 15 inches and the stainless 420 steel blade is 8.7 inches long. The handle is made of stag horn with an antler medallion with silver pins serving as the pommel. This dagger weighs 10.9 ounces. The leather sheath is set with silver decorations.

The classic Dagger Byzantium

BYZANTIUM DAGGER

This is an example of a unique, classic Byzantium dagger. The weapon is 15 inches in total length and the stainless 420 steel blade is 8.3 inches long. The blade is decorated with gold etched figures and brass and copper are worked into the guard and pommel. The sheath is made of metal as well and this large dagger weighs 12.9 ounces.

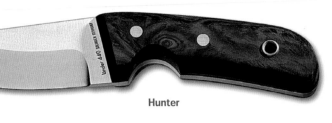

Hunter

blade with a skinning hook and a slim blade. The accompanying sheath is made of woven Cordura nylon.

HUNTER FOLDER

This folding hunting knife has a stag horn handle 5.5 inches long. The large droppoint blade is 5 inches in length and is made of stainless 440C steel. The somewhat shorter blade with its blunt skinning point is 3.9 inches long. The knife has a sawing blade and corkscrew as well. The large blades are locked with a backlock system. The bolster is made of nickel silver.

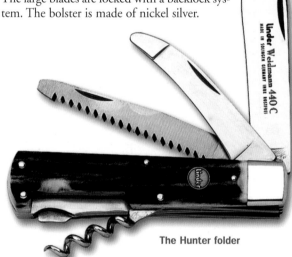

The Hunter folder

The Hunter Combo

HUNTER

The hunting knife shown here is a custom version with a blade made of stainless ATS 34 steel. The total length of the knife is 8.2 inches and the length of the blade is 3.9 inches. This is an integral knife, which means that the blade, guard and pommel are all made of one piece of steel where the extra steel is ground away. The handle is made of stag horn and it weighs 6.7 ounces. The next version is an integral knife as well, made of stainless 440C steel. The total length of the knife is 8.2 inches and the blade is 3.9 inches long. The handle plates are made of Cocobola wood. A beautiful deep finger slot in the handle serves as a guard. This knife is also available with a 2.8 or 4.7 inch long blade. The last model is another custom version with a handle made of amboina wood and a bolster made of aluminum. The droppoint blade, made of stainless 440C steel, is 3.2 inches long and the knife weighs 6.7 ounces.

HUNTER COMBO

This combination system consists of a handle made of Kraton and multiple blades made of stainless 420 steel that can be interchanged. This set consists of a skinning knife, hatchet and an ax, a saw blade for wood and bone, a typical skinner

PATHFINDER

Linder makes a number of pathfinder knives. The knife shown here is 10.2 inches in total length. The blade is made of 440C steel and is 5.5 inches long. The handle is made of synthetic material, has a metal colored pathfinder's emblem and a steel

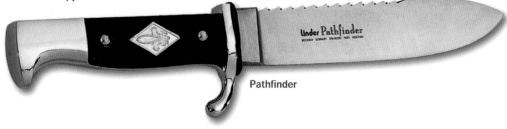

Pathfinder

Pocket knife

length of 2.75, 3.5 or 4.33 inches. The backlock model has a handle 3.9 inches in length. The blade is made of stainless 420 steel. The handle has a steel bolster and plates made of pakka wood.

guard and pommel. The knife weighs 7.2 ounces and comes with a leather sheath. At the top end of the blade back is a row of unique saw teeth, but the knife is available without these teeth as well. Linder also makes a version with a blade length of 4.3 inches.

POCKET

The knives from the Pocket series all have backlock systems. The top knife shown here is made of different materials: with a blade length of 4.0; 4.3; 4.7 or 5.1 inches. The blade is made of stainless 420 steel. The knife has handle plates made of red-brown pakka wood and stainless steel bolsters. The knife also comes with a handle of 3.9 inches, with handle plates made of emerald pakka wood. The decorated bolsters are made of steel. The last version has a standard clip-point blade of 3.9 inches, a saw blade with a

POCKET AUTOMATIC

This luxurious stiletto is 7.9 inches in total length. The stainless 420 steel blade is 3.3 inches long, which means it is within the limits set by German legislation. For most other European countries the

The modern Pocket model

limits are a blade that is no longer than 3.7 inches and wider than 0.55 inches. The thumb stud for servicing the spring mechanism is in the bolster, just on top of the blade pivot. The handle is made of pakka wood.

The luxury Pocket Automatic stiletto

screwdriver point and a built-in bottle opener. The 4.7 inch handle is made of stag horn and the knife has aluminum bolsters.

POCKET

The knife shown here comes from a series of pocketknives with modern shapes. It has a stainless 420 steel blade and is made with or without partial serration of the edge. The handle is made of aluminum with inlaid Kraton plates. The linerlock model is made with a handle

POCKET METAL

The knife shown here goes by the model name of Skelton 1 and has a 4.3 inch long handle. The blade is made of stainless 420 steel. The handle is made of the same steel, but it is sand blasted. The Skeleton series consists of six models, each with a skeleton handle. This knife is especially striking because of the screw top on the blade pivot. The handle is 4.25 inches long and is foldable. The blade is made of stainless 420 steel.

The skeleton shaped Pocket Metal knife

POCKET WOOD

The top knife shown here has a backlock system. The handle is made of pakka wood

Knives from the Pocket Wood series

and is 3.1, 4.0 or 4.3 inches in length respectively. The droppoint blade and bolsters are made of stainless 420 steel. The middle knife has a backlock system and the clippoint blade and bolsters are made of stainless 420 steel as well. This knife is made with a pakka wood handle that is 4, 4.3 or 5.1 inches in length. The bottom knife has a liner-

The Pocket Zac by Linder as a stiletto

lock system. The beautiful bolster, with its flowing lines, is made of stainless steel. The handle plates are made of red-blue pakka wood.

POCKET ZAC

This small knife is a stiletto, 4.7 inches in total length. The stainless 420 steel blade is 1.77 inches long, so is easily within the maximum length allowed. The bolster is made of blued steel. The spring mechanism is served by a large and long stud on the left side of the handle.

SCUBA

This diving knife, appropriately called 'Scuba,' is 8.6 inches in total length and has a blade length of 4.3 inches. The blade is made of stainless steel and it has a series of saw teeth on the back, as well as a cutting hook for cutting through rope or wire. The handle is made of Kraton in red and black. A synthetic diving sheath with a leg strap comes with the knife.

SKINNER

This large skinner is made by Linder in 9.6 or 10.4 inch sizes. The blade is made of stainless 440C steel that is 5.1 or 5.9 inches long. The handle is made of

The Linder Scuba diving knife

Cocobola wood, has a deep finger slot and is 4.5 inches long in both versions. The knife weighs 7.4 or 7.9 ounces respectively. The bolster and pommel are made of nickel silver The Skinner comes with a brown leather sheath.

The large Skinner

TOOTHPICK

The model name Toothpick does not mean that one should niggle around between one's teeth with it, which could be very dangerous. The total length of the knife is 12.8 inches. The blade is made of 440C steel and is 7.9 inches long. The handle is made of stag horn and is 4.9 inches long. The guard and pommel are made of polished brass. The knife weighs 13.8 ounces. It is also made with a Cocobola wood handle.

LUPTÁK

home@memedics

Jozef Lupták completed his studies at the University for Applied Arts in Prague, Czech Republic in 1970 where he studied sculpture. Then he worked as a renovator of historical weapons. He has been making knives since his school days and in the

The logo in the blade of the Lupták knives

1980's he started forging Damasteel. Since then, he has devoted himself entirely to applied arts. Nowadays, he lives and works in Devin, a town close to Bratislava linked to the ancient Celtic tribes that inhabited the area.

KNIFE NO. 1

This integral knife was made of one piece of Damasteel, including the handle and the ring, which serves as

the pommel. The top knife, of cable Damascus, has silver rings in the round pommel. The knife is 7.7 inches long in total and has a blade of 3.7 inches. The bottom knife, in a Celtic design, has a wild Damascus blade, forged from the chain of a chainsaw. The blade is 3.7 inches long and the total length of the knife is 7.3 inches.

Integral Knife

KNIFE NO. 2

This knife has a wonderfully forged blade made of cable Damascus in a patchwork pattern. The bolster is made of nickel steel; the handle is of desert ironwood and the spacers are of green emerald. The knife is 9 inches long in total and has a blade of 4.1 inches.

KNIFE NO. 3

The capricious pattern of the Damascus for the blade was forged from a distributor chain, used in engines. The handle, of yellow taxis wood, has beautiful nerve patterns. The pommel is of band Damascus. This knife is 10.4 inches long in total and has a blade of 5.5 inches.

KNIFE NO.4

Knife No. 4 is made of cable Damascus, forged in wavy mosaic up to the blade. The bolster is of nickel steel and the handle of palissander wood. The pommel is of the same Damascus as the knife. The total length of the knife is 9.25 inches and the blade is 4.5 inches long.

A knife made from cable Damascus and desert iron wood

A beautiful knife
with a blade made band strip Damascus

KNIFE NO.5

This knife is of cable Damascus, forged in a wavy pattern. The blade is 4.7 inches long and the total length of the knife is 9.25 inches. The handle is of stag horn and has spacers of palissander wood.

L'VOV

www.rusartknife.urbannet.ru/gallery.html

Gennady Nikolaevich L`vov was born in Moscow in 1961. He studied instrument engineering and molding metal at the Vladimir Polytechnic School. During his youth he spent a lot of time daydreaming outdoors. This can be seen in the beautiful etching on his blades. In 1989 he went to work as the head of the engra-

Knife No. 4 with wavy cable Damascus

KNIFE NO.6

Knife No. 6 has a blade and pommel forged from a motor chain into a capricious Damascus pattern. The handle is made of a large bone with spacers of green marble. The Damascus pommel follows the contour of the bone precisely. This knife is 8.9 inches in total length and the blade is 4.5 inches long.

Knife No. 5 with a handle made
from stag horn

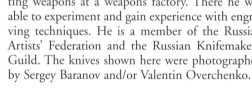

KNIFE NO.7

Knife No. 7 has a blade of cable Damascus forged in a sinuous pattern. The handle is of the unique serpentine stone from Cuba. The knife is 9.8 inches long with a blade of 5.1 inches.

ving department for exclusive work done on hunting weapons at a weapons factory. There he was able to experiment and gain experience with engraving techniques. He is a member of the Russian Artists' Federation and the Russian Knifemakers' Guild. The knives shown here were photographed by Sergey Baranov and/or Valentin Overchenko.

Knife No. 6

The knife from serpentine stone

Gennady Nikolaevich L'vov with his master sign top right and below that the logo of the Russian Knifemakers' Guild

BACKWATER

Gennady made this knife in 2003 for the 'Blades of Russia 2004' exhibition in the Uspensky Belfort of

a dry birch with a large knot. He whittled it down until only the burl lump was left over and left it to dry for a year. In order to expose the exquisite nerve structure of this beautiful piece of wood, 40 percent of the original burl had to be cut away. Gennady prepared the wood himself, treating it with linseed oil, turpentine, wax and resin.

The steel used for the blade was stainless 95X18 or 440C steel, tempered to 56 HRC. Gennady's knives espouse a few basic rules: a knife cannot be aggressive in its shape, but must radiate peace and quiet; its Russian character must clearly be visible and the Slavic, Finnish and Norwegian influences must be evident; and, last, a knife must not only be pretty, it must also be highly functional.

LODGE

This knife was made for the exposition 'Blades of Russia 2001' and is now in the weapons museum of the Kremlin in Moscow as part of a series of 'Russian' knives. The engraved and etched depiction on the blade depicts a hunting party in Fall. It shows the home of a forester who offers them food and invites them to take a bath in the separate bath house. This house and place really exist, not far

The Backwater hunting knife from 2003

the Kremlin in Moscow. The Backwater knife is part of a series entitled 'Messhera.' The river Pol'a depicted on the blade springs in Shatura and deltas into the big river Kl`azma. The townsfolk of Krivadino who live on its banks have been breeding beavers since 1918, and old, protected beaver dams are still in evidence there. One of the adjacent creeks inspired the artwork on the blade.

The knife is 9.6 inches long and the blade is 4.5 inches long and 1.1 inches wide. The knife rests on a small birch plank. For the handle, Gennady found

from Moscow in the province of Shatura, close to the town Nikitinskaya. A forester used to live here during the 1950s, with his wife, two children and a horse. Everyone in the area knew the house and extraordinary characteristics were attributed to the spring water from the well. Today the house is in ruins.

The knife is 10.2 inches long with a 5.2 inch stainless 95X18 (440C) steel blade, tempered to 56 HRC. The handle is made of birch burl wood.

The Lodge knife from 2001

M

MACKRILL

www.mackrill.co.za

The emblem of Mackrill Custom Knives

Mackrill is a small South African family company that currently produces fifty handmade knives per month, but production can be increased to dou-

The silver California Bowie

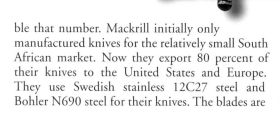

ble that number. Mackrill initially only manufactured knives for the relatively small South African market. Now they export 80 percent of their knives to the United States and Europe. They use Swedish stainless 12C27 steel and Bohler N690 steel for their knives. The blades are

hollow ground, then tempered under vacuum conditions to 58-60 HRC. The hardening is done by Mackrill itself. The handles of Mackrill knives are made of the most beautiful indigenous materials from South Africa: ivory from hippopotamus teeth, horn from the Cape buffalo and kudu, giraffe hoof and the tusks of warthogs. For wood they use wild olive, ebony and red ivory. Mackrill specializes in exclusive scrimshaws done in freehand on the handle material. Sheaths and cases are made of wood, often inlaid with silver and gold. The bolsters and pommels are made of copper, stainless steel and, on request, gold or silver. Mackrill also make replicas of historical pieces, custom-made knives and collector's knives in limited editions. They also do hunting trophies and personal or corporate gifts. Company logos, family coats of arms, and more can be photo-etched onto the knife.

CALIFORNIAN BOWIE

This Bowie knife is impressive because of the many precious metals used in it. The handle and the sheath is made of silver, the guard is made of macumé and the blade from stainless Sanvik 12C27 steel. The fittings on the sheath are made of brass and lapis lazuli. An engraving of a mineworker washing ore in search of gold is on the sheath.

DAMASCUS DAGGER

This dagger has a blade made of beautiful wild Damascus. The extra large guard is shaped like a claw of a bird of prey. The guard and pommel are made of silver and the handle from hippopotamus ivory, inlaid with silver wire and the horn of a Cape buffalo. The black spacers are made of buffalo horn as well. This beautiful dagger comes in an attractive wooden case.

The lovely Damascus Dagger

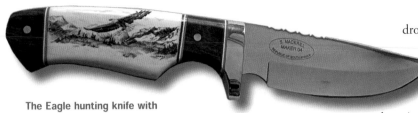

The Eagle hunting knife with
a beautifully colored scrimshaw drawing

EAGLE OVER THE MOUNTAINS

The handle of this fixed knife is made of lead wood and hippopotamus ivory. The Scandinavian blade is of Sanvik 12C27 steel and the guard and pins are made of brass. A colored scrimshaw drawing of an eagle gliding through the air over a mountain decorates the handle.

GRAND SLAM SHEEP SET

This beautiful set of four identical fixed knives depicts the four most important sheep breeds in South Africa: the Big Horn, the Dall, the Desert Sheep and the Stone Sheep. The sheep are etched

The Pula and the Cape Buffalo folding knife

in scrimshaw on the hippopotamus ivory of the handles of all four knives. The ends of these handles are made of sheep horn. The guards and handle pins are made of brass and the blade is made of Sanvik 12C27 steel.

PULA FOLDER / CAPE BUFFALO FOLDER

These linerlock folding knives are real 'gentlemen's knives.' The handle of the Pula knife is made of mother-of-pearl from a pula shell. The bolster is stainless steel engraved with fantasy figures. The liner of the locking system is made of spring steel and the

droppoint blade is made of stainless Sanvik 12C27. One of the folding knives has a drop-point blade made of Sanvik 12C27 Steel The handle of the Cape buffalo folding knife shown here is made of warthog tusks and Cape buffalo horn. There is a scrimshaw drawing of a male elephant on the ivory. The short droppoint blade is Sanvik 12C27 Steel. A leather sheath and a wooden chest come with the knife.

SABRE ANTELOPE

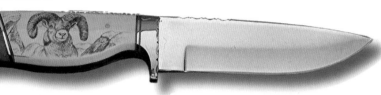

The Grand Slam Sheep

This fixed integral knife is striking for two reasons: the beautiful scrimshaw drawings of a sabre antelope on the hippopotamus ivory handle plates, attached with brass pins; and the pommel, made of bright blue turquoise. The droppoint blade is made of Sanvik 12C27. The bolster (which is also a type of guard due to its shape) and the spacers are made of brass. A part of the blade back has a wavy decorative edge filed in.

MADARIC
www.knives.cz

Lubomír Maďarič comes from Brno in the Czech Republic, famous for its ancient weapons industry. Many modern weapon systems are based on the inventions of weapon designers from this area. Other than firearms, Brno is also known for its knife makers. Maďarič started making knives in 1972 as a hobby and he has been doing it full time since 1993. Since 1997, he has been making military knives in close cooperation with the Czech military, including special combat

The beautiful Mackrill Sabre
Antelope knife

The emblem of Maďarič and the weapon shield of the BMAC Guild

knives, such as the Charon and the Lupus for the Special Forces and the police. Almost all of his blades are made of Czech 14260 steel with

The 'Best Fighter' knife of the 2004 knife exhibition at Brno

a hardness of 58 HRC. The handles are made of leather, walnut wood or duralumin. The combat knives are phosphated for protection against rust and reflection.

Maďarič was the chairperson of Bohemian Cultellatores until 1998, when the organization split into two opposing sides: one considered knives utilitarian objects while the other viewed them as art. The two opposing groups were the ANBC: Asociace Nožířů Bohemia Cultellatores, chaired by Josef Pok; and the BMAC: Bohemiae et Moraviae Artes Cultellatores, chaired by Maďarič. The permanent members of the art society are Jaroslav Brixi, Jaroslav Čech, Petr Pospíšil, Jan Slezák and Miloslav Petráček. Thanks to the expansion of the European Community, Europe has gained access to the beautiful knives from this country.

The Madaric Charon

CAPTURED HUNTER

The Captured Hunter knife is a sort of parody of hunting. The bears are not being hunted here, but have got the better of the hunter. He is being kept in check by one bear and has to wait on two other card-playing bears. The knife is made of stainless 440C steel. The high-relief depiction of the bears was done by Julius Mojžíš, an artist who often cooperates with Maďarič. The total length of the knife is 10.4 inches. The blade is 5.5 inches in length and the handle is 4.9 inches long.

CHARON

Maďarič does things differently when it comes to the design and production of custom combat knives. He has a model collection of this type of knives, often furnished with traditional handles made of leather rings. This is not the case with the Charon, however, as the handle is made of walnut wood, stained dark. The Charon is 12 inches in total length with a handle of 6.5 inches, and a blade 5.5 inches long. The knife has a firm guard and the blade is partially serrated. The false incision at the top blade runs half the length of the knife. This knife comes with a black leather sheath. The Czech aphorism

The Captured Hunter by Maďarič

engraved on the blade, 'POT ŠETŘÍ KREV,' means 'Sweat Saves Blood.'

GERONIMO

The Geronimo combat knife looks very similar to the Charon, but the handle is made of leather rings. The knife also has a steel bayonet-like pommel with a shackle. The black phosphated blade looks very much like that of the Charon, but it is 6.7 inches long. The slogan 'Vivere Militare Est,' engraved on the blade means: 'Long Live the Military.' The total length of the knife is 11.8 inches and the handle is 5.1 inches long. This large, heavy knife comes with a black leather sheath. At the 1998 Brno Super Show, it dominated the 'Fighting Knife' category and was awarded 'Knife of the Year 1998.' Geronimo was nominated for a prize at knife show in Thiers in France that year as well.

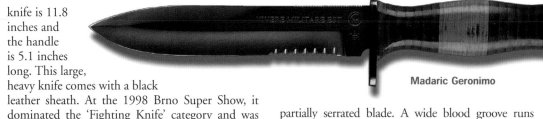

Madaric Geronimo

Green Beret combat knofe

partially serrated blade. A wide blood groove runs down the middle. The handle is made of leather rings and closed off with a thick, steel, bayonet-like pommel with a shackle. The Lupus B is roughly similar, but it has a dark walnut handle with wide, diagonal grooves. The Lupus C is similar to the Lupus A, but has the smooth pommel of the Lupus B. The knives come with black leather sheaths, but a tactical Kydex sheath would not go badly with it either.

GREEN BERETS

The Green Berets combat knives are an ode to the American soldiers who fought in the Vietnam War, with the fifth Special Forces group. This is engraved in the blade. The 11.8 inch long Green Berets have Bowie blades that are 6.3 inches in length and handles that are 5.5 inches long. The blades, the steel guards and the steel pommels with shackles are phosphated matte black. The handles are made of leather rings, covered with epoxy resin and polished after they dry out. The knives come with black leather sheaths.

MOUFLON

The Mouflon decorative knife won a prize at the knife show in Vienna in 1998. It is a beautiful knife, with beautiful engravings. The pommel is shaped like a sculpted mouflon head. The guard is in the shape of a leg with a hoof. On the left side of the blade, a mouflon buck is depicted. On the right side is a ewe – a female mouflon. The legs were beautifully carved with a scene of a hunter and his hounds. The leather sheath is imprinted with a picture of a mouflon buck. The blade was made of Damasteel. The knife is 11.0 inches in total length and the blade is 5.5 inches long.

The Madaric Lupus in the Lupus C, Lupus B and Lupus A (from top to bottom) versions

LUPUS

The Lupus is actually a small military dagger that only differs slightly from the Green Beret in the blade and handle. The dimensions of the knives are similar, however. The blade is 6.3 inches long, the handle is 5.5 inches long and the knife has a total length of 11.8 inches. The Lupus A has a wide, double-sided,

PIRANHA

The Piranha is a combat dagger with a double cutting edge that does not run over the entire length of the blade. Toward the point, the blade becomes somewhat wider and at the point there is a short serration. The Piranha has a blade of 6.3 inches and is 11.2 inches long in total. The handle is made of duralumin and is 4.9 inches long. This combat dagger is dark green with a gray or black

The elegant Mouflon collector's knife

The Meyerco
Big Rascal

tionary sheath locking system for diving knives. He has more than sixty different patents listed under his name. He also started a company that produced nylon sheaths, which he sold a few years later to Fiskars. Collins was initiated into the American Cutlery Hall of Fame in 1996.

While Collins was busy forging himself a solid reputation as a knife designer, Bill Meyer was very busy as a marketing manager and owner of a successful wholesale company in the United States. He also had a passion for interesting sports knives. Because of this, he decided to start up a company that produces an exclusive and unique range of sport knives: Meyerco. At the 1995 American Blade Show, Meyer called on a countless number of producers and designers. There he discovered that many designers design a bestseller once in a while, but that one designer who was successful almost all the time was Blackie Collins. A business deal was quickly reached. The first Meyerco knife was the Strut' n' Cut, which won the prize for the most innovative knife in America in 1997. Since then, Meyerco has introduced many well-known knives, including the Speedster, the Rascal, the Tactical and the Rescue One.

Big Rascal

The Big Rascal folding knife, designed by Blackie Collins, has a linerlock in the handle made of Fiberesin, synthetic material reinforced with fiberglass. The total length of the knife is 7.36 inches. The clippoint blade is made of stainless 440 steel with a smooth or partially serrated edge and is 3.11 inches long. The knife weighs 2.88 ounces. On the right of the handle is a stainless steel carrying clip.

Bolt-Action

The Bolt-Action folding knife has a patented locking system, designed by Collins. When opening the knife, the blade shoots to the front with a spring rod. In order to unlock the blade, the sliding stud at the top of the handle must be pulled back somewhat and the blade can be folded back in. The total length of the Bolt Action is 7.25 inches. The clippoint blade is made of stainless 440 steel and is 3 inches in length. The knife is made with a smooth or partially serrated edge, as well as with a gut hook. The Bolt-Action weighs 2.78 ounces. The handle is made of Fiberesin and there is a stainless steel carrying clip on the right side.

The Bolt-Action knife

Buddy System

The Buddy model has a Kydex sheath which allows it to be carried upside down around the neck with a lanyard. The knife is locked in place in the sheath with the patented lock, which can be released with a stud on the sheath. The total length of the knife is 5.12 inches. The blade is made of stainless 440 steel and is 2.126 inches long. The handle is made of Fiberesin and weighs only 1.6 ounces.

The Buddy System neck knife

Buddy System II

Buddy System II

The Buddy II is the same length as the Buddy, but the blade is somewhat longer, at 2.25 inches. The knife can also be carried upside down around the neck in a Kydex sheath with a patented locking system: a large button drops into the Fiberesin handle when the knife is drawn. The Buddy II weighs 2.2 ounces.

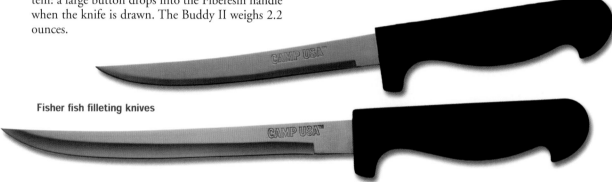

Fisher fish filleting knives

Fisher

The Fisher fishing knife has a long and narrow blade made of stainless 420 steel, 6.25 or 7.87 inches long. Its total length is 10.5 or 12

The ProGrip knife

inches. The ergonomic handle of the Fisher is made of black, polypropylene synthetic material. The knives weigh 1.92 or 2.1 ounces respectively.

ProGrip

The ProGrip series consists of folding knives of two different sizes. The small ProGrip is 6.5 inches in total length. The clippoint blade is made of stainless 440 steel with a

smooth or partially serrated edge and is 2.64 inches long. The knife weighs 2.6 ounces. The larger type is 8.25 inches long, with a 3.62 inch blade, made with a smooth or partially serrated edge, or with a gut hook blade point. This model weighs 5.1 ounces. The handle is made of rubber and does not have a carrying clip. A woven nylon sheath comes with the knife. The ProGrip has a backlock system.

Razor Knife

The 2003 Razor is a working knife for all sorts of tasks. Blackie Collins designed it with a hollow blade attachment into which all sorts of break-off utility knives or Stanley knives can be attached. The total length of

the Razor is 6.26 inches and it weighs 4.2 ounces. On the right of the Fiberesin handle is a stainless steel carrying clip.

Rescue One

The Rescue One has a blade made of stainless 440 steel. The blade has a blunt point with a short smooth piece in the cutting edge. The rest of the edge is serrated for quickly cutting through vehicle seatbelts and similar materials. The handle is made of Fiberesin with a 75 HRC tempered steel point for breaking windows at the end. The knife is locked with a backlock system. The total length of the Rescue is 8.0 inches, the

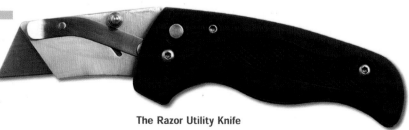

The Razor Utility Knife

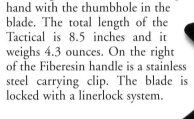

The Rescue One knife for emergency services

blade is 3.5 inches long and the knife weighs 2.73 ounces. On the right of the handle is a stainless steel carrying clip.

SKINNER

The Skinner is a standard shaped, integral skinning knife with a handle made of rubber coated steel. Meyerco produces the Skinner in two different sizes. The total lengths of the knives are 4.37 or 5.5 inches. The stainless 440 steel blades are 2.5 or 3.27 inches long and the Skinners weigh 2.24 or 4.32 ounces respectively. Possession of such a skinning knife is illegal in some countries. This is not due to the gut hook on the blade, but because of the handle that stands transversely to the blade.

SPEEDSTER

The Speedster has a special opening system designed by Blackie Collins. This is called 'speed-assist.' With this system, the blade still

**The Speedster with
the 'Speed-Assisted' system**

needs to be opened with the thumb stud, but it is supported by a spiral spring system. By definition, this is not a stiletto. The push button at the top of the blade pivot is a locking button which closes the blade. The Speedster knife is made with a smooth or partially serrated edge. Meyerco also produces these knives with a titanium coating of the blade, shown here. The total length of the Speedster is 7.13 inches. The stainless 440 steel clippoint blade is 3.386 inches long and the knife weighs

2.26 ounces. The handle is made of Fiberesin and a stainless steel carrying clip is on the right side.

TACTICAL

The Tactical folding knife has a spearpoint blade, made of stainless 440 steel and is 3.62 inches in length. The knife is made with a smooth or partially serrated edge. This knife can be opened with one hand with the thumbhole in the blade. The total length of the Tactical is 8.5 inches and it weighs 4.3 ounces. On the right of the Fiberesin handle is a stainless steel carrying clip. The blade is locked with a linerlock system.

Skinner

TACTICAL 2004

The new tactical folding knife from 2004 has a large, wide, stainless 440 steel blade with a smooth or partially serrated edge. The length of the blade is 3.25 inches and the total length of the opened knife is 7.5 inches. The Tac-

Meyerco Tactical

The new Tactical model from 2004

MIVILLE-DESCHENES
www.amd.miville-deschenes.com

Canadian knife maker Alain Miville Deschenes comes from French Quebec. He started collecting knives as a boy. After studying photography and information graphics 3D, he worked in

tical has a speed-assist blade as well. The push button in the Fiberesin handle is for releasing the linerlock system. The knife weighs 2.6 ounces.

The Traditional

TRADITIONAL

The traditional knives of Meyerco inspire nostalgia. The Turf is a real Grandpa knife, like my own grandfather used to carry. The old-fashioned, wide blade turns on a large, brass blade pivot and the handle plates are made of real bakelite attached with brass pins. A pioneer oxen wagon is etched into the blade. The Turf is 6.5 inches long. Its stainless 420 steel blade is 2.75 inches long and the knife weighs 4.8 ounces. The traditional pocketknife has three blades: a sheepfoot, a clippoint blade and a so-called pen knife. The length of the largest blade is 2.5 inches and the total length of the knife is 5.75 inches. The bolster is made of steel and the handle plates of bone. The knife weighs 2.78 ounces. The Trapper has a bone handle as well and weighs 5.40 ounces. It has two blades: a clippoint and a so-called spey point. Each blade is 3.5 inches long. The total length of the Trapper is 7.36 inches.

WOOD LOCKBACK

The Wood Lockback knives have, as the name indicates, handle plates made of wood. The bolsters are made of stainless steel or brass. The knives are 5.75 or 8.5 inches in total length. The stainless 420 steel blades are 2.5 or 9.5 inches long and are locked with the backlock system. The Wood knives weigh 2.78 or 6.46 ounces.

that field for a long time as a website programmer, integrator, information graphics designer, project manager and production leader. Since 1998, he has been a multimedia teacher and provides staff training at companies. He also designs websites and is a photographer, consultant and multimedia project leader. He has been making knives for a number of years, having learned

Knife maker's emblem, such as
Alain Miville-Deschenes etches on his knives

about the craft through magazines and the Internet. It took many hours of studying before he felt confident enough to set up a workshop in his house. The actual work was a bit shaky at first since there is a big difference between theory and practice. Once a knife is completed, however, the reward is great. He only makes utility knives, and his designs are very ergonomic and practical, but beautiful as well. Alain has an extended range of models and styles. Each knife comes with a handmade

The Wood Lockback

some lovely filing work. Dusty engraved the bolster and pommel beautifully. The handle is made of stabilized giraffe bone, attached with the usual extremely detailed engraving work on the rivets. The total length of the knife is 11.5 inches and the blade is 6.25 inches long. The knife has a leather sheath and a protective cover.

The wild Predator

PREDATOR

This knife lives up to the reputation of its name, as it does indeed look like a predator. A few decorative holes were drilled in the contrast Damasteel blade. The lines were preserved with the half holes in the long false incision. The drawings on the Damasteel are very beautiful with a type of zebra stripe running to the bolster, engraved by Dusty himself with plant motifs. The handle is made of stabilized horn from the African waterbuck and attached with mosaic pins. The knife is 11.25 inches in total length and has a blade 6.0 inches long.

TALON

The Talon seems less rough, but it does look like an animal claw, as its name suggests. The Damasteel blade, forged by Jim Ferguson, has a unique structure. The engraving work on the bolster was done by Dusty. The handle of the Talon is made of legal elephant ivory. The knife is 11.5 inches long and the blade is 6.5 inches in length.

Talon

**The beautiful
Talon blade in detail**

MUELA
www.mmuela.com

Eladio Muela made his first knife more than fifty years ago. It was a good piece of craftsmanship and thus started the story of a factory that produces hundreds of different models of knives and enjoys fame all over the world. Eladio's first knife led to several orders for more and soon knife collectors were on the look-out out for his knives. Difficult times followed, as Eladio did not have any machines to relieve him of some of his workload. Making the knives by hand, however,

The Muela logo

deepened his self-taught craftsmanship and determination. The quality of his materials and the personal finishes of each knife contribute to his growing popularity. The latter is still an important aspect of all

Muela products. Still, it did not take long for him to outrow his workshop. Due to the increased demand for Muela knives, he exchanged the original workplace for a large factory. International orders lead to a more extensive selection of models over the years. Muela's attendance at many national and international exhibitions and knife fairs led to even greater name recognition all over the world.

Aguila, the Damascus Bowie by Muela

Today, Muela is a modern knife factory with modern equipment, capable of handling large orders from all over the world. Part of the company, however, is still dedicated to certain models that demand old-fashioned craftsmanship. The excellent finish of these unique models gives them an advantage over other the products of other manufacturers. The current production capacity of the factory is about 350,000 pieces per year. Starting from the forging of the steel, with different characteristics required for different model types, each step in the process is done in the factory with no outside involvement. Modern computer driven

machines do the work, from stock removal of the metal strips of stainless molybdenum vanadium steel to pre-shaping the half-finished items. The knives are then shaped mechanically, ground, polished and tempered. Much of this work is done by machine under the supervision of highly trained personnel. Many Muela models have traditional stag horn handles selected, prepared and attached at the factory. Muela even has its own leather department where the leather is processed into sheaths. Once the production process is finished and all quality control measures have been taken, the knives go to the finishing department, where they are given a final polish and the Muela logo is applied.

AGUILA DAMASCUS BOWIE

The Aguila Damascus Bowie is a beautiful hand-made hunting knife. The solid silver pommel is in the shape of an eagle head and the silver guard is

The traditional Bowie

shaped like two raptor's claws, complete with feathers and the characteristic scaled hide. The blade is made of Damasteel with a beautiful structure. The handle is made of Cocobola wood. This knife is made in a numbered, limited edition. The total length is 14.4 inches, the blade is 9.06 inches long and the handle length is 5.32 inches. This Damascus Bowie weighs 16.6 ounces.

ALCE

The Alce model consists of a series of knives of different material, available in two different sizes. The blade of the large type is 4.72 inches long, with a hefty serration at the top of the blade back. The blade of the smaller knife is 4 inches long and does not have any serration. The handles of each of the models of

The Alce

are 3.75 inches long. The Alce I has a black synthetic material handle with a synthetic material pommel and guard. The handle of the Alce II is black as well, but the

The Big Mountain

guard and pommel are brass-colored. The Alce III has a military green handle with a black guard and pommel. A black leather or camouflage sheath made of braided nylon comes with the knife.

BIG MOUNTAIN

The Big Mountain series is a set of large Bowie knives with black synthetic material handles with finger slots. The guard and pommel come in black or brass color, as preferred. The large Bowie has a handle 4.92 inches and a blade 8.66 inches in length. The total length of this large knife is 13.6 inches and it weighs 14.5

The Buffalo hunter

made of nickel steel. The handles of these decorative knives are made of laminate wood, varnished in various attractive colors. The Buffalo knife has a handle 4.72 inches and a blade 6.5 inches long and it weighs 11.3 ounces.

ounces. The somewhat smaller Bowie has a handle 4.92 inches long as well, but the blade is 7.09 inches long and it weighs 13.05 ounces.

BOWIE SERIES

This series was modeled on the original Bowie knife. The handle is made of laminate wood and the guard and pommel are brass. This series of large Bowies has handles 4.92 inches in length. The blades are 8.66 or 7.09 inches long. The weight varies between 14.1 and 16.4 ounces. The smaller Bowie knives have handles that are 4.5 inches long, blades 5.5 or 6.25 inches and they weigh 7.9 or 9.9 ounces respectively. The smallest

COLIBRI

Colibri

The name Colibri suggests something small and this is indeed the case. The Colibri knife is 6.1 inches in total length, with a 3.5 inch long handle and a blade

The Cuchillo hunting folder

2.75 inches in length. The knife weighs from 2.65 to 3 ounces. The handle is made of stag horn, laminate wood or special nut burl wood.

CUCHILLO PLEGABLE

This hunter folding knife has a wonderful shape. It is still a traditional knife with a liner-lock system, however. The extra long blade, which protrudes far from the handle, is specially intended for the mercy killing of wounded game. The handle is 5.31 inches in length and the blade is a whopping 7.09 inches long. The knife weighs 15.5 ounces. The bolster and pommel are made of brass and the handle from laminate wood.

Bowie in this series is 7.7 inches in total length. The handle is 3.7 inches long and the blade is 3.5 inches in length. The Bowie knives are also available with or without a blood groove.

BUFFALO

The Buffalo was inspired by the Bowie knife. The large Buffalos have blades made of stainless 440C steel and guards and pommels

Escuderos hunting dagger

The Muela Grizzly skinner

ESCUDEROS

Escuderos hunting daggers are also intended for the mercy killing of wounded game, but they are large enough to cut meat as well. The dagger is 15 inches in total length, has a handle of 5.5 inches and a blade of 9.5 inches. The weight varies between 14.1 and 17.6 ounces. The guard is made of brass and the handle from stag horn, with or without an antler crown.

GRIZZLY – SIOUX

This Grizzly skinning knife has a wide blade with deep finger slots that serve as a type of integrated guard and a large gut hook at the top of the blade. A second finger slot is in the 4.5 inch long laminate wooden handle. Its blade is 6.75 inches long and the knife weighs 8.8 ounces. The accompanying Sioux has a wide running blade of 4 inches, but it does not have a gut hook. The handle is 4.5 inches in total length and the knife weighs 7.8 ounces.

MAGNUM – ALCARAZ

The Magnum knives shown here were derived from the large Bowie hunting knives. The largest Magnum has a 6 inch stag horn handle with an antler crown and a blade of 10.75 inches. The total length stands at a respectable 16.1 inches and this monster weighs 25 ounces. The somewhat smaller Magnum has 5 inch long handle, a blade of 9.06 inches and it weighs 16.6 ounces. The Alcazar is somewhat smaller and has a handle of 5 inches, a blade of 8.66 inches and it weighs 13.4 ounces. These knives

Magnum and Alcaraz

have guards made of solid brass and the handles without antler crowns have pommels made of brass as well.

MARINA

The Muela Marina diving knives are made of special stainless molybdenum vanadium steel and are resistant to seawater. The sheaths are made of ABS synthetic material and come with rubber straps.

The Marina

The knives are recognizable because of their slim pointy spearpoint blades with fine serrations in part of the cutting edge and a rough serration at the top of the blade back. The synthetic material handle has an ergonomic shape and is ribbed for a sta-

Scorpion

ble grip under water. The Marine knives have blades of 4.7 or 5.5 inches and come in blue, yellow, red and black.

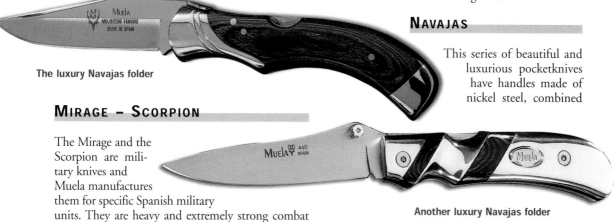

The luxury Navajas folder

MIRAGE – SCORPION

The Mirage and the Scorpion are military knives and Muela manufactures them for specific Spanish military units. They are heavy and extremely strong combat knives with long clippoint blades 7.09 inches in length. The handles are 4.5 inches long and the knives are a whopping 11.6 inches in total length. The knives weigh 12.35 ounces each. A section of the blades have rough serrations that serve excellently for cutting through ropes. The handles are made of rubber and the guards of black steel. The shackles in the handles are protected with brass bushings. The Mirage has a somewhat unusual blade shape. The Mirage and the Scorpion are also available with black protective layers.

The traditional Podenquero and Macareno hunting dagger

NAVAJAS

The Navajas folding knife has a beautiful Mediterranean shape. The handle is decoratively arched and the brass bolster and pommel

go well with the varnished laminate wood. The knife has a frontlock with a short locking rod in the top of the casing. The knife is 8.5 inches in total length. The blade is 3.74 inches long and the handle length is 4.72 inches. The knife weighs 6.7 ounces.

NAVAJAS

This series of beautiful and luxurious pocketknives have handles made of nickel steel, combined

Another luxury Navajas folder

with beautiful, varnished, laminate wood. A finger slot in the bolster makes a wonderful line pattern. The blade is 3.15 inches long and is made of stainless 440C steel. The handle is 4.0 inches long and the knife weighs 3.5 ounces.

PODENQUERO – MACARENO

The Podenquero and the Macareno hunting daggers are ceremonial daggers which bear witness to the traditional South European fondness for hunting. This is evident in the shape of the guard, which consists of a beautifully sculpted dog head or swine head, made of pure sterling silver. This hunting dagger is still made by hand in a limited and numbered edition. The Podequero knife has a handle 6.25 inches in length, a blade 10.24 inches long and weighs 24.7 ounces. The Macareno has a particularly wide blade and weighs a little bit more at 26.5 ounces. The length of the handle is 7.09 inches and the blade is 10.0 inches long. The handle is made of stag horn, with or without an antler crown.

The Luxury Podequero hunting dagger

The Muela Scorpion

PODENQUEROS LUXURY

Both of these Podequero hunting daggers are somewhat simpler versions of the previous series. The guard is made of solid brass and the handle made from stag horn is adorned with an engraved hunting scene. The handle is 5.0 inches long and the blade is 10.2 inches in length. This dagger weighs 22.9 ounces.

SCORPION

This Scorpion combat knife has a somewhat different shape from the Scorpion mentioned earlier. The large Scorpion has a blade of 10.75 inches and the length of the rubber handle is 4.5 inches. The small Scorpion has the same handle, but the blade is 7.48 inches long. The knives weigh from 12.7 to 14.1 ounces. They are made with a blank blade or with a black protective layer.

XA SERIES

The XA Series of folding knives have very elegant shapes. The steel casing has slim handle plates made of varnished Micarta, which looks very similar to

STORM – HORNET

The Storm is a dreaded combat knife. This integral knife has a shackle in the butt and is made of stainless 440C steel. The ridged guard is integrated into the 5.5 inch long blade. The 5.31 inch long handle is shaped by two rounded plates, made of Micarta, varnished dark to look very much like laminate wood. The Storm weighs 10.05 ounces. The knife is made of blank steel

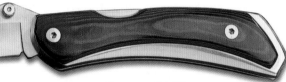

The beautiful XA

or has a PTFE synthetic material protective layer. A similar model is the Hornet, but this version is actually a double-edged dagger. The Hornet has a handle of 5.31 inches and a 5.71 inch blade and weighs 9.5 ounces.

The Storm and the Hornet dagger

laminate wood. The slim blade has a thumb stud for opening and closing the knife with one hand. The handle is 4 inches in length and the blade is 3.35 inches long. The knife weighs 3.17 ounces.

The large Tornado

TANTO – TORNADO

Both of the Tornado combat knives are large and heavy for rugged work. The Tornado Tanto has a blade 7.48 inches in length, a handle of 5.31 inches long and it weighs 12.7 ounces. The Tornado with the clippoint has a partial serration on the edge. The handle is the same length as the Tanto, but the blade is 7.09 inches long.

VARETO AND VIPER

At first glance, both of these knives look somewhat primitive with their ribbed stag horn handles. Upon closer inspection, however, one sees that they have beautiful Damasteel blades. These knives were shaped in the traditional way and are made by hand in limited, numbered editions. The Viper has

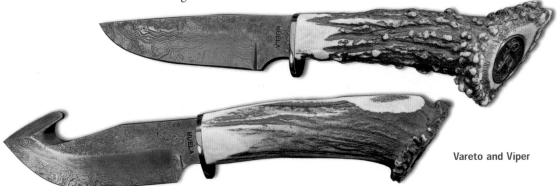

Vareto and Viper

a 4.33 inch long blade with a large gut hook at the top. The handle is 4.72 inches long and has an antler crown that serves as the pommel. The other knife, the Vareto, has a standard hunting blade that is 4.33 inches long. Each of these knives weighs around 6.3 ounces.

for his handles. His designs are inspired by Old Japanese traditions. Clients can choose the finish of the knives from the range of model series. A few years ago he added the ancient Japanese forging technique, known as *shibuichi atama,* to his repertoire.

MAGATAMA

The Magatama is a beautiful folding knife that is misleadingly simple. The casing and blade are made of stainless 440 steel. Inlaid plates made of mother-of-pearl are on both sides of the casing. This knife has a spring pressure system for the 3.03 inch blade. The total length of the Magatama is 7.7 inches.

MIYAMA SKINNER

The Miyama Skinner folding knife is 5.2 inches in total length. The casing and the blade are made of stainless 440 steel. The length of the blade is 2.24 inches. The handle is inlaid with mother-of-pearl plates, made of abalone shells.

MOKUME

The Mokume is a folding knife with a Damasteel blade. The bolster is made of mokume Damascus:

NARUSHIMA

www.nori-messer.de

Noriaki Narushima was born in Tokyo, Japan in 1954. After completing his studies in mechanical engineering at the Technical University of Tokyo, he spent two years working at a machine factory. He then

The logo of Noriaki Narushima

The Magatama folder

embarked on an extended journey through the United States and Europe. After his return to Japan, he went to work as a designer of industrial machines and made knives in his free time. Ever since 1984, he has been taking part annually at the Japan Knife Show in Tokyo. During a visit to Germany in 1985, he met Dietmar Kressler, who became his taskmaster. In

mokume, or *mokume gane,* means 'wood grain.' Mokume gane was developed by Denbei Shoami, a Japanese swordsmith from the Akita prefecture from the northwest of Japan. This Damasteel is a combination of steel layers, copper, brass and silver or nickel silver and sometimes even gold for decorative purposes. The Mokume knife is 7.2 inches in total length. The Damasteel blade is forged by Johannes Ebner and is 3.2 inches long. The casing is made of mother-of-pearl.

The Miyama Skinner

1987, he married a German woman and has been living in Germany ever since. Narushima mostly makes handmade folding knives from valuable steel. He prefers using hard wood, mother-of-pearl and semi-precious stones

The Mokume folder

OUGI

The Ougi is a folding knife with a blade and casing made of stainless 440 steel. The 3.03 inch blade is beautifully hollow ground. The casing is inlaid with *shibuichi*, a mixture of copper and silver. The fan on the shibuichi is made of silver and gold. The total length of the knife is 7.7 inches.

SHOUJOU

The Shoujou folding knife has a casing and blade made of stainless 440 steel. As with the Ougi, the casing has inlaid plates of shibuichi with a death mask made of gold and silver on it. The blade is 3.03 inches long and the total length of the knife is 7 inches.

The Ougi knife with inlaid Shibuichi

TAKE KOZUKA

This traditionally shaped knife has a handle and sheath made of African black wood, a large shrub

Shoujou

indigeous to Africa, related to the rose. The knife has a 3.7 inch Damasteel blade. The total length of the knife is 8.5 inches.

The Take Kozuka knife which has a handle and a sheath made from African Blackwood

NEALY

www.budnealyknifemaker.com

Bud Nealy, knife maker

Bud Nealy was born in Yonkers, New York in 1941. He studied percussion at the Manhattan Music School and worked for 35 years as a musician. He was the person behind the drums in Broadway shows such as *Chorus Line, Grease, Irene* and *Promises.* He was also part of the Glen Miller Orchestra, the First Mood Quartet, the Insect Trust and Jaro (Jazz Artists Repertory Orchestra). He also accompanied many artists, such as Connie Francis, Kenny Rogers and the jazz artists Phil Woods, Al Cohn, Urbie Green and Mose Allison.

Bud Nealy started his knifemaking career in 1980 and actually learned the trade by himself. He mostly uses the stock removal method where excessive material is removed from a strip of steel and then filed until the desired shape is achieved. He learned how to forge motifs into the steel from Daryl Meier and Rob Hudson. Albert Anderson taught Nealy how to make *mokume gane* and he learned various other techniques from other knife makers. He has been a member of the Knifemakers' Guild since 1990, as well as a member of its German and Italian sister organizations. Nealy is the patent holder of a special sheath system that can be easily concealed. He has also developed various models for special military and police units from around the world.

The Amuba knife

His knives have been featured in *Blade Magazine, Fighting Knives, Knives Illustrated, Gun Digest, American Handgunner, Excalibur, Cibles, La Passion des Couteaux* and other magazines. He has designed many knives for knife producers such as Al Mar, Columbia River Knife & Tool (CRKT) and Boker Baumwerk from Solingen, Germany. Nealy designed the Multi-Concealment-Sheath (MCS) system in 1990 and patented it in 1993. the system allows the knife to be carried concealed in nine different ways. Nealy always tries to design knives that are slim in shape and lightweight. He believes that people do not carry heavy knives and they are therefore not handy when one needs them. Nealy takes part in exhibitions around the world and his knives are offered for sale in specialist outlets. Currently he is working on the design of a combat knife for the American Special Forces Group 10.

The Black Aikuchi knife

AMUBA

This typical Amuba knife was based on a design by a master in Eastern fighting techniques, Ralph Mroz. The blade is made of stainless-34 steel and is 3.75 inches in length and the steel is 0.094 inches thick. The total length of the knife is 6.75 inches. The handle plates are made of black G-10 synthetic material with Torx screws. A tactical Kydex sheath with the so-called Dual Lock belt clip, a patent of Bud Nealy, comes with the Amuba. It is also available with a Damasteel blade, forged by Daryl Meier or with a blade with a black synthetic protective layer.

APPALACHIAN TRAIL

The Appalachian Trail is a compact working knife that can be used for all sorts of tasks while out hiking or camping. The blade is made of stainless-34 steel and is 3.5 inches long. The handle plates are made of gray-green Micarta. The knife comes with a Kydex sheath with the Dual Lock system and has a belt strap made of feather steel with which the knife can safely be attached to a backpack, a bicycle frame or to a boot.

BLACK AIKUCHI

The Appalachian Trail

The Aikuchi was the first knife that Nealy designed for his Multi-Concealment-Sheath (MCS) system. This model was based on a Japanese combat knife from the fifteenth century. The blade back has a maximal steel thickness and it runs through to the point, providing optimal strength and perforation power. The cutting edge is ground hollow. Nealy makes the Aikuchi with a blade of stainless ATS-34 steel or S30V steel. The knife is also available with a Damasteel blade by Daryl Meier. This Damasteel consists of a core of 52/100 ball bearing steel with rolled up 80-layered Damasteel, made of high and low carbon steel.

CAVE BEAR SERIES

Nealy designed the Cave Bear series with the recent terrorist events in the back of his mind. This series consists of the Cave Bear, the double-edged Cave Bear II and the smaller Cave Cub. These knives are meant for unconventional warfare fought in caves, desert areas and dark alleys. This knife has an upward slanting thumb rest, a deep index finger slot as a guard and a downward slanting handle end. The spearpoint blade of the Cave Bear is 4.25 inches

The Cave Bear

**The Kwaito with a Damasteel blade
by Daryl Meier**

long and 0.09 inches thick. The total length is 8.5 inches. The Cave Bear II dagger has the same measurements, but the thickness of the blade is 0.125 inches. The smaller Cave Cub has a blade 3.75 inches long and is 7.75 inches in total length. Nealy makes the Cave Bear knives with stainless ATS-34 or S30V steel blades

The Minisink

or with sandwich Damasteel blades from Daryl Meier. The handle is made of G-10 synthetic material. The knives come with sheaths in accordance with the Multi-Concealment-Sheath (MCS) system.

KWAITO

The design of the Kwaito knife was based on an ancient Eastern combat knife. The spearpoint blade has a thick back that runs over the middle of the blade. The top edge consists of a long false incision, which is partly serrated. The length of the blade is 4 inches. The handle plates are made of black G-10 synthetic material and attached with Torx screws. Nealy uses stainless ATS-34 steel for the blade, but the knife is also available with layered Daryl Meier Damasteel. The Kydex Multi-Concealment-Sheath (MCS) system comes with this knife.

Newport version

MINISINK

The Minisink is a small hunting knife with a blade made of stainless ATS-34 steel that is 3.25 inches long. The handle is made of black G-10 synthetic material. The accompanying sheath has a Dual Lock belt clip made of feather steel.

NEWPORT

The Newport was designed as a boot knife, specifically as a utility knife on a yacht. The sheepfoot blade is made of stainless ATS-34 steel and has a long hollow grind. It is partially serrated for cutting through ropes. The Kydex sheath can be handily attached to the boat with the feather steel Dual Lock clip. The blade is 4.13 inches in length. The handle plates are made of G-10 synthetic material or walnut wood. The G-10 plates are attached with the well-known Torx screws and are available in walnut as well, and the screw holes are filled and polished smooth with the wood.

PESH-KABZ

The Pesh-Kabz by Bud Nealy was based on a Persian design from the fifteenth century, with a modern touch. The blade has a specific shape, with the thick

Pesh-Kabz

and strong blade back running through to the point. The cutting edge has an unusual shape and is ground hollow. Nealy makes this Pesh-Kabz with a stainless ATS-34 steel blade in 3.5 as well as 5 inch lengths. The handle is made of G-10 synthetic material. The Pesh-Kabz comes with a special Kydex sheath of the Multi-Concealment-Sheath (MCS) system. This sheath can be carried in nine different ways.

PTK – PICK TACTICAL KNIFE

The PTK or Tactical Knife was designed by Michael Pick, an American grandmaster in Eastern combat sports and instructor of the American Special Operations groups. This combat knife is currently being tested by various professional groups stationed in different conflict zones across the globe. The blade is made of stainless ATS-

PTK

34 steel with a black protective layer and is 5.0 inches in length. It is 0.187 inches thick and the edge is partially serrated. The total length is 10.63 inches. A unique feature of this knife is the deep thumb rest. The handle is made of black G-10. A Kydex sheath with a Dual Lock and a Tek-Lok belt clip come with it.

The Alpina

The logo of Nieto

NIETO

mnieto@adeca.com

The Spanish company Miguel Nieto S.L. is located in Albacete, a city in southeastern Spain, a region famous since the sixteenth century for its knife manufacturing. Records from this time show that the craftsmen of the time kept registers of knives made for clients. The client indicated the size and shape of the desired knife. The name of the client was often engraved on the blade. This work was mostly done at homes or in small workshops. A forefather of the Nieto family worked in such a workshop.

The Nieto knife factory started manufacturing knives in the nineteenth century. Old records, however, contain depictions of knife makers called Nieto. It is very apt that 'nieto' translates to 'grandchild,' since the secrets of forging are still passed from father to son in the company. One of these sons was Miguel Nieto, the founder of the current company. After many years of sacrifice and hard work, he succeeded in opening his own factory. The current generation learned their trade there and the result is rich experience in the area of knife production.

Nieto uses only 440C quality steel, tempered to 58-68 HRC. The Nieto Company is an important knife producer in Spain and exports specialized knives to more than 50 countries.

For example, the thin and beautifully decorative knives are specifically intended for the South European and South American markets. The robust and heavy hunting knives are intended for Northern Europe and the North American continent. Since 2000, Nieto has been innovating and has changed its assortment extensively, with an emphasis on single hand folding knives.

ALPINE

The Alpine series consists of a number of knives in the Bowie style. The large clippoint blades are made of stainless 440C steel. The wooden handles are made of stained laminate, referred to as stamina

The Campera folder

wood. The total lengths of the Alpine knives are 7.8, 11.7 or 14.0 inches respectively. The lengths of the blades are 4.3, 7.1 or 9.1 inches. The knives weigh 5.3, 7.6 or 9 ounces each. The guards and pommels are made of brass colored light metal alloys known as *zamak*. These knives come with black leather sheaths and are also available in combination versions of large and small knives.

CAMPERA SERIES

The Campera is a robust folding knife with four large finger slots in the handle. The bolster is made of brass-colored, light metal called *zamak* and the handle plates are made of scratch proof ABS-synthetic material. The Campera is 5.51, 7.2 or 8.5 inches in total length and the handle length is 3.15, 4.1 or 4.8 inches. The clippoint blade is 3.1 or 3.7

The Caza hunting knife folder

inches long
and locks with a
backlock system.
The knives weigh 3.2
5.6 or 6 ounces each.

CAZA SERIES

This Caza folding knife
series have a clippoint
blade made of stainless 440 steel
and are 2.8, 3.1 or 3.5 inches in length. The knives
have a backlock system. The handles are 3.0, 3.5 or
3.9 inches long and have a brass bolster with handle
plates made of laminated stamina wood. The total
lengths of the knives are 5.7, 6.7 or 7.5 inches
respectively. The Caza weighs from 5.3 to 6.3
ounces each.

The Caza series

The large Cetreria knife

This type of Caza has the same dimensions as the
previous Caza series. Both bolsters are made of
brass-colored, light metal, zamak, and the handle
plates are made of red stained stamina wood.

CETRERIA

The Cetreria is a large and
sturdy utility knife.
The blade is
made of stain-
less 440C steel
and is 5.1, 6.7
or 8.3 inches in
length. The handle has a
guard made of brass and the wood used is laminated stamina. The total length of the Cetreria is 10.4,
11.9 or 15.0 inches and it weighs from

7.1 to 12.0 ounces. A black leather sheath comes
with the knife. The smaller knife has a skinner
blade with a typical upward slanting blade point.

CETRERIA DAGGER

These Cetrerias have double-sided dagger blades
made of stainless 440 steel 5.5, 7.5 or 7.9 inches in
length. The handle is
made of stamina
wood or synthet-
ic stone and is
4.3, 4.8 or 5.6
inches long. The
total length is 9.8,
12.3 or 13.5 inches. These daggers have solid brass
guards and are therefore relatively heavy at 7.1 to
9.9 ounces. They come with black leather sheaths.

The Cetreria dagger

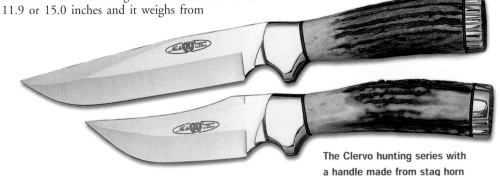

**The Clervo hunting series with
a handle made from stag horn**

CLERVO

This hunting knife has a beautiful handle with a guard and pommel made of nickel silver. The handle itself is 5.3, 5.2 or 5.7 inches long and is made of stag

A series of Combate daggers

horn from India. The stainless 440 steel blade is 5.1, 5.9 or 6.7 inches long and the total length of the knife is 10.4, 11.7 or 11.9 inches. The knife weighs 7.1 to 12.0 ounces, excluding the black leather sheath.

COMBATE DAGGER

The Combate dagger series consists of two daggers of different lengths with polished or bead blasted blades made of 440 steel, 3.7 or 4.7 inches long and partially double-edged and serrated. The 4.0 inch handles and the guards are made of thermoplastic. The total length of the Combate is 7.8 or 8.7 inches and it weighs 5.3 or 6 ounces.

COMBATE KNIFE

Combate series

in length respectively and weigh 4.9, 6.0 or 7.8 ounces each. They come with synthetic material sheaths in black or camouflage colors.

The modern Ergonómico folder

ERGONÓMICO I

The Ergonómico I folding knife has a lovely casing made of nickel steel with four finger slots and inlaid plates of ABS synthetic material. The handle is 3.4, 4.4 or 4.6 inches long respectively. The droppoint blade is made of stainless 440C steel and is 3.0, 3.3 or 3.7 inches long. It is locked with a backlock system. The total length is 6.4, 7.8 or 8.3 inches and the knife weighs from 3.2 to 4.9 ounces.

ERGONÓMICO II

The Ergonómico II folding knife has a casing with finger slots made of nickel steel and with drop shaped holes to reduce the weight. The knives weigh only 2.5 to 3.9 ounces each. The blade is made of stainless 440C

The Combate knives have polished and bead blasted blades, made of stainless 440C steel. The total lengths of these blades are 4.3, 7.1 or 9.1 inches. They have false incisions on the blade back which makes them look double edged. The handles are 3.6 or 4.8 inches long and are made of thermoplastic, as are the guards and pommels. The knives are 8.0, 11.9 or 13.9 inches

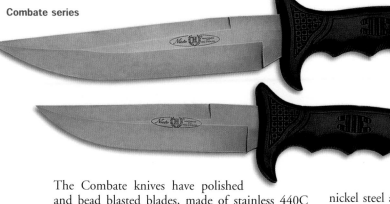

The Ergonómico with steel casings

Ergonómico hunter

steel that is 3.0, 3.3 or 4.0 inches long. The total length is 6.4, 7.8 or 8.7 inches. The Ergonómico II has a backlock system.

Ergonómico Caza

The Ergonómico hunting knife looks like an integral knife, but it is not. The handle, bolster and pommel are all made of nickel steel and are 5.2 or 5.3 inches in length. The inlaid plates on the handle are dark gray synthetic material or olive wood. The blade is made of 440 steel that is 5.1 or 6.7 inches long. This knife is 10.3 or 12.0 inches in total length and weighs 7.1 to 12.0 ounces.

Ergonómico Metálico

The Ergonómico Olivo folder

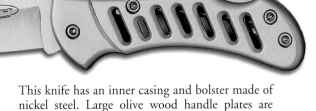

This Ergonómico Metálico series has casings made of nickel steel with different shaped holes for decorative purposes as well as for reducing the weight. The handle is 4.1 or 4.6 inches long and has a stainless steel carrying clip on the right side. The blade of 440 steel is 3.1 or 3.5 inches long and is locked with a backlock system. The total length is 7.2 or 8.1 inches and the knife weighs from 2.1 to 3.5 ounces. Both knives come with black leather sheaths.

Ergonómico Olivo

This beautiful knife has a linerlock system for its 3.5 inch long blade. The casing is 4.6 inches long and is made of nickel steel with inlaid plates of olive wood. The total length of the knife is 8.1 inches and it weighs 2.1 ounces.

Ergonómico Olivo II

The Ergonómico Metálico

This knife has an inner casing and bolster made of nickel steel. Large olive wood handle plates are attached to the casing. In combination with the finger slots this makes for a lovely knife. The blade is 2.2, 2.8, 3.1 or 3.9 inches long and has a backlock system. It is 4.9, 6.3, 7.5 or 9.1 inches in total length and it weighs 1.9 to 3.4 ounces.

Ergonómico Pólar

This is a folding knife with a Mediterranean shape in a modern cover. The nickel steel handle has decorative round holes for a stable grip and to reduce the weight. The length of the handle is 3.8, 4.7 or 5.3 inches. The blade does not have a real locking system,

The beautiful Ergonómico Olivo II

but is stopped by spring pressure. As is usual with Nieto, it is made of stainless 440C steel and is 3.1, 3.9 or 4.5 inches long. The total length of the Ergonómico Pólar is 6.9, 8.1 or 9.8 inches and the knife weighs between 3.9 to 5.6 ounces.

The Ergonómico Pólar

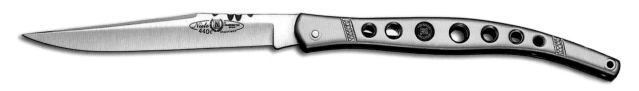

JUNGLA

The Jungla is a somewhat older model than Nieto, but it is still doing very well. The handle is made of leather rings impregnated with artificial resin and then

The Jungla knives

polished. The guard is made of brass and the pommel from nickel steel. The length of the handle is 5.3, 5.7, 5.2 or 6.7 inches. The blade is made of stainless 440C steel and is 5.9, 6.7 or 8.3 inches long. The Jungla is 10.4, 11.7, 11.9 or 14.9 inches in total length and comes with a black leather sheath. The knife weighs from 7.1 to 12.0 ounces.

KANGURO

The Kanguro is a type of adventure knife. It comes with a camouflage sheath, but this has nothing to do with military use. The handle is made of ABS synthetic material with a guard and pommel made of black zamak. The blade, made of 440 steel, is

The Light

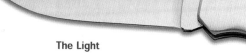

4.3, 7.1 or 9.1 inches long and covered with a black synthetic protective layer. A row of dangerous saw teeth are on the blade back. The total length of the knife is 8.0, 12.0 or 14.0 inches and the knife weighs from 3.9 to 7.4 ounces.

The Montana

LIGHT

The light series has a casing made of lightweight aluminum and it weighs only 2.1 to 3.2 ounces. Inlaid plates of ABS synthetic material are in the handles. The total lengths are 6.4, 7.1, 7.8 or 8.3 inches. The clippoint blade is 3.0, 3.1, 3.3 or 3.7 inches long and locks with a backlock system.

MONTANA

The Montana knife is made in five different sizes. Each size has a specific purpose. The handles are 1.6, 2.2, 3.5, 4.6 or 5.0 inches long and are made of ABS synthetic material. The guards and pommels with shackles are made of black zamak. The blades are made of 440C steel and are 2.0, 2.8 4.3, 7.1 or 9.1 inches long. The

The Kanguro

knives are 3.5, 5.0, 7.9, 11.7 or 14.0 inches in total length and weigh between 2.1 and 8.5 ounces. They come with a black leather sheath.

MONTERÍA

Montería is the Spanish word for hunting big game. Processing big game with this knife should not be a problem. The clippoint blade is 7.0 or 7.9 inches of stainless 440C steel. The handle is made of stamina

The Nieto Montería

wood and is 5.3 inches long and comes with or without a brass guard. Both knives have integrated guards in the blade. The total length of the Montería is 12.4 or 13.2 inches and it weighs 7.4 or 9.9 ounces. The knife comes with a leather sheath.

2.8, 3.1 or 3.5 inches long and is locked with a backlock system. The total length of the knife is 6.3, 7.1 or 7.9 inches and it weighs 3.5 to 6.3 ounces.

The Olivo knife in two different lengths

Olivo

The Olivo hunting knife has a beautiful shape. The olive wood handle is 5.3 or 5.7 inches long. The bolster and pommel are made of nickel steel. The stainless 440C steel blade is 5.1, 5.9 or 6.7 inches long and the total length is 10.4, 11.7 or 12.4 inches. The Olivo weighs 7.1 to 12 ounces and it comes with a black leather sheath.

Sevilla

The Radice folder

Radice

The Radice is a luxurious folding knife with a handle made of amboina wood and a bolster from nickel silver. The length of the handle is 3.5, 3.9 or 4.3 inches. The blade is made of stainless 440C steel, is

The Sevilla series consists of a number of beautiful, paper-thin South European knives with brass bolsters and handles made of stamina wood or imitation horn. The blades are 3.1, 3.9 or 4.5 inches long and do not really lock, but have spring pressure systems. The total lengths of the knives are 6.8, 8.6 or 9.6 inches and the weights vary from 1.9 to 3.4 ounces.

The Sevilla series

TOLEDO

The Toledo is another series of large knives, but this series has mini versions as well. It has a handle

The Toledo

length of 1.6, 3.5, 4.3, 5.4 or 5.8 inches, made of thermoplastic with a guard and pommel made of zamak. The blade is 1.97, 4.33, 5.91, 7.1 or 9.1 inches long and it has a decorative edge on the blade back. The total length of the Toledo is 3.5, 7.8, 10.2, 12.5 or 14.9 inches and it weighs 3.0 to 8.8 ounces.

VERSALLES

The Versalles does not come from Versailles, but from the Nieto factory in Albacete. It is a very beautiful folding knife with a toplock system and a locking rod trigger at the back of the handle which looks like a backlock. The bolster is made of nickel steel and Forprene synthetic material is used for the handle plates. The knife has a blade of 3.1 to 3.5 inches and it is 7.2 or 8.1 inches in total length. The Versalles weigh from 2.8 to 3.5 ounces.

The Versalles folder

OPINEL

www.opinel.com

The emblem of the French Opinel

In 1885, Joseph Opinel and his father ran a small forgery in the small French town of Albiez-Le-Vieux in the Savoie region. They made various agricultural tools for the local farmers and Joseph forged a few pocket knives for friends on request. The grinding machines in the small workshop were run by waterpower, from a mountain stream that ran past the house. Eventually he got more orders for knives. In 1890, Joseph designed a prototype for his Opinel knife and soon started producing it in twelve different sizes. The old model had a shackle in the knife handle so that it could be carried on a necklace or a cord.

Joseph Opinel had himself officially recorded as a knife maker in 1909. In accordance with a law from 1565, issued by the French king Charles IX, knife makers had to put their master signs on their products as a guarantee of quality. Joseph chose a blessing hand topped with the crown of the Savoie region from the days when it was still a dukedom. The first success came when he won a gold medal at the industrial exhibition in Turin in 1911. Opinel knives gained fame and Joseph started exporting them to Italy and Switzerland in 1914. In 1920, he

moved to Cognin. Joseph's two sons, Marcel and Leon, expanded the company. Joseph Opinel passed away in 1960 and his sons were succeeded by his grandson, Maurice Opinel, in 1974. The company currently employs 105 people, half of whom are women. Opinel produces around 4.5 million knives a year and exports around 35 percent of its products to more than 50 countries. Maurice Opinel currently runs the company with his son Denis.

The Opinel knife was added to the Good Design Guide of the Victoria and Albert Museum in London in 1985. This is a collection of the 100 most beautiful products in the world. Opinel knives are very simple. Only after close study can one appreciate the purity of their shape and the precise manufacturing technique.

CARBONE ORIGINEL SÉCURITÉ

The safety ring around the blade pivot was added in 1955. This is the so-called Virobloc, a simple but ingenious system. As soon as the blade is folded away from the handle, the ring can be turned a quarter of the way around the hinge point, which

A complete series of Opinel knives

The original Opinel
security knife with
the Virobloc system

blocks the blade. The blade of the Opinel Originel
is made of carbon steel. The length of the blade is
2.8, 3.1, 3.3, 3.5, 3.9 or 4.7 inches. The total
length of the opened knife is 6.3, 7.1, 7.5, 8.7 or
10.2 inches. The handle is available
in beech, oak, nut or olive wood. The
handle is 3.5, 3.9, 4.1, 4.3, 4.7 or 5.5
inches long and the knife weighs, depending
on the length, 1.4 to 2.0 ounces.

CARBONE MINI

The Opinel Carbone mini knives are made according to the original model from 1909. The blade of
the knife is only held open with spring pressure
since the knife does not have a locking system. The
round nail on the bolster is the blade pivot. The
blade is made of carbon steel and is 1.4, 1.6, 2.0 or
2.4.0 inches long. The handle is made of beech
wood and is 2.2, 2.4, 2.8 or 3.1 inches long. The
total length of the knife is 3.5, 3.9, 4.7 or 5.5 inches and it weighs from 0.71 to 1.59 ounces.

INOX COULEURE SECURITÉ

The Opinel Carbone Mini knife

The colored Opinel Inox knives come in several
sizes. All versions feature the Virobloc safety ring
for locking the opened blade. The stainless steel
blade is 2.6 or 3.3 inches long. The handle is made
of beech wood and is 3.5 or 4.3 inches long. The
wood is treated with varnish in blue, yellow, red or
green. The total length of the knife is 6.1 or 7.7
inches and it weighs 1.6 or 1.9 ounces.

INOX COULEURE MINI

The stainless steel Opinel mini knife has a 2.4 inch
beech wood handle varnished blue, yellow, red or
green. A hole is drilled into the handle to which a

The Opinel Inox security knife

INOX SECURITÉ

The real Opinel security knife is made with a stainless steel 2.0,
2.8, 3.1, 3.3
or 3.9 inch blade.
The well-known Opinel
Virobloc turning ring on the bolster
locks the blade when it is opened. The handle of
the original Inox version was made of beech wood
and was 2.8, 3.5, 3.9, 4.1 or 4.7 inches long.
Opinel uses other wood types for the newer versions, such as Brazilian rose, Bubinga, oak and walnut. The total length of the Inox is 4.7, 6.3, 7.1,
7.5 or 8.7 inches and the weight varies from 1.1 to
2.0 ounces.

The cheerfully colored Opinel Inox

short lanyard with a large key ring is attached. The
blade is 1.6 inches long and the total length of the
opened knife is 3.9 inches. The knife weighs 0.71
ounces. The blade is locked in the same way as the
Carbone Mini.

The colored Opinel Mini knife as key ring holder

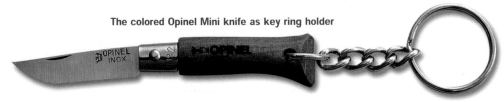

The Design

INOX DESIGN

The Opinel Design knife has a handle made of beech wood artfully painted in colored patterns. It is actually a standard Inox knife with a handle length of 4.3 inches. The stainless steel blade is 3.3 inches long and is locked with the Virobloc safety ring. The total length of the knife is 7.7 inches and it weighs 1.9 ounces.

INOX EFFILÉ

This knife has an extremely long and thin, stretched steel blade 3.1, 3.9, 4.7 or 5.9 inches in length that is locked with the Virobloc safety ring system. The handle is made of beech, Bubinga, oak, ash tree, elm, cherry, olive, palm or walnut wood and is 3.9, 4.7, 5.5 or 6.7 inches long. The total length of the knife is 7.1, 8.7, 10.2 or 12.6 inches. The knife weight varies from 1.4 to 2.5 ounces.

INOX OFFICES COULEURE

production process and a high level of craftsmanship. David Bloch tests his products extensively for sixty days a year in the field. He tested his skinners and caper knives on whitetail in South Ohio, on wild boars in California and on large kudus in South Africa. Outdoor Edge cooperates with various American and international hunting and nature conservation organizations. This is very possible in America as hunting and nature conservation tend to go

The logo of Outdoor Edge, left, with the emblem of the Kodi hunters on the right

hand in hand and there are fewer distinctions between hunting and nature conservation than in Europe.

The Inox Effilé or Slimline series

Opinel designed this fixed knife as a type of office knife. It can be used as a letter opener or to peel an apple. The handle is made of colored beech wood and is 4.3 inches long. The stainless steel blade is 3.3 inches long and the total length is 7.7 inches. The knife weighs 1.9 ounces.

KIT CARSON MAGNA

The Magna folding knife was designed for Outdoor Edge by custom knife maker Kit Carson. He made his first knife in 1972 and he decided to keep making them, along with his son Jody. Kit retired from the

The Inox Slimline in olive wood

OUTDOOR EDGE
www.outdooredge.com

Outdoor Edge is a knife factory, wholesaler and internet shop all in one. It was founded in 1988 by David Bloch, who wanted to make the best possible tools for hunting by combining functional design, an extremely modern

American military as a sergeant first class in 1993. During his military career he had spent a long time with combat arms divisions, as well as the cavalier and the armor infantry. Immedi-

The Inox Offices Couleure

The Kit Carson Magna

ately after his retirement he started a fulltime career as a knife maker. The Magna is no ordinary folding knife, but a real workhorse for any task. The knife has a clippoint blade that is 4 inches long. It is a single hand knife with a thumb stud on the blade, which is locked with a linerlock. The Magna knife is made with a smooth or partially serrated edge. The handle is made of cold pressed 6061-T6 aircraft aluminum and is 5.25 inches long. Vertical and horizontal ridges in the handle ensure a stable grip. The total length of the Magna is 9.25 inches and it weighs 7 ounces. A stainless steel carrying clip is on the right handle plate. The Magna is also available with a handle made of Zytel synthetic material.

inches in total length. The blade is 2.5 inches long and the Kraton thermo rubber handle is a comfortable 4.8 inches long. The large Kodi Skinner has a 4.37 inch blade and is 9 inches in total length. The Kodi Saw is 9.25 inches long with a saw blade of 6 inches. The complete set weighs 16 ounces. Outdoor Edge provides lifelong guarantees with the Kodi-Pak.

PARAGREE FOLDING KNIFE

The Paragree Folder was designed by custom knife maker Darrel Ralph. He has his own style, which combines natural elements with modern technology. Ralph has more than twenty-five years of experience producing precision parts, applied tools, metallurgical tech-

The Kodi-Pak hunting set

KODI-PAK

The Kodi-Pak consists of a short cutting knife for precision work, a large skinning knife with a gut hook at the blade point and a large saw with diamond strength teeth for bones and antlers. It is easy to dismember shot game into manageable pieces with this set: the blades of these knives are made of stainless AUS-8A steel and the rubber Kraton handle ensures a stable grip, even during hard and slippery working conditions. The Kodi-Pak is handily kept in a leather combination sheath, but the three parts are also sold separately with their own sheaths. The short Kodi Caper knife is 7.36

niques and cad-cam programming as well as computer driven process techniques and he also completed his education as an expressive artist. He was a lecturer at knife-making courses at the Montgomery College and the Bill Moran Knife Forging School. The Paragree is a sturdy utility knife with a solid stainless steel skeleton casing and a framelock construction. The handle is furnished with a several holes in order to reduce the weight and provide a solid grip. The stainless AUS-8A steel blade is 3 inches long and is made with a smooth or partially serrated edge. There is a thumb stud on both sides of the blade and a detachable steel carrying clip on the right handle plate. The total length of the Paragree is 7 inches and it weighs 3 ounces.

SPORTSMAN'S MULTI-TOOL

This multifaceted tool actually serves as a mobile mini-toolbox. It is an indispen-

Paragree Folder

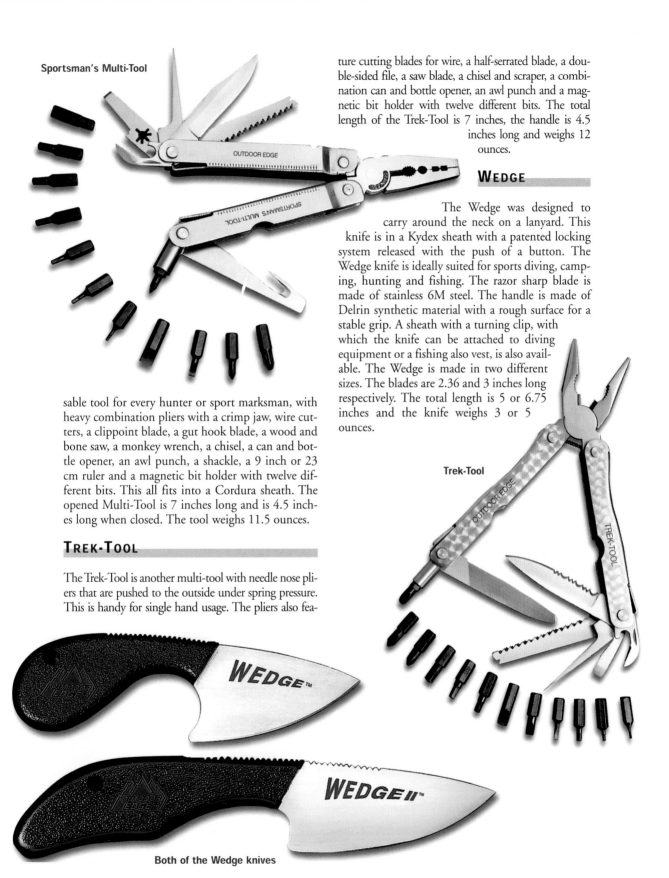

Sportsman's Multi-Tool

ture cutting blades for wire, a half-serrated blade, a double-sided file, a saw blade, a chisel and scraper, a combination can and bottle opener, an awl punch and a magnetic bit holder with twelve different bits. The total length of the Trek-Tool is 7 inches, the handle is 4.5 inches long and weighs 12 ounces.

WEDGE

The Wedge was designed to carry around the neck on a lanyard. This knife is in a Kydex sheath with a patented locking system released with the push of a button. The Wedge knife is ideally suited for sports diving, camping, hunting and fishing. The razor sharp blade is made of stainless 6M steel. The handle is made of Delrin synthetic material with a rough surface for a stable grip. A sheath with a turning clip, with which the knife can be attached to diving equipment or a fishing also vest, is also available. The Wedge is made in two different sizes. The blades are 2.36 and 3 inches long respectively. The total length is 5 or 6.75 inches and the knife weighs 3 or 5 ounces.

sable tool for every hunter or sport marksman, with heavy combination pliers with a crimp jaw, wire cutters, a clippoint blade, a gut hook blade, a wood and bone saw, a monkey wrench, a chisel, a can and bottle opener, an awl punch, a shackle, a 9 inch or 23 cm ruler and a magnetic bit holder with twelve different bits. This all fits into a Cordura sheath. The opened Multi-Tool is 7 inches long and is 4.5 inches long when closed. The tool weighs 11.5 ounces.

TREK-TOOL

The Trek-Tool is another multi-tool with needle nose pliers that are pushed to the outside under spring pressure. This is handy for single hand usage. The pliers also fea-

Trek-Tool

Both of the Wedge knives

P

PACHI

www.pachi-knives.com

Emblem of Pachi

Francesco Pachi started making handmade knives in 1991. His first knives were for friends and acquaintances, but his clientele gradually grew. Within a relatively short time, he became one of the leading knife makers in Europe. Francesco Pachi is known worldwide because of his unique contrast Damasteel. As an artist and lover of nature, he can express natural shapes in his knives with little effort. He combines modern steel types with ancient techniques and works the finest engravings into his knives. His wife, Mirella, is an artist and she specializes in extraordinary scrimshaw depictions. Most Pachi knives are *objects d'art*, but they are also intended for daily use. Nowadays he travels to all the great knife shows in Europe and North America where his creations are on display. His knives are made using the stock removal method, which means that the excess material is removed from a complete strip of metal and filed down to the knife shape. He makes many different models and uses a great number of different materials. He also does the hardening of the steel himself. His knives come with leather sheaths and corduroy protective covers. When designing his creations, he often gives shape to his own feelings, but he also works to the specifications of clients.

CITY KNIFE

The City Knife is a fixed knife 5.8 inches in total length. The droppoint blade is made of polished stainless ATS-34 steel. Decorative filing work was done on the blade back. This looks like a serration, but it is not. Pachi used stainless steel for the bolster. The handle of the knife has handle plates made of black mother-of-pearl, attached with golden rivets.

DROP HUNTER

This hunting knife has a droppoint blade made of stainless RWL-34 steel. There is a typical serration in the blade back and the total length of the knife is 9.0 inches. The bolster is made of stainless steel with an Indian escutcheon done with braids on the bolster. The handle is made of mammoth ivory and attached with steel pins. Mirella Pachi worked a beautiful scrimshaw depiction of an Indian into the ivory. The drawn medallion around the neck of the Indian is inlaid with lapis lazuli.

The Drop Hunter with a beautiful scrimshaw drawing

The City Knife by Pachi

The Fine Folding folder

FINE FOLDING

This beautiful folding knife is 6.5 inches in total length. The carbon Damasteel sheepfoot blade has a typical Pachi separate decorative serration at the top back. The bolsters are made of mosaic Damasteel. The thumb stud on the blade is attached with golden Torx screws. Pachi used mother-of-pearl for the handle plates.

The 'Lions' folder

FOLDING UTILITY 'LIONS'

This knife has a beautiful blade made of carbon Damascus. The unique bolster was forged from mosaic Damasteel. The thumb stud on the blade is attached with golden Torx screws. The mammoth ivory handle plates feature beautiful scrimshaw drawings done by Mirella Pachi. Two lionesses are depicted on the left handle. Two cubs are on the right side, waiting for their mother. The knife is 7.0 inches in total length.

FOLDING UTILITY 'METEORITE'

This knife has a blade and bolster made of the Damasteel for which Pachi has achieved worldwide acclaim. A real meteorite was worked into the Damasteel. The thumb stud on the blade, the Torx screws and the shackle at the back of the bolster are all made of gold. Pachi made the handle plates from Mammoth ivory. The knife is 7.0 inches in total length.

GREY HERON

The Grey Heron depicted in the scrimshaw drawing is standing among reeds. The beautiful colored drawing on the walrus ivory handle plates was done by

The Meteorite folder

Mirella Pachi. The blade and bolster are both of increadible beauty. That Francesco Pachi obviously went all out in making this Damasteel is evident in the precise details of the bolster. The knife is 7.5 inches in total length.

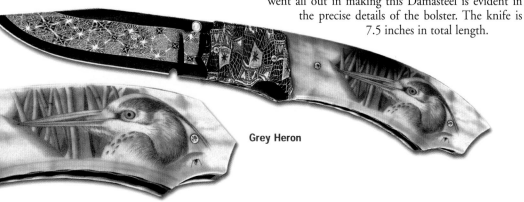

Grey Heron

Bowie Hunter

The 4.9 inch long handle is made of snake wood and the knife weighs 13.4 ounces. The guard is made of stainless ATS-34 steel and is inlaid with the initials of the client. A leather sheath and a leather covered presentation box come with the knife.

BOWIE FIGHTER

Dog & Snake

This knife is made of stainless Schneider Damascus. The Bowie blade is 8.7 inches long and 0.24 inches thick. The total length is 14.6 inches. The guard, tang and pommel are all made of stainless Damasteel. The handle is 5.9 inches long and has plates made of mammoth ivory. The knife weighs 22.9 ounces.

BOWIE HUNTER

The Bowie Hunter is a unique knife with a half round hand protector. The stainless Schneider Damasteel blade is 10.0 inches long and 0.24 inches thick. The handle and hand protector are made of stainless 440C steel with hunting engravings by J. Cech. The grip itself is made from the horn of the sambar deer. This large knife is 16.1 inches in total length and weighs 28.2 ounces. The knife has a special leather sheath with two strap nooses.

Panther & Snake

DOG & SNAKE

The Dog & Snake is an integral knife, made of one piece of stainless ATS-34 steel. The total length of the knife is 6.3 inches and the blade is 2.95 inches long. The knife was designed to be carried in a sheath on a cord around the neck. It only weighs 2.82 ounces and can, of course, be carried in other ways as well. The handle is partly openwork and decorated with engravings of a dog and a snake done by J. Cech.

LION & ELEPHANT

Lion & Elephant

This large hunting knife is called Lion & Elephant and is 11.4 inches in total length. The 6.5 inch long blade is made of stainless ATS-34 tool steel and is 0.23 inches thick. The bolster is made of ATS-34 steel as well and was beautifully engraved with a lion and elephant head by V. Klihavcová. The Cocobola wood handle is 4.9 inches long and the knife weighs 17.6 ounces. The steel rivets of the handle plates are engraved to look like animal eyes.

PANTHER & SNAKE

This integral knife has a beautiful blade made of Schneider ladder Damascus and a handle that is worked with trees, branches, plant motifs, a panther and a snake. J. Cech did the engraving on this knife. Inlaid plates of mammoth ivory are on both sides of the handle. The knife is 8.1

Wolves

inches in total length. The blade is 3.7 inches long and about 0.2 inches thick. The knife weighs 4.9 ounces.

WOLVES

This collector's knife is 8.7 inches in total length. The blade is 4.1 inches long, 0.2 inches thick and made of stainless Damasteel. The blade is openwork over its entire length and engraved with wolf figures in the woods by J. Cech. The bolster is made of stainless ATS-34 steel and engraved by Cech as well. The handle is 4.5 inches long and the knife weighs 9.9 ounces. A leather sheath and a leather covered presentation case come with it.

POSPÍŠIL

Za Sidlistem 2146/13
CZ-14300 Praha-4 Komorany
Czech Republic

The logo of the
Czech and Bohemian Knifemakers' Guild

Petr Pospíšil is a Czech knife maker from Prague. His knives have very tight and stylish shapes. He mostly makes unique hunting knives either indi-

vidually or in very small series. The blades he uses are mostly forged by hand, including the Damasteel that he forges by himself. Sometimes he also uses Damasteel made by other Czech knife makers. Pospíšil prefers using bruyere, palisander and ebony wood for the handles. Until 1998 he was a member of

Fox

Bohemian Cultellatores. After the organization split, he became a permanent member of the BMAC: Bohemiae et Moraviae Artes Cultellatores. Petr Pospíšil was awarded the prize for best engraver at the international knife fair in Brno in 2004.

FOX

The Fox is a large skinner knife, 9.1 inches in total length. The 4.3 inch long blade was made of Damasteel by Pulis in Slovakia. The guard is made of brass and beautifully engraved. The handle is 4.7 inches long and is made of polished giraffe bone. Vlada Klihavcova made a beautiful scrimshaw drawing of young foxes on the bone.

NARVIK

This large Narvik hunting knife has a 5.1 inch long blade, forged from a vehicle spring. The blade is 0.16 inches thick and tempered to 58 HRC. The total length of the knife is 9.8 inches. Petr made the handle of the Narvik from ebony and birch wood. The bolster and pommel are made of brass.

The knife for which Petr Pospíšil won the award as best engraver at the Brno exhibition o f2004

The Narvik knife

SCARLETT O'HARA

This knife is dedicated to Scarlett O'Hara from the novel *Gone with the Wind*, by Margaret Mitchell. The book was filmed by Victor Fleming with Vivien Leigh and Clark Gable in the leading roles. The knife is 12.2 inches in total length. The 6.3 inch long blade consists of 360-layered Damasteel, forged by Puli. The guard is made of brass and engraved by J. Cech. The handle is 5.9 inches long and is made of buffalo horn.

SWISS DAGGER

This Swiss dagger has a beautiful, 80-layered Damasteel blade. It is 5.9 inches long and is forged by Latka from Slovakia. The red-flamed drawing on the steel is a result of a special etching tech-

The Scarlett O'Hara hunter

nique. The total length of this dagger is 11.2 inches. The handle is made of bruyere wood and the guard and pommel from brass.

The Swiss Dagger with a wonderful blade

TAIGA

The Taiga has a large blade of 6.3 inches, forged from stainless Czech AK9 steel. The total length of the knife is 11.2 inches. The handle is made of dark bruyere wood. The bolster, spacers and pommel are made of brass. A large emblem, which is not visible in the photo, of a Russian eagle was engraved on the brass pommel by J. Cech.

The Taiga hunter

PULI

wchristina@dwa.dunaferr.hu

The logo of Puli with the knife maker Károly Szabados on the right

Hungarian knife maker Károly Szabados was born in 1944 in Budapest. He was educated as a tool maker and made his first custom knife during his technical education. After finishing school in 1961, he went to work as a toolmaker at the Dunai Vasmü (Donai Iron Works) in Dunaújváros. This company is currently known as Dunaferr Dunai Vasmü. During his breaks he secretly made knives there from all sorts of material. His boss quickly learned of Károly's hobby and commissioned him to make special knives as bribes. In 1990, Károly decided to start working independently. He founded his own workshop in Dunaújváros a city south of Budapest, under the name of Puli. He was given the predicate of 'knife maker and national artist' by a Hungarian panel. Today he is famous in his native country as well as internationally for his handmade knives.

He mostly uses stainless 440C steel tempered to 58-59 HRC for his hunting knives, but other steel is used upon request. ATS-34, CPMT-440V, powder Damascus from Schneider or Balbach, D2 or RWL-34 steel is also used for his collector's knives. These special steel types are tempered to 58-62 HRC. He uses noble woods, mammoth ivory, mother-of-pearl and anything he can lay his hands on or anything the client requests for handle material. Károly developed an interesting safety system for his hunting knives, which prevents the hunting knife from easily falling out of

that the blade runs straight through to the back. The handle plates are made of ebony with inlaid plates of mammoth ivory. The integral bolster is engraved and finished to a high gloss.

An elegant Gentleman's Knife

the sheath and getting lost. Once the knife is sheathed, it is held in place by a locking pin that must be depressed manually for the knife to be drawn from the sheath.

GENTLEMAN'S KNIFE

This decorative knife seems at first glance to be a luxurious stiletto, but most certainly is not. It is a fixed knife with a slim, narrow blade which would not be out of place in a beautiful office and would and could serve very well as a letter opener. It is an integral knife, which means

HUNTER

This integral hunting knife is made of one strip of metal using the stock removal method. The same goes for the knife shown at the bottom, with the guard and pommel forming part of the blade steel. The inlaid plates are made of stag horn. The blade of this hunting knife has a so-called parabolic grind. This means that the middle part of the blade is the thickest part. In the direction of the blade back, the steel tapers in

A set of hunting knives by Puli

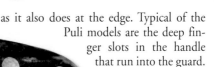

as it also does at the edge. Typical of the Puli models are the deep finger slots in the handle that run into the guard.

HUNTER SPECIAL

This hunting knife is a luxury version of Pull's standard hunting model. It is also an integral knife with a beautifully engraved bolster where deep finger slots create the effect of a guard. The handle plates are made of stabilized stone and attached with mosaic pins. A lovely sheath made of legal snakeskin comes with the knife.

A couple of Puli hunters

An extra luxurious hunter

PYRASTER
www.pyraster.hu

Tanusítvány

The emblem of the Hungarian company Pyraster

The Pyraster company was founded in 1988 by knife smith Fazekas Jozsef. The company name comes from the Latin name for the wild pear tree: Pyrus pyraster. Fazekas is self-taught. He was a trained metalworker and as a result knew how to handle steel and iron, but he only mastered the technique of Damasteel after years of trial and error. The day-to-day forging is still done by Fazekas himself and a trainee smith.

He forges his knives from crude steel. For Damasteel he uses C60 steel, combined with carbon or wolfram steel or S132 and C45 steel. His Damasteel consists of 300 to 1,500 layers. All of the blade steel is forged to shape by hand. Each knife is a unique object and no two knives look the same. Fazekas makes not only knives, but all kinds of swords and daggers as well. He cooperates closely with various Hungarian artists for unique decoration work. The carving on the handles is done by Tamas Seres. Attila Harmat provides the particularly detailed scrimshaw drawings. Fazekas has been present at top international exhibitions since 1998.

HUNTER NO. 3

This lovely hunting knife has a blade made of Turkish Damasteel. Fazekas forged it from C60 steel, combined with standard steel. The blade is tempered to 57-59 HRC and is 6.3 inches long. The guard and pommel are made of Damasteel as well. The handle is made of specially selected and smoothly polished mammoth ivory.

HUNTER NO. 4

This hunting knife has a torsion Damascus blade, made of 176 layers with C60 and standard steel. It is 6.3 inch-

Damascus Hunter

es long and tempered to 57-59 HRC. The handle is composed of ebony, polished mammoth ivory and bank-sia, an Australian pine tree.

Hunter No 4

HUNTER NO. 5

This hunting knife has a blade made of 88-layered torsion Damasteel made from C60 steel and stan-

HUNTER NO. 7

This is another Damascus hunting knife. The blade is 3.9 inches long and is made of 88-layered, wavy

Knife No. 7

dard steel and tempered to 57-59 HRC. The blade is 6.3 inches long. The guard is made of nickel, combined with ebony. The handle is of ebony, cow horn and padauk wood. Padauk is a West African

Damascus, forged from C60 and standard steel. The handle is composed of padouk and bank sai wood. The bolster and spacers are made of nickel steel.

Knife No. 5

wood type with the botanical name of Pterocarpus soyauxii and it mainly grows in Cameroon. It has a very fine grain and a reddish color.

HUNTER NO. 6

HUNTER NO. 9

This Damasteel hunting knife has a blade made of 176-layered, wavy Damascus forged from C60 and

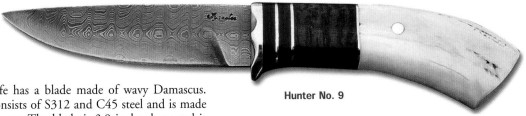

Hunter No. 9

This knife has a blade made of wavy Damascus. which consists of S312 and C45 steel and is made of 176 layers. The blade is 3.9 inches long and is tempered to 57-59 HRC. The guard is made of nickel steel. The handle is a combination of bruyere wood and wood from the wild pear, the Pyrus pyraster.

wolfram steel and tempered to 59 HRC. The length of the blade is 4.3 inches. The bolster and spacers in the handle are made of nickel steel. The handle is composed of ebony wood, snake wood and the incisors of a warthog.

Hunter No. 6

DAGGER NO. 10

This double-sided ground dagger is made of Turkish Damasteel, forged from C60 and standard steel. The large guard and pommel are also made of Turkish Damascus. The blade is 6.3 inches long and tempered to 57-59 HRC. The handle is a combination of ebony and boxwood.

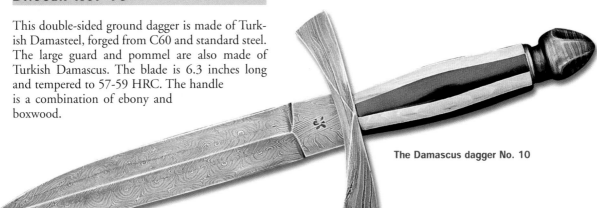

The Damascus dagger No. 10

R

REXROAT

www.rexroatknives.com

The logo of Kirk Rexroat

Kirk Rexroat was born and educated in the state of Wyoming. His style and the design of his knives are as changeable as the weather there. He has an extended range, from small gentlemen's knives right up to large Bowies. A knife must lie well in the hand and maintain its sharpness: these two principles apply to all Rexroat knives.

He started making knives in 1980, after watching his friend make a knife for his father. Kirk started off with the stock removal method: making a knife from one strip of steel. In 1991, he started forging. Since 1997, Kirk has been a member of the American Bladesmith Society, and in 1999, he achieved his master title. His strong points are the variety of his models, the slim lines of his designs and the excellent finish of his knives. Grinding, hardening and polishing all take place in his workshop, which is the best way to guarantee quality. He guarantees all of his products against production and material defects.

Cooperation with Al Mar Knives from Oregon, such as the Nomad and the Shrike, has taught him the techniques needed to design knives for factory production.

AFRICAN BOWIE

The African Bowie is 15.25 inches long. The 10.0 inch long blade is made of Damasteel. The guard and pommel are made of nickel steel and beautifully filed. The handle is made of the wood of the African Blackwood tree with mammoth ivory spacers.

CALIFORNIA FOLDING DAGGER

This is a brilliant folding dagger with a blade and bolster made of mosaic Damascus. The length of the blade is 3.75 inches and the total length of the knife is 8.5 inches. The handle plates are made of mammoth ivory with inlaid pieces of Damascus and scrimshaw. The casing plates are made of gold anodized titanium with beautiful filing work. The handle plates and bolster are fixed with gilded screws.

African Bowie

The California folding dagger

Damascus Dagger

DAMASCUS DAGGER

This Damascus Dagger has a 10.5 inch blade made of torsion Damascus of 1084 and 15N20 steel. The guard and pommel are made of blued steel and beautifully filed. The handle plates are made of mammoth ivory.

DON'T FENCE ME IN BOWIE

This large Bowie is 15.25 inches in length. The blade is made of special mosaic Damascus into which well-known rodeo horses and their riders were forged. The blade is 10.0 inches long. The handle is made of walrus ivory with a Damascus inlaid plate and pommel. The back of the handle is finished with decorative filing work.

RIBONI

www.riboni-knives.com

The emblem of Riboni

Claudio Riboni was born in 1973 in Truccazzano, north of Milan in Italy, where he still lives. He has been making custom knives since 1994. Initially he only made fixed hunting knives for his friends and acquaintances, but his clientele gradually increased. Since 1998 he has been making folding knives for hunting as well, and these currently make up around eighty percent of his work. Riboni has been a member of the Italian Knifemakers' Guild since 1996 and he

currently introduces members to the trade as well. Riboni decided in 2002 to work full time as a knife maker and he spends more than ten hours a day in his basement workshop. Other than knives he also makes bows and arrows. He has taken part in all sorts

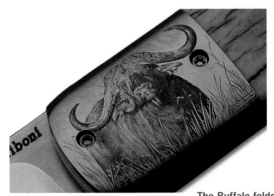

The Bowie with the extraordinary mosaic Damascus

of knife exhibitions in Atlanta, Milan, New York and Paris. His clientele come not only from Europe, but also from North America and Asia as well.

BUFFALO IDEAL

The Buffalo folding knife by Riboni has a linerlock system. The bolt rod is made of 6L4V titanium and the inner casing from stainless steel. Riboni used stainless RWL-34 steel, tempered to 61 HRC, for the blade. This folding knife has a 3.9 inch long blade and the total length is 7.9 inches. Riboni used mam-

The Buffalo folder with
a beautiful scrimshaw drawing

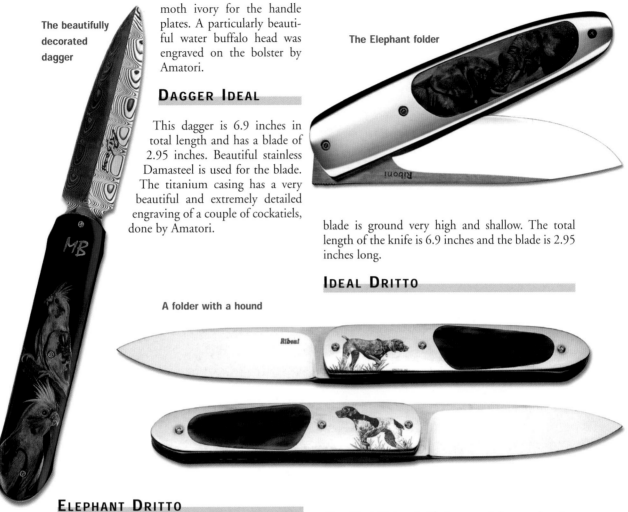

The beautifully decorated dagger

moth ivory for the handle plates. A particularly beautiful water buffalo head was engraved on the bolster by Amatori.

DAGGER IDEAL

This dagger is 6.9 inches in total length and has a blade of 2.95 inches. Beautiful stainless Damasteel is used for the blade. The titanium casing has a very beautiful and extremely detailed engraving of a couple of cockatiels, done by Amatori.

The Elephant folder

blade is ground very high and shallow. The total length of the knife is 6.9 inches and the blade is 2.95 inches long.

IDEAL DRITTO

A folder with a hound

ELEPHANT DRITTO

The Elephant folding knife has a casing made of stainless steel. Inlaid plates of mammoth ivory attached to the casing feature beautiful scrimshaw drawings of romping elephants. The RWL-24 steel

The Ideal Dritto knife has a stainless steel casing with inlaid plates of mammoth ivory and beautiful engravings of hounds on either side.

LION

This fixed hunting knife and bolster are made of stainless RWL-34 steel. Amatori engraved the lioness and cub in such detail that they almost look like a photograph. The handle plates are made of mother-of-pearl.

The Lion folder

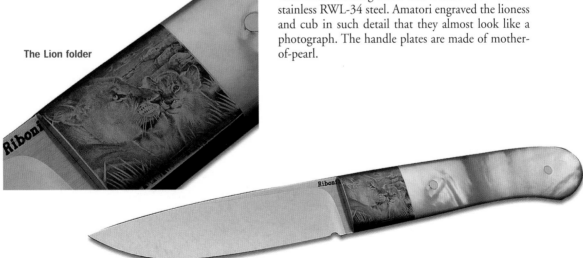

Premium Large

PREMIUM

The Premium folding knife has a linerlock system. The bolt rod is made of 6L4V titanium and the inner casing of stainless steel.

Riboni used stainless RWL-34 steel or mosaic Damasteel for the blade. The Premium knife is made in three different sizes: the small folding knife is 6.3 inches in total length and has a blade of 2.4 inches; the somewhat larger Medium Folder is 7.1 inches in total length and has a blade of 3.15 inches;

through each other. The bolster is made of mosaic Damascus and etched in a special way. The handle plates are of mother-of-pearl.

Premium Medium

The Premium folding knife has a Damascus blade with an unforgettable Damascus pattern. The casing is made of stainless steel with inlaid plates of spiro-graphic Damascus.

Premium Small

Premium Spirograph

and the largest knife has a 3.9 inch long blade with a total length of 7.9 inches.

The Premium Medium folding knife has a specially forged blade of wavy Damascus. The bolster is made of special mosaic Damascus and the handle plates from mother-of-pearl.

The Premium Small folding knife has a Damascus blade with a special wavy structure. It looks as if various wave motifs are woven

These unique knives have extraordinarily beautiful blades made of very complicated, mosaic Damasteel. The casings are made of titanium. Amatori engraved animal figures with exceptional precision on the handles. The bolsters are made of Damascus as well.

Premium Titanium

WILDLIFE

The Wildlife is an integral dagger, ground on both sides and made of one strip of steel. The handle is mostly worked open with small sculptures of animals trekking in a long line around the middle, made of mammoth ivory and held in position by four monumental trees. A great eagle is hovers above them, his wings touching the treetops. A portrait of an Indian is engraved in the pommel.

WILDPARC

This Bowie has a stainless steel blade worked open over virtually its entire length with a sculpture of a landscape with wild animals. The story starts on the left at the bolster: a castle with a castle garden that runs into a park with high trees that support the back of the blade. From the left to right, a great number of wild pigs with their piglets can be seen. A few does look on from the direction of the blade point.

The weapon shield of the BMAC Guild

In 1994, he took part in a knife exhibition with his first collection of knives. Articles about his knives quickly appeared in national hunting and weapons magazines. This led to orders from Russia and the United States. He experimented with bone, stag horn and mammoth ivory and also applied himself to molding bronze and silver.

The Wildlife dagger

Wildparc Bowie

This beautiful knife is 13.8 inches in total length. The handle and the bolster are made of two different colors of mammoth ivory.

RUSNÁK

www.knife.cz/noziri/rusnak

Josef Rusnák was born in Pilsen, Czechoslovakia in 1953. After undergoing a technical education as a mechanical engineer, he went to work in knife making. His artistic interest dates back to 1975 when he made a few oil paintings. In 1977, he made his first engravings and small sculptures. He also restored various sculptures by the old masters and his work was praised in Pilsen and in the neighboring town of Marianske Lazne.

He always tries to combine different materials, sometimes with surprising results. Rusnak has always gone his own way and is not influenced by historical or modern motifs. When developing a new project, he always makes a great number of sketches first. This phase can be time consuming as he always looks at all the angles beforehand. If the idea has not been completely developed, he puts the plan away in a closet for a number of months or even

The Ying-Yang knife from 2004

Dusk, the award winner
for the most artistic knife
at the Brno 2004 exhibition

years. He then looks at it again, makes some adjustments and goes to work. He is absolutely convinced that this way he makes the best knives he can possibly make.

In 2001, Rusnak acquired a license to work with gold. In 2002, he became a member of the Bohemian and Moravian BMAC Knifemakers' Guild. He started producing a series of folding knives in cooperation with Ameri-

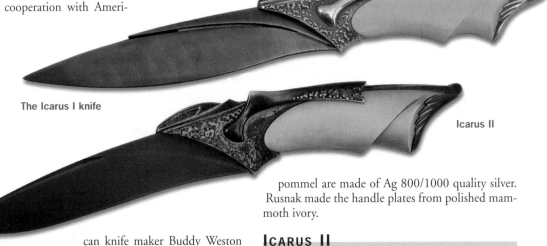

The Icarus I knife

Icarus II

can knife maker Buddy Weston in 2003. Rusnak is not only a knife maker, but also a restorer of metal works of art and jewelry. He has taken part in a great number of local and international knife exhibitions in Prague, Brno and Paris. In 2003, he won the 'Brno Super Special 2003' prize and the most artistic knife in 2004.

DUSK

This unique and futuristic knife won the award for the most artistic knife at the great knife exhibition in Brno in 2004. The blade is made of Damasteel. The handle is made of silver, gold and mother-of-pearl. The handle plates are made of polished white mammoth ivory.

ICARUS I

The Icarus I has a modern shape, with a series of flowing lines. The blade is made of fine Damasteel. The bolster, the top edge of the handle, and the pommel are made of Ag 800/1000 quality silver. Rusnak made the handle plates from polished mammoth ivory.

ICARUS II

The Icarus II knife is similar to the Icarus I. The blade of this knife is made of etched, stainless, ATS-34 steel, however. The bolster, the back of the handle and the pommel are all made of bronze in an antique finish. The rest of the handle is made of polished yellow mammoth ivory.

'Memory of Africa'

Space Legend II

MEMORY OF AFRICA

This knife with the beautiful name of 'Memory of Africa' is made of Damasteel. In the corner of the open worked blade, a piece of the sun, made of virtually pure gold (986/1000), can be seen. The frame of the handle is made of stainless ATS-34 steel. The

SPACE LEGEND II

This knife has a very refined construction and is technically much more complicated than it appears. It is a folding knife with a linerlock system made in cooperation with American knife maker Buddy Weston. The handle is partially worked open and has

A new design
from 2004 by
Josef Rusnak

bolster and a part of the blade were worked open with a depiction of a lioness relaxing in the shade of a large tree on the right. On the left, a lion looks fixedly at the beholder. The handle plates are made of giraffe bone.

a moonscape on both sides. An inlaid piece of mother-of-pearl is used as background between the two images. This depiction extends to the Damasteel blade with a golden sun at the top.

The Flash II is 8 inches in total length. The droppoint blade is made of stainless AUS-8 steel and is 3.5 inches long. The blade has a smooth or partially serrated edge, is bead blasted and comes with a black protective layer or a colored titanium nitride layer, if desired. The handle of the Flash II is made of Zytel, anodized aluminum or even titanium and is 4.5 inches long. The knife weighs 3 ounces.

The Flash II

The Government Agent combat knife

GENTLEMAN

The Gentleman is a beautiful flat knife with a stylish shape. There is a double-sided thumb stud on the blade or a slot in the blade on the Gentleman Mini. The blades and handles of both of these knives are made of stainless AUS-8 steel. The total lengths of the Gentleman knives are 6.5 and 4.6 inches respectively. The blades are 2.75 and 2 inches long each and the knives weigh 3.5 and 1.5 ounces respectively. The blade is locked with a backlock system.

GOVERNMENT AGENT

The Government Agent is a field knife, based on a combat knife of the American military. The blade used to be made of 440A steel, but it is currently made of stainless AUS-6 steel and has a dark gray protective layer. The length of the blade is 6.2 inches. The 5.1 inch long handle is made of Kraton with a checkered motif on the surface so that the knife can be held firmly in hand. The pommel is made of tempered steel that can be used as a hammer in case of emergency. The total length of the Government Agent is 11.25 inches and it weighs 8.3 ounces. A Kydex sheath comes with the knife.

MAGNADOT

The Magnadot folding knife has a fiberglass reinforced Zytel handle and a partially serrated edge. The blade used to be made of 440A steel, but nowadays SOG makes it from stainless AUS-6 steel. The blade is 3.6 inches long and the total length of the knife is 8.25 inches. The Magnadot has a backlock system and a double-sided thumb stud on the blade and it weighs 4.5 ounces.

The Magnadot Folder

The Gentleman Mini

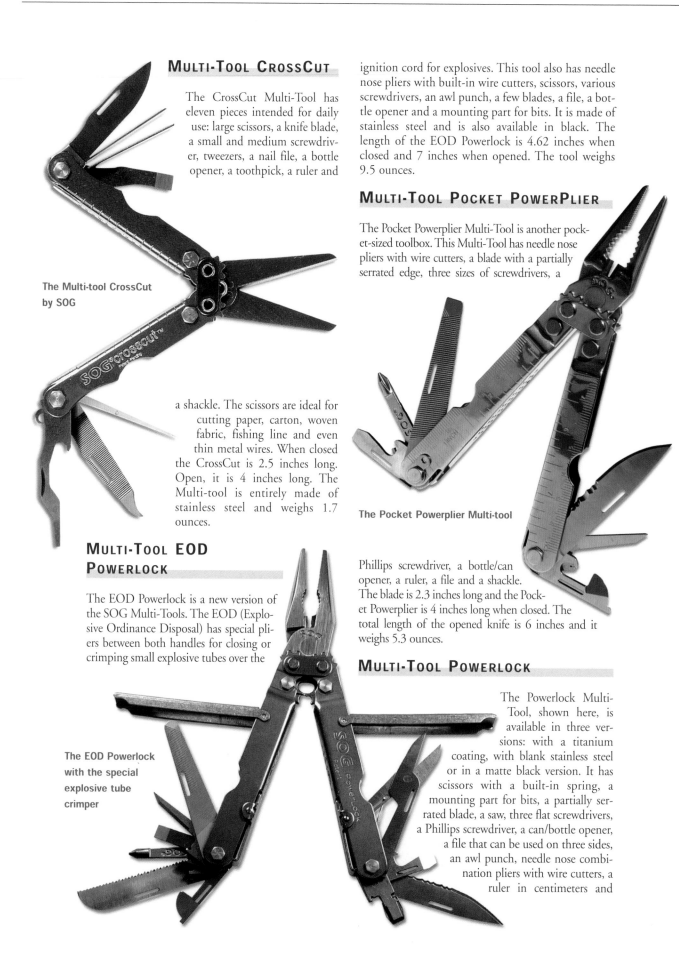

MULTI-TOOL CROSSCUT

The CrossCut Multi-Tool has eleven pieces intended for daily use: large scissors, a knife blade, a small and medium screwdriver, tweezers, a nail file, a bottle opener, a toothpick, a ruler and

The Multi-tool CrossCut by SOG

a shackle. The scissors are ideal for cutting paper, carton, woven fabric, fishing line and even thin metal wires. When closed the CrossCut is 2.5 inches long. Open, it is 4 inches long. The Multi-tool is entirely made of stainless steel and weighs 1.7 ounces.

MULTI-TOOL EOD POWERLOCK

The EOD Powerlock is a new version of the SOG Multi-Tools. The EOD (Explosive Ordinance Disposal) has special pliers between both handles for closing or crimping small explosive tubes over the

The EOD Powerlock with the special explosive tube crimper

ignition cord for explosives. This tool also has needle nose pliers with built-in wire cutters, scissors, various screwdrivers, an awl punch, a few blades, a file, a bottle opener and a mounting part for bits. It is made of stainless steel and is also available in black. The length of the EOD Powerlock is 4.62 inches when closed and 7 inches when opened. The tool weighs 9.5 ounces.

MULTI-TOOL POCKET POWERPLIER

The Pocket Powerplier Multi-Tool is another pocket-sized toolbox. This Multi-Tool has needle nose pliers with wire cutters, a blade with a partially serrated edge, three sizes of screwdrivers, a

The Pocket Powerplier Multi-tool

Phillips screwdriver, a bottle/can opener, a ruler, a file and a shackle. The blade is 2.3 inches long and the Pocket Powerplier is 4 inches long when closed. The total length of the opened knife is 6 inches and it weighs 5.3 ounces.

MULTI-TOOL POWERLOCK

The Powerlock Multi-Tool, shown here, is available in three versions: with a titanium coating, with blank stainless steel or in a matte black version. It has scissors with a built-in spring, a mounting part for bits, a partially serrated blade, a saw, three flat screwdrivers, a Phillips screwdriver, a can/bottle opener, a file that can be used on three sides, an awl punch, needle nose combination pliers with wire cutters, a ruler in centimeters and inches and a shackle. When closed, the Powerlock is 4.6 inches long and when opened, it is 7 inches long. The tool weighs 9.5 ounces. The additional pieces lock in position as soon as they are opened. In order to fold them back again, the lock on the handle must be depressed.

Powerlock

a large screwdriver. All of the large bits automatically lock after they are opened. The total length of the Switchplier is 6 inches and the blade is 3 inches long. The Switchplier weighs 5.5 ounces. The additional pieces are made of stainless steel and the handle is of 6061-T6 aluminum.

OUTLINE

The SOG Outline is a so-called neck knife. It can be used as a type of backup weapon that is carried on a cord around the neck. In a relatively safe continent such as Europe, a weapon like this is not really a necessity, but there are also unsafe places here on earth. This knife sits safely in the patented Kydex sheath, even if it is carried upside down. The knife has a stainless steel AUS-6 steel serrated blade of 2.5 inches and it is 4.6 inches in total length. The skeleton handle is open so that it can be handled with one or more fingers in a hole which is also handy for opening bottle caps. The Outline weighs 1 ounce.

MULTI-TOOL SWITCHPLIER

The Switchplier has heavy combination pliers with a large lever to exert extra pressure. This Multi-Tool opens automatically under spring pressure and can therefore be used with one hand. It contains a knife blade, a bottle opener with a small screwdriver, a Phillips screwdriver, a can opener with a medium sized screwdriver end and a three-sided file that can also be used as

The Outline neck knife

The SOG Multi-tool Switchplier

The Pentagon dagger

PENTAGON

The Pentagon daggers are meant as backup weapons for military and police personnel. The blades of both knives are ground double with a serration on one side. They used to be made of stainless 440A steel, but SOG currently makes them from AUS-6 steel. The length of the blade is 5 inches and the total length of the knife is 9.75 inches. The 4.75 inch long handle is made of checkered Kraton for an optimum grip. The Mini Pentagon has a handle made of fiberglass reinforced Zytel. The knife is 7.75 inches in total length and has a blade of 3.5 inches. The Pentagons weigh 5.8 or 3 ounces respectively. They come with a tactical Kydex sheath that can be carried in many different ways.

PENTAGON ELITE

The Pentagon Elite I and II are folding knives of a different format, with single ground knives 3.9 and 5 inches long. The blade is made of stainless bead blasted AUS-8 steel and has a two-sided thumb stud. The Pentagon Elite has an assisting spring for easily opening and a separate safety stud for locking the closed blade,

a turning notch that grips into the foot of the blade. Once it is latched, the blade is locked. Because of the wedge shape it stays put and is self-adjustable and immune to wear. The knife and the Arc-Lock have

The typical Sculptura folder

been tested extensively. It took a weight of 118 pounds to damage the locking system. When converted this means a weight of 1,184 pounds on the bolt ridge.

SCULPTURA

The Sculptura knife is a small folding knife with a blade made of AUS-8 steel that is 2 inches in length. The new Arc-Lock system is applied to this knife as well. The total length of the opened knife is 4.75 inches. The handle is made of transparent Zytel and has a detachable stainless steel carrying clip. The arched casing of the Sculptura is ergonomic in shape. The knife weighs 2.1 ounces.

SEAL KNIFE SERIES

The Pentagon Elite I

The Seal Pup is the smallest of the tactical Seal knives and it is derived from the Seal 2000 commando knife. The small format makes it ideal for underwater work. The blade used to be made of 440A steel, but SOG currently uses stainless AUS-6 steel with a powder coating. The blade is 4.75 inches long and the knife is 9 inches in total length. The knife weighs 5 ounces. Zytel with Kraton is used for the handle and the knife has a Kydex sheath. The Seal 2000 was chosen as the standard knife for the US Navy SEALs after extensive testing and evaluation by Ameri-

which also acts as additional security for the opened knife. When opened, the knives are 8.6 or 10.75 inches in length respectively. The handles are made of Kevlar-reinforced Zytel. The knives weigh 4.3 and 6.8 ounces each. A detachable stainless steel carrying clip is on the right handle plate. This knife is particularly popular among American police officers and is part of the standard equipment of many police corps. It features the Arc-Lock system, designed by Spencer Frazer:

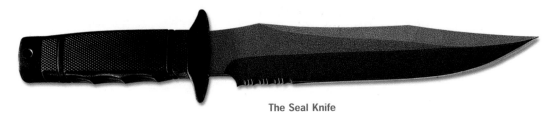

The Seal Knife

The Tomcat II

can authorities. The knives were tested for the breakability of the blade point, the breaking point of the blade, the sharpness and the wear resistance of the edge, the ease with which the handle could tear loose, the effect of 14 days in salt water, diesel oil, heat, hacking, hammering, penetration ability, cutting six different types of rope and nylon lines, silence and reflection. It was also extensively tested in the field. The Seal 2000 has the new Kydex sheath with the Groove. The knife has a blade of 7 inches, it is

The Seal Revolver turning knife

12.25 inches in total length and the Kraton handle is 5.25 inches in length. The Seal Tigershark is the largest combat knife in the Seal series. The blade is 9 inches long and the total length of the knife is 14 inches. The handle is made of Kraton and is 5 inches long.

SEAL REVOLVER

The Seal Revolver is a new concept from SOG and it falls in the survival knife category. The standard blade has a partial serration and can be turned into a saw blade with a twist of the hand. This system was developed by Robbie Roberson. The handle is made of stainless AUS-

The SOGwinder folder

6 steel and is 4.75 inches long. The total length of the knife is 10 inches. This knife has a Zytel handle, weighs 6 ounces and comes with a Kydex sheath.

SOGWINDER

The Sogwinder is a somewhat older model. It has a droppoint blade with a double-sided thumb stud. The blades used to be made of 440A steel, but are currently made of AUS-6 steel. The length of the blade is 2.75 inches and the total length of the

knife is 6.5 inches. The handle is made of Kraton and it weighs 3.5 ounces. Until 2000, SOG also produced a large version of the Sogwinder. This knife had a blade length of 3.75 inches, was 8.25 inches in total length and weighed 8 ounces. The Sogwinder has a backlock system for the blade.

TOMCAT I AND II

The old Tomcat model had a spearpoint blade made of 440A steel and had a single thumb stud on the blade. SOG came out with a new and improved version in 1998 with a kind of Bowie blade made of stainless AUS-6 steel, 3.75 inches in length. It is locked with a backlock system. The new Tomcat II has a double-sided thumb stud on the blade. The old as well as the new model were developed by Spencer Frazer. The handle has inlaid plates of Kraton between stainless steel bolsters. The Tomcat II is also available with handle plates made of Cocobola wood. The total length of the knife is 8.25 inches and it weighs 8 ounces.

TWITCH I AND II

This new knife model was designed by Spencer Frazer. It has SAT (SOG Assisted Technology) for smooth opening. A protruding ridge at the foot of the blade can be pushed back with the thumb so that the knife can be opened effortlessly with one hand. An additional safety stud is integrated in the knife. This safety feature works when the knife is opened and when it is closed. The handle is made of anodized 6061-T6-aluminum and has a blade made of stainless AUS-8 steel. The Twitch is made in two differ-

The Twitch

ent lengths. The blades are between 1.9 to 2.7 inches long and the total length of the knife is between 4.75 to 6.2 inches. The knife weighs 2 or 3 ounces.

The Mini X-Ray Vision

VISION

The SOG Vision is a new design with a blade made of stainless ATS-34 tool steel. The length of the Tanto-shaped, partially serrated blade is 3.75 inches and the total length of the opened knife is 8.37 inches. The knife has the patented Arc-Lock system and a double-sided thumb stud on the blade. A transmutable carrying clip is on the titanium handle and the knife weighs 4 ounces.

The X-Ray Vision is produced in two different shapes with a handle of cost effective Zytel and a detachable carrying clip. The large X-Ray Vision has a blade made of stainless ATS-34 steel that is 3.75 inches long. The total length of the knife is 8.4 inches and it weighs 3 ounces. The smaller model, the Mini X-Ray Vision, is 7 inches in total length and has a blade of 3 inches. The Mini X-Ray weighs 2.6 ounces. The three Vision versions are all supplied with the Arc-Lock system.

X-42 AUTOCLIP

The X-42 AutoClip folding knife was developed through an entirely new concept and is produced in two formats. It is the first SOG knife with a blade made of the new stainless BG-42 steel. This tool steel is normally used for bullet layers and jet propelled motor parts. It is an exceptionally strong and wearproof metal and it can be cryogenically tempered to 59-60 HRC. BG-42 steel is not widely used in the knife industry, as it is expensive and difficult to work with. The blade of the X-42 AutoClip has a modified Tanto shape with a double-sided thumb stud for quick opening. The X-42 is made with a smooth or partially serrated edge. The blade is also available in a choice of a bead blasted or a black tita-

nium nitride protective layer finish. The length of the blade of the X-42 AutoClip is 3.6 or 2.9 inches. The total length of the knife is 8.25 or 6.75 inches and the knife weighs 2.6 or 1.5 ounces. The handle is made of fiberglass reinforced Zytel with a cast on carrying clip. The holding force of the carrying clip can be adjusted with the thumb wheel at the back of the handle.

X-42 FIELD /RECONDO

The X-42 Field Knife has a blade made of BG-42 steel as well. The droppoint blade is 5.4 inches long. At the top of the blade back is a deep serration that serves as a thumb rest. The blade steel runs right through to the protruding shackle at the back of the handle. The length of the knife is 10.65 inches and it weighs 6.5 ounces. The handle plates are made of Zytel. The X-42 Recondo got its name from a particular unit of the American military forces, the MACV Recondo School, established in 1966. Special Forces were trained in long-distance reconnaissance tactics and commando operations. Those who completed the training could accomplish various tasks, including infiltration and extended periods of operation

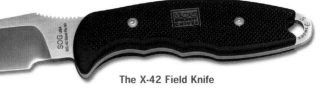

The X-42 Field Knife

inside enemy territory. They were referred to as the 'Recondos,' a synonym for courage and trust.

The X-42 Recondo was designed by Spencer Frazer in the spirit of this school and its recruits. The blade is made of the new BG-42 steel and is 5.3 inches long. The total length of this integral knife is 10.5 inches and it weighs 6.3 ounces. The handle plates are made of fiberglass reinforced Zytel. The X-42 Recondo is made with a matte bead blast finish and a partially serrated edge, as well as with a matte black protective layer of titanium nitride. The knife comes in a tactical Kydex sheath. The new SOG Kydex sheath is certified for military units and para-commandos.

The X-42 Mini AutoClip

The Hunter knife

ground, was tempered by Paul Bos to 60-61 HRC and finished to a high gloss. The handle is made of the sambar stag crown, leather discs and nickel silver with pieces of buffalo horn on both sides. The guard is made of polished 416 steel. A beautifully decorated leather sheath made by Treestump Leather comes with the knife.

HUNTER

This large Hunter is 11.6 inches in total length and has a 7.1 inch long hollow ground blade made of A2 steel. The cutting edge was polished to a high gloss and the blade back was polished by hand. The steel was tempered by Paul Bos. The guard was made of stainless 416 steel. The lower part of the handle, just above the guard, was made of stabilized birch from Finland, separated by nickel silver spacers from the rest of the handle, made of burl wood from a thuya tree. The leather sheath was made by Treestump Leather.

PERSIAN HUNTER

This decorative knife is 10 inches in total length. The hollow ground blade is 0.156 inches thick, 4.9 inches long and made of stainless 154CM steel, tempered by Paul Bos to 60-61 HRC. Bob van Gelder used stabilized

The graceful Persian Hunter

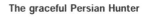

walnut burl wood and beautiful masur burl wood with spacers made of nickel silver for the handle. The guard is made of stainless 416 steel. The leather sheath was made by Treestump Leather.

SCAGEL CAMP KNIFE

The Scagel Kamp Knife is based on an old sailor knife design. The large 9.2 inch blade, made of stainless 154CM steel that is 0.187 inches thick and convex

The Scagel Kamp Knife

SPYDERCO

www.spyderco.com

The Spyderco emblem

Spyderco, an American knife factory from Golden, Colorado in the Rocky Mountains, was founded in 1978 and initially only produced knife grinders. Today, the company is the inventor and patent holder of the single hand knife with the round thumbhole in the blade. Many producers have been applying Spyderco innovations since 1982. In 1981, the company introduced the CLIPIT Worker model, with a thumb hole in the blade and a patented handle clip, so that it could be carried easily on the belt or in the pocket. The next breakthrough came in 1982 with the market release of the CLIPIT Mariner, the first production knife with a special serrated edge, referred to as SpyderEdge. This is a serrated system with one large and two smaller serrations all along the edge. This serration, a sharp recessive notch next to the edge, makes for a larger cutting surface over the same length than a straight non-serrated edge. It is a typical feature of Spyderco knives and increases their cutting ability. The serration points protect the sharp inlets, making it more wear resistant. The SpyderEdge is particularly well suited to cutting through rope, safety belts, carton, rubber hoses and leather. With some practice, the SpyderEdge is also very well suited to precision work, such as skinning, cutting paper and cutting thin planks.

Spyderco works in cooperation with internationally renowned designers, such as Bob Terzuola, Wayne Goddard, Michael Walker, Jess Horn, Frank Centofante, Bill Moran, Tim Wegner and Jot Singh Khalsa. A variety of custom knife makers have been involved in designing different Spyderco knives, for example, the C63 Chinook II by James A. Keating, the C68 Gunting by Bram Frank, the C83 Persian Folder by Ed Schempp and the C84 Karambit by

The Spyderco B01 SpyderFly from 2004

Warren Thomas, to mention only a few.

Spyderco uses three types of locks for its folding knives: the frontlock, the linerlock and the ball bearing Lock. A number of Spyderco knives designed for use in or on water have a notched handle, which allows the knife to dry out well. Most Spyderco knives have casings made of fiberglass-reinforced nylon, this is an extremely strong, but lightweight material. Spyderco also designs some very special knives. After the terrorist attack on the World Trade Center of 11 September 2001, the owners and employees of Spyderco designed The World Trade Center Knife to

The Spyderco C01 Worker from 1981

commemorate the brave police and the firefighters. In the black handle is an inlaid silhouette of the New York skyline with the Twin Towers. Spyderco issued these knives with beautiful wooden chests. There were 2819 copies made, one for each life claimed by the attack. All profits from the sale went to the New York Police and Fire Widow's and Children's Benefit Fund.

B01 SPYDERFLY

Spyderco introduced the SpyderFly, the first butterfly knife it produced, upon the request of its clients in 2004. The handles are made of cast steel and stainless VG-10 steel was used for the blade. This knife weighs 6.6 ounces

The C02 Mariner folder by Spyderco

and is 9.75 inches long when opened and 6 inches long when closed. The hollow ground dagger blade is 4.13 inches long and 0.118 inches thick. The handles are locked with a latch, but only when the knife is closed. In some countries such as the Netherlands and other European countries, butterfly knives with a blade longer than 3.5 inches, with more than one cutting edge, are forbidden.

C01 WORKER

Model C01 Worker was the first and oldest model made by Spyderco. It is a pity that it does not have this traditional folding knife in its production line anymore. The 2.75 inch long blade is made of stainless GIN-1 steel. The length of the opened knife is 6.5 inches. The handle is made of stainless 440C steel and is 3.86 inches long. The C01 Worker weighs 3.7 ounces and locks with a frontlock system in the top of the handle. This single hand knife has the typical Spyderco thumb hole in the blade and a serrated SpyderEdge. A carrying clip is on the right of the handle.

C02 MARINER

The Spyderco C02 Mariner folding knife was first produced in 1982, but it is unfortunately not produced by Spyderco anymore either. The blade has the typical thumbhole as well and the SpyderEdge serration over the entire length of the edge. The 3.62 inch long blade was made of GIN-1 steel. This knife is 8.39 inches in total length and the stainless steel handle is 4.76

The Spyderco C07 Police folder

inches long. A wide groove in the middle of the handle allows the blade and casing to dry out well after it is used in water. The knife weighs 4.5 ounces.

C07 POLICE MODEL

The Police Model has been around since 1984. This folding knife has a linerlock system and weighs 5.6 ounces. The stainless steel handle is 5.31 inches long. The total length of the opened knife is 9.44 inches. The typical blade used to be made of GIN-1 steel, but since 2000 it has been made of VG-10 steel. It is a cross between a spearpoint and a sheepfoot blade and is hollow ground. The blade is 4.13 inches long, 0.118 inches thick and comes with a smooth edge, a long SpyderEdge or with a partial serration. The C07 Police knife used to weigh 5.5 ounces, but the modern version weighs 5.6 ounces. The knife shown here is the new version produced since 2001. The difference is the dent in the frontlock system called a 'David Boye dent.' David Boye, a custom knife maker, invented this dent in the bolt rod to reduce the chances of the locking system being depressed accidentally when the handle is gripped tightly.

C08 HARPY

C08 Harpy

This folding knife got its name from the claw of the Harpy, the largest eagle in South America, and was designed for cutting through ropes, lines or nets while fishing. The arched shape of the blade ensures that whatever one is cutting will not slip from the point. This folding knife has a frontlock system. The knife shown here was the original model from 1987. It has the same groove in its stainless steel handle as the C02 Mariner. The C08 Merlin, introduced in 1993 as the C21 Merlin, has a handle made of fiberglass-reinforced nylon. In 1997, the

handle was made of G-10 synthetic material and the blade was of ATS55 steel. In 1999, the handle material was changed to fiberglass nylon and the David Boye dent was introduced in 2001. The stainless steel version then got the name C08 Harpy and the C21 became known as the C08BK Merlin. Both knives have blades made of stainless VG-10 steel. The C08 Harpy is 6.5 inches in total length and has a blade of 2.75 inches. The blade is 0.118 inches thick. The handle is 3.88 inches long and the knife weighs 3.75 ounces. The C08BK Merlin has a somewhat longer blade at 2.87 inches and it is somewhat lighter at 2.5 ounces because of the synthetic material.

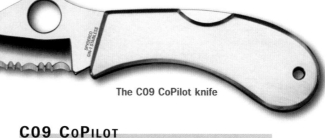

The C09 CoPilot knife

C09 COPILOT

This small folding knife was designed in 1987. It was originally intended for air travelers when small knives could be taken through security. Spyderco even consulted the American aviation authorities and a maximum blade length of 2 inches was approved. The shape of the blade made of GIN-1 steel is similar to the high back of a Boeing 747. This knife has a frontlock system and the well-known SpyderEdge serration. The handle is 3 inches long and the total length of the opened knife is 5 inches. The knife weighs 2.5 ounces. A relatively large carrying clip is on the right handle so that the knife can serve as a money clip as well.

C10 ENDURA, ENDURA SS AND ENDURA TRAINER

The Endura was first brought to the market in 1990, but several versions were designed. The original model was 8.5 inches in total length, had a blade 3.75 inches long

The C10 Endura

and weighed 2.75 ounces. The blade was originally made of G-2 steel, but this was later changed to stainless AUS-8 steel. The handle was 4.8 inches long and made of Kraton synthetic material. The Endura was the first knife to have a carrying clip that could be mounted the other way around, with the blade facing up. In 1999, the steel type for the blade was changed to AUS-6, but in 2001 Spyderco switched back to VG-10 steel. The C10BK Endura

The C10TR Endura Trainer

model has the David Boye dent in the bolt rod. The synthetic material version, with fiberglass reinforced nylon, which is 8.78 inches in total length with a 3.94 inch long and 0.118 inch thick blade, has been produced since 2001. The knife weighs 3 ounces and the blade is ground flat. The stainless steel Endura has also been produced since 2001 with a total length of 8.5 inches, a blade length of 3.75 inches and it weight of 5.5 ounces. These knives are made with a SpyderEdge, a smooth edge or a 50/50 combination. The stainless steel C10-SS blade is ground hollow.

C10TR ENDURA TRAINER

The Endura is also available in a trainer version. This knife was specifically designed to practice combat sports safely. It looks it many ways just like the real knife, but the blade is not sharp and the point has a different shape. All Spyderco training knives have red handles to indicate that the blade is not sharp. The Endura Trainer is 8.78 inches in total length. The blade is 3.94 inches long and the handle length is 4.92 inches. The blade is made of stainless AUS-6 steel and the knife weighs 3 ounces.

C11 DELICA AND DELICA SS

Like the Endura, the Delica is one of Spyderco's classic models and has been in production since 1990. Like the Endura, it is available in a few different versions: the classic Delica, the stainless Delica and the Trainer. The original Delica folding knife had a blade made of stainless AUS-6 steel. This knife was modified in 1998. The

new blade was made of ATS-55 steel, but this was changed back to VG-10 steel in 2001. The old model is 6.81 inches in total length, has a handle length of 4.0 inches and a blade of 2.87 inches. The knife weighs 1.75 ounces. A version with a stainless steel handle known as the C43 Delica II appeared in 1996 (see C43). This was transformed to the C11 Delica Stainless in 1999. This type has, just as the C10 Endura, extra screw holes for the carrying clip to be turned around so that the knife can be carried upside-down. The stainless steel blade of the C11 Celica SS is made of AUS-6 steel. This knife is 7 inches in total length. Its blade is 3 inches long and it weighs 4 ounces. The new C11BK Delica has a handle made of fiberglass-reinforced nylon. The measurements are the same as the stainless steel C11, but it weighs considerably less at 1.9 ounces. This model has been made with the David Boye dent in the blade since 2001. The new Delica knives are available with smooth edges, SpyderEdges or a combination of the two. The blade is 0.098 inches thick. The Delica is one of Spyderco's greatest sales successes.

C11TR DELICA TRAINER

The Delica Trainer was not really developed as a practice knife for the military or the police, but more as a marketing device. Clients can get used to opening the knife at

The Delica C10TR Trainer

the counter with one hand without any nasty little accidents because of the razor sharp blade. It is, of course, also well suited as a training knife for combat sports. The Delica Trainer has a blunt AUS-6 steel blade and the same measurements as the two other versions.

The C11 Delica

C83 SCHEMPP PERSIAN FOLDER

This Oriental-looking folding knife from 2004 was designed by Ed Schempp. It weighs 5.4 ounces and is 8.25 inches long when opened. The handle is 4.75 inches long. The Persian VG-10 clip blade is 3.5 inches long and 0.118 inches thick. Along with the Spyderco thumbhole, Ed Schempp's logo is etched into the blade. The ergonomically shaped blade is made of Micarta and has polished steel bolsters. This

C83 Schempp Persian Folder

folding knife has a frontlock system. On the right of the handle is a stainless steel carrying clip.

C84 WARREN THOMAS KARAMBIT

Warren Thomas is known as a custom knife maker, but he worked on the design of the Karambit in 2003 with Spyderco. This distinct folding knife was introduced in 2004 and has a blade inspired by the kujang, an ancient knife shape from Indonesia. The claw-like, arched blade is used for harvesting vegetation, but it is also a formidable self-defense weapon. The entire knife is made of stainless VG-10 steel and it weighs 5 ounces. The handle is 5.03 inches long and the total length of the opened knife is 5.47 inches. The blade is 2.13 inches long and 0.098 inches thick. The Karambit has a linerlock integrated in the right casing plate. A small steel carrying clip is on the right side.

The Karambit knife by Warren Thomas

C85 YOJIMBO

This folding knife from 2004 was designed by Martial Blade Craft master Michael Janich and Michael Snody built the prototype. The knife is well suited for combat sports. It weighs 3.6 ounces and is 7.81 inches long when opened and 5 inches long when closed. The CPM-S30V blade has an adjusted Wharncliffe sheepfoot blade. The shape is almost a complete triangular shape reminiscent of the Stanley knife. The design ensures good contact with whatever is being cut and it provides little resistance when it is used to stab. The blade is 2.88 inches long and 0.157 inches thick. The handle is made of blue G-10 and tapered so that it can be used as a combat weapon as well.

C87 SCORPIUS

Ed Glesser designed this knife in 2004 according to the idea that form follows function. He describes it as an 'urban-tactical utility knife.' The entire knife was

C85 Jojimbo from 2004 by the duo Janich and Snody

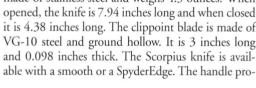

made of stainless steel and weighs 4.3 ounces. When opened, the knife is 7.94 inches long and when closed it is 4.38 inches long. The clippoint blade is made of VG-10 steel and ground hollow. It is 3 inches long and 0.098 inches thick. The Scorpius knife is available with a smooth or a SpyderEdge. The handle pro-

C87 Scorpius, a new design from 2004

vides a good grip and a carefully shaped end that can be used for breaking vehicle windows or keeping an opponent under control. The two large finger slots provide a perfect grip. The extra large Spyderco blade hole was specifically intended for opening the knife while wearing gloves.

C88 Salt I

There is a myth in the knife world that a super steel type that cannot rust exist somewhere. A steel factory in Japan recently turned this myth into reality with the introduction of H-1 steel, a PH steel (precipitation tempered) that is hardened naturally, without the heating process. With one percent nitrogen instead of carbon, this steel type cannot rust. H-1 steel maintains its hard cutting edge, just like many other carbon steel types, but it does not rust or pit.

The Salt I from 2004 is roughly the same shape as the Delica, Spyderco's most popular knife, but it has a number of adjustments, such as a rounded blade point. This folding knife weighs 2 ounces and is 7 inches long when opened. The han-

C88 Salt I

dle is 4 inches long. The blade is somewhere between a clippoint and a sheepfoot blade and is 3 inches long and 0.098 inches thick. Just like the Delica, the Salt has a frontlock system with the David Boye dent in the fiberglass nylon handle. The black steel carrying clip can be removed. Spyderco introduced the Pacific Salt with an H-1 blade in 2004.

FB01 Bill Moran

Bill Moran, one of the grandfathers of the American knife world, designed these two fixed knives on commission from Spyderco in 1995. Each knife weighs 3 ounces and is about 8 inches long. The handles are made of fiberglass nylon with Kraton and the blades are made of VG-10. One has an upward slanting blade and the other has a droppoint blade. The blades are 3.88 inches long each and 0.118 inches thick. The knives are suitable as outdoor knives for hunting, camping or fishing. A sheath made of Kydex comes with the knives.

The FB01 Bill Moran hunter

FB04 Fred Perrin

Fred Perrin, a former commando in the French military, designed this fixed hunting knife in 2002. It weighs 3.7 ounces and is 9.38 inches long. The VG-10 clip blade is 5 inches long and 0.157 inches thick. The handle is made of fiberglass nylon with Kraton inlaid pieces for extra grip. It has a deep dent at the bottom for the index finger, which replaces the guard.

The Fred Perrin FB04

FB05 Temperance and Temperance Trainer

The Temperance was designed in 2001 by Sal Glesser. This sturdy hunting knife is 9.63 inches long and weighs 5.4 ounces. The VG-10 steel blade has an adjusted droppoint of 4.44 inches long and 0.157 inches thick. The blade is available with a smooth edge or with a partial SpyderEdge. The handle, made of fiberglass nylon, has an ergonomic shape as well as four small dimples for certain techniques used in Eastern combat sports. This knife is

The FB05 Temperence knife

also very well suited to hunting, camping and fishing. A Kydex sheath comes with it. There is also a training version available for practicing combat techniques. As with all Spyderco training knives this training knife has a red handle and a blunt point.

FB08 SPOT

The Self Protection Option Tool, or SPOT, is Spyderco's first neck knife – a knife that can be carried around the neck. This fixed knife was designed by Sal Glesser and is available in two types: one made with AUS-6 steel and one with VG-10 and Micarta. The knife is 4.81 inches long and weighs 1.3 or 1.4 ounces. The separately shaped blade looks somewhat like a mirror image of an 'S.' The blade is only 1.63

The SPOT knife from 2003

inches long and 0.118 inches thick. The handle has a so-called skeleton shape and is worked completely open to avoid any unnecessary weight. The first version was made completely from stainless AUS-6 steel and the second is finished with edges of Micarta on the skeleton. A flat Boltaron neck sheath comes with the knife. Boltaron is a new material that consists of recycled ABS and acryl synthetic materials. It is resistant to shock, chemicals and is fireproof.

a Kydex sheath, but since 2004, a Boltaron neck sheath, which can also be carried on the belt, comes with it.

JBK Jester and Jester SS

This basic version of the Jester is a small folding knife that weighs only 0.6 ounces and is 4.4 inches long when opened. When closed, it is 2.5 inches long and it is very well suited for carrying on a key ring or taking along in a bag. The adjusted clip blade is only 1.94 inches long and 0.079 inches thick. The blade is made of AUS-6 steel and is available with a smooth cutting edge or a SpyderEdge. The handle is made of green fiberglass nylon. The Jester SS is made of stainless steel and weighs 1.36 ounces. Otherwise, this version is the same as the standard Jester.

The small Jester folders from 2002 as key ring holders

LBK and LFG Ladybug

LBK Ladybug

Another small folding knife, only 4.31 inches long when open and 2.5 inches long closed. The knife weighs 0.5 ounces. The clippoint blade is made of AUS-6 steel and is 1.94 inches long and 0.079 inches thick. The blade is available with a smooth or a partial SpyderEdge. The handle is made of black fiberglass nylon. The Ladybug with the frontlock has been in production at Spyderco since 1990 and is the oldest model still in production.

FB09 Ronin

A Ronin is a samurai warrior without a master. Spyderco's Ronin is a fixed neck knife, designed in 2002 by Michael Janich. The prototype was made by Michael Snody. This integral knife is 7 inches long and it weighs 3.3 ounces. The nearly triangular Wharncliffe sheepfoot blade is made of VG-10 steel and is 3 inches long and 0.148 inches thick. The handle is made of Micarta with holes in order to reduce the weight. This knife used to come with

FB09 Ronin

Janich/Snody
Ronin

MOKI MKC920 / MKC921 ZEPHYR

The Moki Zephyr folding knife was designed and made for Spyderco by the Japanese knife factory Moki. This folding knife has a frontlock system. The stainless AUS-8 steel blade is made with a smooth or partially serrated SpyderEdge. The blade is 2.87 inches long. The knife is 7 inches in total length and the fiberglass reinforced handle is 4.13 inches long. The Zephyr weighs 2.2 ounces. The Moki MKC921 Elite is somewhat smaller. This folding knife is 6 inches in total length and has a blade of 2.36 inches. The knife weighs 1.4 ounces.

The Moki Zephyr folder

SAKAI GS103 / GS104 BACKPACKER

The Backpacker folding knife was designed and produced for Spyderco by the Japanese company G. Sakai. The blade of this knife is made of stainless AUS-6 steel and the handle is made of anodized zinc with inlaid plates of Kraton. It has the traditional backlock system. The total length of the GS103 is 5.91 inches, the handle is 3.39 inches long and the blade is 2.5 inches long. The knife weighs 2.6 ounces. The GS104 Backpacker is 6.89 inches long, the blade is 3 inches long and the knife weighs 4 ounces.

SAKAI GS105 INTREPID

This knife was designed and made by the Japanese manufacturer Sakai and is produced in various versions. One is made with a interchangeable thumb stud on the blade, but

The Sakai GS105 Intrepid folder

there is also a luxury pocket knife version with a groove in the blade. These different versions are also available with a smooth edge or with a SpyderEdge. The blade is made of stainless AUS-6 steel and is 3 inches long. The handle is 4 inches long and the total length of the opened knife is 6.89 inches. The handle plates are made of Kraton and the knife locks with a backlock. The knife weighs 4.6 ounces.

SAKAI TA-101 PACK RAT / TA-102 ROAD RUNNER / TA-103 FISHER

This Sakai folding knife was designed and made by the Sakai Company from Seki, Japan. Sakai uses stainless AUS-6 steel for the blade and the handle is made of Micarta. The small TA-101 Pack Rat knife is 6.25 inches in total length, has a blade of 2.5 inches and weighs 1.6 ounces. The somewhat larger TA-102 Road Runner is 7.13 inches in total length, has

The graceful Sakai folder

a handle of 4.25 inches and a blade of 2.87 inches. The Road Runner weighs 2.3 ounces. The largest model is the TA-103 Fisher. This knife is 9.06 inches in total length and has a handle length of 5.5 inches. The blade is 3.75 inches long and the knife weighs 4.4 ounces.

The Japanese folder
Sakai Backpacker GS103

Solo SO-01 / SO-02 / SO-03

The Solo knife series dates back to 1998. This knife was designed in the Japanese style and made for Spyderco by Solo in Japan. The series consists of three knives of sequential sizes. The blades of the knives are made of GIN-1 steel and Micarta is used for the han-

The folder series by Solo

dle plates. The knives have linerlock systems. The small SO-01 knife is 5.87 inches in total length. The length of the blade is 2.5 inches and the knife weighs 1.5 ounces. The middle knife, the SO-03, is a lightweight version with a fiberglass reinforced nylon handle. The knife weighs only 1 ounce. The measurements are the same as those of the SO-01. The largest knife, the SO-02, has a blade of 3.39 inches, is 7.64 inches in total length and weighs 1.9 ounces.

T02 SpyderSaw

The SpyderSaw from 2002 has a saw blade 4.88 inches long, designed for use while camping, hunting, pruning or other activities in the garden. It saws through wood, bone and fiber rich material with ease. This folding knife weighs 2.98 ounces and is 10.44 inches long when opened. The handle of the knife is 5.88 inches long. The blade is made of stainless AUS-6 steel and the handle from black fiberglass nylon.

The T02 SpyderSaw

WTC World Trade Center Knife

The owners and employees of Spyderco wanted to do something after the attack on the World Trade Center on 11 September 2001 to commemorate the brave policemen and firefighters. The World Trade Center Knife was designed for this reason. All profit from sales of these knives go to the New York Police and Fire Widow's and Children's Benefit Fund. This folding knife has a ball bearing lock. It weighs 5.30 ounces and is 8 inches long when opened. The handle is 5.0 inches long. The length of the sheepfoot blade is 3.44 inches and has a SpyderEdge over the entire cutting surface. The steel is 0.118

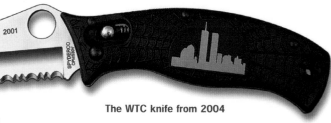

The WTC knife from 2004

inches thick. An inlaid piece made from the steel pillars of Tower 1 and shaped like the skyline of New York with the Twin Towers is located in the black handle. Spyderco issued these knives in beautiful wooden cases. There were 2819 copies made, one for each life claimed by the attack.

T

Design and Investigation Bureau for Sport and Weapons. He started making knives in 1990 and his first object was a broadsword. His work was displayed at an exhibition of the 'Artists of the Tula Region' in 1990. In 2001, he became a member of the Russian Knifemakers' Guild.

GOLD HOP

The Gold Hop knife was made in 2001. It is a sturdy knife on a stand. Tatarnikov made this knife in cooperation with Butovsky. The blade was forged by Kurbatov. The total length of the knife is 11.7 inches and the length in the sheath is 12.2 inches. The length of the blade is 6.6 inches. The exact number of grams of gold and silver used for this knife is not known.

JUNGLE

Tatarnikov made the Jungle knife in 2003. Victor Soskov forged the blade and the engravings were done by Butovsky. Filatov did the fine inlay work in the wood. The total length of the knife is 9.8 inches and the blade is 5.1 inches long. There are knives that come about after a single breath but there are also knives where the artists needs to search for the right image. Tatarnikov could not find the precise way to combine the beauty of the

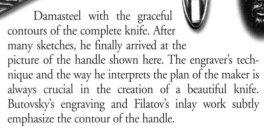

TATARNIKOV

www.rusartknife.urbannet.ru/gallery.html

Konstantin Nikolaevich Tatarnikov with his master sign and the guild logo

Konstantin Nikolaevich Tatarnikov was born in Tula on 27 October 1961. He had no artistic education and went to work as an apprentice rifle stock maker at the Central

The Jungle knife with a bolster and beautifully engraved pommel

Damasteel with the graceful contours of the complete knife. After many sketches, he finally arrived at the picture of the handle shown here. The engraver's technique and the way he interprets the plan of the maker is always crucial in the creation of a beautiful knife. Butovsky's engraving and Filatov's inlay work subtly emphasize the contour of the handle.

THISTLE

Tatarnikov made the Thistle knife in 2002. The blade was made by Soskov, the engraving work by Butovsky and Kuznetsov made the presentation case. The materials used were Damasteel, walnut, silver and gold. The total length is 10 inches and the blade is 5 inches long. The work on the knife started with

The Gold Hop collector's knife

the finished blade, made by Soskov. The brilliant forging pattern in the steel and the shape of the blade were determining factors for the final design.

THORBURN

thorburn@icon.co.za

André Thorburn was born on 12 May 1956 in Johannesburg, South Africa. His two daughters, Elize and Marlene, have been helping him make knives since they were children.

A chance meeting with Roelf Swanepoel in 1989

André Thorburn at work

sparked his interest in the knife making trade. He contacted the South African Knifemakers' Guild, attended a few courses and sold his first handmade knife to a friend in 1990. He was accepted as a member of the Guild in 1995. Business went so well that he became a fulltime knife maker in 1996. André made his first linerlock knife after an inspirational week in the workshop of Buzz Bezuidenhout from Durban. He started teaching courses for beginning knife makers himself and is never too busy to give advice and help. He has sold many knives to foreign clients through Knifeart.com on the Internet among others

and good shops such as Sharp Edge Sharp Shooter.

He attends many local knife shows in Johannesburg and Durban and is often present at various hunting fairs. In 2001, he became a member of the German Knifemakers' Guild and was also accepted as an aspiring member of the American and Italian Knifemakers' Guilds. He wins regular awards at international knife fairs for his work.

He specializes in engraved hunting knives and folding knives. He uses unusual materials, such as mother-of-pearl, mammoth ivory, desert iron wood and Amboyna burl wood as well as local products, such as giraffe bones and hippopotamus teeth. For his blades, he uses Swedish Damasteel, 12C27 Sandvik steel, stainless 440C Bohler steel from Austria, BG42 steel and unique Damascus types forged for him by Darryl Meier and Etttoré Gianferrari, Damascus artists from Cape Town. His liners are made of titanium and he sometimes gives the 304 steel bolsters some color through an electrochemical process. The engraving work of the knives is done by Helene van Wyk and the scrimshaws are done by South African artists Sharon Burger and Melodie de Witt. His wife works full time with him: she is in charge of marketing, making leather sheaths and the etching work. He is always open to new ideas and his motto is: 'Only dead fish follow the stream.'

Abalone Folder

ABALONE FOLDER

The Abalone folder got its name from its handle made from reconstructed mother-of-pearl from Abalone shell. This beautiful knife has a bolster made of stainless 304 steel with the surface worked into ridges. The blade is made of Swedish 12C27 Sandvik steel, polished by hand to a high gloss. The knife was originally designed for a double-edged

Damasteel Folder

TEREZA

This Tereza hunting knife has a special blade made of Odin-powder steel tempered to 57-60 HRC. The blade is 5.5 inches long and 0.1575 inches thick. The nickel steel bolster was beautifully engraved with flowers by Takáts Sándor. The yellow hearts of the flowers were made of 24kt gold. The handle is 5.7 inches long and the handle plates were made of polished mammoth ivory. A scrimshaw drawing was made in the ivory by Harmat Attila. The total length of the knife is 11.2 inches.

The Tereza hunter

WIENER WALZER

This is an integral knife with the blade and guard made of one piece of CPM-420X steel. The guard was beautifully engraved with a thistle in the relief technique. At the top of the guard is a strip of polished gold and the monogram plate is made of gold as well. The handle is 5.3 inches long and made of mammoth ivory attached with beautifully engraved mosaic pins. The blade is 4.5 inches long and 0.24.0 inches thick. A beautiful leather sheath covered with treated python skin comes with the knife.

Wiener Walzer

V

VALIANT

www.valiantco.com

The Valiant Trading Company was established in Perth, Western Australia. This company deals in knives, cleavers or *parangs* and kerisses from South East Asia. In order to promote these products, Valiant stimulates small-scale production in various parts of Indonesia. The knives are forged by hand, locally, in small quantities, from spring steel or Damasteel using the old methods. This work is done by craftsmen whose trade knowledge has been handed down through the centuries from father to son. This goes for the forgers, as well as the wood carvers or *mranggi*, which is why no two knives are the same, even when they are produced in a small series. They do work with certain specifications, but the measurements are 'general.' The length, thickness and width, as well as the pattern of the Damascus, do not have fixed guidelines. The quality is excellent, nevertheless. These knives are outstanding working tools as they have been per-

(royal residence). A keris, or kris, is an Indonesian dagger, which originated in Java. The blade is forged straight or winding, referred to as the parmor technique, whereby the steel types with and without nickel are forged together in traditional patterns to form Damasteel. The shape and forging motifs on the blades are authentic to the respective areas, based on antique examples, the company's own collections or from museums. The handles and sheaths are made of local wood types in the traditional way. The assortment available at Valiant is a true treasure house from the Orient.

PARANG LANGGI
TINGGANG FROM BORNEO

A *parang* from Borneo was originally a large cleaver used to clear a path through the jungle. The parang shown here is a traditional and ceremonial object. The handle was cut from buffalo horn and is too beautiful and vulnerable for daily work. The sheath is made completely from ironwood and decorated with traditional Borneo figures. The

Example of a Keris from the Valiant collection

The parang Langgi Tinggang from Borneo

fected by hundreds of years of practical experience. They are also beautiful decorative objects of exceptional quality.

In addition to dealing in newly produced traditional knives, Valliant also restores antique knives and swords and does a flourishing trade in antique and affordable kerisses that can be admired on their website. The antique material comes directly from the Indonesian kampong and *kraton*

Damasteel blade is forged by hand. It is 23.25 to 23.75 inches long and about 0.315 inches thick. The total length of this parang is between 30 and 30.5 inches and it weighs between 38.8 and 42.3 ounces.

Damascus Klewang Penai

KLEWANG PENAI FROM CELEBES

This traditional *klewang* comes from Celebes and is made in accordance with ancient traditions. The blade is made of Damasteel and forged from car-

The Damascus Golok from Java

bon steel from vehicle leaf springs. The right blade is about 19.5 inches long and the steel is 0.25 inches thick. The total length is 32 inches. The beautifully decorated handle has an integrated guard and is made of buffalo horn. The sheath is made of ironwood and adorned with decorative pieces of horn and brass spacers. The klewang weighs 19.4 ounces on its own and 31.7 ounces with its sheath.

A Javanese Damascus Golok Cikerouh

JAVANESE GOLOK

This is a traditional sword or *golok* from Java. The blade is made of hand-forged Damasteel and is 15.75 inches long and 0.25 inches thick. The han-

Damascus Golok Cinghol

dle is made of water buffalo horn into which finger slots are sanded and polished. The sheath is made of iron wood and the spacers from buffalo horn. The total length of this golok is 24 inches and the knife weighs 19.4 ounces.

JAVANESE GOLOK CIKEROUH

This *Golok Cikerouh* has a blade made of hand forged Damasteel as well. The length is 13.75 inches and steel is 0.25 inches thick. The handle is made of buffalo horn and cut out very artfully. Ironwood, with spacers made of bone and horn, is used for the sheath also embellished with wood carving work. The total length of this dagger is 22.5 inches and it weighs 16.9 ounces.

JAVANESE GOLOK CINGHOL

This traditional *Golok Cinghol* comes from Java. The sword has a blade made of hand-forged Damasteel that is 16 inches long and 0.25 inches thick. The handle is made of beautifully carved buffalo horn. The sheath is made of ironwood with

horn adornments. The total length of the knife is 22.5 inches and it weighs 27.2 ounces.

JAVANESE KERIS

This Keris from Java has a blade made of Damasteel that is more than one hundred years old. The blade has a *pamor Adeg Salur*. The length of the

blade is 14.75 inches and the total length is 20 inches. Artfully carved teak is used for the handle. The spacer or *mendak* is made of sterling silver. The traditional sheath is made of teak and is carved in the *batik* style. The handle has spacers made of bone. This

A Damascus Keris from Java

Keris weighs 16.6 ounces. The actual spirit of the Keris resides in the pamor. The forging pattern is proof of the craftsmanship of the smith, the *Empu*. There are many different Damascus motifs for Indonesian kerisses and swords. *Pamor* means mix, which alludes to the mixing of the

A standard Kujang

various metals. Magic powers are often ascribed to Kerisses. There are evil Kerisses that carry anathemas with them. Kerisses are mostly good, however, and protect the owner against malicious spirits and other evils.

JAVANESE KUJANG

This ceremonial *kujang* decorative sword comes from Java. The decorative blade, forged from vehicle springs and decorated in a beautiful etching technique, is between 8.25 and 8.75 inches long. The steel thickness of the blade is 0.25 inches. The

The Javanese Damascus Wedung

handle is cut from mahogany and the sheath from rasamala wood. The total length of the kujang is between 15.5 and 16 inches and it weighs between 16.2 and 17.6 ounces.

JAVANESE KUJANG BIKANG

This *Kujang Bikang* from Java is a ceremonial knife as well. The separate blade is 6.5 inches long and the steel is 0.25 inches thick. The blade is molded by hand and furnished with etched decorations in the steel. The handle and sheath are made of teak. The total length is between 12 and 12.5 inches. The knife weighs between 13.1 and 14.1 ounces.

JAVANESE WEDUNG

This wide and short Javanese sword is called the *Wedung*. It has a hand-forged Damasteel blade that is between 10 to

Kujang Bikang

10.5 inches long. The solid, octagonal thorn at the handle is 0.5 inches thick. The blade is filed into the traditional shape at the back. The finely carved handle is made from buffalo horn. The sheath is made of ironwood and decorated with carving. The total length of this wedung is between 16 and 17 inches and it weighs between 22.9 and 24.7 ounces.

CALOK FROM MADURA

This was originally a rice harvesting knife from Madura. The curved blade is made of Damasteel, forged by hand. The length of the blade is 14.75 inches and it is 0.25 inches thick. The handle is made of buffalo horn with brass spacers. The sheath is made to measure from ironwood and has

Damascus Calok from Madura

the same curve as the blade. The total length is 22 inches and the weight is 19.75 ounces.

PEDANG RUSA FROM MADURA

A traditional Damascus Pedang Rusa from the Indonesian island of Madura

The Malaysian Lawi Ayam

This traditional sword comes from the Indonesian island of Madura, located at the top of Java. The blade is made of hand-forged Damasteel and is 14.5 inches long and 0.189 inches thick. Stag horn is used for the handle. The short knob is beautifully cut and the long spur is left in its original state. The sheath is made of iron-wood. The total length of this sword is between 25 to 26 inches and it weighs between 23.3 and 24.7 ounces.

LAWI AYAM FROM MALAYA

This was originally a traditional decorative sword for ceremonial purposes. The curved blade is forged by hand from spring steel. The length of the blade is between 8.5 and 9 inches and it is 0.217

inches thick. Beautifully carved mahogany is used for the handle and the sheath. The total length of this *Lawi Aayam* is between 13.75 and 14 inches. It weighs between 10.6 to 12 ounces.

PARANG GINAH FROM MALAYA

This was originally a harvesting knife from Malaysia, but it is also used as a ceremonial sword. The blade is forged by hand and is between 14.25 and 14.75 inches long. The thorn at the end of the handle is 0.374 inches thick. The handle is made of buffalo horn. The guard and pommel are

made of brass. The *parang* is between 20 and 20.5 inches in length and weighs between 15.5 to 17.6 ounces.

PHILIPPINE BARONG

A Damascus Parang Ginah from Malaya

This short sword originated in the Philippines. The blade, forged by hand in the traditional way from Damasteel, is 12 inches long and 0.311 inches thick. The handle is made of smoothly polished buffalo horn without any adornments. A wide brass ring is between the handle and the blade. The sheath is made of carved ironwood. The total length of this *barong* is between 19.5 and 20.5 inches and it weighs between 42.3 to 45.9 ounces.

Damascus Barong from the Philippines

The Philippine
Sanduko Bolo

PHILIPPINE SANDUKO BOLO

This is a traditional sword from the Philippines, with a Damasteel blade, 15.5 inches in length, that is forged by hand. The steel thickness of the blade is 0.311 inches. The handle is made of the usual buffalo horn, has a round horn guard with brass spacers and features a beautifully carved head. The sheath is made of ironwood with horn spacers and

The Sumatran Klewang Maremu

a figure made of buffalo horn. The total length of this *sanduko bolo* is between 19.5 and 20.5 inches and it weighs between 42.3 and 45.9 ounces.

SUMATRAN KLEWANG MAREMU

This sword comes from Sumatra as well. It has a hand-forged Damasteel blade 18 inches long and 0.311 inches thick. The

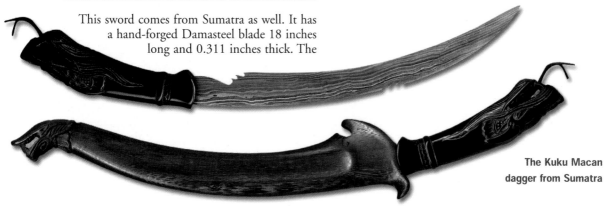

handle is made of buffalo horn and cut out very finely. The total length of the sword, inclusive of the sheath, is between 24 and 25 ounces. The sword weighs from 25.4 to 26.5 ounces. The sheath is made of ironwood and decorated with carving.

SUMATRAN KUKU MACAN

This ceremonial *Kuku Macan* dagger comes from Sumatra. The name of this dagger was derived from the original *kuku macan* or 'tiger claw.' Two names for this tiger are used: the one is *harimau* and the other, more indigenous name is *pak macan,* or great tiger. This is a sword that used to be wielded with both hands. Through the centuries it became

smaller and more manageable, however. The handle, made of buffalo horn, and the sheath, made of ironwood, are adorned with traditional carving work in the shape of a snake's head. The curved blade is made of hand-forged

The Kuku Macan
dagger from Sumatra

Damasteel with decorative filing work in the shape of saw teeth. The blade is 8.5 inches long and 0.189 inches thick. Its total length is between 14 to 14.5 inches. This dagger weighs 8.8 ounces.

Parang Lading from Sumatra

Damascus Klewang from Sumbawa

SUMATRAN PARANG LADING

This ceremonial sword comes from Sumatra. The buffalo horn handle is cut in the shape of a *wajang,* or doll's head. The blade is made of hand-forged Damasteel and is between 17.75 and 18 inches long and 0.311 inches thick. The total length of this parang is between 24.5 and 24.75 inches. It weighs between 25.4 and 26.5 ounces. The sheath is made of ironwood and decorated with carvings.

DAMASCUS KLEWANG FROM SUMBAWA

This *Klewang* is based on a traditional model such as that used on the island of Sumbawa. The Damasteel blade is forged by hand. The length of the blade is 19.5 inches and the steel is 0.25 inches thick. The handle is made of buffalo horn artfully carved in the shape of an elephant head. The sheath is made of ironwood and decorated with carving work. The total length of this heavy klewang is 24 inches. It weighs 38.8 ounces.

TIMORESE KLEWANG

This *Klewang* is made in the traditional style of the island of Timor. The blade is made of feather steel and molded by hand into an authentic shape. The length of the blade is 16 inches and the steel is 0.25 inches thick. The handle is made of buffalo horn. The sheath is made of ironwood and decorated with steel pins. The total length of the knife is 24 inches. The Klewang weighs 23.6 ounces.

VICTORINOX

www.victorinox.com

The name Victorinox dates back to 1909 and comes from the mother of the founder of the company:

The logo of Victorinox

Victoria, combined with the indication of stainless steel: inox. The company was founded by Carl Elsener in 1884. Along with twenty-five other knife makers, he tried to form a cooperative called the Swiss Knives Association. Most of the participants did not even last one year due to strong competition from Solingen in Germany. But Carl Elsener, kept at it. In 1891, he delivered his first batch of military pocketknives to the Swiss Army. This knife was relatively heavy with wooden handle plates, a long blade, a short blade with a screwdriver end and a

The old emblem from 1909

separate can opener. On 12 June 1897, he developed a lighter model: the Officer's and Sport Knife. It did not please the Swiss Military leaders, however, and it was not taken up as standard equipment. Many troops bought this knife themselves, nonetheless. The interest from abroad was even greater.

After the Second World War, the PX shops of the American Military sold many Swiss Army Knives to their troops. This knife was even part of the standard equipment for the crew of the space shuttle. Since

Timorese Klewang

then more than 400 different models have been designed. The company currently has more than 950 employees at the Swiss canton of Schwyz. Their knives are made of steel alloys with chromium and molybdenum. After the tempering process, a hardness of HRC 56 (Rockwell) is reached. Cellidor synthetic material or nylon is used for the handle plates. The Swiss Army Knives have handles made of Alox, an aluminum alloy. The smallest Victorinox knife is the Classic with a handle of 2.25 inches. The largest model is the SwissChamp XXLT with 73 different tools. It consists of 64 parts and is no bigger than the palm of one's hand. 450 different operations are necessary to make it. Despite all of the innovative high-tech products, the name Victorinox will forever be associated with Swiss Army Knives.

ALPINEER LOCK-BLADE

The blade of this folding knife locks when it is opened with a linerlock. On the Alpineer, the lock can be released with the slide switch in the handle. The total length of the knife is 8.1 inches. The

Alpineer Lock-blade folder

length of the blade is 3.7 inches and the handle is 4.4 inches long. The knife weighs 4.6 ounces and has a corkscrew, a key ring, tweezers and a toothpick. The same model, but with a Phillips screwdriver instead of the corkscrew, goes by the model name of Cowboy.

ALTIMETER

The Altimeter is a highly regarded precision tool developed especially for mountain sports with a built-in digital altimeter. This multi-folding knife is 8.1 inches in total length. The two blades are 2.95 and 1.57 inches long respectively. The length of the handle is 3.6 inches. The knife has the following parts: a corkscrew, a can opener, a small

screwdriver, a bottle opener with a screwdriver end, wire strippers, an awl punch, a key ring, tweezers, a toothpick, scissors, a universal hook, the altimeter in meters and feet, a thermometer in Celsius and Fahrenheit, a ballpoint pen, a steel pin and a mini screwdriver in the corkscrew.

Victorinox Altimeter

AMBASSADOR

The Ambassador is a small, elegant, multi-folding knife with a 2.9 inch long handle. The knife has a large blade of 2.3 inches and is 6.8 inches in total length. It also has a nail file with a point, scissors, tweezers and a toothpick.

Ambassador

The Angler fishing knife

ANGLER

This large model of the Angler knife has a 3.6 inch handle. The two blades are 2.95 and 1.57 inches each and it is 8.1 inches in total length. The knife only weighs 3.2 ounces, including all of its accessories. The knife has a corkscrew, a can opener with a small screwdriver, a bottle opener with a screwdriver end and wire strippers, an awl punch, a key ring, tweezers, a toothpick, a fish scaler with a hook disgorger and a ruler and grip and wire pliers. The same model, but with a large Philips screwdriver, instead of the corkscrew is called the Fisherman.

ARMY CADET

The Cadet is a smaller version of the official Swiss army knife. It has an aluminum handle of 3.25 inches and a blade of 2.7 inches. The total length of the Cadet is 7.8 inches. This knife also has a nail file with a point, a can opener with a small screwdriver, a bottle opener with a screwdriver end, wire strippers and a key ring.

ARMY KNIFE

This is the official pocketknife of the Swiss army. Its forerunner, delivered to the Swiss army in 1891, had wooden handle plates and weighed 5.1 ounces. In 1908, the knife got synthetic handle plates and weighed only 4.4 ounces. Since 1951, the blades and additional pieces have been made of stainless

**The original
Swiss Army knife**

steel. From 1961, the handle has been made of alox, an aluminum alloy. It was still red, but since 1965, it was made in the famous silver color. The Swiss emblem only appeared in 1980. The blade is 3.6 inches long and the total length is 6.5 inches. The blade is 3.95 inches long. This knife has an awl punch, a can opener with a small screwdriver, a bottle opener with a screwdriver and wire strippers and weighs 2.5 ounces.

CAMPER

The Camper is made without an imprint and in a version with a tent and the word 'Camping' on the handle plates. This multi-folding knife has two blades, 2.95 and 1.57 inches in length. The total length of the knife is 8.1 inches. The handle is 3.8 inches long and the knife weighs 3.2 ounces. The knife has a corkscrew, a can opener with a small

Army Cadet

Victorinox Camper

2.95 and 1.57 inches long each and it is 8.1 inches in total length. The knife weighs 3.2 ounces, including all of its accessories.

CLASSIC

The handle of this small folding knife is 2.25 inches long and it has a blade 2.1 inches long. The knife also has a nail file with a point, scissors, a key ring, tweezers and a toothpick. The Classic is available in several colors with a LED lamp and with a built-in ballpoint pen.

screwdriver, a bottle opener with a screwdriver and wire strippers, an awl punch, a key ring, tweezers, a toothpick and a saw blade and a black handle.

CAMPING RANGER

This folding knife is the same length as the Camper, but it is thicker due to the number of extra pieces it has: a corkscrew, a can opener, a small screwdriver, a bottle opener with a screwdriver end, wire strippers, an awl punch, a key ring, tweezers, a toothpick, scissors, a universal hook, a saw blade, a chisel, a nail file with a metal file on the other side, a metal saw and a small screwdriver. The large Camping Ranger knife has a handle 3.6 inches in length. The two blades are

The Classic in various colors

CLASSIC WHISTLER

This knife is 4.3 inches in total length has a handle of 2.25 inches and a blade of 2.1 inches. Other than the large blade and a built-in whistle, the knife also has a nail file with a screwdriver point, scissors, a key ring, tweezers and a toothpick.

Camping Ranger

CLIMBER

The Climber was designed for mountain hikers. The total length of the knife is 8.1 inches and the handle is 3.6 inches long. The blades are 2.95 and

Classic Whistler

1.57 inches long respectively. The knife has a corkscrew, a can opener with a small screwdriver, a bottle opener with a screwdriver and wire strippers, an awl punch, a key ring, tweezers, a toothpick, scissors and a universal hook.

Climber in the standard version

CYBERTOOL 29

Cybertool 29

This multi-folding knife is a small toolbox with a large, 2.95 inch long blade, a smaller, 1.57 inch long blade, a corkscrew, a can opener with a small screwdriver, a bottle opener with a screwdriver and wire strippers, an awl punch, a key ring, tweezers, a toothpick, a needle, screw bits with a series of bits for Phillips and Torx screws, a ballpoint pen, which can also be used to set dip switches on a computer board, a steel pin and a mini screwdriver in the corkscrew.

CYBERTOOL 34

This Cybertool version has all of the features of the previous model, but it also has pliers with wire cutters, scissors and a universal carry hook.

Cybertool Model 34

MiniChamp

NOMAD LOCK-BLADE

This large knife with a lockable blade of 3.7 inches is one of the simplest Victorinox knives. The handle is 4.4 inches long and, when opened, the Nomad is 8.1 inches in length. It also has a corkscrew, a can opener with a small screwdriver blade, a bottle opener with a screwdriver blade and wire strippers, an awl punch, a key ring, tweezers and a toothpick. The Centurion model is virtually the same, with a large Philips screwdriver instead of the corkscrew.

The large Nomad

is 2.2 inches long and the total length of the knife is 6.6 inches. The knife weighs 2.1 ounces. It also has scissors, a nail file with a nail cleaner, a cuticle pusher, a screwdriver with a ruler, a letter opener, an orange peeler with a scraper, a bottle opener with a magnetic Phillips screwdriver and wire strippers, a key ring, tweezers or a toothpick as desired and a ballpoint pen.

MOUNTAINEER

This multi-folding knife for hikers is 8.1 inches in total length, has a handle of 3.6 inches and two blades, 2.95 and 1.57 inches long respectively. The Mountaineer has a corkscrew, a can opener with a small screwdriver blade, a bottle opener with a screwdriver blade and wire strippers, an awl punch, a key ring, tweezers, a toothpick, scissors, a carry hook, a nail file with a metal file, a nail cleaner and a metal saw.

OUTRIDER LOCK-BLADE

The Outrider is one of the large knife series with a handle of 4.4 inches. This knife has a large blade of 3.7 inches that can be locked with a type of liner-lock, a corkscrew, a can opener with a small screwdriver blade, a bottle opener with a screwdriver blade and wire strippers, an awl punch, a key ring, tweezers, a toothpick, a wood saw blade, scissors and a long Phillips screwdriver.

The Outrider Lock blade folder

Mountaineer

Picknicker

The Rambler multi folder

PICKNICKER LOCK-BLADE

The Picknicker is virtually identical to the previous Nomad knife. Only the handle plates are red instead of the black nylon of the Nomad. The large lockable blade is 3.7 inches long. The handle is 4.4 inches long and, when opened, the Picknicker is 8.1 inches in length.

PILOT LOCK-BLADE

The Pilot is virtually the same model as the Trailmaster, but the shape of the large blade is actually a type of Spyderco blade with a long, stretched thumbhole, which makes it easy to open with one hand. The blade is 3.7 inches long and has a separate lock. The handle is 4.4 inches in length. With the large blade opened, the knife is 8.1 inches in total length. The Pilot also has a saw blade, a can opener with a small screwdriver blade, a bottle opener with a screwdriver blade and wire strippers, an awl punch, a key ring and a large Philips screwdriver instead of the corkscrew. The logo of the Dutch Marine Air Force Service is on the handle plate.

The Pilot of the
Dutch Marine
Air Force Services
(MLD)

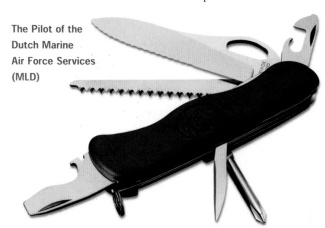

RAMBLER

The Rambler comes from the Classic series with a handle of 2.25 inches and a blade of 2.17 inches. The knife includes the new bottle opener, a magnetic Phillips screwdriver plus wire stripper, scissors, a large nail file with a screwdriver end, a key ring, tweezers and a toothpick. The Manager has an additional ballpoint pen.

RECRUIT

The Recruit is the basic Swiss Victorinox pocketknife. It has two blades 2.7 and 1.57 inches long. The total length of the knife is 7.8 inches and the handle is 3.3 inches long. The knife weighs 2.3 ounces. In addition to the two blades, the knife also has a can opener with a small screwdriver, a bottle opener with a large screwdriver and wire strippers, tweezers, a toothpick and a key ring.

The Recruit
pocket knife

RUCKSACK LOCK-BLADE

With a handle of 4.4 inches, the Rucksack folding knife is another one of the large knife series. This knife has a large blade of 3.7 inches that can be locked with a type of a linerlock. The total length

Rucksack

except for the worn out Helvetia, as good as new, despite having had to fiddle open and disassemble hundreds of weapons through the years. The Spartan has a handle length of 3.6 inches and the blades are 2.95 and 1.57 inches long respectively. The total length is 8.1 inches. This knife does not have a wide range of accessories, but it is suitable for a wide range of technical tasks because it includes a corkscrew, can opener small screwdriver blade, bottle opener with a screwdriver blade and wire strippers, awl punch, key ring, tweezers toothpick and transparent blue or red handle.

of the Rucksack is 8.1 inches and it weighs 4.4 ounces. The knife has a corkscrew, a can opener with a small screwdriver blade, a bottle opener with a screwdriver blade and wire strippers, an awl punch, a key ring, tweezers, a toothpick and a wood saw blade.

SIGNATURE

The Signature folding knife belongs to the Classic Victorinox series. The total length of the knife is 6.6 inches, the handle is 2.3 inches long and the blade is 2.2 inches long. The knife also has a nail file with a screwdriver blade, scissors, a key ring, tweezers or a toothpick as desired and a ballpoint pen. The knife is made in transparent colors of red, blue and green.

SPARTAN

The Spartan is the traditional Swiss folding knife and one of the most successful models made by Victorinox. I still use the old Spartan myself, without the tweezers and toothpick, for my daily weapon work. I received this knife years ago from my old boss, a police commissioner, and it is,

The Spartan multi folder

SPORTSMAN

The Sportsman is a medium-sized knife with a handle of 3.25 inches. It is part of the same series as the Cadet, the Recruit and the Tourist. It has a large blade of 2.7 inches and the total length of the knife is 7.8 inches. It also has a nail file, a corkscrew, a can opener with a small screwdriver

Victorinox Sportsman

The Signature in red transparent handle plates

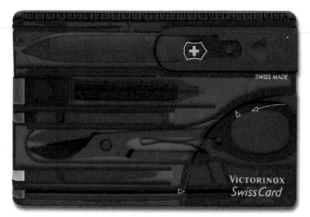

The Victorinox SwissCard in various transparent colors

SwissCard Lite

The SwissCard Lite got its name from the built-in LED lamp. With normal usage the lamp has sufficient energy from its 3V-lithium micro battery to last two years. This version has the same measurements as the standard SwissCard, which is 3.2 x 2.1 inches and 0.138 inches thick. It also looks very similar to it except fot a loose 'Quatro' screwdriver with two screwdriver ends at the four corners for standard screws and two for Phillips screwdrivers. It also has a built-in magnifying glass, a letter opener, scissors, a

blade, a bottle opener with a screwdriver blade and wire strippers, an awl punch, a key ring, tweezers and a toothpick.

SwissCard

The SwissCard is as big as a standard credit card and measures 3.2 x 2.1 inches. It is only 0.138 inches thick and contains a letter opener, scissors, a stainless steel pin, a nail file with a screwdriver point, tweezers, a toothpick, a ballpoint pen and a ruler in centimeters and inches. The SwissCard comes in gray transparent red, blue and anthracite.

The standard
SwissChamp
with 33 pieces

SwissCard Lite

stainless steel pin, tweezers, a ballpoint pen and a ruler in centimeters and inches along the edge. The SwissCard and the SwissCard Lite have won various design awards. The Lite is available in transparent red, blue and anthracite colors.

SwissChamp

This SwissChamp was the champion of Victorinox for a long time thanks to its wide range of accessories. Larger SwissChamps were also developed, such as the XLT with 50 pieces and the XXLT with a whopping 73 pieces. It goes without saying that these knives do not easily fit into one's pocket. The standard SwissChamp is already a very thick knife. This knife has a handle of 3.6 inches and two blades of 2.95 and 1.57 inches respectively. The total length of the knife is 8.1 inches and it weighs 6.5 ounces. The knife also has a corkscrew, a can opener with a small screwdriver, a bottle opener with a screwdriver and wire strippers, an awl punch with a needle, a key ring, tweezers, a toothpick, scissors, a carry hook, a saw blade, a fish scaler with a fish measurer and hook disgorger, a nail file with a metal file, a nail cleaner and metal saw, a small screwdriver, a chisel, grip and wire pliers, a Phillips screwdriver, an eight-fold magnifying glass, a ball-point pen, a stainless steel pin and a mini screwdriver in the corkscrew.

SWISSCHAMP XXLT

The absolute champion among multi-folding knives is the SwissChamp XXLT with 73 accessories. In addition to the 33 pieces of the standard SwissChamp, it has a second carry hook, a great number of screwdrivers, various chisels, pruning-shears, various awl punches and reamers, various screw bits with series of bits for Phillips and Torx screws and, of course, the built-in SwissFlame lighter that also serves as a mini burner.

The SwissFlame with the inbuilt lighter and mini burner

SWISSFLAME

This multi SwissFlame folding knife has an ingenious built-in lighter and mini burner, called a 'laserflame.' This knife has a handle that is 3.6 inches long. The two blades are 2.95 and 1.57 inches long each and it is 8.1 inches in total length. The knife also has a corkscrew, a can opener with a small screwdriver blade, a bottle opener with a screwdriver blade and wire strippers, an awl punch, a key ring, tweezers, a toothpick, scissors, a carry hook, a ballpoint pen, a steel pin and a mini screwdriver in the corkscrew.

SWISSLITE

The small SwissLite knife is one of the famous Victorinox Classic series. This small knife was introduced in 1996 and has a handle of 2.25 inches and a blade of 2.1 inches. The SwissLite also has a nail file with a screwdriver point, scissors, a key ring, tweezers or a toothpick as desired and of course the LED lamp. This knife is made with standard red plates or in transparent blue, red and green versions.

The extended SwissChamp XXLT with 73 pieces

The small SwissLite knives

SwissMemory with
the 64 Mb USB memory
card from 2004

SwissMemory

In 2004, Victorinox introduced a small, multi-folding knife with a handle of 2.25 inches and a built-in USB memory card of 64 Mb. Victorinox developed this new knife in cooperation with a specialist company called Swissbit AG. This small knife comes in two different versions. The first version had a stainless steel blade, scissors, a nail file with a screwdriver point, a ballpoint pen and a red LED lamp. The second version, designed especially for air travelers, only has a red LED lamp and a ballpoint pen. The knife weighs 1.175 ounces. Both versions have a USB memory card that can be taken from the handle. The memory card is equipped with flash technology so that it can function independently from a computer. The SwissMemory can be used with Windows, Mac OS and Linux and is recognized by a computer as an external data storage unit. Additional drivers for Win 98SE and Mac OS 8.6 are available at www.swissbit.com/drivers. The data in the memory card can be protected with SecureLOCK Software. If BIOS is properly defined, this memory card can even be used to boot a PC (USB: Universal Serial Bus that connects to the computer with external equipment for transporting data. BIOS: software for basic establishment of the computer system).

SwissTool

Victorinox released the SwissTool in 1998, a so-called multi-toolbox set with 27 different functions. A featured detail is that both 'paws' of the opened tools can be locked with a sliding stud. This ensures that it will not unexpectedly fold back when one is working hard with the screwdriver or saw blade.

The SwissTool has the following pieces: grip and wire pliers with wire cutters for steel wire up to 40 HRC, a screwdriver of 0.079 inches, a screwdriver of 0.118 inches, a screwdriver of 0.197 inches, a bottle opener with a screwdriver and wire strippers, a screwdriver of 0.295 inches, a normal blade of 3.15 inches in length, a metal file, a metal saw, a wood saw, an awl punch with a needle, a Phillips screwdriver, a chisel, a strong crate opener, a wire bender, a can opener, a ruler of 23 cm and a ruler of 9 inches, a crimper for electric cable and a shackle. The total length of the SwissTool is 4.53 inches and it weighs 8 ounces.

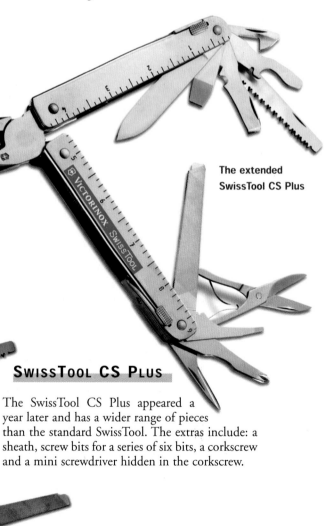

The extended
SwissTool CS Plus

SwissTool CS Plus

The SwissTool CS Plus appeared a year later and has a wider range of pieces than the standard SwissTool. The extras include: a sheath, screw bits for a series of six bits, a corkscrew and a mini screwdriver hidden in the corkscrew.

SwissTool

The Time Keeper
multi folder

TIME KEEPER

The Time Keeper is a medium-sized folding knife with a handle of 3.6 inches. The blade is 2.95 inches long and the total length of the knife is 8.1 inches. The knife has a lid opener, combined with a can opener, a screwdriver and wire strippers, a corkscrew, scissors, a carry hook with a nail file, a key ring, tweezers, a tooth-

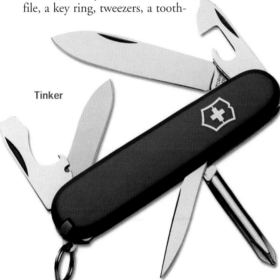

Tinker

pick, a ballpoint pen, a stainless steel pin and a mini screwdriver in the corkscrew. An oval Swiss watch is in the right handle plate.

TINKER

The Tinker is an older model multi-folding knife. It originally had a 3.3 inch handle, but Victorinox increased it to 3.6 inches a few years ago. Because of this innovation, the large blade was also lengthened to 2.95 inches, from the previous 2.7 inch-

es. The total length of the knife changed from 7.8 inches to 8.1 inches. Other than the blades, the knife also has a Phillips screwdriver instead of a corkscrew, a can opener with a small screwdriver, a bottle opener with a large screwdriver and wire strippers, an awl punch, a key ring, tweezers and a toothpick.

The extended
Tinker Deluxe

TINKER DELUXE

This multi-folding knife is, in fact, the standard Tinker with a few additional pieces. Other than the earlier mentioned pieces of the Tinker, the Tinker Deluxe also has scissors, a carry hook and grip and wire pliers.

TOURIST

The Tourist is actually a smaller version of the Spartan and has the same pieces. The handle is 3.25 inches long instead of the 3.6 inches of the larger Spartan, however. The two

Victorinox
Tourist

blades of the Tourist are 2.7 and 1.57 inches long respectively. The knife is 7.8 inches in total length and weighs 2.2 ounces. This knife has a corkscrew, a can opener with a small screwdriver blade, a bottle opener with a screwdriver blade and wire strippers, an awl punch, a key ring, tweezers and a toothpick.

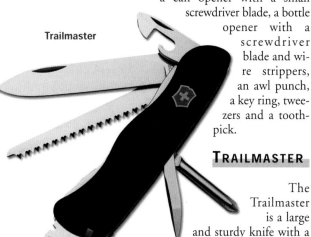

Trailmaster

TRAILMASTER

The Trailmaster is a large and sturdy knife with a handle of 4.4 inches and it is 8.1 inches in total length. This is a simplified version of the Locksmith. The Trailmaster has a single blade of 3.7 inches, a Phillips screwdriver instead of a corkscrew, a can opener with a small screwdriver blade, a bottle opener with a screwdriver blade and wire strippers, an awl punch, a key ring, tweezers, a toothpick and a wood saw blade.

VOYAGERLITE

The Voyager looks similar to the Time Keeper, but the built-in clock is digital. This clock does not only indicate the timer, it can also be used as an alarm and time. The clock is run by a CR1225 lithium battery that has the durability of a standard digital watch. The Voyager knife has a handle 3.6 inches long and two blades 2.95 and 1.57 inches

The Voyager

The WorkChamp with lockable blade

long respectively. The knife also has a corkscrew, a can opener with a small screwdriver blade, a bottle opener with a screwdriver blade and wire strippers, an awl punch, a key ring, tweezers, a toothpick, scissors, a carry hook, the clock mentioned earlier, a ballpoint pen, a steel pin and a mini screwdriver in the corkscrew. Victorinox introduced the Voyager Lite in 2002 with a built-in LED lamp. The functions mentioned earlier were extended with a Phillips screwdriver. The LED lamp and the functions of the clock are all activated with the Helvetia button in the handle. The knife is made in transparent red and transparent anthracite.

WORKCHAMP LOCK-BLADE

The WorkChamp is an older model with a handle 4.4 inches in length and a handy toolkit in pocket format. The knife has a working piece for every possible task. The lockable blade is 3.7 inches long. The knife also has a corkscrew, a can opener with a small screwdriver blade, a bottle opener with a screwdriver blade and wire strippers, an awl punch, a key ring, tweezers, a toothpick, a wood saw blade, scissors, a long Phillips screwdriver, a short Phillips screwdriver, grip and wire pliers and a mini screwdriver in the corkscrew.

VLASOV

www.rusartknife.urbannet.ru/gallery.html

Yoeri Vlasov was born in the city of Tomsk in 1956. His first sculpture was of his parents' hands folded together, carved from burl wood. The image got him accepted into the professional art workshops in the city of Novokuznetsk. He studied there for three years and then got a job as a mechanical engraver in a factory in the weapon-making city of Izhevsk. In 1989, he went to work at the Izhgor design company. In 1992 and 1993 he traveled to France and

Yoeri Anatolievich Vlasov, right, with his master sign, top, and the emblem of the Russian Knifemakers' Guild, below

visited French sculptor and graphic artist Daniel Bigata. Vlasov met Oleg Bobkov in 1994 and, through him, was accepted by the Russian Knifemakers' Guild. He received training as a knife smith from Valery Koptev in Tula. His current work is inspired by art nouveau.

AUTOCRATIC

Yoeri Vlasov designed the Autocratic knife in 2003. This knife was displayed at the knife fair in the Kremlin. A double eagle head was engraved in the pommel, which is the emblem of the Russian state. The knife was made in four months and it is currently still in the possession of the maker. The blade was made of stainless steel and a combination of Russian steel types 95J18 (**95X18**), 110J18 (**110X18**). The rounding in the guard was made of titanium.

The Autocratic knife in a stand

The Little Corporal

The blade is 7.2 inches long, the total length of the knife is 12.2 inches and the stand is 6.5 inches high.

THE LITTLE CORPORAL

The Little Corporal knife was made by Yoeri Anatolevich Vlasov in 2003 at Nizhni Novgorod with a historical reference to Napoleon. The blade was forged by Egor Aseev from Tula. The knife maker, Gennady Kopylov, a friend from Moscow and a member of the Russian Knifemakers' Guild, also worked on it. This knife, was made over a period of three months for an exhibition in the Kremlin in 2004. It is currently in a private collection in Moscow. A copy was donated to the Weapons museum of the Kremlin. It is made of mosaic Damascus, stainless steel and ebony. The total length is 13.6 inches and the blade is 7.5 inches long.

VENUS

Vlasov made the Venus of Damascus, also known as 'A Girl with Armor,' in 2000 in Nizhni Novgorod. It is a fantasy knife with a blade forged by Sergey Danilov from Moscow. The knife was made of Damasteel. The mosaic Damascus of the blade was transformed into wavy Damascus. The total length of the knife is 10.2 inches and the length of the blade is 5.3 inches. Vlasov was inspired by the Venus de Milo and designed this knife in 1995. It was only finalized in 2000 for the exposition at the Kremlin the same year. Six months were spent working on this knife and it is currently in possession of a collector in St Petersburg.

The long, slim Venus knife

WALTHER

www.gutmanncutlery.com; www.waltheramerica.com

The logo of Walther

The Walther Company, one of the most important weapons producers in Germany, concluded an agreement with American knife producers Gutmann Cutlery from Bellingham, Washington for the knives that carry their mark. Gutmann have made knives since 1947 under their own mark, Junglee, but also produces knives and tools for Smith & Wesson and Walther. Gutmann sometimes utilizes the services of master knife makers from Seki, Japan as well. Most Walther knives have blades made of stainless 440A or 440C steel, a staple in the knife industry, with excellent cutting qualities, wearproof and rust resistant as it contains more carbon so the edge stays sharp longer.

Walther was founded in 1886 by Carl Wilhelm Freund Walther in Zella-Mehlis. In 1908, the company released its first semi-automatic pistol on the market and production increased during the First World War. During the Second World War, Walther was a part of the war industry. The capitulation of the German military in 1945 meant the end of the Walther factory. The family fled the Russian zone to Heidenheim in the Swiss Alps when they started producing weapons again in an old stable in Ulm. Sales went so well that a large factory complex was built in 1953. The family sold the company in 1993 to German wholesalers Umarex.

ALLIED FORCES

The 2002 design for the large Walther Allied Forces folding knife was inspired by the military units stationed in various conflict areas. These knives are made to deal with the toughest circumstances on land, sea or in the air. The long, narrow blade is 3.94 inches in length and is made of stainless 440A steel. The blade is finished with a matte black protective layer or is matte bead blasted. A double sided thumb stud is on the

The Walther Allied Forces folders

blade. The angular handle has a casing made of pressed aluminum with inlaid plates of palissander wood or Kraton. An adjustable steel carrying clip is on the right of the handle and it also has a shackle. The handle is 4.09 inches long and the total length of the opened knife is 9 inches.

BELIZE

The snake-ridden jungles of Belize in Central America were once the home of pirates and smugglers. This knife is made of stainless 440A steel, is 2.56 inches long and has a flat thumb stud on

The Belize knife

The Collector folders

top of the blade back. The handle is made of light-weight Zytel and is 4.09 inches long. The inlaid plates are made of nut burl wood or from imitation ivory with a scrimshaw depiction of a pack of wolves. A detachable steel carrying clip is on the right of the handle and the knife weighs 1.2 ounces.

COLLECTOR'S SERIES

Walther's famous pistol models appear in the scrimshaw drawings of the Collector's Series on inlaid plates of imitation ivory. The skeleton blade of the knife comes from Seki in Japan, is made of stainless

The Grand Hunter with gut hook

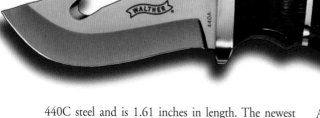

440C steel and is 1.61 inches in length. The newest model in this series has inlaid plates made of quince burl wood. The casing of this knife is fiberglass reinforced Zytel and is 2.36 inches long. The knife weighs 1.2 ounces.

GRAND HUNTER

Gutmann produce the Grand Hunter for Walther. It is more than just a simple hunting knife. The stainless 440A steel blade has a lovely, arched skinner shape and a large gut hook on top of the point. The blade is 4.41 inches. The handle has comfortable finger slots and is made of pakka wood or black rubber. The total length of the knife is 5.86 inches and it weighs 6.6 ounces.

SOLACE

Due to its flat design, this knife is easy to carry concealed and can be within reach in the wink of an eye in case of approaching danger. The Walther Solace inspires confidence if a dangerous situation threatens to spiral out of control so Solace is a very appropriate name for this knife. The blade is made of 440A steel and is 3.5 inches long. This integral knife is 8.25 inches long. Because of the skeleton handle the knife only weighs 4.0 ounces. It comes

WENGER®
THE GENUINE SWISS ARMY KNIFE™

The logo of Wenger

with a Kydex sheath with a belt clip, but can also be carried with a Para Cord around the neck.

WENGER
www.wenger-knife.com

Swiss knife factory Wenger was founded in 1893 as Fabrique Suisse de Coutellerie in Courtetelle as a direct result of the success of Carl Elsener with his Swiss Army knife in 1891. The forerunner of the Wenger factory got its first military commission in 1901 for a soldiers' knife with a wooden handle. In 1950, the company decided to use stainless steel. A certain synthetic material that Wenger refers to as grilon was used as handle material. During the 1960s,

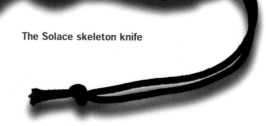

The Solace skeleton knife

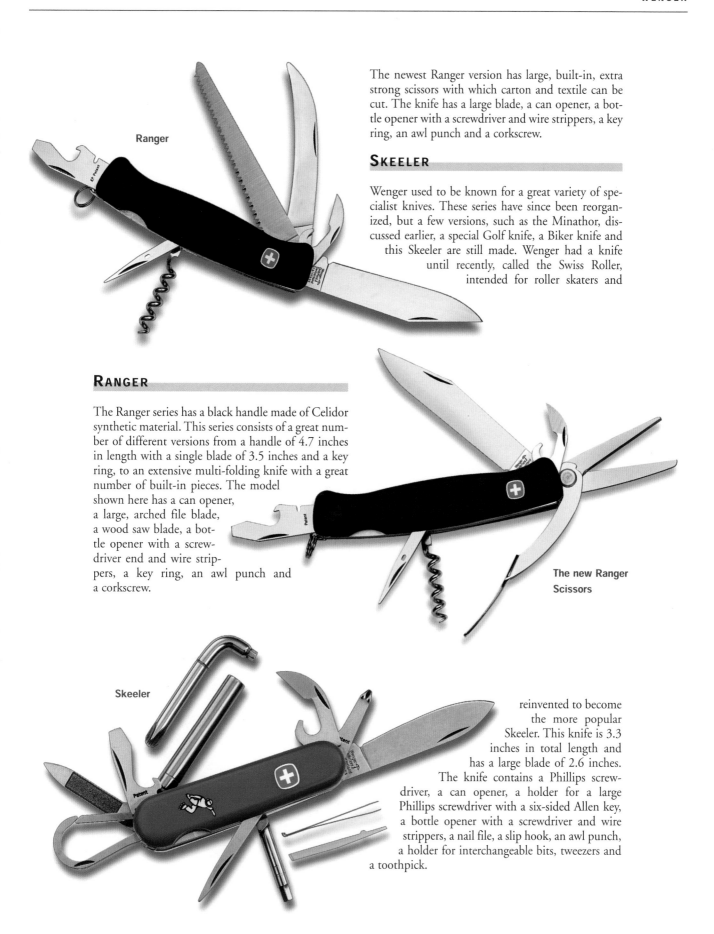

Ranger

The newest Ranger version has large, built-in, extra strong scissors with which carton and textile can be cut. The knife has a large blade, a can opener, a bottle opener with a screwdriver and wire strippers, a key ring, an awl punch and a corkscrew.

SKEELER

Wenger used to be known for a great variety of specialist knives. These series have since been reorganized, but a few versions, such as the Minathor, discussed earlier, a special Golf knife, a Biker knife and this Skeeler are still made. Wenger had a knife until recently, called the Swiss Roller, intended for roller skaters and

RANGER

The Ranger series has a black handle made of Celidor synthetic material. This series consists of a great number of different versions from a handle of 4.7 inches in length with a single blade of 3.5 inches and a key ring, to an extensive multi-folding knife with a great number of built-in pieces. The model shown here has a can opener, a large, arched file blade, a wood saw blade, a bottle opener with a screwdriver end and wire strippers, a key ring, an awl punch and a corkscrew.

The new Ranger Scissors

Skeeler

reinvented to become the more popular Skeeler. This knife is 3.3 inches in total length and has a large blade of 2.6 inches. The knife contains a Phillips screwdriver, a can opener, a holder for a large Phillips screwdriver with a six-sided Allen key, a bottle opener with a screwdriver and wire strippers, a nail file, a slip hook, an awl punch, a holder for interchangeable bits, tweezers and a toothpick.

Snowboarder

STANDARD

The Standard series varies from a super simple knife to an extended multi-tool. A unique version is the commemorative knife 'Patrouille des Glaciers.' A bronze-colored, engraved plaque with a depiction of the Bertol mountain cabin in Arolla is on the handle. The Gletscher Patrouille was introduced during World War II by Rodolphe Tissičres and Roger Bonvin, both captains of the 10th mountain brigade of the Swiss army. The idea was to guard against attack from the enemy on mountain passes. In order to train the troops, military competitions were held for three man plows that had to go down the mountain pass from Zermatt to Verbier in one push. The first Gletscher Patrouille started in April 1943 and completed a distance of 39 miles at an altitude of 24,934 feet in 12 hours and 7 minutes. After the war, similar competitions were held for mountain guides. The knife shown here was made in commemoration of the 2002 journey.

The standard has a large blade, a can opener, a smaller blade, a bottle opener with a screwdriver and wire strippers, a key ring with a lanyard, an awl punch, a corkscrew, tweezers and a toothpick.

SNOWBOARDER

The Snowboarder is a variation of the old Biker with everything on board for adjusting boot clamps on a snowboard. It looks very similar to the Skeeler, except for the bit holder, but it does have a key ring that can be attached to the handle. The knife contains a large blade of 2.6 inches, a Phillips screwdriver, a can opener, a holder for a large Phillips screwdriver with a six-sided Allen key, a bottle opener with a screwdriver and wire strippers, a nail file, a slip hook, an awl punch, a corkscrew, tweezers and a toothpick.

A special Standard knife

Another knife from the Standard series

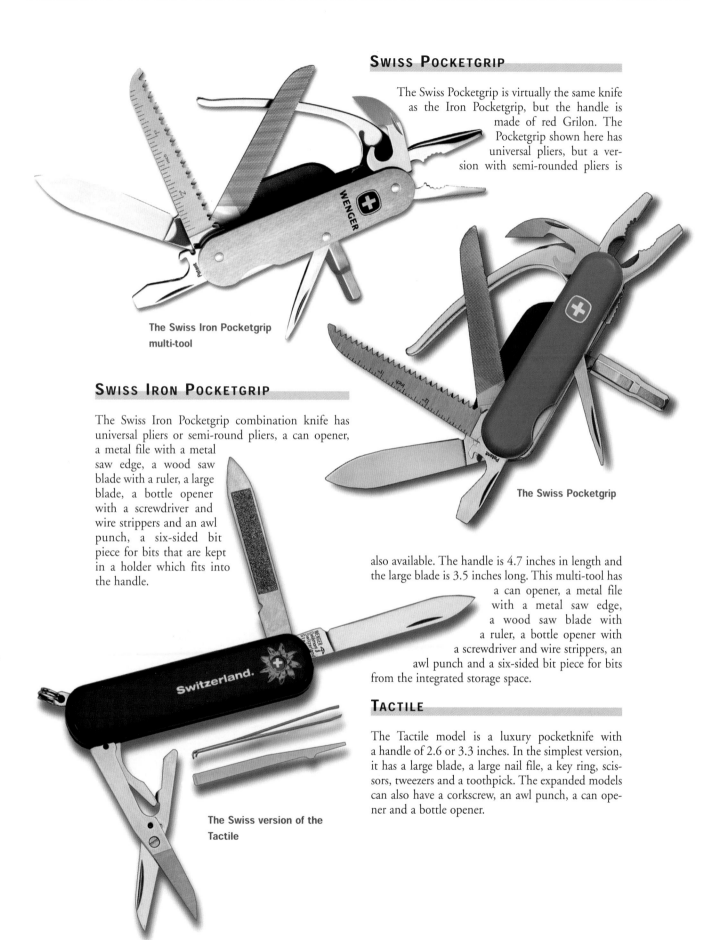

SWISS POCKETGRIP

The Swiss Pocketgrip is virtually the same knife as the Iron Pocketgrip, but the handle is made of red Grilon. The Pocketgrip shown here has universal pliers, but a version with semi-rounded pliers is

The Swiss Iron Pocketgrip multi-tool

SWISS IRON POCKETGRIP

The Swiss Iron Pocketgrip combination knife has universal pliers or semi-round pliers, a can opener, a metal file with a metal saw edge, a wood saw blade with a ruler, a large blade, a bottle opener with a screwdriver and wire strippers and an awl punch, a six-sided bit piece for bits that are kept in a holder which fits into the handle.

The Swiss Pocketgrip

also available. The handle is 4.7 inches in length and the large blade is 3.5 inches long. This multi-tool has a can opener, a metal file with a metal saw edge, a wood saw blade with a ruler, a bottle opener with a screwdriver and wire strippers, an awl punch and a six-sided bit piece for bits from the integrated storage space.

TACTILE

The Tactile model is a luxury pocketknife with a handle of 2.6 or 3.3 inches. In the simplest version, it has a large blade, a large nail file, a key ring, scissors, tweezers and a toothpick. The expanded models can also have a corkscrew, an awl punch, a can opener and a bottle opener.

The Swiss version of the Tactile

WILKINSON SWORD

www.wilkinsonsword.com

Henry Nock founded the Wilkinson Sword Company in 1772. He was trained in Birmingham as a weapons maker , but moved to London and quickly made himself a name by producing innovative de-

The commemorative model of the English commando dagger

signs for firearm locks, prompting the English government to order 10,000 flintlocks. Wilkinson Sword became the largest weapons factory of the time and Henry's son, James, was named the official weapons maker to King George III. When Henry died, management of the company passed on to his son-in-law, James Wilkinson. This company made firearms for the English military and for dignitaries.

James Wilkinson was not very innovative, but his son Henry Wilkinson was. He had an excellent technical education behind him and he published various weapon books such as *Engines of War* (1841) and *Observations on Swords* (1848). After he took the company over from his father in 1824, he moved to Pall Mall, close to the Board of Ordnance, his best clients. He developed several patents. The quality of swords from this time was not overwhelmingly good, as the steel was not strong enough in battle. Henry, in 1844, developed a sword and bayonet testing machine called the *Eprouvette* that is used to the present day. Each individually numbered sword that withstood a difficult test was given a proof mark and a certificate as a guarantee of quality.

tract, Latham decided to focus production on swords and knives. The scandal after the battle in Sudan in 1885 lead to an important breakthrough. The British bayonet swords were so bad that they bent and broke off. The Board of Ordnance immediately took steps and ordered 150,000 bayonets. This meant a considerable capacity extension and Wilkinson Sword had to move to Chelsea.

Around the turn of the century, the company started producing a greater variety: the safety razor Pall Mall in 1898, followed by typewriters, bicycles, motorbikes, vehicles and hunting and sports articles. The uniting factor in all its products was quality and modern shapes. The First World War kept Wilkinson very busy with the production of two million bayonets and a blossoming trade in ceremonial swords and daggers. Wilkinson Sword has been making swords of high quality for more than 230 years. This is well summed up in the motto of the company: 'Semper Qualitas Suprema,' or 'Always the Finest Quality.'

DARTMOOR KNIFE

The Dartmoor Combination Survival Knife was designed for the most difficult circumstances, from the tropics to Antarctica. When developing the knife, the company cooperated closely with survival instructors of the commando-training center, namely RM Lympstone of the Royal English marines. The knife is

The Dartmoor survival knife

In 1858, due to health reasons, Henry could not run the company anymore and his manager, John Latham, took over. Due to a reduction in the government con-

13.5 inches in total length. The droppoint blade is made of stainless 440C steel tempered to 57-58 HRC. The blade is 7.25 inches long and 0.25 inches thick. The blade is bead blasted against reflection and the knife weighs

22.6 ounces. The handle is made of shock resistant nylon-6-polyamide with a top layer of thermoplastic rubber. The pommel and guard are made of stainless steel. The handle is hollow and serves as a storage space for survival equipment. This kit contains total length. The blade, made of stainless Sheffield carbon steel, is 7 inches long and 0.25 inches thick. British Paratroopers, the British Special Air Service, the British Special Boat Section and the Royal Marines as well as foreign military forces, such as the

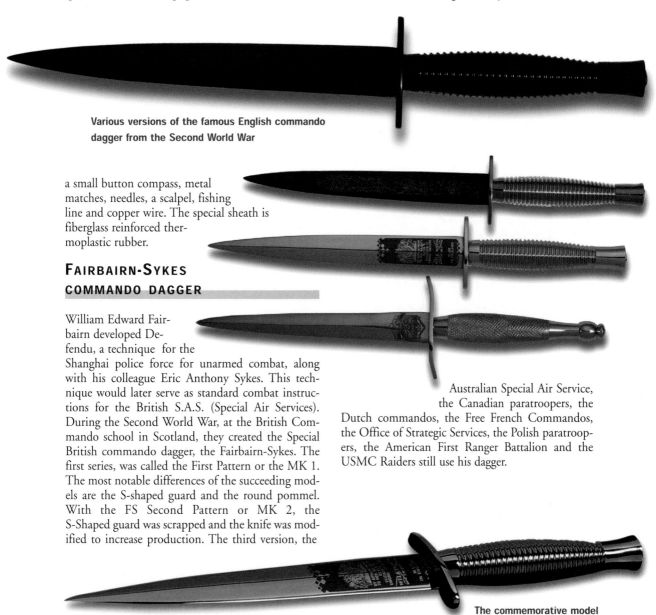

Various versions of the famous English commando dagger from the Second World War

a small button compass, metal matches, needles, a scalpel, fishing line and copper wire. The special sheath is fiberglass reinforced thermoplastic rubber.

FAIRBAIRN-SYKES
COMMANDO DAGGER

William Edward Fairbairn developed Defendu, a technique for the Shanghai police force for unarmed combat, along with his colleague Eric Anthony Sykes. This technique would later serve as standard combat instructions for the British S.A.S. (Special Air Services). During the Second World War, at the British Commando school in Scotland, they created the Special British commando dagger, the Fairbairn-Sykes. The first series, was called the First Pattern or the MK 1. The most notable differences of the succeeding models are the S-shaped guard and the round pommel. With the FS Second Pattern or MK 2, the S-Shaped guard was scrapped and the knife was modified to increase production. The third version, the

Australian Special Air Service, the Canadian paratroopers, the Dutch commandos, the Free French Commandos, the Office of Strategic Services, the Polish paratroopers, the American First Ranger Battalion and the USMC Raiders still use his dagger.

The commemorative model by Fairbairn-Sykes

Third Pattern or MK 3 is the most famous and is produced to the present day. This matte black model has a straight pommel and a ribbed handle 4.7 inches in length. The FS commando dagger is 11.7 inches in